THE
PIANO

King Palmer is an Associate and Licentiate of the Royal Academy of Music and a Fellow of the Royal Society of Arts. He has had a rich and varied career in music – conducting orchestras, choirs, operettas and musical plays, as well as his own light orchestra (BBC) and recording sessions in this country and abroad. A prolific composer in many different styles – from solo voice to military and brass bands – King Palmer has also written and lectured widely on various musical topics, including musical composition, orchestration, church music and the piano.

D0715850

TEACH YOURSELF BOOKS

THE
PIANO

King Palmer
Associate of the Royal Academy of Music

TEACH YOURSELF BOOKS

Hodder and Stoughton

British Library Cataloguing in Publication Data
Palmer, King
  The Piano—3rd ed.—(Teach yourself
  books)
  1. Piano—Performance
  I. Title
  786.3′041 MT220
ISBN 0 340 40212 1

First published 1957
Second edition 1981
Third edition 1986
Reissued 1992
Impression number   10 9 8
Year   1998   1997   1996   1995   1994   1993

Typeset by Rowland Phototypesetting Ltd, Bury St Edmunds, Suffolk.
Printed in Great Britain for the educational publishing division of Hodder &
Stoughton Ltd, Mill Road, Dunton Green, Sevenoaks, Kent TN13 2YA by Clays
Ltd, St Ives plc.

Contents

Preface   vii

1   How to Use This Book   1

2   The Instrument   4
     The piano action. The pedals. Choosing a piano. Looking after
     a piano.

3   Theory of Piano Music (1)   9
     The pattern of the keyboard. The octave. Self-testing
     questions.

4   Beginning to Play   16
     Your position at the piano. How fingering is indicated.
     Finding notes on the piano.

5   Theory of Piano Music (2)   21
     Leger lines. Octave signs. Beats and bars. Repeat marks and
     signs. The value of notes. Dotted notes. Time-signatures.
     Grouping of notes. Rests. Self-testing questions.

6   Theory of Piano Music (3)   32
     Tones and semi-tones. Scales. Degrees of the scale. Sharps,
     flats and naturals. Accidentals. The pattern of major scales
     (and key-signatures). The minor scale. The chromatic scale.
     Double-sharps and double-flats. Invervals. Chords, arpeggios
     and broken chords. Self-testing questions.

7   How to Practise   51
     Finding the key of a piece. What to look for.
     Counting time. The metronome. Intensity and speed.
     Training the ear. Sight-reading. Some final points.

vi   *Contents*

8   Fingering   65
    Printed fingering. The principles of fingering. Changing
    fingers on the same note. Scales. The chromatic scale.
    Arpeggios and broken chords.

9   Theory of Piano Music (4)   74
    Syncopation. Notes of embellishment. Self-testing questions.

10   Phrasing   80
    Phrasing and cadences. Phrasing.

11   Tone Production   87
    The piano keys. Legato. Staccato. Finger position. Forearm
    rotation.

12   The Pedals   92
    The damper pedal. The left pedal.

13   Technique and Interpretation   96
    Scales. Arpeggios and broken chords. Skips and leaps. Trills.
    Chords. Interpretation. Accompaniment and melody.
    Rubato. Accents and pauses. Phrase endings.

14   Tension and Relaxation   105
    Tension and relaxation and the pianist.

15   Improvisation   109
    Triads. Modulation. Melodic decoration.

Demonstration Lessons   123

1   'Melody' (Robert Schumann)   124
2   Scales and Arpeggios   132
3   Reading Music at Sight   138

Glossary of Musical Terms used in Piano Playing   144

Index   149

Preface

Since I first wrote *The Piano* for this series it has been reprinted many times but only small revisions have been possible, and I have long felt that I should like to write an entirely new book which would take into account new ideas about piano playing, and my own continuing thoughts and experiences as a teacher and musician. This book has now been completely rewritten and reset.

Quite a few people have told me that they have learned to play the piano with the help of my book, but in fairness I have not heard them play. I think, however, that this book should be able to impart sufficient knowledge to enable someone to *enjoy* playing the piano, and perhaps to give enjoyment to others. It may even be the means of revealing some hitherto undiscovered talent, so that the reader will be persuaded to take piano lessons from an experienced teacher.

Of the many adults who do have a real desire to play, some, who have studied piano playing at any earlier period of their lives, would like to remind themselves of things they have almost ceased to remember; but, like others who have never played at all, they may wonder how much progress they are likely to make. I think that, given the desire and will to learn, it is never too late to start. Of course if one is older it may take longer but then one may have a little more time to spare.

I hope that would-be pianists who read this book will find it of help in one way or another. Perhaps, also, it may sometimes help piano students when they are trying to resolve problems of theory and technique which present themselves in their teacher's absence.

In preparing this book I have been greatly encouraged by the interest shown by many of my friends. I am especially grateful to Harold Britton and Brian Black for reading the whole book in typescript, and for offering many helpful comments and suggestions; and to Helena O'Connell for patient and thoughtful help in preparing the manuscript for press.

Notes on American usage

1 American 'cancel' = British 'natural' (after sharp or flat sign).

2 There is a distinction between British and American usage of the words 'tone' and 'note'. In British usage 'tone' usually means either (a) the interval of a major second (i.e. two semitones); or (b) the quality of a musical sound; and 'note' either (a) the actual written or printed sign which represents the pitch and duration of a musical sound; or (b) an actual sound of musical pitch; or (c) the finger-key of a piano, organ, etc. In American usage 'tone' (from the German 'ton') may be used to describe an actual sound of musical pitch, whereas 'note' is usually reserved for the written or printed sign. Thus 'three notes higher' (British) becomes 'three tones higher' (American).

3 Distinctions between British and American names of the varieties of notes and rests will be found on pages 25 and 30.

4 'Measure', an old English term, is used in America as the equivalent of British 'bar'; in America, 'bar' is often reserved for British 'bar-line' (see page 20).

5 *Degrees of the scale.* British 'submediant' is sometimes American 'superdominant'; sometimes, also, British 'leading note' becomes American 'subtonic' or 'leading tone'.

1

How to Use This Book

Perhaps you have never played the piano, and have just opened this book. Or perhaps you did play long ago, and have almost forgotten how. If you came to me for a first lesson, the situation would be rather different. I could ask whether you had a musical background, if you could read music, why you wanted to play the piano, what music you had heard and enjoyed. I could even invite you to try a few aural tests, which would give me some idea of your musical ability.

But whether you choose to take lessons from a teacher or to learn what you can from a book (or perhaps even from both) there are certain objects and skills that you will need before you can make a start. The first is a piano to play on and, unless you already possess one, or have access to one for regular practice, your first concern will be to obtain a suitable instrument. This is considered in Chapter 2, which also discusses ways of looking after a piano, and gives a brief description of how the instrument works.

Then, if you are not already able to read music, you will need to learn some theory – about notes, time, scale formation, and so on. Large doses of theory can be indigestible, so I have introduced it gradually, in four chapters which can be studied separately, so, if you wish, you will be able to start playing something simple at an early stage.

When you can read music you will need some to play from. Music can be borrowed from some public libraries, but if you are a beginner you should have a small basic collection of your own. It need not be expensive, and could comprise these items:

A book of scales
Scale books published by the Associated Board are suitable; the Grade Four book would last a beginner a long time.

A book of easy studies
Either of these would be suitable:
Graded Pianoforte Studies, Preliminary, 1st and 2nd Series (Associated Board).
Preliminary Exercises for Piano, Hanon, ed. John Thompson (Chappell).

A book of easy pieces
A Keyboard Anthology, Book One, 1st, 2nd and 3rd Series (Associated Board).
Classics to Moderns, Book One (Yorktown Music Press).

A book of aural tests
Part One (Associated Board).

A book of music paper
Writing music is an important part of learning it, so you will need this. Some of the music examples in this book are printed along, rather than across the page. It is recommended that those which are to be played should be copied in to a book of music paper; this will provide you with a valuable lesson in note-reading and also enable you to read the music from the piano.

These books will probably last you for a year or so, unless you are able to put in a considerable amount of practice, and so make exceptional progress. After that you can, if you wish, continue with studies and pieces in the same series, but in a higher grade. By this time, however, you will probably be able to make suitable choices on your own, either to buy, or to borrow. If you would like special music for sight-reading, the *Read and Play Series* (Grade One) by Thomas A. Johnston (Hinrichsen) is useful. If you have had previous experience of piano playing, you will be able to make a start with pieces and studies of a higher grade, and to make appropriate choices accordingly.

In writing this book I have, as far as possible, arranged the chapters progressively, but learning is a personal undertaking, and it is not really possible to lay down hard and fast rules. I suggest, therefore, that first you should read through the entire book (except for the Demonstration Lessons) fairly rapidly. After this, study each chapter in depth, with cross-references to other chapters, and to the index and glossary of terms, whenever necessary. Most chapters can be studied in any order you wish, but whenever possible they should be applied to music which you are practising. The four chapters on Theory of Piano Music should be studied in order, but they need not be taken all together. As soon as you feel confident to tackle a simple study or piece you should do so. But it is important that you should check your knowledge of theory by answering the Self-Testing Questions, which you will find at the end of each of these four chapters.

Do make early and frequent use of the Demonstration Lessons which, for convenience, are together at the end of the book. They will show you, step by step, how to play a simple piano piece, scales and *arpeggios*, and how to read music at sight. The basic principles in these lessons are of vital importance, as also are those discussed in Chapter 7 (How to Practise); this chapter should be studied at a fairly early stage. Chapter 14 (Tension and Relaxation) is also, I think, of great importance, and has been the subject of my concern for many years.

If, after reading this book, you feel that you would prefer to work to a more rigid (and less personal) plan than the one I have suggested, then one of the published methods which is divided into lessons could be studied side by side with this book. One such method is *Piano Lessons with Fanny Waterman and Marion Harewood*, Books One to Three (Faber Music).

If you are using this book to teach a young child, the books of studies and pieces cited should be replaced by one or two of the many small albums which are specially written for children. Some of these are so attractively produced and illustrated, that perhaps the best course might be to ask your dealer to produce a suitable selection, and allow the child to make the choice. The series of *Piano Books* by Carol Barratt and Wendy Hole (Chester Music), and the *Piano Albums for Children* (Universal Edition) are particularly good examples of attractive productions.

2

The Instrument

The piano action

Although the early keyboard instruments contributed something to the modern piano, their actions are quite different. The clavichord has the simplest and most direct action, housed in an oblong box; a key, when depressed by a gentle rocking motion of the fingers, causes a brass blade (called a 'tangent') to touch the string. The harpsichord, whose shape is somewhat similar to that of the modern grand piano, has an action in which the strings are plucked by plectra (of quill or leather) set at right angles in wooden 'jacks' which rise when a key is depressed and then fall back into position. Harpsichords have several sets of strings, and sometimes two or more keyboards, and hand-stops and pedals. Virginals (rectangular) and spinets (five-sided or triangular) have single keyboards with one set of strings, which are also plucked by plectra. In the sixteenth century, a small virginal was often placed on top of a larger one, thus forming a 'pair of virginals'.

The modern piano action is based on the idea of the Italian, Bartolomeo Cristofori who, about 1709, introduced a keyboard mechanism fitted with hammers (instead of harpsichord jacks), capable of producing loud and soft (*piano* and *forte*) sounds; from this we get the word 'pianoforte'.

If you look inside a grand piano, you will see that the strings are arranged in groups: the higher notes have three strings to each note, and each of the lower notes has either two thicker strings or a single thick string. If you press down a key fairly quickly you will see that a felt-covered hammer will strike the string (or group of strings) and that whether the key is held down or released the hammer will at once fall back, so that the string is free to vibrate. A felt-lined 'damper' will also spring away from the string when the key is depressed, and fall back on the string when the key is released, thus stopping the sound. The shortest strings, having very little sustaining power, are not fitted with dampers.

The quantity of sound (i.e. the loudness or softness) that can be obtained from a piano string depends upon the extent to which the string is made to vibrate, and this in turn depends upon the amount of energy with which the piano key is depressed. If put down very slowly indeed the hammer may not reach the string, and there will be no sound. If depressed a little faster there will be a soft sound and, as the speed of depression is increased, so the sound will also increase in loudness. An important characteristic of piano sound is that once a string has been struck, the sound will immediately begin to fade. The pianist, unlike most other performers (e.g. violinist, flautist) is thus unable either to maintain a single sound at a constant level, or to increase or diminish it at will.

The pedals

The modern piano usually has two pedals. The one on the right is the 'damper' or 'sustaining' pedal (often miscalled the 'loud' pedal). The effect of this pedal is to keep the dampers raised from the strings so that the notes which have been sounded will continue to sound when the keys are released until the vibrations of the strings come to an end. Since the damper pedal raises *all* the dampers, it releases, in addition to the note sounded when a key is depressed, a series of higher and weaker sounds called 'partials' or 'harmonics'. Although these partials are normally unheard, unless they are made prominent, they do help to enrich the sound. A simple experiment will illustrate this. Depress the damper pedal and hold it down, then depress Middle C key with some force (see Example 3.2 for position of Middle C). Now *silently* depress the C key next above Middle C (having found its position from Example 3.2), and release both the damper pedal and the Middle C key. The upper C (being a partial of Middle C) will continue to sound because its damper is still raised, though the other dampers have fallen. This harmonic enrichment has to be taken into account when using the damper pedal. When conflicting harmonies occur, the pianist has to decide whether or not the resultant clash is artistically desirable.

Some pianos, such as the Steinway, have a third, middle pedal. This 'sostenuto' pedal, when used instead of the damper pedal, keeps certain dampers up when it is depressed, while allowing other dampers to remain down, and thus enables the performer to sustain an isolated note or chord (mainly below Middle C), while higher changing notes are not affected.

The left pedal (called 'soft' or *una corda*) is used to reduce or alter the quality of sound. On upright pianos this pedal, when depressed, usually moves the hammers closer to the strings, so that they travel a shorter distance with less speed. On grand pianos it moves the keyboard and hammers sideways, so that two strings instead of three (or one instead of two) are struck.

The damper pedal is used frequently; the soft pedal infrequently. Either may be used on its own, or both together.

Choosing a piano

If you are buying a piano the choice needs to be made with care as a good piano is a very costly instrument. Pianos are made in many shapes and sizes. Grand pianos, in which the strings are horizontal, are usually considerably more expensive than upright pianos in similar condition; the larger grands are not suitable for small rooms, although baby grands take up very little space. Upright pianos vary in size and structure, and although the tone of the largest upright may compare favourably with that of a small grand, small upright pianos often have a much weaker tone. Most good upright pianos are over-strung, the strings being arranged diagonally, one set crossing the other; the length of the bass strings is thus greater, and the tone fuller, than that of vertically strung pianos. The dampers are usually under the hammers, but are sometimes over them; the under damper system is usually better, since it gives more weight to the keys.

If the purchase of a secondhand piano is contemplated, and it has not been reconditioned by a reputable piano repairer, it is usually essential to have the piano inspected by an expert, as the cost of restoring a neglected piano may be excessive. Some of the defects to look out for are rusty strings, warped hammers and dampers, a cracked sound-board, worn or moth-ridden felts, pedals which stick or rattle, a stiff action, and ivory keys which are nearly worn through. If faults such as these exist, only an expert can judge whether restoration is possible and worthwhile.

Apart from outright cash purchase, it is possible to buy a new piano on a five year purchase plan, or to rent a piano (credit sometimes being given for part of the rental charge, if purchase is decided upon at the end of a specified period). Local instrument dealers will usually supply details. It is also sometimes possible to arrange to use a piano at a school or church hall for regular practice – perhaps in return for a small donation.

Looking after a piano

A piano does not improve with age: if subjected to hours of practice a day, it will eventually show signs of wear and tear. Hammer and damper felts will develop ridges where they come in contact with the strings, and, unless renewed, the tone will be affected (sometimes, as a temporary measure, the hammer felts can be 'pricked'). Nevertheless, a good piano can last a century or more if it is properly looked after and regularly played.

The position of the piano is important. It should not be in a draught (e.g. under an open window), and it should never be put into a room, or against an outside wall, which is damp: if it is, rust may form on the strings, and the hammers and dampers may warp. Central heating may also cause grave problems. Although a piano should not be left for long winter periods in a room without heat (this is unlikely if it is regularly played on), a position close to a hot radiator may not only play havoc with the tuning, but may also cause the sound-board to crack. If central heating is unavoidable, the use of a suitable humidifier may be the only way to alleviate the situation.

A piano needs to be tuned at regular intervals by an experienced tuner, who is also able to deal with any other problems which may arise. Good tuners are in short supply, but it may be possible to make a contract with one of the leading piano makers or suppliers for a piano to be tuned two or three times a year. As a first step a local music shop may be able to offer advice. It is as well to ask the tuner to keep your piano up to standard *pitch* (A = 440 cycles a second).[1] If you wish to check the pitch yourself you can buy a small metal tuning fork from your music dealer.

Should anything go wrong with the piano action it is wise not to touch it yourself, but to leave it to an expert; it is quite easy to break a hammer or string.

---

[1] *Pitch* is used to describe how high or low a particular sound is, see page

3

Theory of Piano Music (1)

The pattern of the keyboard

Look at the piano keyboard, and you will see that the white and black keys form a regular pattern, with the white keys at equal distances from each other, and the black keys grouped in twos and threes.

Example 3.1

This basic pattern is repeated throughout the entire length of the keyboard. Depress, with one finger, the white keys in order, starting from the extreme left of the keyboard, and you will hear the sounds becoming gradually higher until, at the extreme right, the highest sound is reached. Look inside the piano, and you will see the shorter and thinner the string, the higher the sound or pitch.

Now look at Example 3.2, which is a diagram of the complete keyboard on the average piano (some pianos have extra keys). Please ignore, for the moment, the music notation above the keyboard diagram, this will be explained very shortly.

Example 3.2

You will see that the white keys are named after the first seven letters of the alphabet – ABCDEFG – and that this series is repeated each time the seventh letter (G) is reached; also that the white keys immediately to the left and right of the *two* black keys are, respectively, C and E, and the white keys immediately to the left and right of the *three* black keys are, respectively, F and B.

Your first task is to memorise the pattern of the piano keys; to know the names of the white keys, and to be able to find them on the piano. Start by naming (and playing with one finger) all the As, Bs, Cs etc. on the keyboard. When you can do this easily, try naming different white piano keys at random, and finding them on the keyboard.

The *average* piano keyboard has fifty white keys, seven of which are C keys; of these seven keys, the fourth C from the left (or right) is known as *Middle C*. Middle C is a 'landmark', and it is important that you should memorise its position, so that you can find it quickly, as this will help you to read from printed music. Its position should be studied carefully; first from Example 3.2, and then on the piano keyboard.

How piano music is written

Piano music is written on two sets of five parallel lines called *staves*. These staves, which are bracketed together, are distinguished from one another by two different signs called *clefs*. The *treble clef* (𝄞) is normally placed on the upper stave, and the *bass clef* (𝄢) on the lower stave. The treble clef is also known as the 'G' clef, because the lower part of the clef sign encloses the note G. The bass clef is also known as the 'F' clef, because a pair of dots is placed on either side of the fourth (F) line.

Example 3.3

Musical sounds of different pitch (i.e. height or depth) are shown by little oval characters called *notes*, which are placed on the lines of the stave, and in the spaces between the lines. In addition, a note may be placed above each stave, and another note below the stave. Usually, treble notes on the upper stave are played with the right hand, and bass notes on the lower stave with the left hand.

In theory, the treble and bass staves may be combined to form a single *great stave* of eleven lines and ten spaces, with the names of the notes in alphabetical order; in practice, two five-line staves are easier to read. The middle (sixth) line of the great stave is then introduced on a short line, either below the treble stave, or above the bass stave, if a note appears on it; this note is then called Middle C (Example 3.4).

You should now memorise the names of the notes on the lines, and in the spaces, of each stave. You will find it easier to do this if the lines are separated from the spaces.

You may find it helpful to associate the names of the notes with a sentence or word, e.g.

Treble notes on the lines:	Every Good Boy Deserves Favour.
Treble notes in the spaces:	FACE
Bass notes on the lines:	Gold Buttons Dress Fine Actors.
Bass notes in the spaces:	All Cars Expect Grease.

(If you make up your own sentences, you may find them easier to remember – Example 3.5.)

Example 3.4

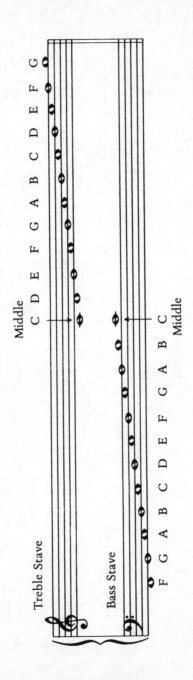

Example 3.5

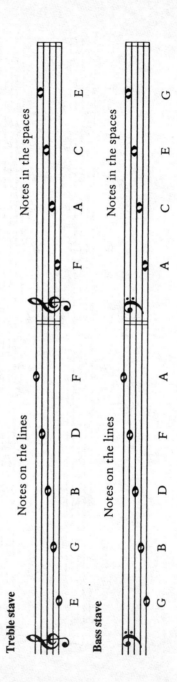

Treble stave

Notes on the lines

E   G   B   D   F

Notes in the spaces

F   A   C   E

Bass stave

Notes on the lines

G   B   D   F   A

Notes in the spaces

A   C   E   G

The octave

The distance from any white note to the next white note of the same name on the piano keyboard is called an *octave* (i.e. eight notes). (Although the notation of the black piano keys has not yet been discussed, it should be noted that the distance from any black note to the next black note of the same name is also an octave.) Thus, Example 3.6 (a), which is Middle C on the piano, is an octave below (b), and an octave above (c).

From the diagram of the piano keyboard (Example 3.2) you will see that the *average* piano has seven octaves, starting and finishing on the note A.

Example 3.6

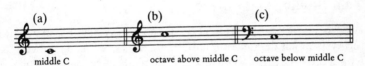

Self-testing questions

Preliminary remarks

Write the answers to these questions in your music book, without reference to this chapter. Check each answer with the appropriate music example (the number of this is shown in brackets at the end of the question). In a few questions, a page of the text is given, instead of, or as well as, the number of the music example. If your answer is wrong, try the question again.

1 Write, on a stave in your music book, a treble clef sign. Then write: a) the five notes on the lines; b) the four notes in the spaces. Put a letter name under each note. (*Example 3.5*)
2 Do the same with the bass clef. (*Example 3.5*)
3 Write on the stave: (a) Middle C in the treble clef; (b) Middle C in the bass clef. (*Example 3.4*)
4 Write these notes in the treble clef: (a) A in a space; (b) D on a line; (c) E in a space; (d) E on a line. (*Example 3.5*)
5 Write these notes in the bass clef: (a) G in a space; (b) D on a line; (c) G on a line; (d) A in a space. (*Example 3.5*)
6 Write: (a) the C above Middle C in the treble clef; (b) the C below Middle C in the bass clef. (*Example 3.6*)

4

Beginning to Play

Your position at the piano

Advice about your position at the piano is only possible in general terms as much depends on variable factors such as height, build, length of arms, legs and fingers. So that while it can be said that you should sit at the centre of the keyboard, your distance from it, and the height of your seat, are to some extent matters of individual choice. If you have an adjustable piano stool you will be able, by experiment, to find the height that suits you best. If you use a chair, adjust the height, if necessary, by adding a cushion, and be careful to sit well forward. There is no 'correct' height; some pianists prefer a fairly high seat, others a fairly low one.

In general, you should sit at such a height, and at such a distance from the keyboard, that when your arms are naturally bent, your fingers will fall easily on the white keys, and just about reach the black keys when your fingers are stretched out a little.

This means, for example, that if the thumb is playing a white key, it will normally be in the same position whether the next key to be played is white or black; if the thumb is playing a black key, however, it will be stretched forward, and the whole hand positioned over the black keys.

Your elbows should hang loosely and naturally, fairly close to the body, and not be lifted too high. As a rough guide, your forearms need to be almost level with the keyboard, and your elbows a little higher. The ball of your right foot (not the toe) should rest firmly on the damper (right hand) pedal, ready for action. As the left pedal is used less frequently, the left leg can be further back (perhaps just in front of the piano stool). At times the left leg can carry the weight of the body, so it is worth experimenting to find a position which seems natural and comfortable.

Your hands should normally be cup-shaped (imagine you are holding an orange in each hand), so that the fingers are bent and rounded, with the tips playing vertically into the centre of the keys; your finger nails will need to be kept short. The thumb plays with the side, not the tip, and should be slightly bent so that it rests on the key about as far as the root of the nail. These finger positions are only approximate, and modifications may be necessary when black keys and certain styles of playing are involved.

How fingering is indicated

In modern piano music, notes to be played by the thumb of either hand are numbered 1, and notes to be played by the other fingers, in order, 2,3,4,5. These small figures are printed above or below certain notes. Some music (usually advanced) is not fingered at all, and the pianist has to work out suitable fingering in accordance with general principles which will be discussed later in this book. (Should you come across music which was printed in England many years ago, an obsolete form of fingering may be used, in which the thumb is marked with a +, and the fingers, in order, 1,2,3,4.)

Finding notes on the piano

The preliminary exercises in Example 4.1 will help you to read printed music and to find notes on the piano. You should first name the notes in each group, and then play them. At first you may do this by looking down at the keyboard, finding the first note of each group, and then playing all the notes without looking at the music. As soon as possible, however, you should practise these exercises without looking at your hands.

Be careful to use the fingering printed below each exercise. You will see that where notes proceed in alphabetical order, the fingers are used in that order, but that if a white key is left out, the corresponding finger is also left out. This is more fully explained in

Example 4.1

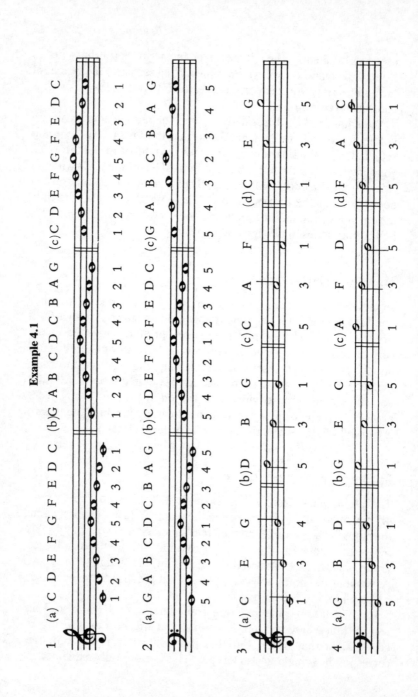

Example 4.2

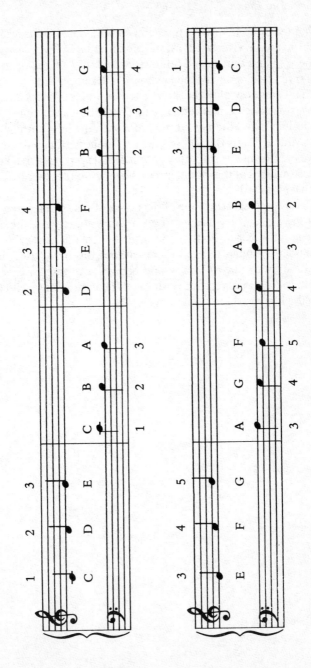

Chapter 8. To help you, the names of the notes are printed above each exercise. Exercise 1(a), starts on Middle C; if you are uncertain where to find this, or the other starting notes, on the piano, please refer to the diagram of the keyboard in Example 3.2.

You can now play the short exercise in Example 4.2, using the fingering which is marked. The first three notes are played with the right hand, and the next three notes with the left; both hands start on Middle C. In this exercise, every note is of equal value. Play fairly softly and as smoothly as you can. Try to raise one key at the precise moment that you depress the next, so that there are no gaps between sounds.

You could also start one of the books of easy studies (see page 2). At this stage, it is quite in order, if you wish, to write the names of the notes in pencil, so that you can rub them out as soon as you feel confident enough to read them without this aid. Also, since it is quite easy to play in the wrong octave, it is wise to check, from Example 3.2, the relative position of the written note with the note on the keyboard.

5

Theory of Piano Music (2)

Leger lines

If we add together the number of notes which can be written on the lines, and in the spaces, of the two staves, and also include the single notes above and below the staves, together with Middle C, we have a total of twenty-three notes. But since there are fifty white notes on the average piano, short *leger lines*[1] are used when notes are too high, or too low, to be written on the staves (the little line on which Middle C is written is, in fact, a leger line).

The names of the notes on the leger lines above and below the treble and bass staves are shown in Example 5.1.

Example 5.1

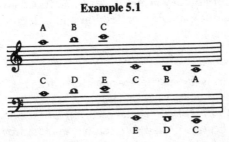

You can, if you wish, memorise these notes, but you may find it easier to learn them gradually, as they occur in the music you are playing.

[1] Only a few leger lines will be found in easy piano music. Additional lines, which occur in more difficult music, are shown in Example 3.2.

Octave signs

Since high leger lines are often difficult to read, the sign *8va* (or *8*) may be placed above certain notes, which are then played an octave higher than they are written. When the sign *8va* or *8va bassa* is placed *below* notes, these are to be played an octave lower.

Example 5.2

When the figure *8*, or the words *Con 8va*, are placed below a note, the written note and the note an octave below it must be played together.

Beats and bars

At some time or other you may have scanned poetry to determine its structure, and the number of 'feet' in a line. If, for instance, you were scanning:

His Spírit flútters líke a lárk

you might stress those syllables marked with an accent(´), and pass over the other syllables more lightly.

In music there is also a regular recurrence of stronger and weaker accents, or *beats*. Strong beats can be separated by one or more weaker beats and beats can be grouped into rhythmic[1] units called

[1] Rhythm, though hard to define, takes in everything connected with the 'time' side of music (beats, bars, accents, phrases, etc.). But it goes much deeper than this, implying natural, living, 'breathing' performance, as opposed to mere mechanical time-keeping and accuracy. It might be called the 'heart beat' of music.

bars, which are marked by drawing perpendicular lines across the stave, called *bar-lines*.

Example 5.3

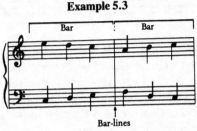

Each bar may consist of a group of two, three or four beats, and the beat immediately after each bar-line is normally the most strongly accented.

Example 5.4

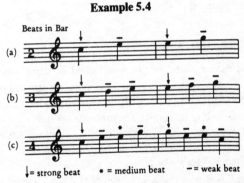

You will see that in Example 5.4 the bars of two and three beats consist of a strong beat followed by one or two weaker beats; but that in the bar of four beats the first beat receives the strong accent, the third beat a medium accent, and the second and fourth beats weaker accents.

Double-bars, repeat marks and signs

Two bar-lines placed together are called a *double-bar*, and are used to mark the end of a movement. Dots placed to the left of a double-bar mean that the preceding movement is to be repeated. Placed to the right of a double-bar they mean that the movement which follows is to be repeated (Example 5.5).

Example 5.5

The words *1ma Volta* and *2da Volta*, or the figures *1* and *2*, when printed over bars where a repetition occurs, mean that the bar or bars marked *1ma Volta* are to be omitted when the music is played a second time, and the bar or bars marked *2da Volta* played instead.

The sign *DC (Da Capo)* means that the music is to be repeated from the beginning of the movement.

The sign *DS (Dal Segno)* means that the music is to be repeated from the sign ⅗ .

The word *Fine* (the end) is sometimes placed over a double-bar to mark the conclusion of the piece.

The values of notes

If all melodies consisted of notes of equal value, music would be a dull affair (Example 4.2 does, but this serves a special purpose, and could scarcely be called a beautiful melody). So in order to show the length of time that different sounds are to last, we use notes of several different kinds. The shape of the actual notehead is the same, but the centre can be left white, or blacked in,[1] and different kinds of 'tails' can be added.

Example 5.6 shows the appearance of each kind of note, and its value in relation to other kinds of notes. The English names are used in this book, although the American names are perhaps more logical, since they show at a glance the relative values of different notes, by dividing whole notes into fractions.

When writing music, the tail of a note is usually upwards if the head is below the third line of the stave and downwards if the head is above the third line. If the head is *on* the third line, the tail can go either way. With chords, or part-writing, this may not apply. It is as well to study some printed piano music, to exemplify this.

---

[1] Several times in my teaching career I have been asked whether this has any connection with the white and black keys of the piano, so perhaps I had better say that it has not.

Example 5.6

Dotted notes

A dot placed after a note increases its value by one half. A dotted semibreve is therefore equal to an undotted semibreve plus a minim. The effect of placing dots after each kind of note is shown in Example 5.7.

Example 5.7

(Two dots (less usual) increase the value of a note by three-quarters.)

Time-signatures

Figures called *time-signatures* appear at the beginning of a piece of music, immediately after the clef signs on the stave. They may also appear during the course of a movement, if the original time-signature is changed.

Example 5.8

The upper figure shows the number of beats in each bar; the lower figure the value of each beat. Thus the time-signature in Example 5.8 shows that there are three beats, each of the value of a crotchet, in a bar.

The notes which make up a bar of music will not necessarily be of the same duration as the beats. A bar of $\frac{4}{4}$ time, for example, might contain four crotchets, or might consist of any combination of notes which are the equivalent of four crotchets.

In Example 5.9, bar one contains one semibreve; bar two, two minims; bar three, eight quavers; and bar four, one minim, one crotchet and two quavers; but each bar contains the equivalent of four crotchets.

Example 5.9

Similarly, a bar of $\frac{2}{4}$ time contains two crotchets or their equivalents, and a bar of $\frac{3}{4}$ time three crotchets or their equivalents.

Each beat in a bar may have the value of a plain (i.e. undotted) note. This is called *simple time*, and each beat may be divided into halves, quarters, etc. Alternatively, each beat may have the value of a dotted note; this is called *compound time*, and each beat may be divided into thirds, sixths, etc. Example 5.10 will make this clearer.

Example 5.10

Baa, Baa, Black Sheep

Equivalent beats (undotted)

Drink to me only with thine eyes

Equivalent beats (dotted)

Example 5.11 shows the time-signatures in common use, together with the value in notes of one complete bar. Bars which may be divided into two, three or four equal beats are said to be, respectively, in *duple*, *triple* and *quadruple* time. (Note that the alternative signs, ₵ for $\frac{2}{2}$ for C for $\frac{4}{4}$, are sometimes found in early editions of music. They are now less often used, as past inconsistencies tended to make them confusing.)

Example 5.11

	SIMPLE TIMES		COMPOUND TIMES	
	Time Signature	Value of one bar	Time Signature	Value of one bar
DUPLE	¢ or 2/2	𝅗𝅥 𝅗𝅥	6/4	𝅗𝅥. 𝅗𝅥.
	2/4	♩ ♩	6/8	♩. ♩.
	2/8	♪ ♪	6/16	♪. ♪.
TRIPLE	3/2	𝅗𝅥 𝅗𝅥 𝅗𝅥	9/4	𝅗𝅥. 𝅗𝅥. 𝅗𝅥.
	3/4	♩ ♩ ♩	9/8	♩. ♩. ♩.
	3/8	♪ ♪ ♪	9/16	♪. ♪. ♪.
QUADRUPLE	4/2	𝅗𝅥 𝅗𝅥 𝅗𝅥 𝅗𝅥	12/4	𝅗𝅥. 𝅗𝅥. 𝅗𝅥. 𝅗𝅥.
	C or 4/4	♩ ♩ ♩ ♩	12/8	♩. ♩. ♩. ♩.
	4/8	♪ ♪ ♪ ♪	12/16	♪. ♪. ♪. ♪.

Grouping of notes

In printed music, notes are often grouped together by joining the hooks of their tails.

Example 5.12

In simple time, notes, when joined, are grouped in twos, fours, eights, etc. In compound time they are grouped in threes, sixes, nines, twelves, etc.

Example 5.13

Simple times

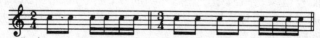

Compound times

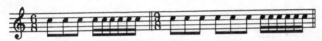

Occasionally, three notes may be played in the time of two notes of similar value. The group of three notes is then called a *triplet*, and the sign $\widehat{3}$ is placed above it.

Example 5.14

Other irregular groupings are sometimes used:

Name	*Sign*	*Effect*
Duplet	$\widehat{2}$	Two notes played in the time of three.
Quadruplet	$\widehat{4}$	Four notes played in the time of three.
Quintuplet	$\widehat{5}$	Five notes played in the time of four.
Sextolet	$\widehat{6}$	Six notes played in the time of four.
Septuplet	$\widehat{7}$	Seven notes played in the time of four (or, occasionally, six)

Rests

In music there are often short periods of silence between sounds, and to represent them a set of signs called *rests* is used. Each rest is equivalent in duration to a note of the same value.

Some rests are rather similar, and may be confused. The semibreve rest *hangs* from the fourth line of the stave, whereas the minim rest *sits* on the third line. Also, when the sign Γ is used to represent the crotchet rest, the hook is to the right; the sign for the quaver rest is similar, but the hook is to the left (see example 5.15).

A silent bar is indicated by a semibreve rest; several bars' silence is shown by a rest with a number over it.

A pause $\frown$ over a note or rest means that it is to be prolonged a little; the exact length is left to the performer's discretion.

Example 5.15

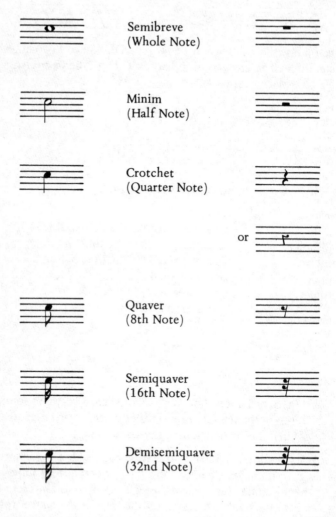

Semibreve
(Whole Note)

Minim
(Half Note)

Crotchet
(Quarter Note)

or

Quaver
(8th Note)

Semiquaver
(16th Note)

Demisemiquaver
(32nd Note)

Self-testing questions

(Please see preliminary remarks in Chapter 3, page 15.)

1 (a) Write the notes C, D, E, F on the treble stave, and write above them the sign which indicates that these notes are to be played an octave *higher* than they are written. (b) Write the notes F, E, D, C on the bass stave, and write below them the sign(s) which indicate that these notes are to be played an octave *lower* than written. (*Example 5.2*)

2 Write notes on the first three leger lines (a) above the treble stave; (b) below the treble stave; (c) above the bass stave; (d) below the bass stave. (*Example 5.1*)

3 'Beats' are grouped into rhythmic units. What are these called, and how are they 'marked'? (*Example 5.3*)

4 (a) Which beat in a bar is normally the most strongly accented? (b) In a bar of two or three beats, which are the 'weak' beats? (c) In a bar of four beats, which is the 'medium' beat, and which are the 'weak' beats? (*Example 5.4*)

5 What is a 'double-bar', and how is it shown on the stave? (*Example 5.5*)

6 Write on the stave, a note which has the value of (a) a semibreve, or whole note; (b) a minim, or half note; (c) a crotchet, or quarter note; (d) a quaver, or 8th note; (e) a semiquaver, or 16th note; (f) a demisemiquaver, or 32nd note. (*Example 5.6*)

7 (a) What is the effect of a dot placed after a note? (b) What is the equivalent of a dotted semibreve? (*Example 5.7*)

8 Write, on the stave, the time-signature of $\frac{3}{4}$. What do each of these figures mean? (*Example 5.8*)

9 Write three bars in $\frac{4}{4}$ time, containing the following notes: Bar one: one semibreve; Bar two: two minims; Bar three: eight quavers. (*Example 5.9*)

10 What is the difference between simple and compound times? Write (a) a bar of crotchets in $\frac{2}{4}$ time; (b) a bar of quavers in $\frac{6}{8}$ time. (*Example 5.10*)

11 Write notes to the value in beats of one bar, of each of the following times (e.g. one bar in $\frac{4}{4}$ time = ♩♩♩♩): (a) $\frac{2}{2}$; (b) $\frac{6}{4}$; (c) $\frac{3}{4}$; (d) $\frac{4}{2}$; (e) $\frac{9}{8}$; (f) $\frac{2}{4}$; (g) $\frac{12}{16}$. (*Example 5.11*)

12 Show how notes may be joined together by writing (a) a group of two quavers; (b) a group of four semiquavers; (c) a group of six semiquavers. (*Example 5.13*)

13 Write a 'triplet' consisting of three quavers. These three notes are played in the time of how many notes of similar value? (*Example 5.14*)

14 Write on the stave a 'rest' which is equivalent to each of the following notes: (a) semibreve; (b) minim; (c) crotchet (write two alternative rests); quaver; semiquaver; demisemiquaver. (*Example 5.15*)

15 How are the following indicated: (a) a silent bar; (b) a pause? (*See page 29*)

6

Theory of Piano Music (3)

Tones and semitones

The height or depth of a musical sound is called its *pitch*, and the difference in pitch between two sounds is called an *interval*. On the piano keyboard, some adjacent white keys have a black key in between, and some have not. Adjacent white keys which are not separated by a black key are said to be a *semitone* (or half-tone) apart; this is the smallest interval in modern music. Adjacent white keys which have a black key in between are said to be a *tone* (or whole-tone) apart.

Scales

A *scale* may be thought of as a 'ladder' of notes, but although we may ascend or descend the notes of the scale one by one, the sounds will not be the same distance apart.[1] In medieval times, church music was based on a complicated system of *modal scales*, each bearing a name borrowed from the ancient Greek word 'modes' (mode = manner). Each scale consisted of 'natural' notes with the basic range of seven notes plus the octave, which, on the piano, would be played only on the white keys. Two of these seven-note modal scales have survived in modern music. They are sometimes called *diatonic* scales (from the Greek word for 'through the tones'),

---

[1] Except for the *chromatic scale*, considered later in this chapter, which consists entirely of semitones.

and are of two kinds, *major* and *minor*.[1] If, starting on Middle C, you play each white piano key in order, up to the C above (or down to the C below), you will have played the scale of C *major*, one octave ascending or descending.

Degrees of the scale

In theory each note of the scale is called a *degree* and is given a name, though it is often more convenient to refer to degrees by numbers, as in Example 6.1. (Usually Roman numerals are used.)

Example 6.1

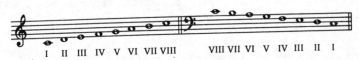

I   II   III   IV   V   VI   VII VIII   VIII VII VI   V   IV III   II   I

The names of the degrees, which are always counted upwards, are:

Degree	Name
I	*tonic*, or *key-note*
II	*supertonic*
III	*mediant*
IV	*subdominant*
V	*dominant*
VI	*submediant*
VII	*leading note*
VIII	*tonic*, or *key-note*

The eighth degree is, of course, a repetition of the tonic, or key-note, an octave higher in pitch.

The dominant, as its name implies, is the 'ruling' note of the scale. Next in importance is the tonic (which is the 'governing' note of the scale). Third in importance is the fourth degree, the subdominant. The seventh degree is called the leading note because of its strong tendency to lead to the tonic.

[1] The major scale is based on the 'Ionian Mode'; the minor scale on the 'Aeolian Mode'.

Sharps, flats and naturals

Since the scale of C major is formed entirely of natural notes, represented by the white keys of the piano, and these notes are named after the first seven letters of the alphabet (the only letters used in musical notation), how are the black piano keys represented? The answer is that a black key takes its name from the white key either immediately above or below it. Thus the white keys C and D are a tone apart, and the black key in between them may be looked upon as a semitone above C, or as a semitone below D.

If a sharp sign (♯) is placed before a natural note, it raises the pitch by a semitone; a flat sign (♭) before a natural note lowers the pitch by a semitone. Thus, a sharp before C natural makes it C sharp, and a flat before D natural makes it D flat.

Example 6.2

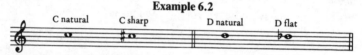

It follows, therefore, that the black piano key between the white keys C and D may be called either C sharp or D flat; and the black key between D and E may be called either D sharp or E flat, and so on. Two sounds of the same pitch, which have different letter names, are said to be *enharmonic*. Example 6.3 shows a section of the piano keyboard, with the enharmonic notes. On the piano, it is wrong to think of sharpened or flattened notes as being played only on the black keys, for example, the notes B and E, when sharpened, and C and F, when flattened, are played on white keys.

Example 6.3

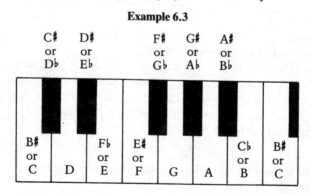

When a sharp or flat has been placed before a natural note, the original pitch can be restored to a subsequent note, of the same letter name, by placing a *natural* sign (♮) before it.

Example 6.4

Accidentals

Accidentals are sharps and flats which are used during the course of a movement.[1] An accidental affects only the note before which it is placed, and any succeeding notes on the same line (or in the same space) on the stave, and in the *same* bar.

Example 6.5

In Example 6.5, each of the four Gs in the first bar is played as G sharp, but the G in the second bar is played as G natural. In practice, a 'cautionary' natural sign would usually be placed before this G – sometimes enclosed in a bracket (♮) – but this is not obligatory.

If a note marked with an accidental is followed by a note of the same letter name in the *same* bar, the second note may be restored to its original pitch by means of a natural sign.

Example 6.6

---

[1] Double-sharps and double-flats are also accidentals. These are explained on p. 45. A natural sign may also be used as an accidental. (See p. 39.)

The pattern of major scales (and key-signatures)

Looking again at the C major scale (example 6.7) you will see that the third and fourth, and the seventh and eighth notes of the scale are a semitone apart, whereas the distance between any other two adjacent notes is a tone. The eight-note scale may, in fact, be divided into two halves, each of which follows the same pattern (tone–tone–semitone). Each half is called a *tetrachord* (a Greek word applied to the four notes of an early instrument), and the two tetrachords are joined together by a tone.

Example 6.7

Scale of C Major

Now play, with one finger, the notes of the C major scale, carefully observing the pattern of tones and semitones on the keyboard, then write the scale in your music book.

So long as this pattern is preserved, a major scale can be formed on any tonic, or key-note. The formation of scales is, however, much easier to understand if they are studied in the right order. If we take the *upper* tetrachord of the C major scale, and add another tetrachord *above* it, we can form the scale of G major. But to preserve the pattern of each tetrachord (tone–tone–semitone) we must raise the seventh note of the new scale by a semitone. This we do by placing a sharp before the note F.

Example 6.8

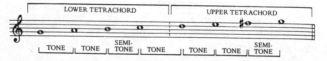

Since this sharp is a vital part of the new scale, it is placed at the beginning of the stave, immediately after the clef sign, and is called the *key-signature*. A piece of music which is founded on the G major scale is said to be in the *key* of G major.

Example 6.9

Scale of G Major

The sharp in the key-signature means that every F in the piece must be played as F sharp, unless the sharp is cancelled by a natural sign. There is thus no need to place a sharp sign before each individual F. (Now play the notes of the G major scale, and write them in your music book.)

In forming the 'sharp' series of major scales, the order goes up in fifths, so that the dominant of one key becomes the tonic of the next. To continue, therefore, we take the upper tetrachord of the G major scale, and add another tetrachord above it, thus forming the scale of D major. Again the seventh note (C) of the new scale is raised by a semitone by the addition of a sharp, so that the new key-signature has two sharps.

Example 6.10

Scale of D Major

(Now play the notes of the D major scale, and write them in your music book.)

By a similar process, we may form the major scales of A, E, B, F sharp and C sharp (key-signatures are shown in Example 6.15). You should now study the structure of these scales in your scale book, and write them in your music book.

If, instead of taking the upper tetrachord of the C major scale, we take the *lower* tetrachord and add another tetrachord *below* it, we can form the scale of F major. But to preserve the pattern of the major scale it is necessary to lower, by a semitone, the fourth note of the new scale. Thus the note B becomes B flat, and we place this flat immediately after the clef sign. It now becomes the key-signature, and affects every B that occurs in the piece. Note that, in the 'flat' series of major scales, the order goes *down* in fifths, so that the tonic of one key becomes the dominant of the next.

Example 6.11

Scale of F Major

By a similar process we can form the major scales of B flat, E flat, A flat, D flat, G flat and C flat (key-signatures shown in Example 6.15, p. 41). Again, you should study the structure of these scales in your scale book, and write them in your music book. You can now, if you wish, start to practise the C major scale, with the help of Demonstration Lesson Two, p. 133. When you can play this fluently, you can practise other scales on the lines suggested in this lesson.

The minor scale

Let us now consider the second kind of diatonic scale: the *minor scale*. A composer chooses the kind of scale which best suits the 'character' of the music. Broadly speaking, music based on the minor scale is often more expressive and less brilliant than music in major keys. Thus, one would expect a funeral march to be in a minor key, and a wedding march in a major key. But there is, of course, much sad and expressive music in major keys, and vice versa.

Although the major scale has remained unaltered during the past few centuries, the minor scale has undergone several changes. The earliest form is based on the modal scale starting on A. (You can hear what it sounds like by starting on the white piano key A, and playing eight consecutive white keys.)

Example 6.12

Modal Scale of A Minor

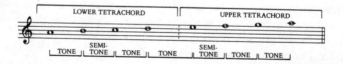

Note that, unlike the major scale, the pattern of the lower and upper tetrachords is not the same; the lower tetrachord has tone–tone–semitone; the upper tetrachord semitone–tone–tone. A peculiarity of this modal scale is that there is an interval of a tone between the seventh and eighth degrees, whereas in our modern scale system these notes are usually a semitone apart. The seventh degree is therefore usually modified. One way of doing this is to sharpen the seventh note of the modal scale. This produces what is known as the *harmonic minor* scale. Again the pattern of the two tetrachords is different.

Example 6.13

Scale of A Minor – Harmonic Form

(Now play the notes of the A minor harmonic scale, and write them in your music book.)

Although the seventh note of the harmonic minor scale is sharpened, the sharp is *not* included in the key-signature, but is regarded as an accidental. (Note that sometimes a natural sign may become an 'accidental'. In the key of G major, for example, the F sharp in the key-signature, which affects every F in the piece, may be lowered a semitone by the addition of a natural sign; a subsequent note of the same letter name can be restored to its original pitch by placing a sharp before it.) However, by sharpening the seventh note, the interval between the sixth and seventh degrees of the scale becomes a tone-and-a-half (i.e. three semitones). To overcome objection to this interval (which, in vocal music, was considered difficult to sing), the *melodic minor* scale was evolved. This scale, as its name implies, was originally used chiefly for the construction of melodies, whereas the harmonic minor scale was used principally in the construction of chords (i.e. harmony).

A peculiarity of the melodic minor scale is that different forms are used when ascending and descending. In ascending, the sixth and seventh notes are sharpened; in descending, they are restored to their original pitch. Again, these sharpened notes are not included in the key-signature, but are regarded as accidentals.

Example 6.14

Scale of A Minor – Melodic Form

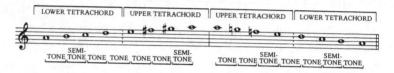

In ascending, the semitones fall between the second and third, and seventh and eighth notes; in descending they fall between the sixth and fifth, and third and second notes. The descending form is, in fact, the same as that of the modal scale. (Now play the notes of the A minor melodic scale, and write them in your music book.)

A minor scale which starts on the same note (or 'tonic') as a major scale is known as its *tonic minor*. But a glance at Example 6.15 will show that the key-signatures of a major scale and of a tonic minor scale are not the same, even though both scales start on the same note. For instance, A minor has a key-signature of no sharps or flats, whereas A major has a key-signature of three sharps.

Major and minor scales which *do* have the same key-signature, however, are said to be *relative* to one another: C major and A minor, for example, are relative because each has a key-signature of no sharps or flats. Each major scale has its *relative minor*, the first note of the minor scale being the sixth note of the relative major. Looking at it another way, the last three notes of the major scale become the first three notes of its relative minor. Example 6.15 shows the key-signatures of relative major and minor scales. As we have already seen, however, the key-signature of the harmonic and melodic scale does not fit exactly, and certain modifications are necessary.

We can now construct a series of minor scales. The process is, in some respects, similar to that of forming major scales. If we take the *upper* tetrachord of the modal scale of A minor (Example 6.12), and add another tetrachord *above* it, we can form the modal scale of E minor. But since the two tetrachords of a minor scale are not identical, we must preserve the pattern of the new lower tetrachord

Example 6.15

Key-signatures of Major and Relative Minor Scales

(tone–semitone–tone) by modifying the pattern of the old (formerly upper) tetrachord (semitone–tone–tone). This we do by adding a key-signature of one sharp, which has the effect of sharpening the second note of the new scale.

Example 6.16

Modal Scale of E Minor

From the modal scale of E minor, we can form the harmonic scale of E minor, by sharpening the seventh note of the scale by means of an accidental.

Example 6.17

Scale of E Minor – Harmonic Form

To form the melodic scale of E minor, we take the modal scale and, when ascending, sharpen the sixth and seventh notes by means of accidentals; when descending, we restore these notes to their original pitch (i.e. the notes of the modal minor scale).

Example 6.18

Scale of E Minor – Melodic Form

Continuing the process, we may form the other minor scales which have sharps in their key-signatures: B minor, F sharp minor,

C sharp minor, G sharp minor, D sharp minor and A sharp minor. (Although you will not be playing music in some of these keys until you are a very advanced player, you should study the *structure* of the scales in your scale book, and write them in your music book.)

The 'flat' series of minor scales is formed by taking the *lower* tetrachord of a modal minor scale, and adding a tetrachord *below* it. The tonic of one key thus becomes the dominant of another, so that the order goes *down* in fifths. But to form the pattern of the new upper tetrachord (semitone–tone–tone), we must *modify* the pattern of the old (lower) tetrachord. Thus, when taking the lower tetrachord of the modal A minor scale, and adding a tetrachord below it to form the modal D minor scale, we add a key-signature of one flat, which produces a semitone between the fifth and sixth degrees of the scale.

Example 6.19

Modal Scale of D Minor

From the modal scale of D minor, we can form the harmonic scale of D minor, by sharpening the seventh note by means of an accidental.

Example 6.20

Scale of D Minor – Harmonic Form

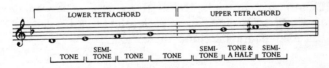

We can also form the melodic scale of D minor by sharpening the sixth and seventh notes of the modal scale, by means of accidentals, when ascending, and by restoring these notes to their original pitch when descending (Example 6.21).

Example 6.21

Scale of D Minor – Melodic Form

By the same process we can form the other minor scales which have flats in their key-signatures: G minor, C minor, F minor, B flat minor, E flat minor and A flat minor. (You should now study the structure of these scales in your scale book, and write them in your music book.)

In the early stages you will, of course, practise only a few of these scales, but it is important that you should understand the general principles of scale formation, which are often misunderstood, and it is for this reason that we have gone into the matter in some detail.

The chromatic scale

The *chromatic scale* consists entirely of semitones. Each octave contains twelve different notes arranged in alphabetical order, though there may be two notes of the same letter name: C and C sharp, D and D flat, and so on. On the piano, all the keys, white and black, are used in order.

The chromatic scale is usually formed by taking the notes of a major scale and 'filling in' the missing semitones, by adding sharps (or naturals) to sharpen notes in ascending, and by adding flats (or naturals) to flatten them in descending. (There are other methods of writing the chromatic scale. Example 8.11 (page 71) shows a different way of writing a chromatic scale starting on D.) Example 6.22 shows the chromatic scale starting on C. The white-headed notes are those of the C major scale; the black-headed notes are those added to form the chromatic scale.

Example 6.22

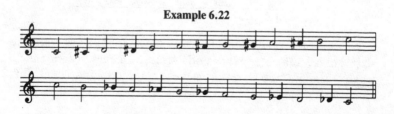

Double-sharps and double-flats

The pitch of a note which has already been sharpened or flattened may be raised or lowered by a semitone, if a *double-sharp* sign (✕), or a *double-flat* sign (♭♭) is placed immediately before the note. A double-sharp or double-flat may be reduced to a single sharp or flat by using the signs (♮♯) or (♮♭); of the note may be raised or lowered a tone, by using a *double-natural* sign (♮♮). Alternatively, the signs for a single sharp, flat, or natural may be used.

Example 6.23

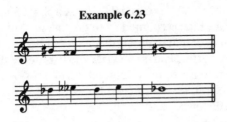

The two passages in Example 6.23 *could* be written thus:

Example 6.24

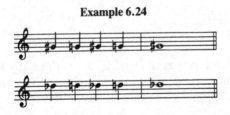

It is often convenient, however, to use double-sharps or double-flats to reduce the number of single flats, sharps and naturals which would otherwise be required. It should be noted that double-sharps and double-flats make it possible for each note of the scale to have three different letter names. Thus C, B sharp and D double-flat are enharmonics (see page 34), as are C sharp, D flat and B double-sharp; D, E double-flat and C double-sharp; and so on.

Intervals

The smallest interval, the semitone, or half-tone, is called *diatonic* when the two notes have different names (e.g. B and C), and *chromatic* when the two notes have the same letter names (e.g. C and C sharp). Intervals can be formed on any note of the scale, but the size of an interval depends on the number of tones and semitones which are included. Thus, the intervals B to C (a diatonic semitone) and B to C sharp (a tone) are both classified as 'seconds', though, as we shall see, one is a minor second and the other a major second.

An interval is calculated by counting the letter names upwards from the lower note to the higher,[1] both letter names being included in the total – thus C to F is a fourth, C to A a sixth, and so on.

Any interval which is counted from the first note of a major scale to any other note of that scale is either *major* or *perfect*. It is useful to relate intervals to the piano keyboard, and to observe the number of tones and semitones in each interval. C to D is a major second (tone); C to E a major third (two tones); C to F a perfect fourth (two-and-a-half-tones), and so on.

Example 6.25

If a major interval is reduced by a semitone (by flattening the upper note or sharpening the lower note) it becomes *minor*. Thus C to E flat, or C sharp to E natural, are minor thirds. A perfect or major interval, if increased by a semitone, becomes *augmented* (e.g. C to D sharp, and C flat to D natural are augmented seconds). A perfect or minor interval, if decreased by a semitone, becomes *diminished* (e.g. C to G flat, and C sharp to G natural are diminished fifths).

Note that, as intervals are calculated by counting the letter names *upwards*, two intervals having identical pitch but different letter names may be differently described. Thus, C to F sharp is an

---

[1] An interval which exceeds the compass of an octave is said to be *compound* (i.e. a *simple* interval to which an octave has been added). A compound interval can be reduced to a simple interval by subtracting seven (e.g. a ninth $(9-7 = 2)$ can be reduced to a second). Compound intervals are calculated by counting letter names upwards (e.g. C to E (three notes above) is a major third; C to E (ten notes above) is a major tenth).

augmented fourth, but C to G flat, a diminished fifth; C to E flat is a minor third, but C to D sharp, an augmented second, and so on.

An interval may be *inverted* by playing either the top note an octave lower, or the bottom note an octave higher. Perfect intervals, when inverted, remain perfect; minor intervals become major; augmented intervals become diminished, and diminished intervals augmented.

Chords

Chords are combinations of notes which are sounded together.

Example 6.26

The simplest kind of chord can be formed by taking any note of the scale, which we will call the bass or *root*, and adding two other notes above it, one a third and the other a fifth from the root. The chord so formed is called a *triad*. Triads can be formed on any degree of the major or minor scale using only the notes of the scale itself.

Triads formed on the degrees of a major scale can be of three kinds:

(a) *Major:* with the two upper notes a major third and a perfect fifth from the root.
(b) *Minor:* with the two upper notes a minor third and a perfect fifth from the root.
(c) *Diminished:* with the two upper notes a minor third and a diminished fifth from the root.

Example 6.27

Key of C Major

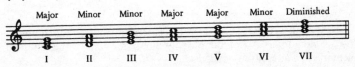

Triads formed on the degrees of a minor scale include, in addition to major, minor and diminished triads, an augmented triad on the third degree, with the two upper notes a major third and an augmented fifth from the root.

Example 6.28

Key of A Minor

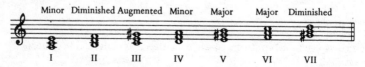

If you play the triads in Examples 6.27 and 6.28, you will probably feel that both major and minor triads sound complete in themselves, but that diminished and augmented triads sound incomplete until they are resolved upon major or minor chords.[1]

Example 6.29

Arpeggios and broken chords

Arpeggios are chords, the notes of which instead of being sounded together are played one after the other.

Broken chords are similar to *arpeggios*, except that the notes are played out of order.

Example 6.30

---

[1] Although a chord is, properly, three or more notes sounded together, the two-note intervals in Example 6.29 can, in the context, be regarded as incomplete major or minor triads.

Self-testing questions
(Please see Preliminary remarks in Chapter 3, page 15.)

1 What is an interval? (*See page 32*)
2 (a) What is a scale? (b) Which two seven-note 'modal' scales have survived in modern music? (c) What are these two scales sometimes called? (*See pages 32–3*)
3 Which adjacent white piano keys are (a) a tone apart; (b) a semitone apart? (*See page 31*)
4 Write the Roman Numerals which refer to the 'degrees' of the scale, and against each numeral write the name of the degree. (*See page 33, and Example 6.1*)
5 Name (a) the 'ruling' note of the scale; (b) the 'governing' note of the scale; (c) the note which tends to lead to the tonic. (*See page 33*)
6 What is the effect of placing before a natural note (a) a sharp sign; (b) a flat sign? (*See pages 34–5, and Example 6.2*)
7 Write, on the treble stave, the notes C sharp and D flat. (*Example 6.2*)
8 Which notes on the piano, when sharpened or flattened, are played on the white keys? (*See page 34*)
9 Each piano black key may be represented as either a sharp note or a flat note. Give alternative names for (a) C sharp; (b) G flat; (c) B flat; (d) D sharp; (e) G sharp. (*Example 6.3*)
10 Write, on the treble stave, the notes F sharp and G flat. Show how these notes may be restored to their 'natural' pitch. (*Example 6.4*)
11 What are 'accidentals', and which notes do they affect? (*See page 34*)
12 What is a tetrachord? (*See page 36*)
13 Write the scale of C major (one octave, treble clef), marking the tones and semitones which make up each tetrachord. Name the interval which joins the tetrachords together. (*Example 6.7*)
14 Show how the scale of G major can be formed on the same pattern. Put a sharp before the note which much be raised in pitch. (*Example 6.8*)
15 Write the key-signature of the scale of G major. (*Example 6.9*)
16 Write the scale of D major (one octave, treble clef), with the correct key-signature. (*Example 6.10*)
17 Write the key-signature and scale of F major (one octave, treble clef). (*Example 6.11*)
18 Which piano keys represent the modal scale of A minor? (*See page 30*)
19 Write the modal scale of A minor. (*Example 6.12*)
20 Write the scale of A minor (harmonic form). (*Example 6.13*)
21 Write the scale of A minor (melodic form). (*Example 6.14*)
22 What does a major scale have in common with its *tonic* minor? (*See page 40*)
23 What does a major scale have in common with its *relative* minor? (*See page 40*)
24 Write the key-signatures of these scales, naming the relative minor of

each: (a) A major; (b) F major; (c) G major; (d) A flat major; (e) B major; (f) D flat major. (*Example 6.15*)

25 Write the modal scale of E minor. (*Example 6.16*)

26 Write the scale of E minor (harmonic form). (*Example 6.17*)

27 Write the scale of E minor (melodic form). (*Example 6.18*)

28 Write the modal scale of D minor. (*Example 6.19*)

29 Write the scale of D minor (harmonic form). (*Example 6.20*)

30 Write the scale of D minor (melodic form). (*Example 6.21*)

31 Write the chromatic scale starting on Middle C (one octave, ascending and descending). (*Example 6.22*)

32 What effect has (a) a double-sharp; (b) a double-flat? What are the signs for these? What signs reduce double-sharps and double-flats to single ones? (*See pages 45–6, and Examples 6.23 and 6.24*)

33 Write the intervals of a major scale, marking each 'perfect' or 'major'. (*Example 6.25*)

34 What is (a) a chord; (b) a triad? (*See page 47*)

35 Write the triads in the key of C major, marking each 'major', 'minor', or 'diminished'. (*Example 6.27*)

36 Write the triads in the key of A minor, marking each 'major', 'minor', 'diminished', or 'augmented'. (*Example 6.28*)

37 Which triads sound complete in themselves, and which sound incomplete until resolved upon major or minor chords? (*See page 49, and Example 6.29*)

38 Write in the key of C major (a) an *arpeggio*; (b) a broken chord. (*Example 6.30*)

7

How to Practise

Any readers who may aspire to become professional concert pianists will probably have realised that they will have to find an outstanding teacher, and follow his (or her) advice. The road to virtuosity is long and hard, demanding not only a high degree of inborn talent, but also the ability and desire to devote many hours a day to soul-searching practice and study, in the burning pursuit of a goal which may, in the end, prove elusive.

If you are playing the piano purely for your own pleasure (and possibly that of some others) careful practice is still essential if you wish to make real progress; but when music is a part-time creative (or re-creative) activity, practice will necessarily be on a more limited scale. We need not therefore devote much space to 'over-practice' which, for the would-be virtuoso, may sometimes result in strained fingers and hands, and is a waste of physical and nervous energy.

However, even short periods of 'aimless' practice may, instead of proving beneficial, serve only to develop and perpetuate faults. Properly directed practice is therefore of first importance and can transform periods of drudgery into periods of enlightenment.

If you are doing other work during the day, you may find that the only time you are able to set aside for practice is when you are not feeling at your best. If you have real enthusiasm for the piano this should not be too much of a problem, but a few general guidelines may be of help.

In the early stages of piano playing, hands and arms will be subjected to unfamiliar sequences of muscular exertion, and periods of practice should be quite short. As muscles become stronger practice periods may be extended gradually, so long as a break is made whenever hands, arms or mind begin to feel tired or tense. It is worthwhile, now and again, taking the hands from the keyboard, and letting the arms fall limply to the sides for a few moments, so that any stiffness and tension are relieved. In longer periods complete changes of body posture are essential from time to time. These can be combined with some small mental or physical relaxation or enjoyment – a walk around the room, a cup of tea, reading a book for a few minutes, for example.

There may be times when playing something will provide solace from grief or disappointment, or relief from anger or frustration, but attempts to practise under conditions of stress, or great tiredness, are not usually rewarding. Practising is, of course, a highly individual experience, and your personal approach is therefore of great importance. If you are studying on your own, or with minimal help from a teacher, you may feel the lack of encouragement and support which every good teacher ought to offer. Nevertheless, you must be reasonably optimistic about your prospects, however small. Those who say 'I can't do it' never can, unless and until they are persuaded otherwise.

One of the disappointments of practising, especially for the mature adult beginner, is that at times progress appears to be non-existent, and when things seem to be getting worse instead of better, the would-be pianist begins to wonder whether he, or she, really has the necessary talent for even the most modest achievements. Progress, however, is seldom a continuous process of advancement, but rather a matter of 'three steps forward and two backwards'. It is important to recognise this *before* discouragement sets in, and to see the problem in its right perspective. Compare today's performance with yesterday's, and you may decide that today's careful practice has been a waste of time. But perhaps yesterday's mood was more perceptive (or your energy cycle more active). Compare today's performance with that of a week or a month ago, and your true progress may be more apparent.

Although 'aimless' practice is to be avoided, it is often a mistake to set yourself too rigid a target or timetable. Ten minutes scale practice, timed with a stop watch, is likely to be less useful than the resolve to practise a single scale for as long as the undertaking seems to be worthwhile, and you are able to give it undivided care and attention. It is usually undesirable to practise one thing for a very long time to the exclusion of everything else, though this may sometimes be necessary for examination purposes. Also, it is usually desirable to have two or more pieces in progress at a time, preferably in contrasted styles. Occasionally, it may be good to have a 'playing' of anything and everything which takes your fancy (including piano duets if you can find a partner) simply for your personal pleasure and amusement.

Before starting to practise, try to have a clear idea of what you are going to do. If you start a technical exercise without understanding *why* you are playing it, you will not be able to identify and correct any faults which may occur. And if you are studying an unfamiliar piece, you will not get far if you fail to observe the key- and time-signatures. Everything you play – scales, *arpeggios*, pieces, studies, sight-reading – needs to be prepared in the mind before you start. 'If you don't know, don't go', says a manual on car driving. Or, in the words of Liszt, 'Think ten times and play once!'. Concentration, interest, observation and listening are the essential ingredients of worthwhile practice.

Finding the key of a piece

It is not always easy to decide the key of a piece of music, simply by looking at the key-signature. A movement, for example, with two sharps in the key-signature could be in either D major or B minor, since both keys share the same key-signature. As a general rule the last lowest note in the left hand will usually be the key-note.[1] Thus, in Example 7.1 the final note in the left hand is B, and the piece is in B minor.

In easier piano music, the final note in the left hand will almost invariably be the key-note, but accidentals may often provide useful clues. For example, a melody with a key-signature without sharps or flats could be in C major or in A minor. In C major, one would

---

[1] 'Key-note' is used in preference to 'tonic', because this term is used by The Associated Board, and other leading bodies, in connection with aural tests, etc.

Example 7.1

Prelude

Chopin
Op.28, No. 6

expect to find G naturals in the melody, as in Example 7.2(a). If sharps appear, it is likely that these are accidentally sharpened leading notes in the key of A minor, and that the piece is in that key, as in Example 7.2(b).

Example 7.2

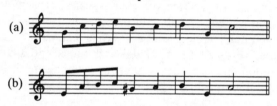

Experience in hearing and analysing phrases before playing them will help you identify a key with some confidence.

What to look for

Before studying a new piece, always look through the music slowly and carefully, taking note of anything which may help you to understand it. What is the name of the composer, his nationality, and when did he live? What is the style and character of the music? Is it romantic, grave or gay? And is there a description which may help (nocturne, minuet, etc.)? You should not play Bach like Beethoven, still less like Debussy. Look at the phrasing, cadences and so on, and try to get as complete a mental picture as possible of how the piece should sound.

It may be useful to number the bars (lightly in pencil which can be rubbed out later); then, from time to time, you can write down the numbers of those bars which present special difficulties, and the nature of these; you can then practise these bars separately, making notes of your progress. (To save time, you could number every fifth bar.)

The first essential is accuracy – correct notes, time-values, fingering, and so on. Until you can play with reasonable accuracy, you cannot really begin to interpret the thoughts of the composer. So, begin by isolating difficult passages one by one as you go along, correcting faults before they become habits. Consider phrasing. Singing over passages will help you to appreciate the shape of the phrases, how the music moves along, and where cadences and climaxes occur. What kind of finger technique will you use, and where, if at all, might the sustaining pedal be appropriate?

It is a great help if you can memorise some of the music, even if, at first, you are able to remember only a few bars at a time. This applies particularly to the opening bars of a piece; if you know them by heart, you will be able to give your complete attention to your playing – to watch your hands, to judge the appropriate tone level, and so on. It will also help you to make a good start when you are playing at a performance or examination, and thus to feel more confidence in your ability.

When practising, however, do not fall into the habit of *always* starting at the beginning. The opening bars may be the easiest, and more time may need to be spent on difficult bars. It is better to isolate phrases (usually of two or four bars) which need most attention, and to concentrate on these. Of course you should also play the piece right through from time to time. Sometimes it is useful to start in the middle of a piece and play to the end; or even to start with the last phrase, and work backwards phrase by phrase. It is important that you should be able to begin at *any* bar.

Counting time

In order to give each note or rest exactly the right duration of sound or silence, you must learn to count time accurately. When practising, it is helpful, particularly in the early stages, to count aloud. You may not find this easy, but it will come with practice, and audible counting will enable you to establish the shape and phrasing of the music, as well as to keep in correct time. Time is usually counted by the number of beats in each bar. In a bar of $\frac{2}{4}$, $\frac{3}{4}$ or $\frac{4}{4}$ time, for example, each beat is represented by one crotchet or its equivalent (see Example 5.9), and each crotchet (or its equivalent) is therefore counted as one beat:

Example 7.3

From Example 7.3 you will see that two quavers (= one crotchet) are counted as one beat, and one minim (= two crotchets) as two beats. If, however, the music is slow, you could subdivide each crotchet into two half-beats, calling the second half-beat 'and'.

Example 7.4

To a Wild Rose (Woodland Sketches)   *MacDowell*
                                                                        Op. 15, No. 1

Although, when this piece is being learnt, you will find it useful to count '1 and 2 and' throughout, when you know the music really well, and can sing the whole phrase from memory, you should be able to 'think' in terms of: 1 and 2– 1 and 2– 1 and 2 and 1–2–, and so on.

Observe that in Example 7.4 there is no precise indication of speed, although 'with simple tenderness' suggests that the music is not fast, as does the expressive melody. The appropriate speed is of course a matter for individual feeling and judgement.

It is not always easy to decide the appropriate speed for a piece of music, and how to count it. The markings of the composer (sometimes very few, or even none at all) may give some indication: *adagio* means slow, but how slow?; *allegro* means lively, but how lively? Qualifying terms may also help: e.g. *adagio non troppo* (not too slow); *allegro assai* (very fast). In deciding the appropriate speed of a movement, start by looking right through it so that, first, you can be guided by the character and style of the whole movement, and secondly you can take into account the fastest passages. If the movement begins with crotchets and proceeds to semiquavers, the speed at which you will be able to play the semiquavers must be considered when deciding the overall speed.

It is always helpful to sing a melody which is being practised at the keyboard, and also to sing it away from the keyboard (e.g. in the bath); by doing so, the phrasing and general character will be made clearer.

A bar of $\frac{6}{8}$ time would normally be counted as two dotted crotchets.

Example 7.5

The Wild Horseman (Album for the Young)   *Schumann*
                                                          Op. 68, No. 8

If, however, the music is slow, a bar of $\frac{6}{8}$ time could be counted as six quavers.

Example 7.6

Romance from Sonatina in G   *Beethoven*

Similarly, a bar of $\frac{9}{8}$ or $\frac{12}{8}$ time could be counted either as three or four dotted crotchets, or as nine or twelve quavers.

Where triplets occur, each group of three should be counted as one.

Example 7.7

Minuet in F   *Mozart*

The metronome

This is a clock-like instrument which has a flat steel pendulum which swings from side to side with a click; variations of speed are obtained by moving an adjustable weight up and down the pendulum. A graduated scale behind the pendulum covers a range from about 40 to 208 ticks (or beats) to the minute.

Sometimes a metronome marking is added by the composer (or music editor), to indicate the speed at which the music should be played. Thus, ♩ = 120 means that if the weight is placed opposite 120 on the scale, the metronome will give 120 ticks to the minute, and that each crotchet has the value of one tick. Metronome marks are not always to be relied on; for example, in the works of some composers, such as Schumann and Grieg, they should not be taken too literally.

Apart from indicating the speed of a piece of music, the metronome may sometimes be a useful aid when practising; if it is left ticking while you are playing, any deviation from the beat should be evident. It is seldom advisable to keep the metronome ticking for long periods, however, as mechanical time-keeping is no substitute for a sense of rhythm, and constant reliance on the 'tick' is likely to weaken rhythmic feeling.

Intensity and speed

Words, abbreviations and signs which indicate the relative intensity of sounds are called dynamics: for example *piano* (*p*) = soft, *forte* (*f*) = loud, *crescendo* (*cres.* or <) = increasing in volume, *decrescendo* or *diminuendo* (*decresc* or *dim*, or >) = decreasing in volume (see Glossary of terms, page 144).

The dynamic range will vary according to the period of the music. In much early music there are no original dynamic indications, and although these are often added to printed music by modern editors, they are only in the nature of suggestions. Up to Beethoven's time, *pianissimo (pp)* and *fortissimo (ff)* were usually taken to mean 'as soft' or 'as loud' as possible. Since Beethoven's time, some composers have increased the range to *ppp, fff*, or even *pppp,* etc. This must be taken into account when playing music for the older keyboard instruments (including early pianos); since these instruments were not capable of nearly such a wide dynamic range as the modern piano; the range of dynamics when playing Mozart, for example, will be quite different from the range when playing Liszt or Debussy.

Dynamics need to be carefully thought out. If, for instance, a *forte* is followed by a *piano*, the level of tone must be such that a satisfactory contrast is produced. In Example 7.8, *forte* tone must be maintained throughout the first bar, and there must be a *sudden* drop to *piano* at the beginning of the second bar.

Example 7.8

Sonata No. 14 in D Major　　　　　　　　　　　　　　　　*Haydn*

Crescendos and *diminuendos* need to be well planned, especially if they extend over a number of bars, so that they are made gradually, and not exhausted so quickly that a level tone is reached too soon, instead of continuing the rise or fall. The sign >, or the words *sforzando* (*sf*) or *forzato* (*fz*) (It. literally, 'forcing') indicate that the note or chord so marked is to be strongly emphasised with an accent. It is important, however, that the strength of the accent should be related to the passage in which it occurs; in a *forte* passage, it is obvious that the accent will have to be far heavier than in a *piano* passage.

Variations of speed, such as *accelerando* (*accel*) = quickening the pace, or *rallentando* (*rall*) or *ritenuto* (*rit*) = slowing down, also need to be carefully planned, so that the increase or decrease in speed is made gradually, according to the speed of the music, and the length of the phrase involved.

Training the ear

Critical listening is the basis of all good piano playing, and at least a few minutes (say three or four times a week) should be devoted to ear-training. The books of aural tests published for grade examinations held by The Associated Board and other examining bodies may be used for practice. For some of these tests, you will need to enlist the help of a musical friend to play for you, but there are several tests that you can practise on your own.[1]

1 Close your eyes, and play a note at random on the piano, keeping your finger on the key. Sing the note, and check the result by playing it again (try to keep within the range of your voice).
2 Play the key-chord and key-note[2] of a major scale. Choose, at random, any note of the scale (2nd, 3rd, 4th, etc.) and sing it, checking the result by playing it. Example 7.9 shows the procedure.

Example 7.9

Scale of D Major

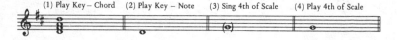

At first you may find that you need to sing up from the key-note to the fourth note, as in Example 7.10.

[1] Alternatively, there are aural cassettes available, one for each Grade 1–8, from Sound Wise, 23 Frithville Gardens, London W12 7JG.
[2] Key-chord = the major triad formed on the key-note (see page 33).

Example 7.10

As soon as possible, however, try to 'think' up the first three notes of the scale, singing only the fourth note. Later, with practice, you should be able to think from the key-note directly to the note you have to sing.

3 From the test book play two notes together (i.e. a two-part interval). Describe the interval (major third, perfect fifth, etc.), and check by counting letter names from the lower note to the higher, etc. (see page 46).

4 From the test book, play a short melodic phrase twice, having first played the key-chord. Sing the phrase, and check by playing it again.

5 From the test book, sing at sight a group of three or more related notes (or a short melodic phrase), having first played the key-chord and key-note, but *not* the phrase. Check by playing the phrase. Simple melodies (folk tunes and hymns, etc.) can also be used for sight-singing.

6 From the test book, play a short melodic phrase twice and clap the rhythm. Check by playing the phrase again. Also clap the rhythm *before* playing it. (This does, of course, presume that you are able to play the phrase *accurately*.)

7 Sing from memory a short melodic phrase from a piece you are studying, then try to write it in your music book. Check with the printed copy. (If necessary, look at the key, and play the key-note on the piano before you start.)

Sight-reading

Sight-reading is to some extent a natural gift; certainly it presents fewer problems to some pianists than to others, even though the latter may be the more accomplished pianists. Those who find sight-reading difficult may, however, develop what ability they have to a reasonable standard by intelligent and regular practice.

Sight-reading is first a matter of observation; the eyes must take in clefs, time- and key-signatures, notes, phrasing, dynamics, and so on. Then, the fingers must make the appropriate response to what the eyes have read, and the ears have heard. And since we must read at least a few notes ahead of what we are playing, the memory must then retain what has been read until the fingers have translated it into sound. In addition, the sight-reader must judge the appropriate speed, style, and interpretation of the music.

Although, in normal practice, it is often useful to be able to watch the hands (having memorised the music to be played), with sight-reading this is not possible. It follows that you must be able to find notes on the piano easily and accurately, without having to glance down at your fingers. Practising scales or short phrases with closed eyes (or with the fingers on top of the closed piano cover), can be useful; also naming a note at random, and trying to find it on the keyboard without looking. The 'feel' of a chord can also be memorised by placing the fingers on the keys, lifting them, and then trying to play the chord with the eyes closed.

When sight-reading from printed music, start quite slowly and try to play strictly in time. Instead of stopping each time you make a mistake (as we all do sometimes), return to the places where the mistakes occurred *after* you have finished the movement, and meanwhile try to carry on calmly.

Instead of thinking of the name of each note, try to hear the sound it represents; this may not be easy at first, but practice in reading through music *before* playing it is a great help. Try also to understand the harmonic and melodic pattern of the music. Watch for *cadences* (see Chapter 10) and sequences. (A *sequence* is a more or less exact repetition of a melody (with or without harmony), at a higher or lower pitch, as in Example 7.11.)

Example 7.11

Remember to look as far ahead as you can, so that the grouping and phrasing of the notes is apparent, and there is a feeling of the music 'going somewhere'. Difficult chords may have to be read upwards from the lowest note.

Demonstration Lesson Three gives detailed advice about sight-reading, and should be studied with care.

Memorising music

Memory implies two things: the capacity to retain knowledge, and the power to recall it. The accuracy with which we retain knowledge depends on how deeply it interests and impresses us; an association of ideas also helps us to remember.

Memory for music depends on three forms of perception: visual, aural and tactile. Some people have great powers of visual perception, and are able to see a page of music in the mind's eye. Those who do not possess this 'photographic' memory will find that music is easier to visualise if the complete shape is concentrated on, before the music is analysed in detail. Points to look for are (a) the pattern or the melody, harmony and fingering; (b) passages, if any, which are repeated, either exactly or in sequence; (c) passages which are based on familiar figures, such as scales, broken chords, or *arpeggios*. Writing out music (a few bars at a time) is often a useful aid to memory.

Aural perception enables the ear to take in the general 'design' of the music as well as the details. It can be developed by careful ear-training and listening. Tactile perception means that the pianist is able to memorise the *feel* of the fingers as they play. Practice with closed eyes (as recommended in the previous section on sight-reading) will help to develop this faculty (scales and *arpeggios* should be included).

Since nervousness often makes memorising difficult and causes memory failure, it is wise to avoid too much conscious effort; at times it is better to read or play music through, noting the various points, without *trying* to memorise it.

It is often also helpful to break up the music into small parts, perhaps even a bar or two at a time. First look at the notes in the right hand, and name them aloud. Now close your eyes, and try to 'imagine' these notes; then, with the eyes still closed, play them five times. Repeat with your left hand, and finally with both hands together. This procedure takes time, but may bring rewarding results.

Some final points

If you know a pianist of approximately the same ability as yourself, try to arrange some duet-playing. There is a large selection of music for four hands at one piano, some of it quite easy. Duet-playing is enjoyable and it is also valuable as an exercise in sight-reading and time-keeping, and for the exchange of ideas with other pianists.

Opportunities of playing before an audience should be welcomed, even if it consists of one or two friends only. They will help you to acquire self-confidence, particularly if you are apprehensive about appearing before an examiner in grade examinations (though you will find that he, or she, is quite human, and will try to put you at ease).

The cassette (or tape) recorder also offers unique opportunities for self-criticism. By playing back your recordings of pieces, studies, scales, and so on, you can not only note your weak points, but also the progress you have made since your previous recording.

Most of your practice periods should include written work. Scales, *arpeggios*, chords, and so on are much more easily understood and remembered if you write them in your music book before playing them. It is also good practice (and fun) to compose and play short melodies. At first, these could be phrases consisting of a few notes; based, perhaps, on suitable words (e.g. FADE, DEAF, BEAD).

Finally, no one should *have* to practise except, perhaps, the very young. Practice is seldom worthwhile unless it is undertaken willingly, and for good reasons – to improve technique and interpretation, to prepare for performance and examination, to provide a yardstick with which to measure progress, and encouragement to go further. Given real desire to learn to play, the necessary self-discipline will follow.

8

Fingering

Printed fingering

Most piano music has fingering marked, and you are advised to avoid unfingered music, especially in the early stages. Printed fingering, however, is intended for pianists with average-sized hands, and if, after trying the suggested fingering for a reasonable period, you find that some of it does not suit you, do not hesitate to alter it. Methods of fingering have changed over the years. Once, for example, the use of the thumb on black keys was not allowed, but it is now freely used in passage work. The development of *legato* pedalling has also resulted in changes of fingering, so that music by Bach, if played without pedal, may be fingered differently from music by Chopin or Debussy.

When playing scales and exercises, it is best to use printed fingering where possible, as it is usually devised with a special purpose in mind, but alternative fingerings are sometimes possible. When music has little or no fingering marked, work out the most simple fingering you can (the easiest is usually the best). Once you have decided on the fingering, try to memorise it and stick to it. Some pianists confuse themselves by using different fingering each time they play, thus making accurate performance almost impossible.

The principles of fingering

The basic principles of fingering are not difficult to understand. In a passage of five consecutive notes, played on the white keys, the five fingers are used in order. (In the examples which follow, the fingering above the notes is for the right hand, and that below the notes for the left hand.)

Example 8.1

In a passage which lies under the hand (i.e. which does not exceed a five-note span), when any white note is left out, the finger which would play that note is also left out.

Example 8.2

Passages exceeding five consecutive white notes are fingered by passing the thumb under the fingers, or the fingers over the thumb.

Example 8.3

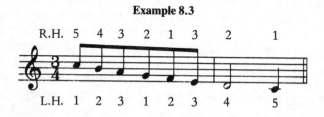

Note patterns

Sequences (groups of notes forming a pattern which is repeated higher up, or lower down, the keyboard) may often be fingered alike.

Example 8.4

The fingers are sometimes contracted to allow one or more fingers to be omitted, so that a passage will lie more easily under the hand. Thus, in Example 8.5, in which both upper and lower parts are played by the right hand, the fourth finger is followed by the second, even though these consecutive notes are only a tone apart.[1]

Example 8.5

For similar reasons, fingers are often extended or stretched. In Example 8.6, consecutive notes, a third apart, are taken by the second and fourth (and by the fourth and fifth, and second and first) fingers of the right hand, and by the third and second (and by the second and first, and third and fifth) fingers of the left hand. Consecutive notes a fourth apart are taken by the first and second fingers of the right hand, and by the fifth and third fingers of the left hand.

Example 8.6

[1] When two parts are played by the same hand, as in Examples 8.5 and 8.7, the upper and lower figures indicate fingering relating, respectively, to the upper and lower parts.

Looking again at Example 8.5, you will see that the first finger is used for each of the two consecutive notes in the lower part. Although, because of this, it is not possible to play the two lower notes absolutely smoothly and without a break, this is compensated for by the smoothness of the melody in the upper part.

Changing fingers on the same note

In Example 8.6, different fingers are used when the note G is repeated by the right and left hands. This device allows the hand to be shifted down (or up) the keyboard, and also allows the repeated notes to be neatly phrased. Sometimes, one finger may be substituted for another while a key is being held down, to obviate a break between notes or to allow a change of position in a passage.

Example 8.7

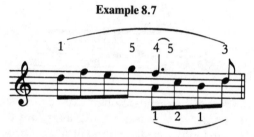

In Example 8.7, the fifth finger is substituted for the fourth (while the key is held down), the change being indicated by a bracket over the figures four and five.

It is sometimes convenient to use the same finger for repeated notes; on the other hand, although the practice of changing fingers is not so strictly adhered to as it used to be, it is often useful. In Example 8.8, the phrasing and shape of the melody is made clearer by the change of finger on the second D, and the fingering is made easier by the change of finger on the first note of the final group of four semiquavers.

Example 8.8

Example 8.9

Scale of C Major

Example 8.10

Scale of A Flat Major

Scales

Let us now look at the fingering of the C major scale (see Example 8.9).

The pattern is 123, 1234, and so on (ascending in the right hand, descending in the left), or 4321 321 (descending in the right hand, ascending in the left). The top note of the scale in the right hand, and the bottom note in the left hand, are played with the fifth finger. All major and minor diatonic scales are fingered on similar principles, but they do not all start with the same fingers. Major and minor scales in the keys of G, D, A and E are fingered like the scale of C major, the thumbs coming together on the key-note, at the end of the first octave. Other major and minor scales may start with different fingers in each hand. The A flat major scale, for example, starts with the second finger in the right hand, and the third finger in the left. It does, nevertheless, follow the pattern 123, 1234, etc (Example 8.10).

The fingering patterns of all major and minor scales should be studied from your scale book, perhaps in the order suggested in Demonstration Lesson Two.

The chromatic scale

The chromatic scale, which consists entirely of semitones, may start on any note. If starting on D, it may be fingered as in Example 8.11.

For chromatic scales starting on other notes, the following rules may be applied:

1 Each hand starts with the appropriate finger, as indicated in Example 8.11. Thus, in the chromatic scale starting on C, the right hand starts with the second finger, and the left hand with the first finger. In the chromatic scale starting on A flat (or G sharp), both hands start with the third finger, and so on.
2 Every black key is played with the third finger. Every white key between two black keys is played with the thumb. Two white keys together are played with the first and second (or second and first) fingers.

Example 8.11

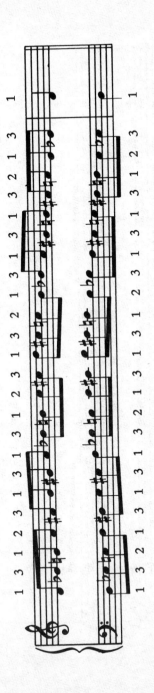

Example 8.12

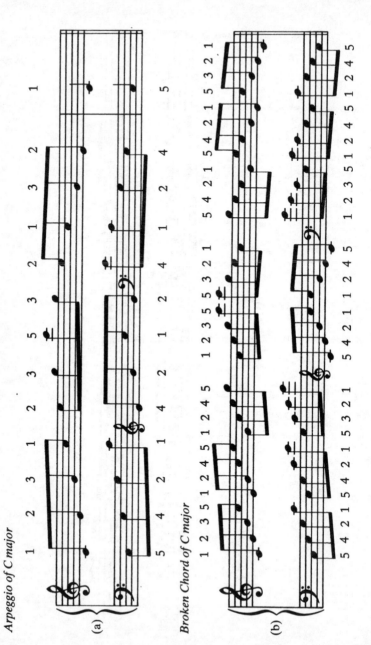

Arpeggios and broken chords

Arpeggio (It. = 'harp-like') means that the notes of a chord are played 'harp-wise' (i.e. in order, but one after the other), instead of being sounded together. The notes of a *broken chord* are similar to those of an *arpeggio*, but they are not in strict consecutive order. The *arpeggio* and broken chord of C major may be fingered as in Example 8.12.

In deciding the fingering of *arpeggios* and broken chords, all the notes of the chord should be considered together. The broken chord in Example 8.13 is fingered:

Example 8.13

The unbroken chord is fingered in the same way:

Example 8.14

	R.H.	L.H.
	5	1
	3	2
	2	3
	1	5

9

Theory of Piano Music (4)

Syncopation

Syncopation is, in general terms, the disturbance of normal rhythm, so that accents fall on beats, or parts of beats, which are not normally accented. The altered accent is often marked with a stress (>).

Example 9.1

Carnaval

Schumann
Op. 9

Notes of embellishment

These are ornamental notes (sometimes known as *grace notes*) which are placed before or after a principal note, and which are usually printed smaller than principal notes.

Ornamental notes were used by the early composers, chiefly to overcome the lack of sustaining power of the early keyboard instruments (spinet, virginals, harpsichord, etc.). The ornamentation of seventeenth- and eighteenth-century music is a specialised subject and is discussed in *The Interpretation of Music of the XVII and XVIII Centuries* (Arnold Dolmetsch), *The Interpretation of Early Music* (Robert Donington), and *Keyboard Interpretation*

(Howard Ferguson). Here we have space to note only the more usual methods of embellishment.

The *appoggiatura*, or 'leaning note', is a small note before the principal note, which takes half the value of the principal note if this is undotted, and two-thirds of its value if it is dotted.

Example 9.2

Written

Played

Written

Played

In modern music, composers give the *appoggiatura* its proper written value.

The *acciaccatura*, or 'crushing note', is written like the *appoggiatura*, but has a slanting stroke through the stem ♪. It is sounded on the beat, as quickly as possible before the principal note, which receives the accent.

Example 9.3

Written

Played

The *turn* (the sign ∽ placed over or after a note) consists of a figure of four notes (note above, note itself, note below, note itself). This figure is played either instead of, or after, the note itself.

Example 9.4

Written

Played

Written

Played

A sharp or flat, placed above or below the turn, means that the upper or lower note is to be sharpened or flattened.

Example 9.5

Written

Played

Written

Played

The *inverted turn* (sign ⌀ or ⅖) is played in the same way as the turn, except that the figure consists of the note below, principal note, note above and note itself.

The *upper mordent* (sign ⩊) consists of three notes (principal note, note above and principal note), played in rapid succession.

Example 9.6

Written

Played

The *lower mordent* (sign ⩊) is played in the same way, except that the three notes consist of the principal note, note below and principal note.

The *trill*, or *shake* (sign *tr*⌇⌇) consists of the rapid alternation of the written note and the note above it; the trill usually ends with a turn.

Example 9.7

Written

Played

In piano music a wavy or curved line is sometimes placed before a chord. A chord so marked is to be *spread*; i.e. the notes are to be played as an *arpeggio* in rapid succession from the lowest note upwards, each note being held as it is played – thus producing a harp-like effect.

Example 9.8

In a book of this size, it is impossible to describe the many rules of ornamentation which apply to music of different periods, particularly the baroque style of the seventeenth and eighteenth centuries. It may be said, however, that baroque trills and turns, with rare exceptions, begin on the upper note.

In well-edited editions of baroque and classical music, however, suggestions for the performance of ornaments are usually included as footnotes; these should, therefore, offer the necessary guidance to the pianist, until such time as enough experience has been gained to attempt a personal interpretation of these complex embellishments.

Self-testing questions
(Please see Preliminary remarks in Chapter 3, page 15.)

1 What is 'syncopation'? (*See page 74*)
2 What is an *appoggiatura*? How does it differ from an *acciaccatura*? (*See pages 75–6 and Examples 9.2 and 9.3*)
3 Write the sign for the 'turn'. Which notes does this figure consist of? (*See page 76, and Example 9.4*)
4 What is the effect of a sharp or flat, placed above or below a turn? (*See page 77, and Example 9.5*)
5 How does an 'inverted' turn differ from a normal one? (*See page 78*)
6 Of which notes does the *upper* mordent consist, and how are they played? Write the sign. (*See page 78, and Example 9.6*)
7 Of which notes does the *lower* mordent consist, and how are they played? Write the sign. (*See page 78*)
8 Write the sign for a trill or shake. Of which notes does it consist, and how does it usually end? (*See page 78, and Example 9.7*)
9 A wavy or curved line is sometimes placed before a chord, how should this chord be played? (*See page 79, and Example 9.8*)

10

Phrasing

Phrasing and Cadences

In verse and prose, punctuation marks (full stop, semi-colon, comma, etc.) are used to shape single words into sentences, clauses, and so on. Apart from serving as breathing spaces, their more important function is to provide 'thinking' places which will enable the reader to take in a number of words as a group, and so give proper meaning to a writer's thoughts. The other factor which gives shape to words is the accentuation of certain syllables, while other syllables are passed over more lightly.

Music also needs breathing and thinking places, and notes are therefore grouped into phrases and sentences by means of cadences.[1] These correspond to punctuation marks, and indicate points of repose – either complete or momentary. A phrase may consist of two or four bars, or sometimes of three, five, six or more bars. A musical 'sentence' may consist of two or more phrases.

Example 10.1 shows four different kinds of cadences.[2] If you play these cadences on the piano, you will find that (a) and (b) give the effect of complete repose, like the full stop, whereas (c) and (d) give the effect of a momentary pause without finality, like the comma or semi-colon. Although cadences appear in various forms,

[1] Cadence = a fall. In speech it is natural for the voice to fall at the end of a sentence. In music there is also often a falling off in flow and movement (but not necessarily in pitch) at a cadence.
[2] The *perfect cadence* is sometimes known as a *full close*; the *imperfect cadence* as a *half close*.

Example 10.1

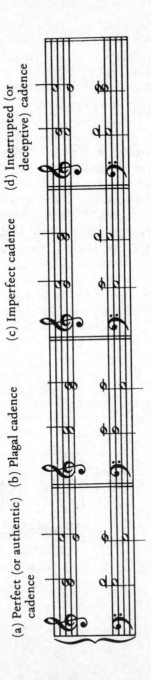

(a) Perfect (or authentic) cadence   (b) Plagal cadence   (c) Imperfect cadence   (d) Interrupted (or deceptive) cadence

which it is not necessary at this stage to analyse individually, it is nevertheless important to be able to recognise points of complete or temporary repose, and to appreciate the feeling of progression towards the cadences. Without this feeling, music would be simply a succession of sounds, with no sense of continuity, of 'going some-where'.

In Example 10.2, the arrows show the progression of each phrase towards its cadence, and when playing these bars this means thinking of phrases rather than beats or bars i.e. from the beginning to the end of each arrow. In addition, the progression from one phrase to another must be considered. In Example 10.2, although the cadence in the second bar may give the impression of a point of slight temporary repose, there must be no halt to the flow of the music. As soon, therefore, as you are able to play the notes with reasonable accuracy you should be thinking from the beginning of the music to the end of the fourth bar. In the second and fourth bars you will see that the chord at the end of each arrow is accentuated (*mfp*); this makes the shape of each phrase abundantly clear. (Note that *mfp* = *mezzo forte piano*: It. = half loud, half soft.)

Example 10.2

Sonata in G Minor

Beethoven
Op. 49, No. 1

Phrasing

In piano music notes may be played in different ways – smoothly, with one note connected to the next, or crisply, with each note separated. The smooth style of playing is known as *legato* (It. = smooth or connected) and the crisp style as *staccato* (It. = detached or separated). Curved lines, called *slurs*, are placed over or under groups of two or more notes of different pitch, showing that these groups should be played *legato*.

Example 10.3

The slur must not be confused with the *tie*, the short curved line which joins the third and fourth notes in Example 10.3. This is used to join together two or more notes of the *same* pitch, the first note being held down, and not sounded again.

Notes to be played *staccato* are indicated by dots placed over or under them. They are usually given approximately half their written value. Two other kinds of *staccato* are sometimes met with. Notes marked with a pointed dash (⸲) are played *staccatissimo*, and held down for about a quarter of their full value. Notes marked with dots covered by a slur are played *mezzo-staccato* (or *semi-staccato*), and are held down for about three-quarters of their full value. In general, all notes not marked with *staccato* signs (even if not covered with slurs) are played *legato*, unless there is some general direction to the contrary, e.g. the word '*staccato*' may be used in place of dots.

Legato slurs *may* extend over entire phrases, but their duration does not necessarily coincide with that of phrases. In Example 10.2, for instance, each bar is slurred, whereas each phrase is actually two bars long. Slurs, therefore, are often used simply to indicate which notes are to be played smoothly and which are not. Just as, in verse or prose, it is not necessary to breathe at *every* comma, so in music we need not break the musical line at the end of every small group of sounds.

Example 10.4

A Little Piece

Not fast

mp

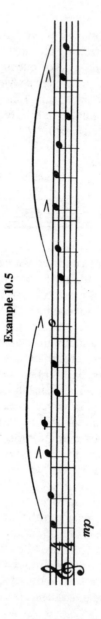

Example 10.5

mp

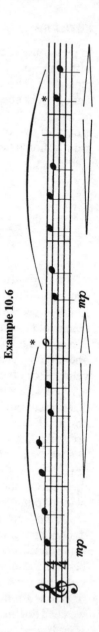

Example 10.6

mp

mp

Schumann
Op. 68, No. 4

As well as thinking from the beginning to the end of a phrase, it is important to appreciate its *shape*, so that you can interpret this in your playing. There is no better way of doing this than by thinking of a phrase as part of a song-melody, and singing it aloud during the process of practising (and *inwardly* when playing, or when you do not want to disturb people (e.g. on a bus). It is good practice to hum over simple melodies, such as folk, hymn or popular tunes, in which the progression of phrases is fairly obvious; this will make it easier to recognise the shape of more intricate phrases when they come along.

Let us now consider the first two phrases of a simple melody (Example 10.4).

Music theory tells us that in $\frac{4}{4}$ time the strongest accent falls on the first beat of each bar, so you *might* be tempted to play the melody as shown in Example 10.5.

However, if you sing the melody phrase by phrase, you will quickly realise that such a mechanical accentuation would completely destroy its shape and flow, and that something like Example 10.6 would be more appropriate. In this interpretation, the melody progresses towards the end of the phrases, and falls away on the notes marked with asterisks.

Here again, as well as thinking from the beginning of each phrase, your overall thinking needs to take in the flow from one phrase to the next, and thus cover both phrases. So we see that although there are accents on the first beat of each bar (except when a beat is displaced in syncopation), these accents may vary greatly in strength, and may sometimes be more apparent in the mind than in the music.

Phrasing in piano music is a complex art which ultimately depends on intuitive good sense and taste, but much can be learned by critical listening and study. In printed music, phrasing indicated by the composer or editor is not always satisfactory and care must be taken, perhaps with the help of an experienced pianist or piano dealer, to seek the best editions. In the early stages some general principles may be of help, provided they are not taken too literally.

When, for example, two notes of equal length are covered by a slur the first note is often stressed more than the second, which is made weaker and very slightly shorter, the finger being raised from the keyboard. A point which arises here is that a sound on the piano begins to fade as soon as it is heard. When two notes are slurred together, therefore, the sound of the first note will have faded a little by the time the second note is played (the slower the notes, the greater the fading). So the second note will need to be played a little more softly than the first, if it is to match. Careful listening and experiment are needed to achieve a perfect balance.

Example 10.7

Aria from Partita in G   *Telemann*

In larger groups of notes, the last note is sometimes shortened slightly by raising the hand from the keyboard, but this depends on the context of the melody. Singing a phrase quite naturally is usually the best way of deciding how it should be treated. Much may be learned by listening to records or tapes of fairly simple piano music and, at the same time, following the printed copy and carefully noting the style of phrasing, and the treatment of phrase and group endings. Suitable recorded pieces include:

Beethoven:	Sonata in G minor, Op 49, No 1
	Sonata in G major, Op 48, No 2
Bartók:	Ten Easy Pieces
	Nine Little Pieces
Schumann:	*Kinderscenen*, Op 15
Tchaikovsky:	Children's Album, Op 39

11

Tone Production

The piano keys

In order to throw a hammer against a string to make it sound, a piano key must be depressed fairly quickly. This requires a certain degree of muscular exertion of the finger – if there is too little, the hammer will merely be lifted, and there will be no sound. The quicker the key is depressed the louder will be the sound. A good sound is not produced, however, by striking the key, but rather by the exertion of the finger, and sometimes the weight of the arm. All tone, loud or soft, needs to be equally well controlled.

Once sound has been produced, it cannot be altered. If a key is held down (with the damper raised) the sound will continue, though it will gradually fade and eventually cease. It is therefore a waste of muscular energy to exert pressure on a key *after* the sound is heard, on the contrary, the finger muscles need to be relaxed at the moment the sound begins, so that the key is held down at its lowest point without pressure.

Arm movements

For tone production different parts of the arm are used for different purposes. A big, round tone may be obtained by using the whole arm from the shoulder, the weight of the arm and hand falling on the keys. To practise this, raise the arms and let them fall limply to the sides, like dead weights. Keeping the arms limp, raise them above the keyboard, and let them drop on to the keys; the fingers will fall naturally into a cup-like position.

When less tone is required (e.g. in slow *piano* and *mezzo-piano* chords), the weight of the forearm, moving from the elbow, may be used.

In more rapid technical passages, the hand may move from the wrist, or the keys may be depressed by the fingers alone. Arm weight may then be dispensed with, the arm being lightly held above the keyboard, with the forearm freely balanced and self-supporting, being neither tight nor relaxed.

Legato

In *legato* playing, one sound is carried over to the next without a break. The duration of a sound therefore depends upon when and how the piano keys are depressed and raised: this requires the most careful practice and listening. The speed at which the keys rise is controlled by the fingers, which do not leave the surface of the keys while they are rising. When moving from one key to another there is a slight rotary movement, as weight is transferred from one finger-tip to the next, rather like a see-saw. The attainment of a smooth *legato* depends on the critical judgement of both eye and ear. The fingers should be watched as weight passes from one finger to another, and the ear must confirm that there is neither a break between sounds, nor 'smudging' (caused by releasing one key *after* another has been put down). Both the beginning and the end of a sound must be listened to.

A true *legato*, such as is possible on the violin, is impossible on the piano because of the nature of the instrument. The pianist's task is therefore to create the illusion of *legato*, often with the help of the damper pedal. Also, because of the percussive character of the piano, a succession of notes played with precisely equal strength often fails to give the impression of *legato* playing. Hence the importance of gradations of tonal strength – rises and falls (*crescendo* and *diminuendo*) in musical phrases. In the early stages such gradations, if used at all, are often exaggerated. Subtlety is only acquired by observation, experience, and the development of the 'inner ear'.

Staccato

Staccato notes are short, and separated from each other by a brief period of silence. *Staccato* playing is made possible by the action of the piano dampers which, by falling back on the strings as soon as the keys are released, bring the sound to an end. True *staccato* is short and crisp, but in deciding the exact duration of *staccato* notes, the style, mood and speed of the music must be taken into account. In Example 11.1, the notes are given half their written value.

Example 11.1

Allegretto

Written

Played

Staccatissimo notes (sometimes marked with dashes) may be given approximately a quarter of their written value.

Example 11.2

Allegretto

Written

Played

Mezzo-staccato notes may be given approximately three-quarters of their written value.

Example 11.3

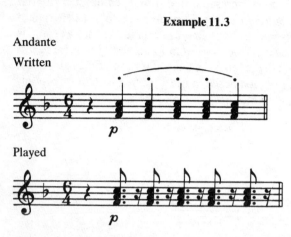

Andante

Written

Played

Staccato notes may be played: with the fingers, which are withdrawn from the keys without waiting for them to rise; with the wrist, which also rebounds rapidly from the keys; with the forearm, the wrist being firm and not allowed to droop; or with the whole arm. The method used depends on the context of the music. In general, finger action may be effective for quick, crisp *staccato*, wrist action for light chords and octaves, forearm action for heavier effects, and whole arm action for *bravura* ('brilliant') passages.

Finger position

For brilliant passage work (scales, *arpeggios* and so on), the fingers should be well curved, otherwise it will not be possible to depress the keys clearly and incisively. The fingers should also be curved when full tone is needed in chord passages, etc.

In *cantabile* (singing) passages, however, an almost flat finger action is often used, the fingers seeming to cling to the keys.

Before trying to produce *any* kind of tone, the appropriate 'tone-colour' should be imagined, so that the mental image can be compared with the actual sound.

Forearm rotation

In piano playing, some kind of rotary action is required almost continually. It is not possible to rotate the hand from the wrist, so that rotary action must come from the forearm and shoulder. In broken octaves the rotary action is most pronounced.

Example 11.4

With smaller intervals, the rotary movement is less obvious, or scarcely perceptible. In forearm rotation, the muscular energy with which a key is depressed must be relaxed as soon as the sound is heard, and transferred to the next key, and so on, backwards and forwards from one key to another. The rotary movement should not be exaggerated though, and the fingers should not be raised higher than necessary. During this movement the hand should be kept on a level with the forearm; there should be sufficient tension at the wrist to ensure this.

12

The Pedals

The damper pedal

In piano music it is customary to use the sign 'Ped' when the damper pedal is to be depressed, and the sign * when it is to be released; alternatively, the duration of the pedalling may be shown by the sign └─────────┘. These markings are not always to be relied on, and a good deal of music has either no pedal markings, or simply a general 'con ped' (with pedal). Although, as a beginner, you will have to rely on pedal markings in the best edited editions you can find, it is important that you should learn to decide for yourself when and how to use the pedal.

The damper pedal has been called the 'soul' of the piano, and when used in a sensitive way it can impart glowing effects of colour to imaginative music, and make possible *legato* passages which could not be played by the hands alone. But it is no easy matter to decide exactly when, and how, the damper pedal should be used; indeed there is often a difference of opinion among experts. (To what extent, for example, should the pedal be used in Bach's keyboard music?) In the early stages you are advised to err on the side of caution, and to start by using very little pedal indeed. Then, as experience is gained, you can gradually add to your pedal technique.

By lifting the dampers from the strings the damper pedal sustains the sound, and also enriches it by setting other strings free to vibrate in sympathy. If, however, the pedal is thoughtlessly used, clarity of phrasing and sound may be sacrificed, and playing which would otherwise be good, spoiled. Let us take a simple example.

Example 12.1

Remembrance (Album for the Young)   *Schumann*
                                                       Op. 68, No. 28

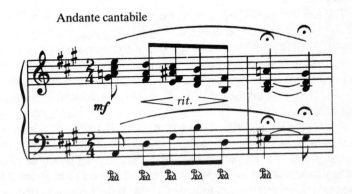

In Example 12.1, if the damper pedal were to be held down throughout the passage, the result would be a meaningless jumble of sounds. Try it and see. It follows, therefore, that the pedal should normally be changed each time there is a change of harmony. If each chord is separately pedalled, as indicated, the passage may indeed be enriched. But how is the pedalling to be done? The normal inclination would be to move the hands and the foot together, depressing the pedal at the precise moment that each chord is played. But a succession of *different* chords can be bound together more smoothly if what is known as 'syncopated pedalling' is used. To practise this, depress the pedal *after* you have played a chord, lift it at the precise moment that you play the next chord, and then depress it again. Syncopated pedalling is by far the most common form, and as a general rule the foot should move after the hand. The time lapse between one movement and the other needs to be very nicely judged. For example, the upper strings of the piano vibrate more quickly than the lower ones, so when playing high chords it may be possible to depress the pedal almost immediately it is raised, but when low bass notes are played (especially if *forte*) more time may have to be allowed for the change of pedal, so that the strings can be completely dampened. The exact duration may vary from piano to piano, so that very sensitive listening and careful experiment is needed to ensure that there is no blurring of consecutive sounds.

Occasionally, the damper pedal may be used 'on the beat' (i.e. simultaneously with the hands) for short, isolated chords, for example.

The top strings of the piano, having no dampers, are not affected by the pedal, and those upper strings which do have dampers are less affected than the lower strings. It is therefore possible to sustain one or more notes in the bass by means of the pedal, while playing light passages in the treble. But, as in all pedalling, it is necessary to try this effect so that the ear can judge whether or not the result will be blurred.

Another principle of pedalling is that the vibrations of the heavy bass strings are strong enough to allow the damper pedal to be changed without stopping the sound completely. In Example 12.2, for instance, the left hand cannot hold down the bass octave, and at the same time play the soft moving chords. If the pedal is held down throughout the bar, it may be found that the last two chords are blurred when the harmony changes. To avoid this, the pedal could be put down as soon as the bass octave is played. Then, after each of the last two chords, the pedal could be lifted and depressed as quickly as possible, the dampers would not have time to check the vibrations completely, so that the bass octave would continue to sound throughout the bar. This technique is known as 'half-pedalling'.

Example 12.2

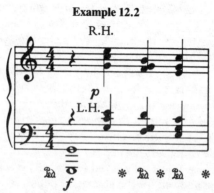

Although there are exceptions to every rule, broadly speaking the damper pedal should not be used in *staccato* passages, or where there are very rapid changes of harmony. It is important that the pedal should be used only for a specific purpose – never to cover up clumsy fingering or inadequate technique. This is why it is usually best to practise for some little time without the pedal, adding it only when a satisfactory degree of accuracy is evident to the ear. When progress has been made in elementary control of the pedal more detailed information may be sought from books such as *Points of Pedalling*, by James Ching (Forsyth), or *Pedalling the Modern Pianoforte* (Oxford University Press).

The left pedal

The use of the left pedal weakens the sound of the strings, producing tone-colour of a veiled or muted quality. The pedal should not be used merely to produce a soft tone which must be obtained from the fingers. The use of the soft pedal is indicated by the words *una corda* (It. = one string) for depression, and *tre corde* (three strings) for release. Sometimes the left pedal and damper pedal are used together.

13

Technique and Interpretation

Scales

Scales and *arpeggios* are the basis of many piano passages, as a glance at almost any piece of piano music will show. Regular practice of scales and *arpeggios* is therefore a major source of the pianist's technical equipment, leading to fluency and agility, and also to control of different tone qualities.

To make scales more interesting they can be played at different speeds, with different gradations of tone, and with different rhythms such as the following:

Example 13.1

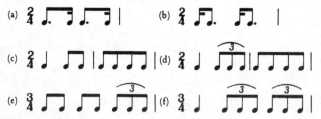

Scales may be played in two octaves or sometimes, for a change, in three or four. The pattern of fingering should be always be studied from the scale book before a new scale is attempted, and this pattern should then be memorised. Each hand should be practised separately, and only when each is reasonably perfect should a scale be played with both hands together.

Example 13.2

Exercises to facilitate passing the thumb under the finger, and the finger over the thumb (repeat each section several times)

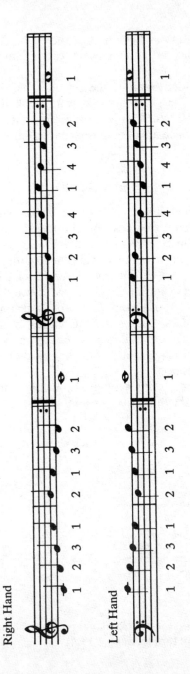

Demonstration Lesson Two should be studied in conjunction with this chapter, and the exercises in Example 13.2 should also be practised.

These exercises are in the key of C, but they can be transposed into other keys, using your scale book if necessary. *Freedom Technique* (Oxford University Press) contains many useful, short exercises which are of help when practising scales, *arpeggios*, etc.

Arpeggios and broken chords

The technical difference between broken chords and *arpeggios* is that whereas, in both forms, the hand is shifted up or down the keyboard, in *arpeggios* the thumb is also passed under the fingers, and the fingers over the thumb (the fingering of each form is shown in Example 8.12). The passing under of the thumb needs to be watched very carefully, and *arpeggios* should be played quite slowly at first, one hand at a time. The wrist and arm must be free, and the wrist raised as soon as the thumb passes under the fingers. The elbow should not be allowed to jerk upwards or outwards when the thumb passes under, but should be adjusted as quietly as possible to the new position.

The exercises in Example 13.3 will help to develop the smooth passage of the thumb and fingers.

Example 13.3

Arpeggio of C Major
(repeat several times)

Right Hand

Left Hand

Unevenness in *arpeggio* playing may be helped by accenting different notes in turn (Example 13.4).

Example 13.4

Skips and leaps

Large skips between notes are often difficult to judge accurately, but they may not appear as large as they look if you think of the first note as a kind of pivot upon which you can swing round towards the second note (the fingers should be over the keys before putting them down). If you are playing a succession of similar skips (octaves, for example, with the thumb and little finger), keep the hand extended so that the distance between the fingers remains the same for each skip.

In leaping to chords from a distance (for example, in the left hand part of a waltz) the feeling again should be of getting over the notes before playing them. Sometimes, with a four- or five-note chord, it is helpful to practise leaping first to the middle notes of the chord before playing it complete. When playing skips and leaps the hand should normally be kept as close to the keys as possible. Awkward passages should be memorised, and practised first with open, then with closed, eyes. When leaping, the arm should be moved from the shoulder. The distance of the 'jump' can be measured by placing the elbow over the first note or chord, and moving it to the second. A good exercise is to prepare the hand for a chord while keeping it above the keys, then to play the chord and repeat it (in other octaves) all over the piano.

Trills

Trills are difficult to play, and should be practised quite slowly and softly, the fingers remaining on the surface of the keys with the muscles relaxed. Any inequality of tone between one finger and another may then be heard and corrected. The comparative weakness of the fourth and little fingers will need to be allowed for when they are used. Notes which are evenly matched in tone and completely regular should be sought. A slow trill, really well played, is better than a fast one which is uneven.

Chords

Chord playing, so far as loudness or softness is concerned, depends on the speed with which piano keys are depressed. For brilliant, heavy chords the keys are moved suddenly downwards, using arm weight from the shoulders. For soft chords the keys are moved more slowly downwards, using forearm weight from the elbows. In chord-playing it is essential that all the notes of a chord should be put down precisely together. 'Ragged' chords are more likely to be heard in very soft music, since it is not always easy to depress several keys together when they are put down slowly.

With *staccato* chords the hand should be allowed to rise with the keys as soon as the sound is heard or has reached the desired length (see Chapter 10, page 83). The hand should not be snatched up, however. Unless the fingers are required to play other notes, they may remain on the surface of the keys.

With *legato* chords only the fingers (not the weight of the arm) should be used to hold down the keys once the sound has been heard.

Interpretation

We can barely scratch the surface of this subject, which needs a book to itself.[1] Interpretation implies an intelligent, commonsense approach to the performance of a piece of music. But intelligence and common sense are personal attributes, and so far as interpretation of music is concerned there is bound to be a wide divergence of opinion. Indeed, without it, music would be dull, as would *Hamlet* if every actor played the title role in the same way. There are, however, certain general principles which are usually accepted, and

[1] *Interpretation in Piano Study* by Joan Last (Oxford University Press) is an excellent book for the serious piano student; as also is her *Freedom in Piano Technique*.

in the Demonstration Lessons some of these have been applied to elementary situations.

Interpretation is, in effect, a creative (or re-creative) element in the performance of music, in which the performer attempts to interpret a piece of music according to his own judgement and personality. Judgement is the outcome of an observation and experience, and in the early stages we must be content to progress very slowly, and to lean heavily on the opinions of performers whose talent and experience we have come to respect.

Nevertheless, it may be useful to discuss some basic matters of interpretation. In studying piano music we should take into account the nature of the music, the composer, and the period during which it was written. We can then decide on the style of playing which would be appropriate. This may lead us to further research to find out how the music was performed at the time it was written. With the early composers – Scarlatti and Bach, for example – this will not be easy, and there may be no conclusive results. But it is always worthwhile, and invariably fascinating, to find out as much as possible about a composer and the times in which he lived. Biographies, programmes on radio and television, records and tapes, reviews and articles in journals and newspapers, all may contribute to the general picture.

It is also important to take note of the 'plan' of a piece, to appreciate the phrasing, chord structure, cadences, and so on, and to realise where the music is 'going'. Most pieces build up to climaxes at certain points, and you should look for these. If a passage is to be increased in intensity towards the climax, the approach should be carefully thought out. A *crescendo* must not be begun too soon or too loudly, or its power will be exhausted before the climax is reached. Similarly, a *decrescendo* must be made gradually.

A phrase may also have a climax – perhaps at the highest, lowest, loudest or softest note. In Example 13.5, for instance, the climax (marked with an *) occurs on the second beat of the second bar.

The study of musical 'forms', which is of considerable importance to the advanced pianist, cannot be entered into in a book of this size. *The Form of Music* by William Cole (Associated Board) is of practical help to the serious student.

Example 13.5

Träumerei (Kinderscenen)

Schumann
Op. 15, No. 7

Andante = 100

Accompaniment and melody

If a melody is played on a violin, accompanied by a piano, the difference in the tone quality of the two instruments will make it easy for the listener to distinguish between the melody and the accompaniment. On the piano, however, there is one basic tone-quality, so that the difference can only be made clear by playing the accompaniment more softly than the melody. Sometimes both melody and accompaniment are played by the same hand; the weight of the arm must then be concentrated on those fingers which are playing the melody, and the accompaniment must be played more lightly with the other fingers.

In Example 13.6 the accompaniment is played by the right hand, and the melody alternately by the left and right hands. In order to play this perfectly smoothly, the tone of the left hand must be matched exactly with that of the right hand.

Rubato

Rubato might well be described as 'robbing Peter to pay Paul'. If, in music of an expressive character, every note of a melody is played with mathematical precision, the result will be dull and mechanical rather than expressive. The pianist will therefore sometimes linger over a certain note or phrase in the interest of more intense

Example 13.6

Liebesträume

Liszt

Poco allegro, con affetto

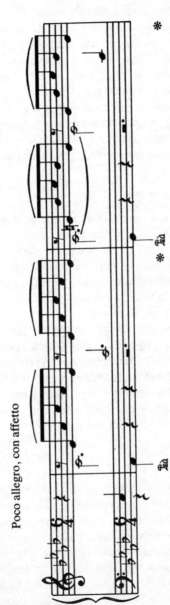

expression. When some notes are minutely lengthened, other notes in the same bar or phrase may be minutely shortened, so that the entire bar or phrase remains the same length as if it had been played strictly in time. These minute variations are too subtle to be expressed in musical notation: they are spontaneous rather than planned, and vary according to the artistic feeling of the performer. The effective use of *rubato* requires a wealth of experience and maturity of judgement. Excessive or exaggerated use can too easily lead to major abuse, but much can be learned by careful listening to the playing of great artists while following the music.

Accents and pauses

Accents can be performed in many different ways, and exactly what is appropriate to a particular note or chord can only be decided after studying the context of the music. Clearly an accent will be less heavy in a soft passage than in a loud one. There will also be a difference between an accented *legato* note and an accented *staccato* one. Generally, a *legato* accent will have more depth, and a *staccato* accent more percussive attack.

A pause over a note shows that it is to be sustained for longer than its normal value. Again the exact length can only be judged in the context of the music which precedes and follows the pause. A pause mark may also be placed over a rest, when this is to be made longer than usual. A pause sign placed over a bar-line indicates a short silence, also, the sign is sometimes placed over the final double-bar, to denote the end of a composition.

Phrase endings

In performance, 'breathing' places between phrases (see page 80) are often indicated by very slight breaks in the musical sound, even when there is no break in the printed music (i.e. when the final note of a phrase is not followed by a rest). In Example 10.6, for instance, the last note of each of the two phrases can be minutely shortened. It is important, however, that such tiny breaks should be subtly 'tailored', according to the character of the music (often they will be 'felt' rather than heard). They must not cause the continuity and 'flow' of the music to be disturbed.

14

Tension and Relaxation

The basis of modern piano technique is the proper use of tension and relaxation of the muscles used in piano playing, as well as the application of arm weight (originating at the shoulder), rotary freedom, and so on. Tobias Matthay (1858–1945), the English pianist and teacher, was one of the first to stress the importance of muscular relaxation.

Tension is often used synonymously with stress to describe a condition of emotional anxiety, and this of course may affect the performance of the pianist, though a degree of emotional tension is a necessary contribution to the intensity of the performance.

Physical tension, however, is concerned with muscular exertion, and without some degree of this kind of tension we should not be capable of any human activity, let alone playing the piano. Physical tension can be necessary or unnecessary, sufficient or excessive. So while we need tension to depress a piano key, we may find that our finger action is inhibited by simultaneous unnecessary tension in other parts of the body. Also, when we have just depressed a piano key, we must learn to control the tension, so that the key is held down without further pressure until such time as we want it to rise. This means that tension must be reduced as soon as the sound is heard.

Although most pianists might benefit from short, regular periods of total relaxation, if you became totally relaxed at the piano the chances are that you would fall off the piano stool! So we need to use 'differential' relaxation, in which unnecessary tension is eliminated so far as is possible, although it is probable that *some* degree of 'residual' tension is always present. Thus, when we are using our fingers we must try to avoid stiffness in other parts of the body, and so on. In short, the more we learn to recognise feelings of tension and relaxation, the more we may hope to bring them under our control.

Differential relaxation may be practised when lying down or sitting in a chair and moving the fingers as in piano playing, while keeping the rest of the body relaxed. Then, still moving the fingers, (a) raise the wrists, (b) raise the elbows, and (c) raise the arms from the shoulders. Differential relaxation, if regularly and correctly practised, will help to reduce many unnecessary tensions, and to produce muscular harmony between the different parts of the body.

Tension and relaxation and the pianist

Deep, easy breathing is extremely important for the pianist. There are times when the breathing has to be matched to the length of a phrase, so that it is not rushed at the end because of shortness of breath. Breathing does, in fact, have a profound effect on the whole nervous system; a few deep breaths will often help to re-establish control over a situation which has become difficult because of some kind of mental anxiety. Because gentle exhalation helps to release unnecessary tension, it is logical to start a piece or scale while breathing out, rather than while breathing in. Try it both ways, and decide for yourself.

If, when practising, you become aware of undue tension or stiffness in any part of the body, stop and relax the muscles. Tense the hands, for instance, and then let go completely, or flex the forearm and let go, or stand with arms falling limply to sides, chin on chest and shoulders flopping forward, like a rag doll.

A useful exercise at the piano is to make small semi-circular movements with the entire arms, from the shoulders to the tips of the fingers. Each movement starts with both thumbs on Middle C, and then travels to the Cs two octaves above and below Middle C, played with the little fingers. This movement, repeated several times slowly and gently, will help to eliminate stiffness, and to introduce a feeling of relaxation.

When practising quick passages such as scales, it is useful to begin by playing each note slowly, quickly moving the finger into the key, then relaxing as much pressure as possible as soon as the sound is heard before moving to the next note.

Another useful exercise to free the wrist of unnecessary tension is to play a chord softly, say:

Example 14.1

Then move the wrist gently and slowly up and down, keeping the fingers lightly on the keys, and making sure that the hand is free from stiffness.

Since all parts of the body are interdependent, stiffness or unnecessary tension in one part is likely to affect another. If, for example, the fingers of the right hand are stiff when playing, the fingers of the left hand may also be stiff, *even when not playing*. A faulty position of one part of the body will therefore have to be dealt with before stiffness in another part of the body can be eliminated. The Alexander Technique, which is taught at many music colleges, is based on the theory that the correct relationship between the head, neck and back can free the whole body from harmful tension. The technique can be learned from a qualified teacher, but quite a long period of study is required.

The ideal in piano playing is to play as well as possible with the least possible effort, but no firm recommendations can be offered to achieve this happy state of affairs. Habits such as raising the shoulders unduly, or hunching them, may cause tensions and wasted effort and should be avoided: but many eminent pianists exhibit similar 'failings'. The most you can do is to take note of your general attitude and playing position, and to try to modify this when you become aware of unnecessary tension or stiffness. Irritating habits however, should be eliminated as soon as possible – foot-tapping, head-wagging, grimacing, etc. Habits resulting from nervousness or excitement (even when practising alone) may be treated by general relaxation away from the piano, and by careful attention to breathing.

For those with special problems, such as the adult beginner with stiff or arthritic fingers, tensing and relaxing the hands between playing may be particularly beneficial. Although, in general, piano playing should help to prevent arthritic fingers from becoming more stiff, care should always be taken to avoid excessive practice, since pain in any part of the body may cause undue tension.

15

Improvisation

Improvisation is music which is created as it is performed, without previous preparation or detailed notation. Improvisation was once considered of great importance, and was a skill much practised by keyboard performers such as Bach, Mozart and Beethoven; in 1747, for example, Bach improvised a fugue on a theme devised by Frederick the Great, which he subsequently developed in his *Music-al Offering*. In modern times, jazz musicians have improvised melodies against a harmonic, or modal, background, and impro-vised passages have appeared in 'aleatory' music, which contains elements of chance, or random selection. Nowadays, improvisation may be applied to a wide variety of skills, ranging from elaborate extemporisations by organists or other keyboard performers, which may involve a high degree of compositional talent, to the reproduc-tion, or harmonisation, of existing music.

Some people have a natural gift for 'playing by ear' music which they have heard, sometimes with a remarkable degree of accuracy. Those who do not possess this gift may, with practice, acquire sufficient skill to enable them to harmonise melodies, and possibly to attempt simple composition, at the piano. To attain this skill, some knowledge of harmonic progression is necessary.

Triads

On page 46 we have seen that triads may be formed on each note of the major and minor scale. The three most important triads are those formed on the first, fourth and fifth degrees of the major or minor scale (Example 15.1).

Example 15.1

These three triads are called *primary triads*, whereas the remaining triads are known as *secondary triads*. In Example 15.1, in which the *root* (fundamental note from which the chord originates) is the lowest note of the chord, the triads are said to be in *root position*. These triads may be in *close harmony* (in which the notes of the chords are kept close together), or in *open harmony* (with gaps between one or more of the upper notes), and any of the three notes may be the highest note.

Example 15.2

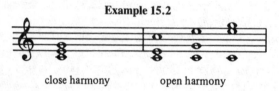

close harmony   open harmony

When harmony is in more than three parts, one or more notes of the triad must be doubled, either at the unison, i.e. the combined sound of two notes at the same pitch (Example 15.3) or at the octave (Example 15.4).

Example 15.3

Example 15.4

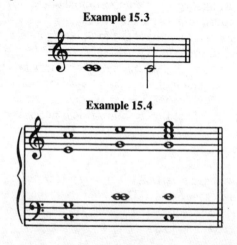

Inverted triads

The notes of a triad may be arranged so that one of the upper notes becomes the lowest; the triad is then said to be *inverted*. Example 15.5 shows the tonic triad of C major in (a) root position with the root as the lowest note, (b) first inversion with the third as the lowest note, and (c) second inversion with the fifth as the lowest note. The chords are usually figured I, Ib, Ic.

Example 15.5

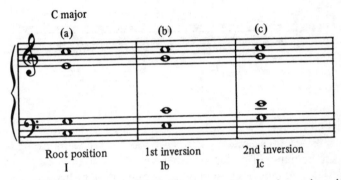

With the three primary chords, in root position or inversion, it is possible to harmonise simple melodies.

Example 15.6

Baa, Baa, Black Sheep

In the third bar of Example 15.6, the second quaver is treated as a *passing note*, i.e. a melody note taken scalewise between two notes which are part of the harmony, and which does not require separate harmonisation.

A more florid accompaniment might be effected by using broken chords in the left hand, on these lines:

Example 15.7

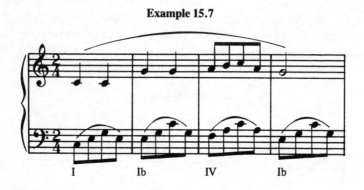

I   Ib   IV   Ib

Secondary triads

The most useful secondary triads are those on the supertonic and the submediant. In major keys the supertonic triad is minor (see page 47), and may be used in either root position or first inversion. In minor keys it is diminished, and is better in first inversion. The most useful progression is from the supertonic to the dominant.

Example 15.8

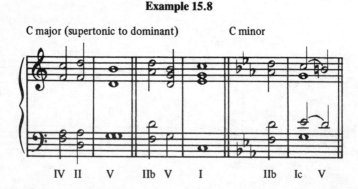

C major (supertonic to dominant)   C minor

IV II   V   IIb V   I   IIb   Ic   V

The submediant triad is mostly used in root position, and is often preceded by the dominant triad, to form an interrupted cadence (see page 81).

Example 15.9

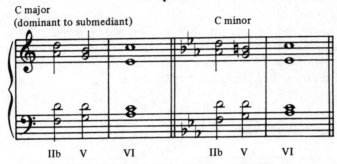

C major
(dominant to submediant)

C minor

IIb   V   VI   IIb   V   VI

Using these secondary chords we could play:

Example 15.10

IVb   Ic   IIb V   VI   IV   I

The last two bars form a plagal cadence (see page 81). In more florid
style, we could play:

Example 15.11

IVb   Ic   IIb V   VI   IV   I

Dominant sevenths

If we add a note to a triad, a seventh above the root, we form a *chord of the seventh*. If the added note is a minor seventh above a dominant root, we form a *dominant seventh* (figured V7). Since this consists of four different notes, it may be used in root position, and in three inversions (figured V7b, V7c and V7D).

Example 15.12

In root position, the dominant seventh may be used instead of the dominant triad. The inversions may be used freely, and are often effective as a half beat between two notes which are a third apart (as at (a) in Example 15.13).

Example 15.13

Other chords

When a fourth note is added to a major or minor triad, a major or minor seventh above the root, a chord is formed which is useful, in root position, to harmonise a melody which moves up the scale.

Example 15.14

Triads with 7ths added above the root

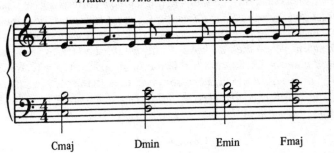

When a note a major sixth above the root is added to a major or minor triad, the following chord is produced.

Example 15.15

Triad with major 6th added above the root

This can often produce a more interesting accompaniment than that provided by the triad.

Example 15.16.

Modulation

Music which constantly remains in the same key often lacks melodic interest and variety of harmonisation; except for some short melodies, therefore, music tends to pass from one key to another and back again. When the new key is firmly established the music is said to *modulate* to that key, and this modulation is often effected by using a *pivot chord* (i.e. a chord common to both the old key and the new one), followed by a *modulating chord* which is usually the dominant seventh of the new key.

Example 15.17

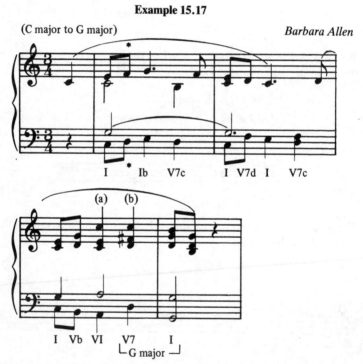

(a) *pivot chord* (VI in C major = II in G major) (b) modulating chord (V7 in G major) * = passing notes

Modulation may also proceed through a chord which has one or more notes belonging to both the old and the new keys; these are known as *pivot notes*.

Example 15.18

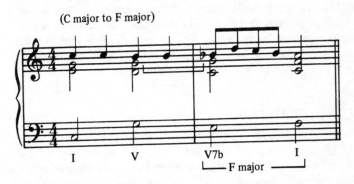

(C major to F major)

I   V   V7b   I

└── F major ──┘

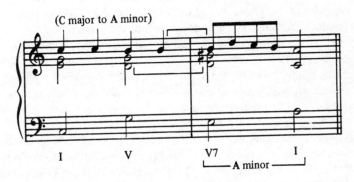

(C major to A minor)

I   V   V7   I

└── A minor ──┘

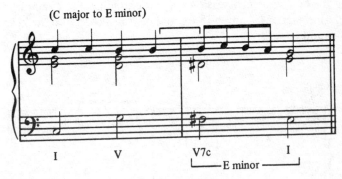

(C major to E minor)

I   V   V7c   I

└── E minor ──┘

⌐ = *pivot note*

Modulation from one key to any other key is possible, but the most simple and natural modulation is when music passes from one key to another key to which it is closely related (i.e. the relative minor (or major), the dominant key and its relative, and the sub-dominant key and its relative). Thus C major is related to A minor, G major and E minor, and F major and D minor.

Melodic decoration

In some music, such as hymn tunes, it is usual to harmonise every note of a melody, but in piano and other music this is seldom necessary or desirable, and more often melody notes move up and down the scale, above a single sustained chord (or broken chord).

We have already mentioned the passing note in the third bar of Example 15.6. Since passing notes do not form part of the chord against which they are sounded, they are called *unessential notes*, whereas notes which do belong to the harmony are called *essential*. Thus, in Example 15.14, the second note of the melody is a passing (unessential) note, whereas all the other melody notes belong to the harmony, and are therefore essential. Passing notes may occur in two parts simultaneously, as in Example 15.17.

All the music examples in this chapter are in the key of C major or minor, and they should be *transposed* (i.e. played at another pitch, and therefore in a different key) into as many keys as possible, so that the harmonic progression becomes familiar. For example, the first four bars of Example 15.6 could be transposed into the keys of B flat and F major.

Example 15.19

Style

Finally, different styles of accompaniment must be considered. In improvising an accompaniment to a melody (existing or invented), the style of the music must be taken into account. As an exercise, let us develop this basic melody in various styles.

Example 15.20

1 As a *march*:

Example 15.21

2 As a *waltz*:

Example 15.22

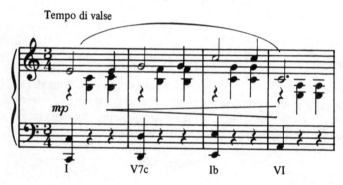

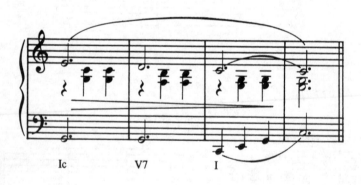

3 As a *lullaby*:

Example 15.23

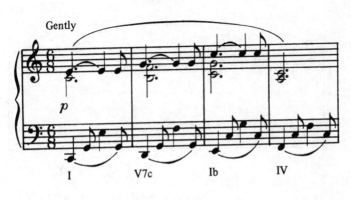

4 As a *blues*:

Example 15.24

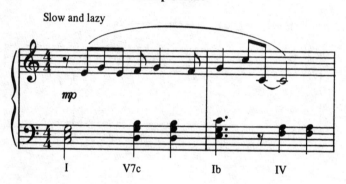

Suggestions for further study

J. Tobin. *How to Improvise Piano Accompaniments* (Oxford University Press)

Dorothy Pilling. *Harmonisation of Melodies at the Keyboard* Books 1 to 3 (Forsyth)

Demonstration Lessons

Introduction

These lessons are designed to show you how to observe, approach, practise and listen to piano music. They include a simple piano piece, scales and *arpeggios*, and sight-reading, so that once you have grasped the 'principles' of study and practice you should be able to apply them to other pieces and situations.

Although the 'demonstration piece' is not printed in full, it is very easily obtainable, and can either be bought quite cheaply, or borrowed from the music section of a local lending library.

Lesson One: 'Melody' (Robert Schumann)
Lesson Two: Scales and Arpeggios
Lesson Three: Reading Music at Sight

Demonstration Lesson One

'Melody' (Robert Schumann)

This is the first of forty-three pieces from *Album for the Young* (Op 68), which Schumann composed in 1848. Although these pieces were intended for children to play, most of them contain technical difficulties, and all need to be played with skill and imagination. This is one of the easier pieces, which would be likely to be graded 'one' or 'two' in piano examinations. It is published by The Associated Board, Peters, Augener, etc. Any edition may be used for the purpose of this lesson, provided that it has been properly fingered and phrased. Your music dealer should be able to advise you about this.

Having obtained the piece, first number the bars *lightly* in pencil; twenty-four bars in all. It will then be easy to locate every bar which is discussed in the lesson, and the numbers can be rubbed out if the copy is on loan.

Before attempting to play anything, sit down and quietly *look through* the piece several times, carefully noting:

Clefs
Both hands are in the treble clef throughout, because in this piece the left hand plays mostly on the upper half of the keyboard.

Key
In this piece there are no sharps or flats in the key-signature, so that the music could be either in the key of C major, or in A minor. Look at the last (lowest) note in the left hand (which is *usually* the key-note); here it is C, and this piece is in the key of C major.

Example 1

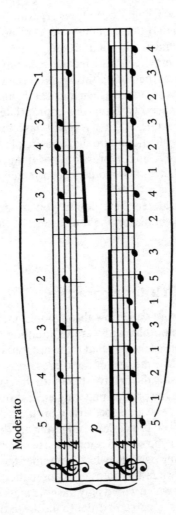

Time and speed

The time-signature is $\frac{4}{4}$ (i.e. four crotchet beats in each bar, also known as *common time*, and sometimes written thus: **C**). Consider the speed at which you will *ultimately* want to play the piece. It is marked *Moderato* (at a moderate speed, not fast). If you have a metronome, and set it about 108 (i.e. 108 crotchet beats to the minute), you may feel that, having carefully considered the style and character of the music, this is about the right speed. The *exact* speed will depend on your own musical feeling and judgement, but whatever the speed you consider appropriate it will take time and patience to reach it. At first you will have to practise very slowly, always *listening* to make sure that you are playing correctly in every detail – time, phrasing, expression, pedalling, etc. It is of the utmost importance that faults should be corrected *before* they become habits.

Having considered these points, you are now ready to place the piece, and this book, on the music desk of the piano, and start to practise.

Points to watch during practice

This piece has a gentle flow throughout, and both hands must be played very smoothly, with careful attention to phrasing. You will see from the phrase marks that there are four one-bar phrases (bars 9, 10, 17 and 18); the rest of the piece consists of two-bar phrases. Start by practising the first two bars with the right hand alone. Try to keep strictly to the printed fingering unless you really feel that some modification is essential, because your hands are smaller or larger than average. The principles of fingering are dealt with more fully in Chapter 8, and you should refer to these if in doubt.

In the opening passage, which lies under the hand, the fingers are used in order when the notes are consecutive. If a note is left out, then the finger which would play the note is also left out. In Example 1, every note is fingered in order to illustrate this point. In passages exceeding a five-note span fingers may be contracted or expanded, to allow a passage to lie more easily under the hand. In a wider span of notes, the thumb may be passed under the fingers (or vice versa), as in scale playing (see page 66). The important point is to use the same fingering always, once you have decided on it.

Play this two-bar phrase quite slowly, *thinking* from the first note to the last note. To secure a perfect *legato* each sound must be carried over to the next sound without a break, one key being raised at the precise moment that the sound of the next key (which is being depressed) is heard. The fingers should remain on the surface of the keys while they are rising. It will be helpful if you can memorise the passage, so you can then watch your fingers and listen critically to what you are playing. And whatever your voice, do *sing* this phrase, as smoothly as you can, and from memory, both when you are practising, and when you are not (e.g. in the street, bath, etc.).

There is also the question of tone production. As well as positioning the fingers correctly (see Chapter 4), try to ensure that your shoulder, arm and fingers are free from unnecessary tension (see Chapter 14). Try to depress the keys by the exertion of the fingers and the weight of the arm, and not by 'striking' them; and remember that it is a waste of muscular energy to exert pressure *after* sound has been produced. On the contrary, the finger muscles should be relaxed at the moment sound begins, so that a key is held down with minimum pressure.

Now try the first two bars with the left hand. They consist almost entirely of quavers, whereas the right hand moves mostly in crotchets. However, the quavers in the first bar are not all of equal importance, those *on* the beats are 'basic' notes, whilst those *between* the beats are 'subsidiary' notes, which add movement. Thus, the first bar could be reduced to this basic pattern:

Example 2

It follows, therefore, that the 'basic' notes should be given slightly more prominence than the 'subsidiary' notes. If the damper pedal is used on each beat (as it can be throughout the piece), the general effect will therefore be:

Example 3

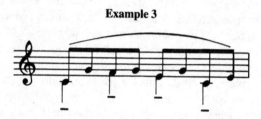

The damper pedal, if used, should be depressed immediately *after* the first note is played, then raised and depressed on the second beat. (This technique of pedalling is discussed in Chapter 12.)

Example 4

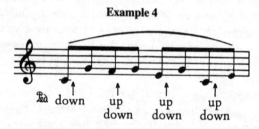

The second bar for the left hand (see Example 1) also consists entirely of quavers, but the first four of these are of equal importance to those played by the right hand.

When you are reasonably satisfied with your performance of the first two bars with each hand separately, try both together. The importance of practising these two bars is apparent when you examine the structure of the piece. Bars 1 and 2 are exactly the same as bars 5 and 6, and *nearly* the same as bars 13 and 14, and bars 21 and 22 (take very careful note of the slight differences). Thus, in this twenty-four bar piece, if you can play bars 1 and 2 you should also be able to play the other six bars mentioned above. Similarly, bars 3 and 4 are the same as bars 7 and 8; and bars 9 to 12 are the same as bars 17 to 20, so that, out of twenty-four bars, no less than fourteen are the same, or nearly the same, which means that, virtually, there are only ten bars which need *individual* practice.

Now consider the tonal balance between the hands. Looking at the piece as a whole, both hands are marked with the same dynamics (*piano* in bar one, *decrescendo* in bar two, and so on), but the right hand is clearly of a different character to the left. Play each separately, and the difference should become apparent. The right hand plays a melody, and the left hand an accompaniment, so the right hand must be made more prominent than the left. In the opening bars, this could mean either that the right hand is played, say *mezzo-piano* and the left hand *piano*, or that the right hand is played *piano* and the left hand *pianissimo*. There are, of course, other possibilities, and the exact solution to the question of tonal balance is a matter for individual thought and taste. The main thing is that the performer should be able to establish a satisfactory contrast between the right hand melody and left hand accompaniment.

Next try bars 3 and 4, again with each hand separately. In bar 4 (right hand) you will probably find it easier to put the fingers over the thumb, thus:

Example 5

Looking again at the first four bars, you will see that although they can be considered to be made up of two two-bar phrases, the music does flow smoothly on throughout the four bars, so that you could think of it as a single four-bar phrase. Exactly how you regard the structure of these four bars does not really matter, so long as you 'think' when you play them, from the beginning of bar one to the end of bar four, and allow the music to flow along smoothly between these points. At the end of bar 4, although there is no actual break in the music, there is the feeling of temporary repose, rather like a comma in verse or prose. The fourth bar does, in fact, 'modulate'[1] for a moment, from the key of C major to the key of G major

---

[1] Modulate = pass from one key to another.

(returning to C major at the beginning of the fifth bar).[1] Because of this feeling of temporary repose, you could make a *very* slight break after the final note in the fourth bar. This should be done so subtly that the break is almost 'felt' rather than heard (like, perhaps, the way that a singer takes a breath between phrases). The important thing is that the rhythmic flow of the music must not be disturbed.

Observe that, in order to make the duration of the crotchet rest in bar 4 precisely one beat, the finger playing G must be raised *exactly* on the count of 4.

Bars 9 to 12 introduce a new idea made up of two one-bar phrases and one two-bar phrase. Think of the melody progressing from bar 9, reaching a climax on the first beat of bar 11, then declining. You may feel that a slight *ritardando* (slowing down) can be made during the last half bar of bar 12, returning to normal speed (*a tempo*) at the beginning of bar 13. Also at this point in bar 12, the lower moving part in the right hand is an 'imitation' of the first half of the bar and should therefore be given slight prominence.

Finally, when you have reached the stage where the fingering, notes, time, phrasing, and so on are reasonably secure, play the piece right through without stopping, noting any mistakes as you go along. Some passages will need to be isolated, and practised again on their own, but it is very important that you should appreciate the unity of the piece, so that you can follow the line of the melody and accompaniment, and the way in which one bar progresses to another.

When you are able to play the whole piece accurately, and with due regard for dynamics (soft, loud, *crescendo*) and phrasing, you can then, be gradual stages, start to increase the speed.

When you come to the final bar of this piece, you may feel that a slight *ritardando* will help to bring the music to a gentle close.

---

[1] Although the fourth bar could be regarded as a 'perfect' cadence in the key of G major, the musical effect is more like that of an imperfect cadence in the key of C major.

Example 6

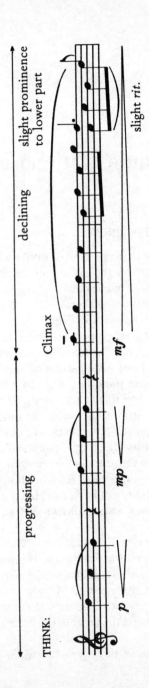

Demonstration Lesson Two

Scales and arpeggios

Do not attempt to play any scale until you understand its structure, know from memory the notes and the fingering pattern, and can write them in your music book.

For the purpose of this lesson, we shall consider the scale of C major. From Example 6.7 (page 36) you will have seen that the C major scale has no sharps or flats in the key-signature, and that like all major scales each octave is made up of two halves, or tetrachords, each having the pattern of tone–tone–semitone, and that the two halves are joined together by a tone. Semitones therefore occur between the third and fourth, and the seventh and eighth degrees of the scale. Other adjacent notes are a tone apart. Now write in your music book one octave of the C major scale (up and down from Middle C), using Example 6.7 as a model if necessary.

Next, pick out the notes of the scale you have written on the piano keyboard with one finger. As you play, study the pattern of the notes, and continue until you can play the scale from memory.

Looking at your scale book, you will see that C major is fingered as in Example 7.

The basic pattern 123, 1234 (or 4321, 321) shows that when the right hand is ascending the thumb is passed under the third finger and fourth finger alternately; when descending, the third and fourth fingers are alternately passed over the thumb. The left hand fingering is the same as that of the right in reverse. Note also that the top right hand note and the bottom left hand note are both played with the fifth finger.

Real progress is only possible when notes and fingering are

Example 7

completely familiar, so start practising first with the right hand, then with the left. This can be done not only at the piano keyboard, but also with the hand resting on a desk or table at odd moments of the day. The fingering can be thought of either in terms of the basic pattern, or of the notes played by the thumb (right thumb on C and F, left thumb on G and C), remembering those top and bottom notes which are played with the fifth finger.

Even when practising away from the piano, try to visualise the notes of the scale (either on the piano keyboard, or in the scale book notation). Visual memory can usually be developed and improved by regular practice.

When you can play note and fingering patterns from memory, you should begin to study the technique of scale-playing. The object of scale practice is to produce a succession of sounds perfectly matched in quality and duration. In the early stages scales should always be played with each hand separately. If a scale is played in similar motion with both hands, weaker fingers (4th and 5th) come together, as do stronger fingers (1st, 2nd and 3rd), so it is hardly possible for the beginner to judge the tonal balance of each hand. Start, therefore, by playing first with the right hand, then with the left hand, two octaves of the C major scale.

Play the scale from memory, so that you can give your full attention to the sounds you are making, and to the movement of your fingers and arms. And, since old habits die hard, make sure that you are using the right fingering from the start (check from time to time with your scale book).

Listening carefully and critically, ask yourself whether each note is perfectly matched, and if not which are the weaker notes; whether each note is of exactly equal duration, and if not which notes are shorter than others; whether there is a true *legato* throughout, since we are trying to play the notes as smoothly as possible.

To match the tone some adjustment of the strength with which the fingers strike the keys will probably be necessary. The thumb, being rather closer to the keys than the other fingers, will need to be raised as high as they are, so that the exertion will not be less. The stronger second and third fingers may need a little restraint, and the weaker fourth and fifth fingers added strength. These are generalisations, since the relative strength of the fingers varies greatly; the ear alone must always be the final judge.

The duration of notes depends upon when and how piano keys are depressed and raised. Since we want to play *legato* one key must be depressed at the precise moment that the previous key is raised, and to ensure that successive sounds are joined together in a flowing sequence, the weight of a finger on a key (just sufficient to hold it down) must be transferred from one finger-tip to another, like a see-saw.

One of the difficulties of scale-playing is the passing of the thumb under the fingers, and of a finger over the thumb. This must be managed with the utmost smoothness and ease. Since it is easier to pass the thumb under after a black key has been played than after a white key, the C major scale, despite its easier key-signature, is technically rather more difficult than some other major scales which have the same fingering pattern (E major, for example).

The thumb, when passing under the fingers, should be moved smoothly and gradually sideways so that it arrives above the key to be played before it is required to depress it. As the thumb is tucked under the hand the arm should glide evenly along, following the movement of the hand horizontally, with no jerking or swinging of the wrist or elbow.

Since it is easier to practise small parts of a scale, the exercises in Example 13.2 (to facilitate the passage of the thumb under the fingers, and of the fingers over the thumb) should be practised and repeated as often as necessary.

The playing position of the fingers also needs to be considered. In the scale of C major, the hands should be curved so that the tips of the fingers play vertically into the centre of the keys. The thumb should be slightly bent, so that the side (with which it plays) rests on the key about as far up as the root of the nail. With scales which include black keys, modifications may be necessary.

Very slow scale practice, with each hand separately, will enable the movements of the hands to be studied closely, so that by gradually eliminating weaknesses and faults a beautifully even scale can be achieved. In detecting faults the ear must *always* be the final arbiter. Small sections of a scale which fail to satisfy the critical judgement of the ear should be isolated, so that a particular problem can be recognised and tackled accordingly. In general, it may be necessary to play a scale more slowly whenever the performance fails to satisfy.

A scale should be played at an increased speed only when it can be played slowly with the right conditions of muscular freedom and relaxation. Unnecessary tensions which may be present when a scale is played slowly are most likely to increase if it is played faster. Increases of speed should be gradual, a *very* little faster each week.

When a scale can be played effortlessly, and from memory, with each hand separately, other ways of playing it may be tried, e.g.

1 With both hands together, starting and ending on the same key-note (i.e. in contrary motion). This will often be found easier than playing with both hands in similar motion, since in many scales the fingers are used in the same order by each hand (when moving in opposite directions).

2 With both hands together in similar motion, with all kinds of dynamic variations (scales played *piano, forte,* or with *crescendo* or *diminuendo,* for example).

3 With each hand separately, and both hands together, in some of the rhythmic patterns shown in Example 13.1, page 96.

4 With each hand separately, the right hand going down and up from the highest and lowest notes of the scale on the piano; the left hand going vice versa.

5 Scales played *staccato* (each hand separately), and with various gradations of tone (*forte, piano, crescendo, diminuendo,* etc.).

Other scales can be added one by one, perhaps in the following order:

G, D, F major	A flat major	E, D minor
A, E major	B major	G, C minor
B flat, E flat major	A minor	B minor

Minor scales can be played in either melodic or harmonic form. The lower grade examinations allow the candidate to choose either form. Higher grade examinations include both forms.

Before starting to practise any new scale, study it carefully in your scale book, and make sure that you can pick out the notes on the keyboard from memory, and that you have also memorised the pattern of the fingering. Practice with closed eyes (of both scales and *arpeggios*) is a valuable way of improving tactile perception.

Arpeggios and broken chords

When playing *arpeggios* and broken chords the wrists should be slightly higher than when playing scales. When passing the thumb under the fingers in *arpeggios*, the elbows should not be raised. The lower grade examinations ask for a small number of broken chords (each hand separately), the higher grades require a number of *arpeggios*.

Before attempting to play an *arpeggio* or broken chord, pick out the notes with one finger on the keyboard, and continue until you can do so from memory.

If you are practising broken chords, you could start with C major, each hand separately (see Example 8.12(b), page 72, for fingering). After this you could practise broken chords in these keys, checking the fingering from your scale book. (Grade 2 contains the broken chords; the higher grades contain *arpeggios*.)

G, D, F major (two octaves)
A, E, D minor (two octaves)

Unevenness in broken chord playing can be helped by accenting different notes in turn (as with *arpeggio* playing) (see Example 13.4, page 99).

If you are practising *arpeggios*, you could start with C major, each hand separately (see Example 8.12(a), page 72, for fingering), and follow on with these *arpeggios*, checking the fingering from your scale book.

G, D, A, E, B, F, B flat, E flat, A flat, D flat

(major and minor, two octaves, at first with each hand separately – eventually with both hands together).

The exercises in Examples 13.3 and 13.4 will help to facilitate the smooth passage of the thumb and fingers in *arpeggio* playing, and to eliminate unevenness. As the consecutive notes in *arpeggios* (and broken chords) are farther apart than in scales, it is more difficult to obtain a completely even performance, and the relative weakness of the fourth finger needs to be carefully watched.

Demonstration Lesson Three

Reading music at sight

Sight-reading is an essential requirement for grade examinations, and for the purpose of this lesson an eight-bar piece has been written, as an example of the kind of test that might be included in Grades 2 or 3. Sight-reading is a most valuable exercise, whether or not you have an examination in mind, and the method of approach described can be applied to other pieces which are to be read at sight.

You will appreciate however that whereas, outside examination conditions, you can take as long as you like to consider a piece before you play it, or you can stop and go back, in examinations the candidate is required to read a piece at sight without stopping, and that only a limited period is allowed for looking through. (It is nevertheless extremely important that you should not start until you have a clear idea of the key, time, style, etc.).

A wrong note or two may not spoil your chances, but many examination candidates lose valuable marks because they begin to play in the wrong key or time, either because they have never acquired the habit of checking such things in advance, or because examination nerves prevent them from doing so. (For 'nerves' there is no infallible remedy, but the breathing and relaxation techniques advocated in this book may often be of considerable help.)

When sight-reading for any purpose you should choose music well within your present range, so that technical problems do not inhibit you. Also, you should try to practise sight-reading before an audience (e.g. one or two friends). Sight-reading is quite different from studying a piece. The main object of sight-reading (and, indeed, of 'performance' also) is to keep going. To do this successfully you must not only play in the right key and time, but also have an appreciation of phrasing, style, dynamics, etc. In other words, you need to develop the ability to proceed calmly, despite mistakes.

Before attempting to play Example 8, look through it slowly and carefully, trying to hear it in your mind. Note the following points:

1 Key
The absence of sharps or flats in the key-signature indicates that the key is either C major or A minor, its relative. The final chord (lowest note A) suggests that the key is A minor, and the sharpened seventh (G sharp) elsewhere in the piece tends to confirm this.

2 Time and speed
The time-signature shows that there are four crotchets to the bar. The Italian term *Allegretto* (animated but not so fast as *Allegro*) suggests a speed that is lively, but not too fast (metronome mark perhaps = c 112). Look through the whole piece and decide the speed at which you will be able to play it *accurately*. On no account try to play it faster than this. If in doubt, play it slower. Count (in your mind) four beats at the speed you have decided upon, before you start to play, and continue counting mentally throughout the piece. If you are playing it fairly slowly, you may find it helpful to sub-divide the beats by counting 'one-and, two-and, three-and, four-and'. Whatever the speed, try to keep in time, even if you make mistakes.

3 Phrasing
Carefully distinguish between *legato* notes (slurred) and *staccato* notes (with dots over or under). *Staccato* notes should normally be thought of as having half the written value (i.e. a written crotchet should be played as a quaver followed by a quaver rest). Notice that in bar 2 (fourth beat) the right hand plays *legato* and the left hand *staccato*. And in order to make the music 'flow', look upon the first four bars as a single phrase, and the last four bars as another, 'thinking' from bar one to bar four, and so on.

Example 8

4 Style

This is a most important consideration. Looking at a piece you have never seen before, how do you decide the appropriate style in which to play it? Some pieces have obvious clues: 'Alla marcia' means 'in the style of a march'. 'Tempo di Gavotta', 'Tempo di Menuetto', 'Tranquillo', 'Scherzando' indicate, respectively, the style of a Gavotte or Minuet, or a tranquil or playful style. But a piece which is marked 'Andante', 'Allegretto', 'Con moto', etc. gives an indication only of the approximate speed. The style must then be judged by looking at the phrasing, dynamics, general characteristics of the melody, harmony, etc. This is a skill which can only be acquired gradually, through experience of many different styles, and intelligent observation.

5 Dynamics

The dynamics range from *piano* to *forte*, with *mezzo-forte* in between. To obtain a noticeable contrast you will have to depress the keys gently for *piano*, more strongly for *mezzo-forte*, and more strongly still for *forte*. Make sure that the keys go down to the key-bed, and that the finger muscles are relaxed at the moment of sound, so that the keys are held down with minimum pressure. And in soft playing take care, when gently depressing a key, that the hammer reaches the string, otherwise there will be no sound. Make the *crescendo* and *decrescendo* gradually, bearing in mind that the *crescendo* during the first three beats of bar 2 can only be made with the left hand, since the right hand is sustaining a note for three beats. On the fourth beat, however, the right hand note must be increased in volume, to match the *crescendo* in the left hand.

6 Fingering

Before you start to play, have in mind the fingering you will be using, at least for the first two bars. Bars 1 and 2 should present no difficulty – each hand lies within a five-note span, so you merely have to start with the thumb, or little finger, and use the fingers in order. Bar 3 (right hand) is less straightforward. To secure a satisfactory *legato* you may find it best to pass the second finger over the thumb on the last beat. In bars 7 and 8, fingering should be chosen which will enable the sixths in the right hand to be played as smoothly as possible.

7 Pedalling

If you have sufficient experience of the principles of pedalling, the pedal may be used when sight-reading pieces like this.

8 Playing

When you are ready, take a deep, gentle breath, and as you exhale start to play (this will help to free the mind and body of unnecessary tension). While you are breathing in, count four beats in the time you have decided upon, then start to breathe out on the first beat of the music.

Example 9 suggests how this piece might be phrased, fingered and pedalled, also that a slight *ritardando* could be made in the last bar-and-a-half, to bring the piece to a gentle conclusion. This example should be closely compared with Example 8.

Example 9

Allegretto

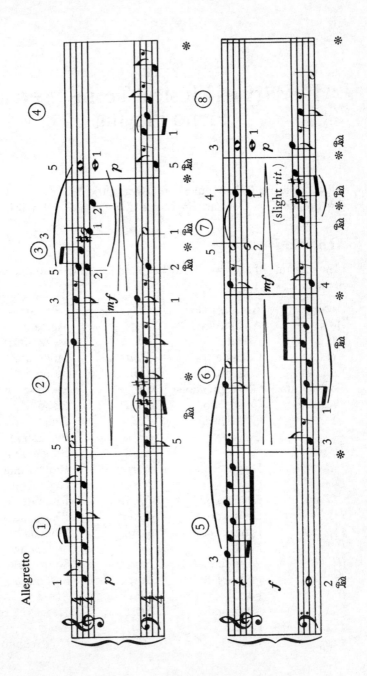

Glossary of Musical Terms used in Piano Playing

All words are in Italian, unless otherwise marked.
F = French G = German I = Italian L = Latin E = English

Abbreviations

(The meaning of each word may be found by referring to that word in the Glossary.)

Accel	Accelerando	*LH (E)*	Left hand
Ad lib	Ad libitum	*Marc*	Marcato
All' 8	All' ottava	*mf*	Mezzo-forte
CD	Colla destra	*Mod*	Moderato
Coll' 8	Coll' ottava	*Mor*	Morendo
Con espress	Con espressione	*mp*	Mezzo-piano
Cres; cresc	Crescendo	*p*	Piano
CS	Colla sinistra	*Ped*	Pedal
DC	Da capo	*pp*	Pianissimo
Decres;		*Rall*	Rallentando
decresc	Decrescendo	*rf; rfz; rinf*	Rinforzando
Dim;		*RH (E)*	Right hand
dimin	Diminuendo	*Rit; riten*	Ritenuto
DS	Dal segno	*Ritard*	Ritardando
Espress	Espressivo	*sf; sfz*	Sforzando;
f	Forte		sforzato
ff	Fortissimo	*Smorz*	Smorzando
fp	Forte-piano	*Sost; sosten*	Sostenuto
fz	Forzato;	*SP*	Senza pedale
	forzando	*Stacc*	Staccato
Leg	Legato	*Ten*	Tenuto
Legg	Leggiero	*VS*	Volto subito

Musical terms

Accelerando	Quickening the pace
Adagietto	Slightly quicker than *Adagio*
Adagio	At a slow pace (between *Andante* and *Largo*)
Adagissimo	Very slow
Ad libitum (L)	According to the performer's fancy
Affettuoso	Tender
Affrettando	Hurrying
Agitato	Agitated
Al fine	To the end (used when an earlier part of the music is to be repeated from the beginning (*Da capo*), or from the sign 𝄋 (*Dal segno*), to the end of the piece, or to the bar marked *Fine*)
All' ottavo	An octave higher
Alla	In the style of; e.g. *Alla polacca* = like a polonaise
Allegretto	Rather fast, but not so fast as *Allegro*
Allegro	Quick (between *Moderato* and *Presto*)
Amoroso	Lovingly; tenderly
Andante	At an easy pace, but less slow than *Adagio*
Andantino	Quicker than *Andante*; but in Beethoven's time sometimes slower
Animato	Animated
Appassionato	Passionately
Assai	Very
A tempo	In time (after *rall* or *accel*)
Bagatelle (F)	A trifle
Ben marcato	Well marked
Berceuse (F)	Lullaby; cradle song
Bis (L)	Twice
Bravura	Brilliance; dash
Brillante	Brilliant
Calando	Decreasing in volume or speed, or both
Cantabile	In a singing style

Colla destra	With the right hand
Coll' ottava	With the octave
Colla sinistra	With the left hand
Con anima	With life
Con brio	With vivacity, spirit
Con espressione	With expression
Con fuoco	With fire
Con grazia	With grace
Con moto	With animation
Con spirito	With spirit, life
Crescendo	Becoming louder
Da capo	From the beginning
Dal segno	From the sign (𝄋)
Decrescendo	Becoming softer
Delicato	Delicate; gentle
Diminuendo	Becoming softer
Dolce	Sweet
Espressivo	With expression
Etude (F)	Study
Fine	The end
Forte	Loud
Fortepiano	Loud, then immediately soft
Fortissimo	Very loud
Forzando; forzato	Strongly accented (see *sforzando; sforzato*)
Furioso	With fury, passion
Giocoso	Joyful
Glissando	A rapid scale played with the finger- or thumb-nail
Grandioso	Grand; magnificent
Grave	Heavy – also used to indicate a tempo slower than *Adagio*
Grazioso	Graceful
Humoreske (G)	A piece of a humorous character

Larghetto	Slow, but less slow than *Largo*
Largo	Broad; slow
Legato	Smooth
Leggiero	Light; nimble
Lentando	Gradually becoming slower
Lento	Slow
Lied (G)	Song
L'istesso tempo	The same time, or movement
Lusingando	Coaxing; caressing
Ma	But
Maestoso	Majestic
Maggiore	Major
Main droite (F)	Right hand
Main gauche (F)	Left hand
Mano destro	Right hand
Mano sinistra	Left hand
Marcato	Marked
Meno mosso	Less movement
Mezzo-forte	Moderately loud
Mezzo-piano	Moderately soft
Molto	Much
Morendo	Dying away gradually
Nobilmente	Nobly
Non troppo	Not too much
Pastorale (I or F)	In a pastoral style
Perdendosi	'Losing itself'; dying away
Pianissimo	Very soft
Piano	Soft
Più mosso	More movement
Poco	A little
Prestissimo	As quick as possible
Rallentando	Gradually becoming slower
Rinforzando	Reinforcing (a note or chord)
Ritardando	Gradually becoming slower
Risoluto	Resolute

Ritenuto	Holding back
Sans (F)	Without; e.g. *sans pédale* = without pedal
Scherzando	Playfully
Sempre	Always
Senza	Without
Sforzando; sforzato	Indicates that a note or chord so marked is to be strongly accented
Slentando	Gradually becoming slower
Smorzando	Dying away
Sostenuto	Sustained
Staccato	Short; detached
Stringendo	Increasing the speed
Svelto	Free; nimble
Tempo	Speed; time
Tempo commodo	In convenient time
Tempo primo	After a change of tempo, the pace first indicated is to be resumed
Tempo rubato	Lit. 'in robbed time'; i.e. a time in which one part of a bar is played slower or faster at the expense of the other part
Tenuto	Held; sustained
Tranquillo	Tranquil; peaceful
Transpose (E)	To read music in a higher or lower key than that in which it is written
Tre corde	Three strings (indicating the release of the left pedal)
Una corda	One string (indicating the use of the left pedal)
Vivace	Lively; brisk
Vivo	Animated
Volto subito	Turn over quickly

Index

accent, 22-3, 74, 85, 104
acciaccatura, 76
accidentals, 35, 39, 40, 42, 54
accompaniment, 102, 129
Album for the Young (Schumann), 93, 124
Alexander Technique, 107
appoggiatura, 75
Aria from Partita in G (Telemann), 86
arpeggios, 48, 73, 79, 98, 137
Associated Board of the Royal Schools of Music, 2, 53, 60, 124
aural tests, 2, 60-1

Bach, Johann Sebastian (1685-1750), 54, 65, 92, 101
Bartók, Béla (1881-1945), 86
Beethoven, Ludwig van (1770-1827), 54, 57, 59, 82, 86
bravura passages, 90
breathing, 106, 108, 138, 142
broken chords, 48, 73, 98-9, 118, 137
broken octaves, 91
cadences, 55, 62, 80-2, 101, 113, n.130
cantabile passages, 90
Carnaval (Schumann), 74
cassettes, use of, 64, 86
Children's Album (Tchaikovsky), 86
Chopin, Frédéric (1810-49), 54, 65

chords, 24, 39, 47-8, 100, 109-18 (see also triads)
Classics to Moderns (Yorktown Music Press), 2
clavichord, 4
clefs, 11, 26, 36, 62, 124
Cristofori, Bartolomeo (1655-1731), 4
Debussy, Claude (1862-1918), 54, 59, 65
duet-playing, 64
dynamics, 59, 62, 130, 141
embellishment, notes of, 74-8
enharmonics, 34, 45
expression, 102, 126
fingering, 17-20, 65-73, 98, 141
Form of Music, The (Cole), 101
forms, musical, 101
Freedom in Piano Technique (Last), 100
Freedom Technique (Last), 98
Graded Pianoforte Studies (Associated Board), 2
grade examinations, 60, 64, 124, 137, 138
grace notes, 74
Grieg, Edvard (1843-1907), 58

harmonics (partials), 5
harmony (*see* chords)
harpsichord, 4, 74
Haydn, Joseph (1732–1809), 59

interpretation, 62, 64, 79, 85, 100–4
Interpretation in Piano Study (Last), 100
Interpretation of Early Music, The (Donnington), 74
Interpretation of Music of the XVII and XVIII Centuries (Dolmetsch), 74
intervals, 32, 39, 45–7, 61

key, 36, 53–4, 125, 139
key-note (tonic), 33, 36–7, 53, 60, 61
key-signatures, 36–44, 53–4, 62, 132, 139
keyboard, 9–11, 16, 17, 20, 32, 36, 57, 86, 88
Keyboard Anthology, A (Associated Board), 2
Keyboard Interpretation (Ferguson), 74
Kinderscenen (Schumann), 102

legato, 65, 83, 88, 92, 100, 104, 134–5, 139
Liebesträume (Liszt), 103
Liszt, Franz (1811–86), 53, 59, 103

MacDowell, Edward (1861–1908), 56
march, funeral or wedding, 38
melody, 24, 39, 54, 57, 63, 68, 85, 102, 109, 111, 118, 119
Melody (Schumann, Op. 68, No. 1), 124–31
memorising music, 63
metronome, 58
Minuet in F (Mozart), 58
modes, 32–3, 38, 42, 43
modulation, 116–18, n.129
mordent, 78
Mozart, Wolfgang Amadeus (1756–91), 58, 59

nerves, examination, 138
Nine Little Pieces (Bartók), 86
nocturne, 54

octave(s), 15, 20, 22, 33, n.46, 90, 94, 99
ornaments (*see* embellishment, notes of)

partials (*see* harmonics)
part-writing, 24
pauses, 104
pedals, 16, 92–5, 128, 142
Pedalling the Modern Pianoforte (York Bowen), 95
phrasing, 55, 56, 62, 80–6, 101, 126, 130, 139
piano
  action, 4–5, 8
  choosing, 6–7
  grand, 6
  looking after, 7–8
  music, 1–2, 3, 11–12, 53, 85, 101
  origin of, 4
  pitch, 8
  position at, 16–17
  Steinway, 6
  stool, 16
  tuning, 7–8
  upright, 6
Piano Lessons with Fanny Waterman and Marion Harewood, 3
Points of Pedalling (James Ching), 95
Preliminary Exercises (Hanon, ed. John Thompson), 2
Prelude (Chopin, Op. 28, No. 6), 54

relaxation, 105–8
Remembrance (Schumann, Op. 68, No. 28), 93
rests, 29–30
rhythm, n.22, 58
Romance from Sonatina in G (Beethoven), 57
rotary movement, 91
rubato, 102–4

Index 151

scales, 32–3, 36–44, 70–1, 96–8, 132–6

Scarlatti, Domenico (1685–1757), 101

Schumann, Robert (1810–56), 57, 58, 84–5, 124–31

sight-reading, 61–3, 138–42

skips and leaps, 99

slurs, 83

smudging, 88

Sonata in G Major (Beethoven, Op. 48, No. 3), 86

Sonata in G Minor (Beethoven, Op. 48, No. 1), 86

Sonata No. 14 in D Major (Haydn), 59

spinet, 4, 74

staccato, 83, 89–90, 95, 100, 104, 136, 139

studies, piano, 2, 20, 53

style, 57, 62, 101, 119–22, 139, 141

syncopation, 74, 85

Tchaikovsky, Peter Ilyich (1840–93), 86

technique, 64, 95, 97–100

Telemann, Georg Philipp (1681–1767), 86

Ten Easy Pieces (Bartók), 86

tension, 105–8

time, counting, 55–8, 139

time-signatures, 26–9, 53, 126, 139

To a Wild Rose (MacDowell), 56

tonal balance, 88, 129, 134

tone-colour, 90, 95, 102

tone-production, 87–91, 96, 99

Träumerei (Schumann, Op. 15, No. 7), 102

triads, 47–8, 109–15

trill, 78, 99–100

tuning fork, 8

turns, 76–8

virginals, 4, 74

waltz, 99

Wild Horseman, The (Schumann, Op. 15), 57

OTHER TITLES AVAILABLE IN TEACH YOURSELF

☐	0 340 56444 X	**Music**	£5.99

King Palmer

☐	0 340 52893 1	**The Guitar**	£4.99
☐	0 340 52933 4	Book/cassette pack	£12.99

Dale Fradd

All these books are available at your local bookshop or newsagent, or can be ordered direct from the publisher. Just tick the titles you want and fill in the form below.

Prices and availability subject to change without notice.

HODDER & STOUGHTON PAPERBACKS, PO Box 11, Falmouth, Cornwall.

Please send cheque or postal order for the value of the book, and add the following for postage and packing:

UK including BFPO – £1.00 for one book, plus 50p for the second book, and 30p for each additional book ordered up to a £3.00 maximum.

OVERSEAS INCLUDING EIRE – £2.00 for the first book, plus £1.00 for the second book, and 50p for each additional book ordered.

OR please debit this amount from my Access/Visa card (delete as appropriate).

Card number

AMOUNT £. ....

EXPIRY DATE ....

SIGNED ....

NAME ....

ADDRESS ....

Carole Matthews is the *Sunday Times* bestselling author of twenty-nine novels, including the Top Ten bestsellers *The Cake Shop in the Garden*, *A Cottage by the Sea*, *The Chocolate Lovers' Christmas* and *The Chocolate Lovers' Wedding*. In 2015, Carole was awarded the RNA Outstanding Achievement Award. Her novels dazzle and delight readers all over the world. She is published in more than thirty countries and her books have sold to Hollywood.

For all the latest news from Carole, visit www.carolematthews.com, follow Carole on Twitter (@carolematthews) and Instagram (matthews.carole) or join the thousands of readers who have become Carole's friend on Facebook (carolematthewsbooks).

Praise for Carole

'All the warmth and wit we expect from Carole ... Perfect' *Bella*

'Matthews is one of the few writers who can rival
Marian Keyes' gift for telling heart-warming tales with
buckets of charm and laughs' *Daily Record*

'Witty, funny and incredibly touching, this is
perfect for lifting the spirits' *Heat*

'Simply brilliant' *Closer*

'A feel-good tale, fun and thoroughly escapist' *Marie Claire*

Novels by Carole Matthews

Let's Meet on Platform 8
A Whiff of Scandal
More to Life than This
For Better, For Worse
A Minor Indiscretion
A Compromising Position
The Sweetest Taboo
With or Without You
You Drive Me Crazy
Welcome to the Real World
The Chocolate Lovers' Club
The Chocolate Lovers' Diet
It's a Kind of Magic
All You Need is Love
That Loving Feeling
It's Now or Never
The Only Way is Up
Wrapped Up in You
Summer Daydreams
With Love at Christmas
A Cottage by the Sea
Calling Mrs Christmas
A Place to Call Home
The Christmas Party
A Place to Call Home
The Christmas Party
The Cake Shop in the Garden
The Chocolate Lovers' Christmas
The Chocolate Lovers' Wedding

THE DIFFERENCE
A DAY MAKES

CAROLE MATTHEWS

SPHERE

First published in Great Britain in 2009 by Headline Review
First published in paperback in 2009 by Headline Review
This paperback edition published in 2013 by Sphere

7 9 10 8 6

A CIP catalogue record for this book
is available from the British Library.

ISBN 978-0-7515-5144-0

Typeset in Sabon by Palimpsest Book Production Limited, Falkirk, Stirlingshire
Printed and bound in Great Britain by Clays Ltd, St Ives plc

Papers used by Sphere are from well-managed forests
and other responsible sources.

MIX
Paper from
responsible sources
FSC® C104740

Sphere
An imprint of
Little, Brown Book Group
Carmelite House
50 Victoria Embankment
London EC4Y 0DZ

An Hachette UK Company
www.hachette.co.uk

www.littlebrown.co.uk

To Bernie Keith and Riley – for all your help and
friendship along the way

Acknowledgements

Thanks to David and Jayne for all things veterinary and countrified and, most importantly, the hair-raising stories about the real-life Hamish. I could have listened to tales about him all day – in fact, I think I did. Once in a lifetime a pet comes along like that – and thank goodness, otherwise no one would have any pants left. He has made such an impression on me and I've never even met him. There is a photo of the original and incomparable doggy on my website for anyone who doubts the existence of such a whirling dervish of a hound.

It might also be pertinent to mention Sue Golden and Andy Bull here who introduced me to David and Jayne in the first place. Thanks so much for that. See how complicated writing a book can be! It's all down to chance, concidence and, mainly, drunken conversations.

Another chance conversation on a tour bus in South Africa brought Carol The Vet into my life and much-appreciated additional material. Also to Louise Davidson for allowing me to spend time on her smallholding and for not making me do anything that involved the non-feeding end of the animals – phew!

Chapter One

Out of the corner of my eye, I see William's face crease in pain. I look up from my Harlan Coben novel which has, up until now, been keeping me gripped. 'Will? What's wrong?'

'Funny pain,' my husband says tightly as he rubs at his chest.

'Indigestion,' is my diagnosis. 'Your toast was burned this morning. And you ate it in three mouthfuls. That'll always do it.'

I sip my take-away latte that I grabbed at the entrance to the station. This morning, the time to eat breakfast eluded me. The rush-hour Tube is packed, as usual. Damp bodies crush together, everyone steaming gently due to the heavy rain out on the street. It's a filthy day out there even though summer is just around the corner and, for once, I'm glad to be squashed on the Underground, pressed up against my husband. I move closer to him and we sway with the movement of the train which is rattling along apace. I'm struggling to hold my book high enough or steady enough to read it, so I abandon it and juggle my coffee into my other hand in an attempt to take another sip.

William rubs at his shoulder and down his arm, muttering to himself as he does so. Beads of sweat form on his forehead and his face has gone pale.

'Are you all right?'

'Hot,' he gasps. 'Very hot.' His fingers fumble with his tie, loosening it, and he lets out a wobbly breath.

'We've only one more stop,' I say. He could probably do with sitting down for a minute, but no one is likely to give up their seat for him. My husband looks clammy and is sweating profusely. 'You'll feel better when you're out in the fresh air.'

I brush his thick, dark hair from his forehead and blow a cool breath on it through pursed lips. Must nag him to get a haircut this weekend – it's long overdue. We've both been so manic that it's simply slipped off the grid. 'Have you got a busy morning?'

William nods. Silly question, really. We're always busy. Last night we were both out late at cocktail parties. It was gone midnight when we fell into bed, too tired for anything more strenuous than a cursory peck on the cheek. I don't think that Will's been home before eleven o'clock all week and we're fast approaching the age where you can only do that so many times in a row without it having a detrimental effect. It would have been lovely to have had a lie-in this morning, but it wasn't to be.

My husband and I work together at the British Television Company. I'm Amy Ashurst, the Executive Producer of a popular sports quiz programme – imaginatively named *Sports Quiz* – that's been running for years. I have a formidable reputation that I don't think I deserve. I'm a pussy cat really, I just have high standards. I adore my work and the buzz around such a successful programme and would probably do it for free if they didn't pay me handsomely for it.

William is Head of Comedy Development and works with

a lot of the up-and-coming comedians to provide showcase programmes for them. He's the life and soul of the party and is responsible for giving breaks to some of the biggest names in entertainment on the small screen today. He doesn't like to brag, but you'd know them all.

There are advantages and disadvantages of working together – although we hardly see each other during the day unless we manage to snatch a rare lunch together in the staff canteen. The difficulty is in the evenings when neither of us can switch off our BTC heads and all we talk about is work. But, as I said, we both love our jobs, so that's no great hardship.

'Try to grab a cup of tea and take five before you launch into the day.' I squeeze his arm. William's never ill. He's a complete fitness freak and runs every day, hail, rain or shine. Not like me who has to be coaxed to the gym once a year. My husband has the constitution of an ox and will declare it to anyone prepared to listen.

'Yes.' His face has an odd waxen look.

'Do you want a sip of this?' I offer my latte, but he shakes his head.

It's about time we had a holiday, I think. We've both been so stretched, with one thing and another, that we haven't had a proper break for ages. Perhaps Will has been working too hard. Maybe I'll have a look at my diary when I get into the office, see if we can squeeze something in.

'You do look a bit peaky,' I tell him, frowning with concern. With that he sags forward and my book and my coffee fall to the floor as I try to catch him. 'William?'

Alarmed commuters step backwards, forming a small circle

of space around him. My husband drops to his knees, clutching at his chest and gasping.

'Help me!' I shout, panicking, my eyes scanning the crowd. 'Help me! Is there a doctor in here?'

Everyone looks at me blankly. Fear grips my stomach. I don't know what to do. What *can* I do? 'William. William.' My husband's fighting for breath.

'I'm a nurse,' a voice says, and a young man pushes his way forward to crouch down beside William, heedless of the spreading puddle of coffee at his feet.

The Tube pulls up at White City. 'This is our stop,' I say hurriedly.

'Let's get him off here.'

We haul William to the door and then half-carry him, shoulders under his arms, to the platform where we lay him down. He continues to gasp, his face turning the colour of putty.

'It's his heart,' the nurse says, opening William's coat and jacket.

His heart? I want to laugh. It can't be. Will's not yet forty-two. Doesn't he know how fit my husband is? He's thinking of doing the London Marathon again next year. William would be the last person in the world to have a heart-attack. He must have got it wrong.

'We need an ambulance,' the nurse barks at me. '*Now.*'

As I fumble for my mobile, I realise that it won't work down here. I scan the platform, looking for a member of the station staff and then I break into a run, pushing through the commuters, searching for help while behind me Will lies unmoving on the platform.

Chapter Two

I pace the hospital room, hours later, still in a state of shock. Then I hear a noise from the bed behind me and I turn to see that my husband has stirred. My own heart contracts again as I stare at him. He looks like a snowman, his eyes like black coals that gaze at me from a too-white face. This man, who's normally so strong and solid, looks as weak as a kitten. I can't get used to seeing him like this. It's just not right.

Going to the bed, I squeeze his hand, mindful of the tubes that enter the back of it. His chest is bared, his hospital gown open, and he's wired up to a heart monitor that beeps steadily now – thank God. 'You gave me quite a scare there, you silly sod.'

'Scared myself too,' William admits. His lips look dry and, as a reflex reaction, I wet my own. 'I thought the Grim Reaper was knocking at the door.'

'I know.' For a while I'd thought that too.

William lets his eyes close again, momentarily. 'Us Ashursts are renowned for our dodgy hearts, Amy.' He tries a laugh. 'Never thought it would bother me though. Assumed mine was as solid as a rock.'

'It might not be your heart. The doctors say that they're going to run all kinds of tests on you to see what caused it.' My husband was whisked straight into hospital and given an initial assessment. They've told us that Will didn't have a heart-attack, that it was simply pain that made him pass out. But we still don't know what caused the pain in the first place. 'You'll be in for a few days yet. But you're out of danger now.' I stroke his hair.

'The consultant asked if I was stressed.'

We both laugh tiredly at that. We're in television. We juggle two careers, two children and a sprawling house. Of course Will's stressed. We both are.

'Have you phoned home?' he wants to know.

'I called Maya.' Maya's our Bulgarian nanny. She's been with us for four years now and, frankly, I have no idea what I'd do without her. My life would fall apart in about ten minutes flat. She's not only fantastic with the kids, but she cooks, cleans, shops, berates tradesmen on our behalf and, generally, assures that our lives run like a well-oiled machine. In return we pay her a king's ransom, give her a top-of-the-range Audi to drive and constantly beg her not to find a nice man, settle down and have children of her own. 'I've told her not to mention anything to the children yet. I'll tell them myself when I get home.'

'You're not going into work today, surely?'

I raise my eyebrows. 'Gav's been on the phone already.' Gavin Morrison – that's my boss. He's a BTC man through and through. The show must go on whatever's happening in your personal life. He wouldn't let a little thing like a suspected heart-attack stand in the way of his ratings war. Sick staff just don't feature on his radar. 'I rang in to say what had happened and that I'd be back tomorrow if all was well. We're recording three shows back-to-back today. He's begged me to go in just to make sure everything's on track.'

'Can no one else do it?'

I shrug. 'You know what it's like.' We don't have enough people to do the jobs that are required already.

Will puffs out his agreement. 'Only too well.'

'I've got so much to do.'

'That's nothing new.'

'No.'

The host of *Sports Quiz* is an ex-footballer who now runs a hotel with fishing rights in Scotland and we have to make the most of him when he reluctantly tears himself away from his country pile and comes down to London to record the programme. He's the ultimate professional and is a joy to work with, but it means a crazily busy day for everyone concerned – including me.

'You look all in,' my husband says. 'It's been a shock for you too. Why don't you go straight home and put your feet up for the day? Tell them to stick it.'

Stick it? That's not like Will at all.

'Or you could jump in the bed next to me?' he suggests.

Smiling, I tease, 'There's nothing much wrong with you.'

'Bravado, I'm afraid,' he admits with a sigh.

The thought of going home and putting my feet up for a couple of hours is very tempting, but how can I possibly leave Will like this? I do feel shaken, all sort of shivery and uncertain inside.

My phone rings again and I grab for it before the nurse

hears it as I'm not supposed to have it on in here. It's my boss again. 'An hour,' he pleads. 'Just come in for an hour.'

If there's any day that I really can't afford to miss work, then it's today. I chew at my lip. I know how pushed my staff will be without me. 'I'll do my best,' I say. 'But I can't promise.' Gavin will just have to put up with that. I hang up.

William catches me glancing at my watch. 'Go on,' he says with an unsteady exhalation of breath. 'Go and give the good old BTC their pound of flesh. You know that Gavin won't let you rest until you do.'

I'm torn with concern for my husband and concern that a dozen other people are depending on me. I called my assistant, Jocelyn, right away this morning to let her know the score and she'll be holding the fort. And she's great. But she's not me. I'd hate for anything to go wrong while I'm not there. My boss wouldn't have called if he wasn't worried too. I check my watch again. If I rush, then I could just get there in time for the first recording. 'I don't want to leave you.'

'There's nothing much you can do here.' My husband takes in his tubes and the array of wires attached to his chest. He appreciates the pressure of my job as his is exactly the same. 'I'll just go back to sleep. I'm very tired.' I hear the catch in his voice.

I lay my head on his shoulder. 'I hate to see you like this. Just a few days of being poked and prodded about and you'll be as right as rain, I'm sure.'

He looks at me bleakly. 'What if I'm not, Amy?'

I laugh at him softly. 'You will be. Of course you will. You're the fittest person I know. This is just a wobble. Nothing more.' I run my thumb over his cheek and he catches my hand and squeezes it. 'You'll be fine. You'll be back at work next week, terrifying all that young talent whose careers you hold in the palm of your hand,' I joke.

Will's gaze goes to the ceiling and I can tell that tears are forming which is so unlike him.

'Close your eyes, darling,' I tell him tenderly. 'Get some sleep. The more you can rest, the better.' I feel terrible for doing this, but I should pop into the studio. Just for a couple of hours, then I'll come back. 'I called into the office for you and everything's under control.'

'I had a dinner organised for tonight with Marty Moran.' The new hot stuff on the comedy scene. 'Can you make sure it's rescheduled for next week?'

I nod. 'Is there anything else I can do for you?'

Will takes my hand and kisses it. 'Just keep loving me,' he says.

'Always,' I assure him. Then he closes his eyes and I wait until his breathing relaxes and he's asleep. Then, giving a last glance to check that his monitor is still beeping steadily and feeling as guilty as hell, I steal away.

Chapter Three

'He works too hard,' my assistant tells me. 'You both do.'

'We love our jobs.'

'You shouldn't be here,' Jocelyn chides, gripping her clipboard tighter as she moves out of my rightful place at the production desk. It seems as if none of the team expected me to turn up today, just my boss. 'You should be at the hospital.'

'I know. I know. Gavin phoned and begged me to come in.'

Jocelyn purses her lips. Her look says that he should have left me alone. Perhaps he should, but we're all under pressure here.

'Go back,' she says.

'I'm here now. Besides, I can't do anything there,' I insist. 'Will was fast asleep when I left. That's all he needs – some rest. He's going to be fine. Really, he is. He's as fit as a flea. They think it might just be stress or something.' I try to console myself with the fact that my husband has a team of experts on hand to jump to attention should one of the myriad machines he's attached to utter a single bleep in the wrong place.

'This is a warning,' Jocelyn continues, warming to her theme. 'Look at the hours you both put it. It's ridiculous. Perhaps you need to slow down.'

If Jocelyn is trying to make me feel old and inadequate then it's not working. Both Will and I thrive on pressure. Or at least I thought we did.

I look out from the gallery. The studio audience are currently taking their seats ready for the warm-up comedian to work his magic on them. 'Shall I send this lot away then?' I wave my arm towards the crowd of people for my assistant's benefit. 'Just say I'm sorry, can't do this today – other, more pressing things on my mind.'

Jocelyn scowls at me. The two opposing panels of famous sports people are currently enjoying the hospitality of the BTC in its most salubrious green room. My very next job is to check on them all. Make sure that they're happy. Some of them enjoy their celebrity status more than others and we see our fair share of diva-like behaviour.

'*I* can manage,' Jocelyn says.

I'm sure she could. My assistant is a very ambitious woman and would love the chance to prove herself in my job. But Gavin made it very clear that it was me he wanted at the helm today and like a fool, here I am.

'Good grief, Amy, people would understand. I know we all like to think that we're irreplaceable, but we can cope without you for a few days. Your husband's ill.'

'He's fine. The doctor said it was just a wobble. A minor wobble.' The doctor didn't *actually* say that, but I'm sure that's what he really meant.

She huffs at me. Neither of us are ever ill. I can't think of the last time either Will or I took a day off work due to sickness. Even if the kids are unwell, Maya deals with it. That's how it has to be. Both Will and I are at the top of our tree – and we didn't get here by taking a day off when we had a cold. We have to be single-minded and focused. William understands why I have to be here even if, in my heart of hearts, I'd rather be sitting next to his bedside watching him sleep, making sure that he really is all right. This place is in our blood. We don't have any choice. We're dedicated professionals. He'd be mortified if he thought I was letting people down because of him. That's just how we are.

'Let's get on with it, shall we?' I smooth back my hair. 'The sooner we finish recording, the sooner I can get back to the hospital.' Today I have to squash down all of my problems and get on with the job in hand. My stomach starts to clench with nerves as the clock ticks down, but that's part of the buzz that I love. That's what keeps me coming back for more. I might be a wife and mother, but I'm also Amy Ashurst, television producer and adrenaline junkie. That's me too.

Chapter Four

We finally wrap the last of the three shows at about ten o'clock and I can leave for the night. All three programmes, apart from the usual minor retakes for fluffed lines, have gone without a hitch. Would that have happened if I hadn't been here?

We do have nights where the guests forget to turn up,

turn up two hours late or, even worse, turn up drunk – but thankfully, this wasn't one of them. Despite being here physically, my mind wasn't entirely on the job and I snatched a phone call to the hospital every time I could, just to make sure that Will was still okay. According to the nurses, he's slept most of the day away, which I'm sure has done him the power of good. He'll be back to his old self before we know it.

'We're all going to Bar Oscar,' Jocelyn tells me. 'Don't suppose you're coming?'

Shaking my head, I say, 'Not tonight.' Ordinarily, I wouldn't miss a chance to socialise with my team. They're a good bunch, fun to be with. We like to hit the hot spots together at least once a week. It's one of the reasons we all work so well together. 'I'm going straight back to see how Will is.'

'Give him my love,' my assistant says.

I make sure that I say my goodbyes to our star presenter and the guest athletes, then I phone a driver and get the car to take me to the hospital.

In the car on the way, I call Maya.

'I put the children in bed at their usual time, Amy,' she says. 'I didn't think that you'd want them to wait up for you.'

'No, no, you did the right thing,' I reassure her, pushing down a pang of longing for my babies. Tom is eight now and Jessica is six, but they're still babies to me. Tom looks just like his daddy, sturdy and solid with a mop of thick, dark hair and midnight-blue eyes. He has his father's competitive streak too and has to excel in everything he does. Jessica favours me – she's slight, elfin-faced and her blue eyes are pale like mine though she seems too laid back to be one of my offspring and excels in absolutely nothing. 'Are they both okay?'

'They're fine.' Now it's Maya's turn to be reassuring.

'I'll see them in the morning.' I feel guilty that once again I've missed their bedtime. They both love it when I'm home in time to read their stories to them, and Will and I try to work it that one of us is around every night of the week even though the co-ordinating of our diaries every Sunday night is a bit like a military operation. I wish I could spend more time with them. But then a paucity of time is the scourge of every working mum.

'I've left your supper ready to be microwaved,' Maya informs me.

'Thank you,' I say. 'You are so good to us. I don't know how I'd cope without you.'

'How's William?'

'I'm just about to find out,' I tell her. 'Don't wait up though.' I know what she's like, she'll force herself to stay awake until I'm home just to make sure that I'm okay. 'We'll talk about it in the morning.'

'Goodnight, Amy,' she says and I hang up, so grateful that I have someone who watches my back.

The ward is in darkness when I arrive and a nurse scuttles out from behind the reception desk to meet me. I give her my name and she says, 'I think that Mr Ashurst is asleep. I'll check his room for you.'

'I won't wake him,' I promise. 'I only want to say good-night.' Actually, just looking at him would be enough. I've missed him so much today. Now that I'm not pumped up on my adrenaline high from work, my fears for his health flood back.

After a moment's indecision, she takes me along to my husband's room.

Will is asleep. His covers are thrown back as the room is unbearably hot and he likes a lot of fresh air in the room. Despite the stifling temperature, he's still looking pale and vulnerable.

The nurse goes through a few cursory checks of the machinery that's monitoring Will, then she creeps out and leaves me alone with my husband.

I stand and watch him, wanting to smooth away the slight frown on his forehead. I love this man so much. We met twelve years ago when I was just twenty-six, and I can quite easily say that they've been the happiest twelve years of my life. I'd been at the BTC since graduating, working my way steadily through the ranks, when Will – already a successful producer at the age of thirty – joined the corporation. We met at a Christmas drinks party for one of the programmes – bizarrely, a dating gameshow. I'd bought a new dress and killer heels as I wanted to dress to impress, make an arrival. The killer heels were so high that I tripped up as I walked into the party and turned my ankle. Will was on hand to break my fall. He got me a drink and put some ice in his handkerchief which relieved my bruised ankle if not my ego. We found a cosy corner where I could hide my shame and put my foot up and, left to our own devices, instead of working the room, we hit it off immediately. That was pretty much that. We dated for a few weeks, decided that we'd both found our soulmate and would look no more. Then, without further ado, I moved lock, stock and two dozen handbags into his spacious flat in Notting Hill. We still live in the same area today, though home is now a three-storey Georgian villa with an enormous private garden and a good line in graffiti on the front wall.

While I'm musing, Will has opened his eyes.

'Hey,' I say. 'You'll get me into trouble with the nurse. I said I wouldn't wake you.'

'It's good to see you,' my husband tells me with a stifled yawn.

I pull a chair next to his bed and lean my elbows on it, gazing at him. 'I was just thinking how much I love you.'

'I love you too,' he whispers in return.

'How are you feeling?'

'Okay,' he says hesitantly. 'This has frightened me, you know.'

'You'll be fine.'

'My father died of a heart-attack at the ripe old age of forty-two,' he reminds me. 'I'd kind of planned on outliving him.'

'You will,' I assure him.

'It makes you think though.' He lets out a shuddering sigh.

'Next week you'll be back at work and will have forgotten all about this.'

'I don't think so.'

'You will. Two weeks max.'

'No,' he says flatly. Will's eyes are troubled as he looks deep into mine. 'You see, Amy, I've been doing a lot of thinking today and I'm not planning on going back to work.'

'Not next week?'

'Not next week, nor the week after,' he says. 'In fact, not ever.'

Chapter Five

'He's gone mad,' I tell Maya as she sets the table for breakfast. I'm wearing a track out of my kitchen floor. Soon I'll be in a trench up to my knees. 'Completely mad. He says he's not going back to work. Work is his *life*. Perhaps he banged his head when he fell. He's talking complete nonsense.'

'Maybe he is just a little worried.'

'I can understand that. But now I'm worried too.' Even more worried than I was before. When we thought he'd had a heart-attack, I was frantic, filled with fear for our future. Now I have a husband who's talking about giving up all our worldly goods, turning off, tuning out and becoming a hippy or something. I am completely beside myself and filled with fear about our future.

Perhaps I shouldn't confide in someone who is technically employed by us, but Maya has also become one of our closest friends over the last few years. She's like family to us. In fact, the only living relative we actually have left now is my sister, Serena. There are no grandparents to rely on for babysitting duties or emergency back-up, no extended-family network. We've no one. No one we can count on. Some people manage to go through most of their adult lives without the devastation of bereavement touching them. Will and I haven't been so lucky. Tragedy isn't a stranger in our lives. William's father died young – at the same age Will is now. I think that's what's frightened him so much. No one wants to bury their parents until they're old and grey. That's how it should be. Yet we hadn't reached our first wedding anniversary when his mother was also taken. She succumbed to cancer, knocking the feet out from under us once again. Within the year, and before our tears were dry, my beloved parents were killed in a terrible coach crash while on holiday in the Austrian Alps. The trip was a treat for my mother's sixtieth birthday and I'd just told her that I was pregnant with her first grandchild. She was so delighted and it still pains me to think that she's never seen my beautiful children. So that's us. Our tight little unit of four against the world. No one else matters now. There are some scattered aunts and cousins, but we've never had time to keep in regular touch with them because of work. Our familial relationships run to exchanging Christmas cards every year. Sometimes we even forget to do that. Maya is our only back-up. There's nothing that she doesn't know about this family. Good and bad. She's seen both William and me in our pants – once together. You can't get much more intimate than that.

'He's talking about packing his job in, Maya. A job which he *adores*. William Ashurst, *workaholic*, is convinced he'd be happier as an unemployed person.'

'He will think differently when he is better. I am sure.' My nanny moves onto arranging a selection of cereal on the table for my children's delectation. She lines up the boxes with military precision, always in the same order, edges neatly aligned.

'I stayed at his bedside until the nurse got fed up and kicked me out.'

'I heard you come home,' Maya says. 'It was very late. And you did not eat your supper.'

I couldn't eat. I still can't eat now. Out of habit, I've poured myself a bowl of Bran Flakes which I'm struggling to stomach. 'All he talked about was wanting to change how we live.'

'Upsets like this make you think in different ways,' she assures me calmly as she gets a jug of fresh orange juice out of the fridge.

'I *like* the way we live,' I tell her. 'I thought Will did.' We have great jobs, great salaries, great help, great kids who go to a great school, a great house in a great neighbourhood. How much better could it get?

'When he comes out of hospital, you must take holiday. That is thing to do.'

'You're right.' I seize on the idea. 'We'll all go. Where do you fancy? Where do you think William would want to go? Perhaps I can book it up today.'

Maya shrugs. 'We could rent big house in France again,' she suggests. 'Your husband is always happy there.'

'Yes,' I agree, animated now. 'He loves it. So do I. All that countryside. All that French bread, cheese and wine. He'll be in heaven.'

'Now that his heart is not so good, perhaps he will be unable to eat those things?'

'Bloody hell.' I let out an unhappy puff. 'You're right.'

19

What's the point of a French holiday when you can't gorge yourself on all that bad stuff? The countryside is all very well, but take away the fab food and there's not a lot to do, is there? Will lives for a wedge of Brie and a glass of Bordeaux.

'Children,' Maya shouts up the stairs. 'Your breakfast is ready. Hurry to the table.'

When Maya tells Tom and Jessica to hurry, they do. When I tell them to hurry, there are snails that could overtake them.

My children clatter down the stairs. They both head straight for the table. 'Don't I even get a hello?' I say.

Jessica comes and gives me a big hug. 'I love you,' I tell her.

'Love you too,' she reciprocates. 'I didn't see you yesterday.'

'You saw me at breakfast,' I tell her, desperately trying to remember whether she did or not. Was it yesterday when Will and I went into work early and missed them? So much has happened since then that my memory has been erased.

Realising that my son is more interested in his Cheerios than he is in me, I go over and ruffle his hair, kissing his reluctantly proffered cheek. 'Where's Dad?' he asks.

I slide into the chair next to him and exchange a weary glance with Maya. 'Daddy's not very well,' I say.

'Is he in bed?' Jessica wants to know as she joins us at the table.

'Yes.' I smile reassuringly at them both. 'But not upstairs. He's in bed at the hospital.' When I see their anxious faces, I hurriedly add, 'Only for a day or two.'

Tom has gone quite pale. 'He's not going to die, is he?'

'Of course not, silly billy,' I say with a forced laugh, but my mind flashes back to the picture of Will lying lifeless on the platform in the Tube. 'He's going to be just fine in no time at all.'

Jessica bursts into tears. 'Why? Why is he in hospital? Can I see him?'

'Of course you can, sweetheart. Maya can take you in as soon as you've finished school today.'

'I want to go with *you*,' she protests with a pouting lip. 'I want to go *now*.'

'I have to go to work.' I'm planning to shoot into the hospital for an hour on my way there, but if I take the kids then the visit will turn into a major expedition. 'You'll have to be a big girl and go with Maya later.'

'I hope Daddy gets better soon.' Jessica sniffs and cuffs her nose.

'So do I, darling.' And I mean that in more ways than one.

Chapter Six

My dear husband has been out of the hospital and at home for two weeks now and he's driving poor Maya mad. Me too, if you really want to know. Don't men make fantastic invalids? I've gone from being terrified that he'll die to wanting to kill him myself with my bare hands.

They kept him in hospital for ten days in the end and have given him every test known to man. What they found, I think, was reasonably reassuring. My husband feels otherwise. The doctor said his heart seemed sound, apart from the odd irregular beat – which surely must be good. Unfortunately, Will's blood pressure was sky high and he now has to take a beta-blocker every day. His cholesterol was pretty bad too, so he's on statins as well as a low-fat diet. No more French cheese for my hubby. He's also taking something to thin his blood. Our GP told him that he needs to have a better work/life balance and I feel that he is taking this way too literally.

'We're going to sell up,' William announces from his armchair in our living room. His feet are up on the pouff where they've been all day, the *Guardian* and his 'medicinal' glass of Merlot discarded at his side.

I widen my eyes behind my husband's head and look at my sister. Her expression gives nothing away.

'I wondered why there was a For Sale board outside,' Serena notes. 'That was quick work. You didn't say you were planning on moving.'

'It's this damn thing,' Will says, pounding a fist in the region of his heart. I do wish he wouldn't do that. Sends shivers down my spine. 'Makes you think.'

'The doctor said you'd hadn't actually had a heart-attack,' I point out. 'Just a scare.'

'It certainly was,' Will says, with a fulsome laugh. 'Most of my family have croaked it when they were still young. I don't want that to happen to me. Scared me into thinking what I'd *really* like out of life.'

'And that's to sell your beautiful home?' Serena sips at the red wine I've poured for her. I hold out my hands behind Will in a what-can-I-do? gesture.

I called Serena to come over and see us today with a view that she might be able to talk some sense into Will. I have tried and I have failed. My big sister is a city slicker – cool and calculating. She'll get right to the nub of this, fight my corner for me as she's always done. I've talked and talked to Will over the last three weeks and he's systematically ignored every single thing that I've said. All of my protests, my objections, my desires, my insecurities have fallen on deaf ears.

'More than that,' my husband tells her proudly. 'We're leaving all of this behind.' His sweeping gesture encompasses the room. My eyes widen further. 'It's only bricks and mortar at the end of the day.'

Bricks and mortar that I've spent the last seven years pouring loving care into, I think. But I say nothing.

Take this living room. I had handmade bookcases of fine oak commissioned to fit our nooks and crannies just perfectly. The curtains alone cost me three months' salary – a not inconsiderable sum. The modern statement chandeliers are hand-blown Murano glass. This room could feature in *Homes & Gardens*, no trouble. And Will wants me to leave it all behind? On a whim? Just like that?

'I've had enough of the stresses and strains of city living,' he continues volubly. 'It's crowded, it's dirty, the pollution's terrible. I never see the children.'

'That's because you're always *working*,' I remind him.

'And now things will be very different, my love.' He reaches behind his armchair for my hand and I supply it. 'I want to feel the wind in my hair, dirt under my nails, connect with the fact that I'm part of nature.'

23

Bang on the head, definitely. I do not know this man.

'This job, this life is *killing* me,' he says. 'Literally.'

It will have to get in the queue, I think.

'I've been on the internet,' Will continues, unaware of my dark and murderous thoughts, 'while I've been recuperating. There are some great properties to be had in the country.'

And some rubbish schools. How much do we pay to get our children perfectly educated and now we're proposing to rip up our former game-plan and throw it all away? Or rather, my husband is.

'And Amy's in full agreement with this?' Serena wants to know.

'Absolutely,' Will says.

I shake my head and mouth a very vehement, 'No!'

Will squeezes my hand again. 'I know that she has some doubts about leaving Town, but she'll love the country life. I'm sure of it.'

I won't!

'Perhaps you could get a place within commuting distance for her so that she continue at BTC? What about that, sis?'

I clutch at the straw that's offered. 'That would be good.'

Now it's Will's turn to shake his head. 'We want to get right away from it all. Properties within striking distance of London are still way too expensive. We want to be remote with a capital "R".'

We don't!

'We'll find other ways to make a living,' my husband says.

'Really?' Serena sounds unconvinced.

'We've given too much to that company over the years and they've been happy to bleed us dry. They badgered Amy

24

to go into work while I was lying in hospital. They're on the phone to me every day asking when I'll be fit to go back. I should have told them to stick their precious job long ago.'

'But how will you live?' Serena asks. And I'm glad she does, because that's exactly what I want to know too and, so far, Will hasn't been able to give me any satisfactory answers. The British Television Company might be a rubbish employer, but are there going to be heaps of other less pressured jobs for us to rush into?

'I could do some freelance work,' Will says. 'So could Amy. If we got a big enough place we could do up a few rooms and do bed and breakfast.'

My mouth drops open. I'm appalled. *Bed and breakfast*? Do I look like a woman who'd be comfortable doing *bed and breakfast*?

'I didn't realise that you liked the country so much,' Serena observes.

'Love it!' Will pronounces decisively.

Since when? I want to scream. One holiday a year surrounded by greenery doesn't make us natural straw chewers. We like the odd stroll among the hills once every blue moon – an hour from the convenient car park and the ubiquitous ice-cream van – but that's our sum and total involvement with the country. We don't possess waxed jackets. We haven't even got wellies! You don't need them for the occasional tootle round Hyde Park – not even in the winter.

'Isn't this a case of the grass is always greener?' my sister suggests, calmly. 'Hasn't that become a cliché? Loads of Londoners up sticks and go to the country every year, only to find that they hate it.'

I think that's a very reasonable observation.

My husband rocks with mirth at the thought. 'Just because you can't get a cappuccino on every corner doesn't make the country a bad place.'

'There are a lot of things – other than the availability of cappuccino – to consider.'

Like the happiness of your wife, I might add.

More hilarity from Will, who has clearly lost his wits.

'You'll be giving up everything that you know, all that's been dear to you for so many years.' Serena is presenting the voice of reason when I bet she's seething inside due the obstinacy of my normally perfectly affable spouse. 'Is that really wise?'

'It's time for a new start. Off with the old, in with the new.'

I really don't like the sound of this at all. I'm rather attached to the old.

'It will be better for the children. Better for us. Besides . . .' A little laugh here from Will. 'I've already given in my notice.'

My wine glass falls from my hand and smashes on our bleached oak floor. There will always be a stain there now. 'You . . . you . . . you didn't tell me,' I stammer.

'You knew I was going to do it,' he says reasonably. 'Graham says there's no need for me to go back at all. How about that?'

Perhaps I can phone Will's boss, Graham Copeland, on Monday and beg for his job back. If I go down on my knees and weep real tears copiously, he might just reconsider. BTC don't like people who no longer want to be part of the family.

They tend to take it personally. Surely they must realise that Will is unwell? Surely they can't have taken him seriously?

'I think we should take this *very* slowly,' I venture.

Will grins magnanimously. 'I think we should go just as soon as we can,' he counters.

This is time for me to make my stand. I look to Serena and she nods her approval. Taking a deep breath, I say, 'William, I'm really not sure about this at all.'

'This is what I need,' he implores. 'How can you consider making me stay here in this hideous rat race? I want to escape – want *us* to escape. I have dreams of providing a better life for all of us – you, me, the children. If we stay here, dealing with all the strains and stresses of modern life, I might not be here to see the children grow up. Do you think about that?'

'Of course I do.'

'This move will be better for all of us,' he insists. 'How can you possibly deny me this chance to grab a new lease of life?'

Chapter Seven

Which is why I find myself less than three months later standing outside Helmshill Grange, a sullen monstrosity of a house, deep in the Yorkshire moors. It's July and it's raining. The clouds are down by my knees. In London it's probably 90 degrees. Our furniture lorry has gone missing – our tables and chairs are probably on their way to Lithuania or some-where. Jessica is crying again. I feel like joining her.

'We're going to live *here*?' she wails in horror. I couldn't have put it better myself.

'Yes, darling.' I hug her to me.

'But it's spooky!'

'It's got character,' I correct. And probably a couple of ghosts.

Tom is wide eyed with horror. 'How will our friends come and play here?' he wants to know.

'With great difficulty' is the answer I fail to give.

I look at the house again and my heart sinks. What was Will thinking of? What was *I* thinking of when I agreed with him? Except I didn't agree with him. Not really. It's just that I allowed him to get swept away with this ridiculous plan for a new life for us when we were all perfectly happy with our other life. That's nowhere near the same as agreeing, is it?

'Will I still be able to do ballet classes here?' Jessica asks tremulously.

'We'll try to find a class just as soon as we're settled.' Which is my way of saying, 'Probably not.' This does not look like a place that has a wide range of leisure activities on every corner.

The house is double fronted and, once upon a time, it was probably very lovely. Now it looks like it needs several grand spending on it simply to make it habitable. The couple who lived here previously had been here all of their married lives and were, I think, a hundred and eight years old apiece and hadn't decorated since their early twenties. They're now snuggled up in purpose-built sheltered accommodation with gas central heating and double glazing in the nearby market town of Scarsby, and I can certainly see why that might be a more attractive proposition.

All the windows need replacing. And the roof. And the front door. The house needs re-wiring, re-plumbing, re-pointing and re-painting. Or bulldozing.

Will bought it over the internet without us actually having been here, purely on the agent's recommendation. Which is so unlike him, as he's previously spent our married life being as reliable as the Swiss rail network. In spite of that, the silver-tongued salesman managed to convince my husband that it was a very desirable property in a very desirable part of the world and that it wouldn't remain on the market for more than five minutes. That bit was true enough. Three minutes later and it was ours.

The picture on the worldwide web was clearly very flattering. We have exchanged our comfortable, well-appointed home in Notting Hill for a house more suited to the Addams Family in the wilds of fuck-knows-where. The gate is hanging off its hinges and the front garden hasn't been troubled by a mower in a very long time. My daughter could go in there and never be found again.

Jessica cries some more and, frankly, I don't blame her. Perhaps she's thinking the same thing as me.

Behind the house is a large open barn in a tumbledown courtyard. The garden stretches out as far as I can see into the surrounding moors, and there's an orchard that might well be ours.

'Look at this!' my husband cries – but in a happy way. 'Isn't it marvellous?'

Mental note to self – I must get myself some of those rose-tinted spectacles he's started wearing since his wobble. I would so like to be able to see life as Will sees it.

When I remain silent, he adds, 'Admittedly it needs some work, but we can do it up slowly. Together.'

I am still stunned into speechlessness. It may surprise you to learn that I haven't the slightest urge to renovate an old wreck. I get men in to do that kind of thing. Polish ones, usually.

'And look at the scenery.' Will waves his arms around.

I can see clouds. Lots of clouds. Grey ones. Grey like underwear you've had for too many years and really should throw out.

'And listen.' My husband cocks an ear in theatrical style. 'Nothing.' He beams at his stunned wife, his weeping daughter and his goggle-eyed, disbelieving son.

I can hear something: sheep. Lots of sheep. All complaining. Their miserable, moaning baas carry across the fields. Sensible things, sheep.

'Breathe in that air!' Will fills his lungs in an exaggerated manner.

I inhale and all that I can smell is poo. Probably from the whingeing sheep.

'Where is supermarket?' Maya wants to know.

Heaven knows how we've persuaded our nanny to come to this godforsaken place with us, but she's here. She too, is now looking as if she bitterly regrets her decision.

'Not too far,' Will assures her. 'It's about half an hour from here to Scarsby.'

Maya gasps. And not with joy.

I turn and take in the rest of the village, unable to look at my new house any longer. An ITV newsreader and her music producer boyfriend are now ensconced in our lovely, lovely home in Notting Hill. They were bowled over by it, they said. I wonder what they'd make of this. I too am bowled over by Helmshill Grange – but not in a good way.

The village of Helmshill looks pretty enough, even to my biased eye. In front of the Grange, there's a neatly mown green, complete with its own textbook duck pond. The green is bounded by a genial-looking country pub and several pint-sized cottages with roses growing round the door. There's a stone water fountain surrounded by a blush of red geraniums. A tiny, picturesque church stands at the foot of the hills. The stone is blackened with age, but the grass round the ramshackle of tombstones is neatly trimmed. I like old churches. Maybe I'll find the time to have a wander round there sometime. So far, so very lovely. The village hall looks too small, even for the populace of this community, but there are more geraniums in hanging baskets flourishing by the door – must be all that rain. However, there's no shop, no post office, no chi-chi little deli selling a wide selection of olives and certainly no café serving frothy cappuccino.

Our nearest neighbour is up on the hill and to the same side of the green as the Grange. The house is an imposing modern stone place with large windows gazing down on the rest of the village in splendid isolation and I wonder, idly, who might live there.

'Let's get ourselves settled in then,' Will says, rubbing his hands together in glee. 'Home Sweet Home.'

Jessica howls again and is comforted by Maya, who is also crying. I have to be strong for them, so I'm digging my fingernails into my palms in an attempt to focus my pain.

To think that I've given up a wonderful, high-paid, life-affirming job for this. A job that I had fought and clawed my way up to for the best part of the last fifteen years and I've walked away from it because my husband wanted me to. I've done it for Will, because that's what marriage is all about. And, try as I might, I'm currently wishing I hadn't.

Maya and the children go ahead of us, but – to be honest – I can't make my legs work. Can shock bring on paralysis?

'Say you like it,' Will urges. He puts his arm round me and gives me a bear hug. I feel that I might break. I'm trying so hard to smile that my cheek muscles are hurting with the effort. 'I wouldn't want to think that you're unhappy.'

'I'm not unhappy,' I tell him. I'm desolate, despairing, desperate and devoid of all hope.

'This is it!' He beams at his new estate with proprietorial pride. 'This is what I've always wanted. My own land as far as the eye can see.' This from a man who couldn't even be bothered to do his own gardening in Notting Hill, a man who'd much rather pick up a book of poetry than a spade. 'Now we'll be living the dream!'

The only thing is, that it's my husband's dream and not mine.

Chapter Eight

Our home, it turns out, is the place where all the spiders in England come on holiday. It's a good job that I haven't seen *Arachnophobia* recently or, indeed, suffer from it otherwise I'd be in a permanent state of terror. Some of them have hairier legs than Will and are wearing hobnail boots.

Our furniture eventually arrived as darkness fell and – all credit to the removal men they unloaded the van in double-quick time. Two charming young men, Paul and Daniel of ShiftIt – movers to the clearly insane – worked frantically until midnight to make sure that we all had beds for the night. The rest of the furniture has been arranged haphazardly in more or less the appropriate rooms.

Despite still being in a state of shock that my husband is happy to swap what we had for *this*, I have forced myself to get out of bed even though I was tempted to stay there with the covers pulled over my head, hiding from bitter reality. From the wealth of packing cases, I've somehow managed to locate my oldest, skankiest clothes. Now, the next morning, Maya and I are setting to in the vast farmhouse kitchen with mops and buckets and gallons of pine-scented disinfectant. Mr and Mrs People Who Lived Here Before were clearly strangers to Mr Muscle. I haven't yet risked opening the Aga as I feel there might be a body in it. Same reason I'm not going anywhere near the cellar.

Maya is still weeping gently as she mops.

'It's not so bad,' I try to reassure her. 'Once we get it cleaned . . .' I falter as I realise that this could take about three years. There are mouse droppings everywhere and I didn't actually think that I knew what mouse droppings looked like. The glass in the windows is opaque with years of grime.

What I don't like to bring to Maya's attention is that she could simply – and justifiably – walk away from all this, whereas I'm trapped by marital duty. When I said 'I do', frankly, I had no plans to be 'doing it' in the country. My nanny could, on the other hand, tell me and Will and the kids to get stuffed and head back to London to find another less mad family to nurture. I hope against hope that she doesn't think of this. She is a girl after my own heart and has the city in her veins. And, like me, she probably feels like slitting one of those veins right now.

Inside, the house is spacious with large, airy rooms – for that read 'draughty'. Maya and I have already cleaned out two of the six bedrooms which have now been designated the children's bedrooms and they're quietly unpacking their toys and games, too shocked to think of squabbling. Never have I seen my offspring so subdued.

We should have got a company in to give the house a thorough clean before we moved in, but I had no idea that it would be so bad. Plus, the truth of the matter is, we are now officially broke. Virtually all of the money from the sale of the house in Notting Hill has been poured into this place. It means that we don't have a mortgage – thankfully – but it also means that we have very little left for day-to-day expenses now that we're both officially unemployed. My husband is convinced that I'm going to be able to get freelance work to top up the pot, possibly at Yorkshire Television or at Granada in Manchester. But I'm not so sure. At best that would be a three-hour round commute for me. Could I do that on a daily basis?

Will, from what I can gather, is planning to turn his hand to country pursuits – whatever they might be – and the words 'bed and breakfast' do still keep slipping into his conversation rather more frequently than I'd like.

My husband is wandering round the house, his rich baritone voice soaring through 'Oh, What a Beautiful Morning' very loudly. And I can honestly say that I've never heard him sing songs from *Oklahoma* before. He's in his element here. This is his dream. Whereas it's my living nightmare.

Of course, his delicate condition now precludes him from doing anything too strenuous and he isn't, therefore, involved in the messy end of cleaning. He's taking on a more supervisory role.

He's moved on to *South Pacific* and the strains of 'Gonna Wash That Man Right Out of My Hair' come ever nearer. 'Missed a bit.' Will points out a dirty patch on the floor as he enters the kitchen. See what I mean?

'You could do something useful,' I suggest. 'Go to Scarsby and buy us some food for tonight.' Don't suppose there's a friendly take-away locally.

'Right,' Will says, in between refrains and he grabs the car keys and leaves.

Sighing, I lean on my mop, just as our nanny gives a bloodcurdling scream as the tail of a mouse pops out from underneath one of the cupboards. I close my eyes. This will all turn out fine. I won't miss my job. I won't miss wearing Jimmy Choos every day. I won't miss sending out for a latte every five minutes. I won't miss the respect or the power. I won't miss hobnobbing it with celebrities from the sporting world. I won't miss my big sister popping round a couple of times a week. All of this I can cope without, as long as this makes my husband happy and keeps him fit and healthy. What would be the point in staying in London if I constantly worried that William wouldn't come home that night? So this is much, much better for us. Right?

I burst into tears.

'Don't cry, Amy.' Maya abandons her mop and puts her arms round me.

'I'm not crying,' I sob, and sniff louder.

I really hoped that work would refuse to accept my resignation, that my boss would hurl himself to the floor and beg me to stay. But he didn't. Gavin Morrison wished me well and waved a fond farewell without a squeak of protest. Even before I went, my assistant, Jocelyn, had been promoted. And, after years of loyal service, made it clear that she couldn't wait to see the back of me so that she could try on my shoes for size.

'We will all adapt,' my nanny tells me firmly.

'I'm sure we will.' I search my pockets for a tissue. While I sniffle, I wonder what I would have been doing in my old life right now. 'Yes. Yes. We'll all adapt. We'll become country bumpkins and love it. It will just take time.'

And I have an eternity at Helmshill Grange stretching ahead of me.

Chapter Nine

When William returns from Scarsby – several hours later – he's bearing two carrier bags overflowing with shopping and there's a definite spring in his step.

'Let me,' I say. 'Should you be carrying that?' His face is pale. Will still tires easily and that worries me. Shouldn't he be on the mend by now if there was really nothing wrong with him? His work/life balance is definitely now more in favour of life – shouldn't that be helping? We haven't signed on with a local GP yet, and I vow to make it my priority. I've been meaning to do it since we got here. He should have someone to keep an eye on him, just to be sure. My husband says that I worry too much. He's decided that he's the picture of robust health now that we've moved to the country. Arteries that were once clogged have miraculously cleared themselves, cholesterol that was high has fallen through the floor of its own volition, apparently. His blood pressure is that of a nineteen year old. Or so he tells me. I'd like a slightly more professional assessment.

'Light stuff,' he assures me. 'The rest is in the boot.'

I take the carriers from him, risking a quick peek to check that he's bought all that we might need. Sure enough there's a couple of cartons of milk and a loaf of bread in there, so I can relax a bit. On the rare occasion that Will ever did the shopping in London, he could come home with absolutely nothing that was on the list but two kilos of wonderfully smelly cheese that he'd fancied and maybe some olives.

Today, he seems to have catered for our more practical needs. The other bag contains loo rolls.

'Why are you grinning like a mad thing?' I want to know as I eye my husband warily. 'What have you done?'

'Nothing, nothing!' He's fidgeting like a five year old.

'Sure?'

I get a giggle in response.

'What's Scarsby like?'

'Wonderful,' he tells me.

Bet it's not.

'I'll go and get the rest of the shopping then,' I say, trying not to sigh.

Plodding out through the kitchen, I go to the car. When I hit the drive, I manage to stifle the half-sob, half-scream that comes to my throat. Now I know what William has been up to in Scarsby. I spin on my heels to find him standing behind me, grinning.

'Like it?' he asks.

My jaw has locked. 'Where's the car?'

'This is it.'

'The *real* car, I mean.'

'There's a great dealership in Scarsby,' he tells me. 'Thought this would be better for us. Now we'll look the part.'

Now we'll look like the Wurzels.

In the drive, in the place where our sleek, black Audi should be, there is the most battered Land Rover that I've ever seen. I think it's supposed to be blue, but there's so much rust on it that it's quite hard to tell.

'Maya won't be seen dead in that.' Me neither.

'It's practical,' my husband points out. 'You've seen how narrow and winding the lanes are – the Audi would have been ripped to bits within weeks. We won't mind if this gets a bit scuffed.'

I won't mind if this is blown up by a nail-bomb. 'We are contractually obliged to provide Maya with a reliable vehicle,' I remind him.

'This old workhorse will go on for years.' Will pats it lovingly. 'Solid as a rock.' The wing mirror drops off.

'Aren't we embracing this country lifestyle a little *too* fully? We can still have some creature comforts.'

Will purses his lips. 'Not sure that we have creature comfort money any more,' he points out. 'This has been a very expensive exercise.'

You're telling me.

'But I have plans,' he says. 'Big plans.'

I hope that those plans involve regaining our sanity, putting this house back on the market at once and heading straight back to London in time for Christmas.

'I feel at home here already,' Will says. He slips his arms round me and squeezes. 'I love you. Thank you so much for doing this. I know that it's a big wrench for you. But we're going to live much more simply from now on. Get back to the things in life that really matter.'

'Which are?'

'Family, friends. Living without stress. You and me.' Will kisses my cheek.

And while I appreciate the sentiment, I can't help thinking that the little bakery at the end of our street that sold seeded Low-GI bread really, really mattered to me too.

Chapter Ten

Two weeks later, deep in the throes of cleaning this place, and I still haven't yet unpacked half of our boxes. My husband has, however, somehow located the copy of *Keeping Chickens* by Audrey Fanshawe that he bought from Waterstones in Oxford Street and it's now on his bedside table. He settles himself in bed, picks up the book with a flourish and flicks open the pages. This is a man I loved for his knowledge of Tolstoy, James Joyce and Thomas Hardy. I shake my head. *Keeping Chickens.*

I give up on Zadie Smith and turn to Will. 'I don't think that I really want to keep chickens.' The only chickens that I like are the organic ones that come in plastic trays from Wholefood Market.

'It will be great,' he tells me in a voice that I'm coming to dread. 'They're wonderful animals. Or are they birds?'

Even I know that they're birds and I haven't even glanced at the chicken book.

'They all have personalities of their own.'

Presumably, he's also gleaned that from Audrey

Fanshawe, as the only experience of chickens that William has is also the organic ones in plastic trays from Wholefood Market.

'We can have our own organic eggs,' he continues excitedly. 'Maybe even sell a few.'

You can also buy them from Wholefood Market, I think, and not have all that fuss – but, as is my way these days, I don't voice that opinion. Instead, I snuggle down next to Will and say softly, 'You've changed so much since your wobble. I hardly recognise you any more.'

He puts down *Keeping Chickens*. 'Don't you like the new, improved me?'

'I'm having a bit of trouble keeping up with you,' I admit, letting my fingers rove over his chest. It worries me that beneath that strong, firm exterior something was going terribly wrong and we were completely unaware of it. Will will have to go for regular check-ups now and will probably be on medication for the rest of his life. That's another thing that worries me – out here in the sticks, will the doctors be up to the standards of the London one he's used to? If he has another wobble, will there be an efficient nurse handy to step in and deal with it? 'In my heart I'm still a hard-nosed television executive with a penchant for killer heels and kick-ass suits. You just seem to have embraced this whole country thing a lot quicker than I have.'

'Wait until we've got a proper smallholding with chickens and sheep and pigs.'

Sheep? Pigs? No one said anything about sheep or pigs.

'Why do we need sheep? There are loads out there on the hills. Can't we just look at those?'

'The point isn't to look at them, it's to rear them and then turn them into tasty dinners.'

'Eat our own sheep?' I don't think so. I like a bit of distance between me and my food. Not that keen on scoffing anything that's been running about in my own backyard. Once you'd tended them, wouldn't they be just like pets? That'd be certain to turn Jessica vegetarian. 'I thought we were just going to have a big house in the country. I don't remember the conversation about a smallholding.'

'I took it as a given,' Will says, sounding offended that I can't read his mind.

I sigh and give in. 'If it's what you want, then we'll do it. I just want you to be happy and healthy.'

'I feel as if I've been given a new lease of life.'

I feel as if I've had mine snatched away from me. But this is it. William loves it here in this big house with its leaking roof and its clanging plumbing and its lights that flicker on and off, so I might as well make the best of it. And I do love this man. I bloody well must do!

'How's the heart bearing up?' I let my fingers walk lower on his chest. He might have been given a relatively clean bill of health – blood pressure and cholesterol notwithstanding – but we still don't really know why it was that he collapsed that fateful day on the Tube so we haven't made love since Will's been ill. We've both been too worried about him exerting himself even though the doctor said – with a laugh – that it's a myth that many middle-aged men die of heart failure while they're having sex with their younger mistress. I'm still worried. He didn't mention what might happen if

42

that same middle-aged man was having sex with his equally middle-aged wife. Do I want to risk it?

'The heart's fine,' he says with a grin. 'Sound as a pound. In fact, it seems to be speeding up quite nicely at the moment.'

'Then I suggest that it's about time that we christened this bedroom,' I say as I fling his damn chicken book to the floor.

'Be gentle with me,' Will teases as he takes me in his arms.

I intend to be. Very gentle. I kiss him lovingly.

And, for a short time, I can forget where we are and what we've done and chickens and sheep and the vague scratching noises that are coming from the attic, and just love my husband once more.

Chapter Eleven

'Jesus!' I exclaim. 'What the hell are *they*?' And I haven't used the Lord's name in vain since the kids were born.

'Chickens,' Will says.

He's just come back from Scarsby in the knackered old Land Rover, blowing exhaust fumes into the ozone layer. If we're embracing a newer, greener lifestyle, it clearly doesn't extend to our choice of vehicle. You could smoke mackerel just holding them near the exhaust for five minutes.

More and more of the scabbiest-looking chickens I've ever

seen are flying out of the back of the Land Rover and onto my drive. They're squawking as if they've been scalded.

We only had the chicken conversation just over a week ago, and I'd hoped that I'd be able to ease myself into the reality of actually owning any. Will normally takes six months to read a book – at least – and I was sure he wouldn't rush out and buy any until he'd gleaned all the knowledge that Audrey had to impart about our feathered friends. But I hadn't bargained on the fact that now he's not working, he has nothing to do with his time. And, of course, there's the matter of his personality transplant.

More and more chickens fill the drive. 'What's wrong with them?' I ask. 'Why are they all bald? Why are they all running round and bumping into each other?'

'I've rescued them,' William tells me.

'From what?'

'They've been kept in terrible conditions.' A bit like this family then. 'The farmer let me have them for five quid each.'

I can't help feeling that my naive husband has been robbed.

One runs into my legs and falls over. 'They're blind.'

'Hmm.' Will scratches his head. 'I thought they might be.'

'What are we going to do with them?'

'Look after them,' Will says, that offended tone creeping into his voice again.

When I imagined chickens I thought of more exotic-looking breeds – Sultans, Polands, Buff Rocks, Gold Sebrights or even the weird Transylvanian Naked Neck for novelty value – (yes, I have been sneaking a look at Audrey Fanshawe's very helpful tome) – not these paltry excuses for poultry.

They're all spreading out now across the garden, banging

44

into things and flapping their wings. 'Where are we going to put them?'

'Ha!' my husband says, and disappears to the back of the Land Rover, lifting out the last remaining chickens as he does. He pulls out a magnificent brochure and points to a building which I take to be a chicken coop. It is the Ritz-Carlton of chicken coops. Yet another person who saw Will coming. 'Da da!'

'We're going to put those manky chickens in that?'

'I thought we'd give them a nicer home than they had. It'll be delivered later today. Fingers crossed.'

Definitely fingers crossed as I'm not having these things in the house if it doesn't turn up.

One of the chickens runs full pelt into the trunk of an apple tree. 'I think we should get someone to look at them. Suppose they've got bird flu or something?'

'They've not got bird flu,' Will says crossly. 'They just need a bit of tender loving care, Ashurst-style. Don't you, my darlings?'

Another chicken falls over.

'Well, I think we should call someone. Maybe a vet.'

'There's a chap in the village,' my husband tells me. 'Lives in that modern house up on the hill.'

Wise man. I bet his windows don't feel as if they haven't any glass in them. 'We should get his number. Phone him.'

'Good idea,' Will says. 'I'll just wait until the sheep arrive and then he can look at them all.'

'Sheep? Sheep? What sheep?' At this point, I start to hyperventilate.

45

Chapter Twelve

Putting on my Joseph trousers and a cashmere wrap cardigan, I wander down to the little school we've enrolled the children in.

It's September, the first day of term and my children weren't very happy at all this morning about starting a new school. I've never seen two kids eat cereal so slowly.

I too am worried about our choice of educational establishment, but for different reasons. Tom and Jessica have been in an exclusive private school until now and I wonder how they'll cope with the change. We've been here over a month now and yet they still haven't met any of the children from the village. There's hardly been anyone around. Most people, it seems, have been on holiday to warmer, more sensible places with fewer sheep and, to be honest, my social skills have been so buried beneath a mountain of gloom that I haven't cared whether we met any of our neighbours or not. So, consequently, we haven't. This morning we hung around in the playground looking new and uncomfortable while everyone else in their cosy cliques ignored us. We might as well have been wearing signs that said *unclean*. Then, when the school bell rang, I left my two at the door of St Mary's with a heavy heart.

Now I can't wait to collect them, to see how they've fared. The school is the size of a Wendy House and has windows just like those in the Gingerbread Cottage. I have to admit there's something quite nice about being able to walk to meet Tom and Jessica. This is a duty that Maya's always performed – out of necessity – as I've always been at work.

This school has the grand sum of twenty pupils and they're all disgorged at once on the stroke of 3.30 p.m. Is this the sort of place though that's likely to turn Jessica into a lawyer and Tom into a plastic surgeon? I bend down to kiss Jessica while Tom, skilfully, skirts my embrace.

'How was school?' I ask cheerily.

'Small,' Jessica says. 'Very small.'

'Did you make any nice friends?'

'No,' she says. 'They all talk funny and I can't tell what they're saying. But they say *we* talk funny.' My daughter looks outraged at that.

'Give it a few days and you'll love it,' I reassure her.

'No,' Jessica says. 'Don't think so. I'd like to go back to my old school.'

'Me too.' Tom kicks at the playground.

'We'll talk to Daddy,' I say as a diversionary tactic.

The Headteacher comes out to talk to me. She's called Mrs Barnsley and is dumpy and is dressed in clothes that my dear mother, even when she was alive, wouldn't have been seen dead in. Mrs Barnsley takes in my designer labels. 'Welcome to Helmshill, Mrs Ashurst,' she says. 'The children have settled in really well.'

'We haven't,' Tom corrects her.

Mrs Barnsley ignores him. 'We hope you'll all be really happy here. This is a small school and we trust that we'll

47

see you on some of the various committees we have. We depend on the enthusiasm of our parents.'

I quite liked it when all I had to do was throw vast quantities of cash every year in fees at the matter. Then I'd felt that I'd done my best by my kids. In all the years that I've had children, I've managed to avoid school committees on the grounds that I've been way too busy. I plan on continuing it that way. In my mind it's one small step from being on a committee to making jam and baking cakes for the summer fayre. If William wants this life so much, then he can be on all the bloody committees. And make the jam. 'Yes, lovely,' I say – two-faced bitch that I am. 'I'd really like that.'

Mrs Barnsley, clearly contented at my malleability, smiles and walks away, task completed and lines of authority drawn.

I hold Jessica's hand as we walk home and, for the first time in our weeks here, start to take in our wider surroundings. Tom idly pulls leaves off the hedges that we pass. My daughter chatters inanely about nothing in particular and I half-tune out.

The village is nestled in a bowl of rolling green hills, crisscrossed with drystone walls at vertiginous angles. Today the sky is impossibly blue and the clouds mimic the white fluffy fleeces of the ubiquitous sheep. Only the sound of bleating and the occasional burst of birdsong breaks the silence. This is a little different to the relentless noise of traffic on Ladbroke Grove outside our previous home. Could I learn to love it here? Would it be so bad to lead a small life in the middle of nowhere with time on my hands to look at the sky? Maybe I'm starting to soften towards this place, after all. Could we all live a life of blissful contentment here? It wouldn't be too bad, would it . . .

'I hate it here,' Tom says, breaking into my musing. 'I want to go home.'

'Me too,' Jessica agrees. 'It smells funny.'

I sigh to myself. My daughter's right. Wherever you go there's the faint lingering smell of manure in the air. Perhaps my happy-ever-after ending still needs more work.

Chapter Thirteen

We cross the green to Helmshill Grange and the sight of its dilapidated exterior takes even more of the spring out of my step. In the drive there's a shiny new Range Rover that I don't recognise.

Then I hear a bleating noise rather close to home and my springless step grinds to a halt. I know exactly what that means. We've got sheep. Despite my hope that Will would change his mind and would be kept sufficiently busy with the blind chickens not to have time to consider any other farmstock, the sheep, it seems, are now ensconced in my garden.

'Go and say hello to Maya,' I tell the children, giving them a gentle shove in the direction of the house. 'She's been baking some cakes.' At least, I hope she has. When I finally steeled myself to risk the Aga, it's taken days to fire up the wretched thing and now the kitchen is as hot as Hades.

I head toward the sheep. There are only three of them, but that seems like more than enough.

'Hello, darling.' Will kisses my cheek distractedly. 'This is the vet.'

'Hi,' the vet says. 'Guy Burton.'

'Hi.' I shake his hand. The vet's very handsome, I have to say. We've met very few of our neighbours yet, but most of them have been ancient, gnarled and unfriendly. Guy Burton very definitely doesn't fit into that category.

The vet is fairer than Will, taller too and more rugged-looking. His eyes are brown, soulful and look like they've seen a bit of life. His face is bronzed and weather-beaten. How old must he be? My age – thirty-eight – or maybe a bit younger? There's a hint of designer stubble around his chin, but it's probably not designer at all; it's likely that he just hasn't shaved today. He looks like a man who wouldn't hog the bathroom mirror. Even so, I bet he makes the hearts of the single girls in Helmshill flutter – if there are any. His accent doesn't sound local and I wonder what someone like Guy Burton is doing in a place like this. Apart from looking at our livestock, of course. Hmm. If I wasn't a happily married woman, perhaps Guy Burton would turn my head. Wonder if he's unattached? Perhaps I could fix him up with Serena. It's about time my sister dated someone who wasn't a married lawyer.

'Welcome to Helmshill,' he says, breaking into my match-making thoughts.

'Thanks.'

'I hope you'll be happy here.' You and me both, I think. Then I point at one of the bedraggled chickens who is currently walking round in a circle, pecking blindly at the ground. 'Are they going to live?'

'I've called that one Christopher,' my husband tells me with loving pride, causing my mouth to gape.

'They've been badly kept in deep litter,' Guy says with a shake of his head. 'We've told that farmer a dozen times. Doesn't listen. The ammonia from their own waste makes them blind. He's lucky that you've taken them off his hands.'

Will says nothing about the large sum of Queen's shilling that has changed hands.

'With a lot of love and some well-aimed antibiotics,' the vet says, 'they'll be fine in no time.'

'How often do they need the antibiotics?' This sounds expensive.

'Daily,' Guy answers.

'You have to come every day?'

'No,' he laughs. 'You put them in. It's just a few drops for their eyes. Nothing to worry about.'

'Oh.' My husband will have to put drops in their eyes.

'And they'll need to be shown where their food is and be lifted up on their perches until they learn to do it themselves again.'

'If you buy healthy chickens, presumably they do all this for themselves.'

'They do,' Guy confirms. At which point I glare at Will. 'It'll be for a couple of months. Maybe a while longer. That's all. Feed them right and they'll perk up in no time.'

'What about the sheep?'

'You've got three very nice old ladies,' the vet says.

Will looks sheepish again – no pun intended.

'Old ladies? Is that a good or a bad thing?'

'They were going to be slaughtered,' my husband volunteers. 'Look at them.'

I do. They're standing in a line, staring straight back at me. They do, in fact, look just like three old ladies; all they're short of is felt hats and handbags. Not only have we got blind chickens, but we've got menopausal sheep.

'How could I let that happen?' Will wants to know.

Spoken like a true townie.

'I thought we'd look after them too,' he continues. 'The farmer told me they'd got a touch of black bag. Or was it blue bag? Some colour bag.' My husband shrugs away the need for technicalities. 'He assured me it wasn't contagious.'

'Blue bag,' the vet confirms. 'It just means that the ewe can't feed her offspring. I don't think you have to worry about that with this little trio, they're not much good for breeding anyway.' Guy Burton addresses me, clearly thinking I'm the more rational of our couple. 'Too old.'

I know how they feel.

'So we can't eat them either?'

'They'll make nice pets,' Will ventures. 'Three lovely old ladies.'

I bet he's got names for them already.

'I should be going,' Guy says. 'Mr Dawkins's cat's not very well. I said I'd call in on the way back to the surgery.'

'Thank you,' Will says. 'Thanks for coming out here.'

'No trouble,' Guy says. 'Have this one on me. I'll just charge you for the drugs. I'll send the bill through.' He hands over boxes and boxes of chicken eye-drops. Yes, he's probably going to go and put a deposit on a new Porsche after seeing the state of this lot. 'I'm sure I'll be seeing more of you.'

I'm sure too, if Will keeps bringing these ramshackle, no hope animals home. Who does he think he is? Bridget Bardot?

We watch as Guy Burton strides to his Range Rover, climbs in and backs out of our drive.

'Seems very nice,' Will says. 'Capable. The sort of chap you could rely on in a crisis.'

'Yes,' I agree.

'Gave me some great tips on keeping chickens.'

I wonder if our vet reads Audrey Fanshawe at bedtime. I somehow doubt it. 'Is that it?' I say wearily. 'There's not a three-legged goat you've forgotten about? I don't think I could cope with any more surprises.'

'Ah,' Will says.

And, with perfect comedy timing, the children come hurtling out of the kitchen.

'Mummy,' Jessica cries ecstatically. 'We've got a kitty!'

Tom adds, 'And a dog!'

Behind them, a big black and brown dog lollops towards me at full tilt. His tongue is hanging to the ground and there's two trails of drool flying in the whirlwind he's creating. He looks completely insane. I hate dogs. They smell and leave hair everywhere. The cat follows him, mincing over the gravel. It's sleek, black and looks as mean as hell. I hate cats too. They've got bottoms like pencil sharpeners and try to eat babies while they lie sleeping in their prams.

The dog bowls into my knees and nearly knocks me clean over.

'This is Hamish,' my husband says, grabbing the dog before it does any more damage and roughing up its ears. This sends the hound into a frenzy of shaking, sending gobs of spit flying all over my lovely Joseph trousers.

I look at my husband and my eyes well up with tears. 'Oh, William,' I say. 'What on earth have you done?'

Chapter Fourteen

'Bloody hell!' I mutter as I get out of bed and step in mouse entrails. I've long since stopped screaming when I do that, so things must be improving. Right?

The cat, Milly Molly Mandy – Jessica's choice of moniker – is the only animal we've acquired that seems to have all her faculties and physical attributes working as they should. However, Milly Molly Mandy also exhibits tendencies that any prolific serial killer would be proud of. 'Hannibal Lecter' would have suited her better as a name.

Our sleek feline friend – or do I mean fiend? – is sitting licking her paws with satisfaction as she surveys the three decapitated and disembowelled rodents she's brought in for our delectation.

'Is this what I have to look forward to every morning?' I ask as I hop towards the bathroom. 'Tortured mouse?'

'If she keeps going at this rate, the few remaining members of the mouse population of Helmshill Grange will soon be packing their bags and seeking safer territory,' my husband observes. 'Isn't that right, Mols?' The cat, needing little encouragement, jumps on the bed and snuggles down in the warm space I've just vacated. I hate animals in the bedroom. I'm not that fond of them in the lounge or the kitchen either.

'Who's a good girl?' Will coos as he caresses her fondly. 'Who's the best mouser in Yorkshire then?'

It's taken very little time for Milly Molly Mandy to worm her way into Will's affection. It will take a damn sight longer with me.

'It's nice to have a home filled with animals and love,' he says dreamily.

Will wouldn't even let the kids have a hamster in Notting Hill. Tom begged for years – every birthday and Christmas – but Will's heart was stone. How times change. And not always for the better.

I shower in an ice-cold drip. The water knocks, shudders and clonks through the pipes. The plumbing is so ancient that by the time the hot water has worked its way reluctantly through the house to the bathroom I could have grown a beard. Unfortunately, even after six weeks or so here, I'm resolutely locked into London speed and haven't the patience to wait that long. Shivering as I towel myself down vigorously, I think, it's still only September – and a ridiculously mild one at that – so what will this place be like in winter? The windows already have proved worthless at stopping even the mildest of breezes. How will they cope with a full-on gale which I'm told that Helmshill is frequently battered with? Come to that matter, how will I cope?

For reasons best known to myself, I'm trying to make a valiant stab at sophistication despite my reduced circumstances, and choose a Diane Von Furstenberg dress to take the children to school. When else am I going to wear the damn thing now?

My husband looks tired again this morning. His face is pale, and dark shadows ring his eyes. Unusually, Will's still lying in bed when I've finished my ablutions. 'Didn't you sleep well?' I ask.

'Like a log,' he says. 'Could just do with a few more hours.'

'Probably all the frenzy of the move is finally catching up with you. It wouldn't hurt to rest for a few days.' I still haven't got round to registering with a GP. Our nearest one is in Scarsby and every time I'm over there I forget to go into the surgery and pick up the forms. 'Why don't you stay there for another couple of hours?'

'Things to do,' he says, and yawns as he throws the covers back, sending the cat scuttling from the bed.

'Did you take your pills yesterday?'

'Hmm . . .' Will scratches his chin.

'Well, don't forget to take them today. That can't be helping. You're getting very absent-minded now that you've become the country squire, William Ashurst.' I have to nag him every day otherwise he'd never remember to take those damn tablets.

'Oh, yes,' he says with a nod. 'Must do. Can you put them out for me?'

I'm going to have to get one of those boxes with the days marked out on them and fill it with Will's medication – just like you do for old people. What would he do without me? I smile at him indulgently. Still, now that I'm not working I can afford the time to spoil him a bit more. That's taking some adjusting to as well. I only get a pang of longing for my old job about ten times a day and have studiously avoided watching television as it only makes me worse. Plus the reception here is so rubbish that it's like watching every show through a snowstorm.

'The hot water's probably just about to make an appearance,' I tell him.

'A nice long shower might liven me up.' He squeezes me round the waist as he passes. 'I'll see you downstairs.'

'Love you,' I say, as he disappears into the bathroom, but I don't know if he hears me.

Chapter Fifteen

Fastening on some diamond earrings, I head for the kitchen. Maya, being her efficient self, has – amid the packing boxes we haven't yet got round to sorting – already laid the table for breakfast. I think she's starting to settle in here now as I only catch her crying once a day now.

She comes out of the scullery, weeping.

'Maya, what's wrong?' Our newly acquired dog, Hamish, is at her heels and is wagging his tail furiously, clearly very pleased with himself. He comes over to me and brushes against my legs, depositing hair and slobber on my dress. His tail thumps against me and it's like being repeatedly hit by a mallet.

'He has tried to eat all of underwear again,' she tells me

tremulously. 'He has opened tumble dryer all by himself and has ruined it completely.'

'No,' I laugh. 'He can't have.'

'He has. He is very naughty dog, Amy.'

Already, I know this. Hamish has been the bane of my life since the day he arrived. He's enormous – way too big, even for a house this size. He's full of energy, full of mischief and now, it seems, full of our underwear. Even in the short time he's been here we've got used to putting anything edible out of his range. He's had Will's breakfast off his plate more than once. My husband finds this trait for snaffling other people's food charming. Dish cloths are a thing of the past. As is anything involving sponge – a particular doggy favourite, it appears.

Now Hamish has apparently moved onto more expensive inedible materials to eat and has learned how to open the tumble dryer. For a dog that dense, I doubt it.

I go through to the scullery, still not quite believing Maya's assessment of the situation. But, sure enough, the tumble dryer door is ajar and there's a pile of suspiciously shredded underwear on the floor. 'Hamish,' I shout. 'Get here! Did you do this?'

But my anger falls on deaf ears and Hamish, quite sensibly, doesn't appear to answer for his crime. This dog can never hear his name being called, no matter how loud, but can recognise the sound of a biscuit tin being opened from the bottom of the garden.

'I think some is missing.' Maya starts to clear up the mess. 'Maybe he has eaten it.'

'Bloody dog,' I grumble – at which point Will arrives in

the kitchen. I bolt from the scullery and greet my husband by waving a shred of black lace at him.

'What's that?'

'The remains of my favourite knickers. He's had a go at all of yours too.'

'Oh, Hamish,' Will says indulgently to the dog who is currently hiding behind his legs. 'Have you been naughty?' Hamish goes into throes of ecstasy and hurls himself to the floor, tummy up, legs akimbo.

Never in my lifeplan did I imagine getting a full-frontal view of canine genitalia before breakfast. 'Where exactly did you get this dog from?' I want to know.

'He's a rescue dog,' he says cagily. 'I told you. He came from a place over near Malhead. He'd been there ages. No one wanted him. Did they, woofer?'

Hamish, on cue, woofs.

'Did you ever question why that might be?'

'They said he was a bit of a handful, admittedly. He's a Gordon Setter,' my husband tells me. 'Fine breed. He's a pedigree.'

Pedigree? The thing looks half-dog, half-stand-up comedian.

'Could just do with a bit of training.'

Could just do with a sedative.

'He's still in his puppyish stage. He'll calm down once he settles in.' The dog's currently trying to mount Will. 'Won't you, boy?'

'He's completely destroyed all of the underwear.'

'No!' Will laughs in exactly the same way I did.

'Yes!'

My husband realises that I'm serious. 'It's probably a chewing phase. He'll grow out of it.'

'I'll have to drive into Scarsby later to get us some more.' I tut. 'That damn vet didn't fix you up with him, did he?'

'No,' Will assures me. 'In fact, Guy warned me that he might be a bit boisterous.'

'Fabulous.'

Jessica comes into the kitchen bearing an armful of Bratz dolls – all of them with their heads chewed off. 'Look what happened to my dollies!'

Hamish hangs his head in shame and tries to slink off. This dog wouldn't make a poker player.

'Bloody dog,' I mutter. Then to my daughter, 'You'll have to keep your bedroom door closed, sweetie. Until Hamish grows out of his "chewing phase".'

'They were my favourites,' she whines.

I hate Bratz dolls, I don't know why I let my child play with them. They wear too much make-up and dress like hookers. If you want my opinion, they actually look better headless. 'Never mind,' I say, casting a steely glance at Will. 'Daddy will buy you some more.'

Tom comes down. He's wearing his school blazer and a bemused expression. 'Look,' he says, holding his arms out. 'It's got holes in it.'

Lots of them. Dog-shaped ones. But if that isn't enough evidence, the silver trails of slime that cover the new uniform condemn Hamish as the guilty party. The dog lowers himself to the floor and tries to look invisible. Quite hard for a great hairy mutt that must weigh at least twelve stones.

'Never mind,' I say even more sweetly than the last time. 'Daddy will buy you another one.'

'But what will I wear today? Mrs Barnsley will go bonkers.'

'Daddy will come to school with us,' I say crisply in Will's direction, 'and explain to Mrs Barnsley exactly what happened.'

Maya helps them to pour out their cereal, while I pull Will to one side. 'That's it,' I whisper fiercely. 'This isn't a home filled with animals and love. It's filled with an eating machine, a serial killer and a variety of chewed things. You're not Doctor flaming Doolittle. No more animals. None. I'm serious.'

'That's fine,' Will says, chastened. 'I hear you. No more animals.'

'Promise me on your children's lives?'

'Yes,' he says. 'After the goats arrive today, that's absolutely it.'

Chapter Sixteen

While the children finish their breakfast, Will and I head outside to tend to our steadily growing flock. With a distinct lack of enthusiasm, I take the chicken duty, while my husband goes to look after the elderly sheep who've been christened Daphne, Doris and Delila.

I'm trying to ignore the fact that the toes of my favourite Kurt Geiger boots have obviously been given a tentative chew by our new dog. Though I've quickly realised that, even given their less than pristine state, they're not the ideal footwear for animal husbandry. It looks as if we're staying here for the duration, so I ought to invest in some decent wellies for us all.

I jump and give a scream as I lift the lid off the feedbin and a mouse scuttles out. Grief. My heart's pounding in my chest like a hammer. Will might think that this place is going to be the panacea for his dodgy heart, but I think it's going to *give* me a dicky ticker. At least I'm not having to scoop out the bloodied remains of one of Milly Molly Mandy's 'playmates'. Getting back to nature is all very well, but sometimes you can just be *too* close to it. I sigh as I measure out the grain for the chickens. Will I ever get used to the amount of small, scary and fast-moving creatures that nature harbours?

Our henhouse is enormous – industrial-sized probably – with room for many more chickens than our scabby dozen. The door has a heart-shaped Perspex window in it – which is a nice touch, but one that the chickens couldn't care less about as they're blind. There's a long, enclosed run next to it where Will has – rather hopefully, I think – installed a large rabbit hutch. Despite my husband's leanings, I have no intentions of having rabbits too.

Working my way along the chickens, I grab each one with a reluctance I previously hadn't known possible. I can feel the expression of extreme distaste on my face. Oh, I so don't like chickens! Particularly not these nervous, moth-eaten ones. I try Christopher first as she looks the most docile. Clearly my husband hasn't got to the bit in *Keeping Chickens* where

Audrey points out that all hens are female. Chris wriggles underneath my hands and squawks as if I'm trying to murder her as I struggle to drip the antibiotics into her unseeing eyes. This makes the rest of the hens scatter, flapping blindly round the chicken coop and scrabbling vainly for the door.

'I'm doing this for your own good,' I tell Christopher firmly. 'Stop fidgeting. You're frightening the others.' To think that in my former life as a television producer of the UK's favourite sports quiz, I used to find the demands of Premiership footballers difficult to deal with.

When I've managed to catch them all – a not inconsiderable feat – and have worked my way through them all administering medicine, my Diane Von Furstenberg wrap dress is thoroughly covered in chicken shit. I then carry each chicken carefully over to the bowl of food and point it in the direction of its breakfast. It's taken me for ever. And I'll have to do it all again later. And tomorrow. And the day after. And the day after that.

When I get back to the kitchen, exhausted, my husband is sitting drinking tea. He has fared much better with the sheep. 'Lovely old things,' he declares with a contented smile. 'No trouble at all. I think they'll really enrich our life.'

Three menopausal sheep? Can't wait to see how. It's a bright, sunny day today. Wait until we're struggling out in the wind and snow to deal with them. Might not be such an attractive proposition then.

Before I've had time to enjoy a cuppa, the children are ready for school.

'Hamish has had his breakfast too,' Jessica informs me, and it's then that I spy the pile of cornflakes on the floor plus the shredded box. I feel my forehead. It's becoming feverish, I'll swear.

'I will clean it all up, Amy,' Maya says with a tut and then she disappears to find the dustpan and brush – which, frankly, has never seen so much action. I don't know how she's putting up with all the extra work she's having to do: if I was her, I'd go on strike. And then I wonder why *I'm* not on strike.

'Can we take Hamish to school with us?' Tom asks.

'What a good idea,' Will says. I'd rather leave the damn thing here, preferably locked in a small room with nothing for him to eat other than the rest of the cornflakes box. Mind you, he'd probably gnaw his way out through the door.

'Come on, boy.' My husband tries to lasso him with the lead while the dog bucks like a bronco. 'I might try to find some dog-training classes,' Will pants as he wrestles with Hamish. This can't be good for his heart.

Ten minutes later and after a great performance the dog is finally harnessed and we set off, rushing as now the children are in danger of being late. Will is yanked down the lane by Hamish, to whom rushing is second nature. It's like trying to take a charging bull for a walk.

'Whoa, boy! Whoa, boy!' Will cries in vain as we all head to the school in double-quick time, my husband's feet being dragged along the pavement as he scrabbles to keep a purchase. No one can be in any doubt about who's taking whom for a walk. I don't think the children have ever had to run to school before.

We arrive in time to see Mrs Barnsely in the playground, giving Will plenty of time to assail the Headteacher with his sob story about Tom's chewed jacket. The redoubtable Mrs Barnsley eyes Hamish warily while, oblivious, he wees on the school gate, and her look says that she hopes our children will be better behaved than our dog.

Leaving Tom and Jessica to their day, my husband and I – and dog – head back to Helmshill Grange. I still can't quite bring myself to call the place home. The hills around us, lush and green, stretch to the sky. The roads are empty – in fact, the only vehicles I've seen this morning have been ones carrying hay. Even though it's now gone nine o'clock there's not another sign of life in the village. This could possibly be the most peaceful place on earth. Or the most dull.

Hamish drags us along the lane, straining at the lead. Will links his arm through mine and I'm not sure if he's trying to be romantic or whether he's trying to get some extra stability.

He turns to me. 'Do you think you can be happy here?'

What can I say?

'I don't know, Will,' I answer honestly. I fail to tell him that I'm having to fight the urge to phone the British Television Company every five minutes to find out what's going on and whether they're missing me. If they begged me to come back, what would I do? Is my husband's health more important than my sanity? Could I go back to my high-powered job, get a place in London during the week and come back here at the weekends? Don't plenty of families live like that these days? I didn't realise that a part of me was defined by my ability to produce great television programmes, but it is. I can't deny it, sad as that may sound. I was proud of what I did. Is anyone going to give me praise or a huge pay rise for nursing some scraggy hens back to good health?

Then I think of Will lying on that station platform as I watched, terrified that his life might be ebbing away from him. Isn't it more important that I'm here with him rather than fretting about the loss of my career and a decent six-figure salary? I don't want to be away from him or the kids during the week. We're a family. We have to do what's best for all of us. And my husband is utterly convinced that we'll all be given a new lease of life by opting out of the rat race. 'Give me time,' I tell him. 'I'm sure it will work out fine.'

'I hope so,' he says. 'I love it here. So do the kids.'

I'm not sure that the kids love it any more than I do, but I decide to let that thought remain unspoken.

Will looks at the crazed hound lurching down the road in front of us. 'You love it here too, don't you, boy?' Hamish yelps in delight. 'I think I'll let him off the lead. Just for a minute or two.'

'Do you think that's wise?'

'I think this dog's brighter than you give him credit for,' Will chides. 'He'll come back when I call him.'

William slips the lead from Hamish's collar and, immediately, the dog bolts for freedom. 'Hamish,' Will shouts optimistically. 'Heel!'

Hamish gives him a look that says not-on-your-nelly, mate. Then he vaults a four-foot wall and heads off into the surrounding hills, barking manically.

'Hamish!'

The dog barks some more and runs faster in response.

'Hamish!' Will sounds very stern now. 'Come back here at once!'

Hamish is rapidly becoming a small black dot in the distance. The deafening noise of his bark recedes.

And I say nothing.

Chapter Seventeen

'If I find that dog worrying my sheep again,' the farmer says in an accent so broad that I can barely understand it, 'I'll bloody shoot it.'

'Thank you,' Will says. 'Thank you so much for bringing him home.'

My husband had trailed through the fields for hours looking for Hamish, but with no joy. Unfortunately, it's bad luck for us that he was found playing with sheep. Probably trying to mount them, if I know Hamish. And I feel I've got his character marked quite well.

'I'm very, very sorry,' Will continues. 'I can only apologise. And pay for any damage.'

What's the going rate for a shagged sheep, I wonder. Later today, I seriously have to bash the phones to see if I can put out some feelers for a new job. I've already tried the two main television stations in the area, but there was nothing going. Everyone, it seems, is tightening their belts. The best they could offer was to tell me to send in my CV and they'd put me on file. It makes me feel like a teenager again, having to scratch around for work. Surely someone must be able to use my expertise? Will was so sure that we'd be able to get freelance work, but where? There's nothing round here. For the moment, replacing our healthy income has proved steadfastly elusive. The bills are mounting here as the cost of feeding and caring for our growing farmyard brood is not inconsiderable. The money that Will raised from selling our lovely, lovely Audi has already been eaten up – literally. One of us needs to start pulling in some serious cash before what little is left of our savings is completely gone.

The farmer grunts. He's wearing a raincoat, flat cap and wellies and a big scowl.

Hamish, thick with mud and smelling like a pigsty, is wagging his tail in our drive, seemingly unaware of his brush with death. There's a piece of orange nylon twine round his neck and Will is clutching it as if his life depends on it.

My husband holds out his hand to the taciturn man. 'William Ashurst,' he says in his friendliest tone. His hand remains unshaken. 'And my wife, Amy.'

At this moment, I'd like to deny that I even know Will, but how would I explain being here? 'Hello.'

He glowers at me too.

'We've just moved here,' Will continues brightly.

'I know,' the farmer says, unimpressed. 'You're the posh incomers.' He looks at our designer chicken coop and our three ageing sheep with disdain.

'We'd love to know our neighbours better. Perhaps we could entertain you one evening. And your good lady wife. If you have one . . .' Will's attempt at bonhomie trails away.

Hamish, clearly mobilised by his master's attempts at

friendship, tries to nuzzle the farmer's nuts. It doesn't go down well. The man's hands go to protect his testicles and he lashes out a kick at Hamish, who nimbly scoots out of the way.

'Keep that bloody dog off my property or I'll bloody shoot it.' With that our neighbour turns on his heels, stamps back to his Land Rover – which is in better condition than ours – and screeches off.

'That went well,' Will observes with a sigh.

'I thought Londoners were supposed to be the miserable bastards,' I mutter.

'Hamish,' Will says, 'we're in trouble with our neighbours now. You're a very naughty dog.'

'You're a menace to society,' I add. 'You're going to have to do something about him, Will. He's like a wild animal.' He certainly smells like one.

'I will. I will,' my husband promises.

'Get the hosepipe on him,' I instruct. 'Or better still, I'll do it.'

'I can manage,' Will insists. 'He'll sit still for me.'

Yes, I think, in the same way he came back when you called him.

'I don't want you to over-exert yourself,' I say. 'The next job on my list is to phone the doctor's and make you an appointment for tomorrow. I'm worried that you're still so tired all the time.'

'I'm fine.' Will flexes his muscles like a old-fashioned circus strong man. 'You worry too much. I'm feeling as fit as a flea.'

'Promise me that you'll take it easy.'

'I will.' My husband kisses my cheek. 'Of course I will.'

As I go back into the kitchen, I wonder if I can find the contents of our wine rack anywhere. A decent glass of red would go down a treat right now, even though it's not yet lunchtime. This is what the relaxing life in the country has done to me – turned me into an alcoholic within two months.

With that thought in mind, my step perks up no end. I could even be moved to whistle to myself. I bound into the kitchen where I find Maya standing in her jacket with her case at her feet. 'I am leaving,' she says.

'What?' That stops me in my tracks, and my momentary lightness of spirit is flattened. 'You can't.'

'I don't like it here, Amy.' Our treasured nanny begins to cry. 'I did not want to come. But I did for you, for children. But I do not like it here. I do not like dog. He tries to sniff my bottom.'

'He does that to everyone.' It's one of his traits I might not have mentioned. Every time you bend over in this house you feel the bump of canine nasal passages between your buttocks. The only person's bottom I haven't seen him try to sniff is Mrs Barnsley's and I'd say that it was a rare moment of wisdom on Hamish's part. 'It means he likes you.' Good grief, I'm defending him now. This is how desperate I am for Maya to stay.

'Well, I do not like him. I not like finding dead mouses in slippers either. This house very windy and cold. What will I do on days off?'

I note that my nanny hasn't actually had a day off since we arrived. She hasn't uttered a word of complaint – until now. That makes me feel terrible. 'We'll sort it all out, Maya. I promise you.'

Maya shakes her head. 'I am too young to live in country.'

Me too.

'Don't do this.' I feel like dropping to my knees. 'Please don't do this.'

She rubs her red eyes. 'My friend telephoned this morning. There is job for me. Back in London. More money and Mercedes Benz.'

Well, that'll sway the loyalties of many a nanny, but I had thought that Maya was different. I thought she was with us because she'd come to love us – as we love her. She's more than a nanny, she's my friend. Here, she's my only friend. 'Take your coat off,' I beg. 'Let me speak to William. We could get you your own little car, perhaps a pay rise. We need you here.'

'I have been on internet,' she says sadly. 'I can catch train this afternoon. I have to call taxi now.'

'Please wait. Don't go without saying goodbye to the children. They'll be devastated. They love you.'

'I cannot see children. That will be too sad. I must go now.'

My husband comes through the door, presumably in search of his wellies to give the dog his hosing down.

'Maya's leaving,' I cry in anguish and grab his arm. 'Tell her not to, Will. Tell her how much we love her. I said that we could buy her a little car. She's not a Land Rover kind of girl.' Any more than I am. I have complete sympathy with her. 'Perhaps we can give her some more money.'

Will sighs and pulls me to him. He lowers his voice when he speaks. 'To be honest, Amy, I'm not sure how long we'll be able to afford to keep Maya on. Things are tight. Now that we're both at home, can't we take care of everything ourselves?'

'The children will be distraught. Maya's been with us for years.' Since Jessica was just turned two.

Will's voice becomes a whisper. 'Perhaps it's time to let her go.'

Turning round, I realise that Maya has heard every word. 'I should call taxi,' she says, head hung low.

If we wanted to, I'm sure that we could find the money from somewhere. Perhaps I should plead more with her, but how can I beg her to stay here with us when I'm not even sure that I want to be here myself? 'I'll drive you to the station,' I say resignedly.

I take the keys to the Land Rover from the hook, fighting down my anger, disappointment and frustration. 'While I'm out, I'll go into Scarsby to try to find some replacement underwear.'

That will get through some more of the money we haven't now got.

Chapter Eighteen

I wave Maya off from Scarsby station, then sit in the Land Rover and cry. Big, fat tears. My once lovely and ordered life has changed beyond recognition and I'm not sure that I want it any more.

When I eventually stop sobbing and feeling sorry for

myself, I crunch the Land Rover into gear and rattle my way into the centre of town. When I say town, don't think urban sprawl, think little little parochial excuse for a town.

Scarsby is a tiny market town with an equally tiny population – none of them under the age of eighty. I've halved the average age just by turning up. There's one main street with a cluster of attractive, traditional Yorkshire stone buildings. The poshest restaurant is a pizzeria and their answer to Starbucks is Poppy's Tea Room. I park in the main square – the only advantage to being in Scarsby as opposed to, say, Knightsbridge, is that you don't have to trawl around for hours looking for a parking space. And it's free as opposed to legalised mugging.

The market is on today. A couple of dozen pensioners amble around the scattering of stalls. A posse of invalid buggies choke the pavements. I wander aimlessly along, taking in the wares for sale. When I looked this place up on the internet – shortly after Will dropped the bombshell that we'd be moving here – the page on Scarsby Tourism said that there was, and I quote, 'a thriving market selling a wide range of desirable and designer goods' and that revived my troubled soul. What the piece failed to say was that Scarsby market carries a wide range of desirable and designer goods – *so long as you want them in Crimplene*. There are orthopaedic shoes, slacks with elasticated waists and floral blouses that even building society employees wouldn't be seen dead in. It doesn't look like I'm going to be able to replace my black lace La Perla underwear here.

From a stall selling CDs, Louis Armstrong's 'Wonderful World' not so much blares out as seeps out at an inoffensive volume. Next to it, I buy a dozen eggs from The Hen Hut in view of the fact that it could be several years before our chickens see fit to lay a bloody thing. There are too many shops selling sturdy footwear and none of them selling heels. In one of the dozens of outdoor clothing shops, I buy a bright red waterproof jacket that's on sale. What it lacks in style, it makes up for in practicality. The jacket makes me look like a Guide leader or a lost rambler. But, very soon, the winter will be upon us and I realise that I don't have suitable clothing for it. If it rained in London, then I simply didn't go outside. Now I don't have that option. Reluctantly, I pick up some green wellies as well. See what I'm reduced to?

Purchases paid for and wrapped in plain brown paper, I then head off to the doctor's surgery and fill in the required forms to register the whole family. Then, having done that, I make an appointment for Will for tomorrow afternoon. That takes a weight off my shoulders. The sooner that he's under the doctor here, the better.

After doing that, I walk over to Poppy's Tea Room to seek succour in a toasted teacake and some hot Yorkshire Tea. I can't face going back to Helmshill Grange yet. I'm cross with Will, I'm cross with myself and, most of all, I'm cross with that wretched dog. If Hamish hadn't kept trying to sniff Maya's bottom, perhaps she would have stayed. But then I realise that our dog is only one small contributing factor to the sum of all parts.

The tea room is buzzing. A veritable crowd of three old ladies, our sheep in human form, huddle together in the corner. They have hats on their heads and patent leather handbags at their feet and give me a sideways glance as I enter. I sit at a table for two by the window and order tea and a teacake from an indifferent waitress – the only teenager I've seen so far.

As I'm waiting for my order, the vet's Range Rover pulls up outside and Guy Burton jumps out.

'Hello, Mrs Ashurst,' he says to me as he comes inside, his smile widening.

'Amy, please.' He leans over to shake my hand.

'How are things?'

Ridiculous, stupid tears, unbidden, rush back to my eyes. I scrabble for a tissue. 'Fine,' I say with a sniff. 'Fine.'

'Oh,' he says. 'That good. Anything you want to talk about?'

I shake my head. 'I'm fine really.'

'Mind if I join you anyway? You're not waiting for anyone?'

'No, no.' I don't know anyone here to wait for.

He pulls out his chair and I realise how tall he is as he folds himself into it. The waitress comes over and she looks decidedly happier than she did when she took my order. The women in the hats watch intently. Well, let them.

'Our nanny's left,' I tell him when the waitress has cleared off again and I've composed myself. 'She's been with us for years. I've just dropped her at Scarsby station so that she can head back to the smoke.'

'Is that the end of the world?' he asks, but not unkindly.

I shake my head. 'No. But it feels like the end of a world that I previously knew very well and rather enjoyed.'

'Finding it difficult to adjust to life in the country?'

'Somewhat,' I say, and manage to find a laugh from somewhere. Then, bravado failing, I let out a shuddering sigh.

Guy waits and studies me and, for some reason, that prompts me to carry on. 'It wasn't exactly my choice to come here,' I explain. 'I did it for Will. He's convinced it's what we need. I packed in a great job and a wonderful city lifestyle. And there are times, lots of them, when I wonder if I did the right thing.'

'You must love him very much.'

'I do,' I say.

Our humungous pot of tea arrives, along with my teacake and Guy's toasted cheese sandwich.

'My husband recently had a health scare,' I go on. 'It was a terrible shock to us.'

'I'm sure.'

'It made him completely reassess his life,' I continue, suddenly unable to stop myself from unburdening my troubles. 'It should have made me do the same, but it hasn't. And now I feel we're singing from a different song-sheet.'

'But you're giving this a go for him.'

'Something like that.'

'Sounds very noble to me,' Guy observes.

'I don't feel very noble. I feel bereft, bad tempered and, to be honest, bloody trapped.'

'It's early days yet,' Guy says sympathetically. 'It took me a long time to learn to love this place.'

'But you do now?'

He nods. 'I've been here five years. Now I wouldn't go anywhere else.'

'Not even for love?'

The vet laughs at that. 'I came here to get away from a broken heart and I don't know that I'd be in a rush to chase another one.'

'Where are you from originally?'

'Surrey. It took them three years to stop calling me an incomer. It took me two to understand what they were saying.'

'And now you're a pillar of the community.'

'I like to think that I perform a vital role here.' I think Guy flushes. 'Speaking of which, how are the chickens coming along?'

'I loathe them,' I confess. 'But I'm giving them their medicine every morning and evening. They reward me by crapping on me.'

He laughs again at that and I join in. 'They'll thank you for it one day.'

'I wish.'

'Just wait until those lovely, organic eggs come rolling in every morning.'

'And, believe it or not, I ought to be getting back for the chickens.' I glance at my watch and then call the waitress over, adding '*That's* a sentence I never thought I'd hear myself utter.'

'It'll get better,' Guy says. 'I promise you. Just give it time.'

'You'll make me cry again.'

'I wouldn't want to do that.' At which I blush like a schoolgirl.

The waitress comes with the bill. 'I'll settle that,' Guy insists.

'Thank you.'

'Amy,' he says softly, and his gorgeous brown eyes look

deep into mine. His hand covers my fingers and it sends an unexpected wave of tingling through my skin. I should pull away, but I don't. Wrong as it is, I like the feel, the strangeness of his skin on mine. 'If there's anything that you need – you, or William – you only have to call me. You've got my mobile number. Don't hesitate to use it.'

'Thank you,' I say. 'I'll remember that.' Finally, I extricate my hand and we exchange an uncertain smile. As I rush out of the tea room, I see the old ladies' heads together, gossiping, fussing with adjusting their hats. That will have made their afternoon.

And, as I head back to my rickety old Land Rover, I can imagine that – if I wasn't a happily married woman, of course – Guy Burton is someone I could definitely come to depend on.

Chapter Nineteen

'Who was that you were with in Poppy's?' Cheryl leaned back against the wall of the staff room and folded her arms.

'How do you know about that?' Guy asked as he washed his hands in preparation for the afternoon consultations.

'I am the all-seeing oracle and know everything,' she told him.

'Then why are you having to ask me?'

'News travels fast here. It was the new incomer, Mrs Ashurst.'

'You really do know everything, don't you?'

Her smile returned. 'Does that mean I get a pay rise?'

'No.'

'You're late for surgery,' the receptionist chided. 'You must have been having a good time. You're never late for surgery.'

'Sorry. It won't happen again.' It was true, the reception was stacked with people sitting with cardboard boxes and travel cages on their laps, eager to bring him their pets. Thanks to Amy Ashurst he was, indeed, going to have a nice backlog. Still, it had been a very pleasant way to make his clients and his receptionist irate.

'So? Is she nice?'

'She's lovely,' Guy said. More lovely than he liked to dwell on. 'So are her husband and children.'

Cheryl wrinkled her nose at him. 'I know, I know.'

There wasn't a lot Cheryl didn't know. She'd been his receptionist since he'd bought the practice five years ago and, also for the last five years, she'd been trying her best to fix him up with every woman in Scarsby and surrounding districts – whether they were eligible or otherwise. They'd once had a tricky conversation about whether he was gay or not. Cheryl claimed that you could never tell these days, and it was fair to say that there wasn't a thriving gay community in Scarsby – as far as he was aware. So, having ascertained that he was, indeed, a red-blooded male despite his lack of interest in dating her dubious friends, she had redoubled her efforts to make his lovelife more interesting. Sometimes he wished he'd invented a boyfriend called Cecil – it would have made life so much easier. The fact that Cheryl had recently married and had a small child herself didn't stop her from looking longingly at him on occasions – something he found exceedingly embarrassing. His favourite employee definitely had a soft spot for him. And he often wondered if her acute interest in getting him fixed up was simply to put him out of harm's way.

'Mrs Todd's here with her bald pussy.'

'I've told you before, Cheryl. It's a hairless cat. A Sphynx cat. A bald pussy is . . . let's not go there.'

'Whatever.' She smirked at him. 'It's puking up all over the place. 'Orrible little thing. She's waiting in consulting room one for you and has been for ten minutes now.'

'I'll be right there.' Mrs Todd was one of his clients who didn't always come here primarily out of concern for her animal companion. She wore lots of leopardskin prints and heavy perfume. Her cat was unusually afflicted by ailments. Most of them minor. Mrs Todd wasn't alone in this. He had a few clients like that. Sometimes in Scarsby, housewives had to create their own fun.

The practice was tucked away in a snug back street, next to Duggley's hardware store – a place where you could buy anything from a few penceworth of plastic wotsit to a ten-ton tractor. The veterinary surgery had become too much work for the previous owner, who'd been keen to retire after a lifetime of rootling in cows' backsides. The price had been right, the timing perfect and Guy had, literally, run for the hills. It was a decision he'd never regretted. Well, only sometimes, in the dead of night when there was no one to hold. But he'd coped brilliantly with all of that lost-love stuff. Or at least he thought he had. Guy pushed away any doubts.

Work was his succour now. The practice was thriving. He wasn't only popular with the bored housewives of Scarsby. Over the years he'd gradually won the grudging respect of the farmers round here. No mean task for a 'soft southerner'. He'd taken out an enormous loan to buy a new, state-of-the-art scanner. He had a new, ultra-keen assistant – Stephen – who mainly ran the surgery while he was left to go out and about on the farms tending to the livestock, charming grumpy farmers who assumed that all you were trying to do was fleece them of their hard-earned cash.

It was a good life. One that suited him. He answered to no one. Except, of course, the bank manager. And Cheryl. And, occasionally, Mrs Todd. She'd be unhappy that he'd kept her waiting. Better put on his best bedside manner.

'They say she's very posh,' Cheryl called after him. 'That Mrs Ashurst.'

'No,' Guy corrected after giving it some thought. 'She's not.' Amy Ashurst was a whole lot of things that stirred up emotions in him that he had thought were long dead, but posh wasn't one of them.

Cheryl's eyes narrowed. 'You've gone all dreamy-looking.'

He snapped his attention back to the surgery. 'Just thinking about that bald pussy,' he quipped.

Chapter Twenty

When I pull into the drive, I can see that my dear husband is fast asleep on a tired-looking wooden bench in the garden under the massive oak tree. Will has attached a birdfeeder to one of the bottom branches and there's a steady stream of blue tits and other brightly coloured birds that I can't name flitting backwards and forwards to it.

My husband is slumped down in the corner of the seat, chin on his chest, arms folded across his tum. Will clearly thinks we've moved to the Mediterranean rather than Yorkshire as a lengthy afternoon siesta features heavily in his daily routine now. Not that I begrudge him it. If he needs to sleep more at the moment then he should.

It looks like William has rooted through all of the packing boxes to find his favourite Panama, which has now fallen forward over his eyes. I always like him in that hat and he looks so comfortable snoozing there – the country gentleman at peace – that it brings a much-needed smile to my lips.

I slide out of the driver's seat and brush the dirt from the car off my dress while I look out over the garden. This really is a very peaceful spot. I wouldn't mind a bit of shut-eye too. Maybe Will and I could curl up in our bed and have a little extended afternoon siesta before the children are due home? The thought sends butterflies to my tummy. Perhaps there are some benefits of living the quiet life in the country. Our sexlife normally has to be fitted in around everything else and is usually conducted in silence in the dead of the night.

Hamish is also fast asleep at Will's feet and is clearly going to make a wonderful guard dog as he hasn't batted an eyelid at the noisy arrival of the Land Rover or the sound of my feet crunching across the gravel. Come to that, neither has Will. I tut to myself and smile, Sleepy Head!

My smile slips slightly when I see that in my absence William has taken delivery of two pygmy goats – one black, one brown – who are now in the penned-off part of our garden, chewing contentedly at the grass. They look adorable, but I bet like everything else in this place, they have 'hard work' stamped all over them.

I sigh. Scene of contentment it might be, but it looks like I'm going to have to do everything myself round this place. All warm thoughts of illicit afternoon delight dissipates. There's so much stuff to do that I daren't even start to think about it or I'd have a panic attack. I realise that this consti-tutes an ideal lifestyle for many people – my husband included – but I wonder why couldn't we have found a smaller, less dilapidated house with central heating that works and not enough land to start our own petting zoo? It's no good complaining though. This is my lot and I'll just have to get on with it.

Anyway, the kids will have to be collected soon. I hope after a few weeks they'll be able to walk home on their own sometimes but, for now, I'm enjoying the routine of taking and collecting them from school. I check my watch. That'll teach me to stay so long at Poppy's Tea Room flirting with what seems to be the only piece of local talent.

Maybe I should go straight down there now and get them. Then I remember that school is a five-minute stroll away and, even if I'm a few minutes late, it's highly unlikely that they're going to be abducted or troubled with a drive-by shooting in this neck of the woods. I have more than enough time to spare to make Will a cup of tea and to have a chat.

That is another good thing about living here. The children should be able to have more freedom and a better quality of life – at least while they're young. What happens when they're teenagers and there's nothing for them to do is anyone's guess. Spend their lives on the internet, no doubt. But we're a world away from that yet. Perhaps we should raid our dwindling funds to buy them some bikes and get out together as a family if Will gets a clean bill of health from the quack tomorrow. Even though I don't much fancy tackling those hills on two wheels. Our doctor in Notting Hill said that William should take gentle, regular exercise. I'm not sure walking that damn dog can be classed as gentle exercise. It's more like hanging on to a speeding train.

I wonder if I should leave Will asleep. He looked so tired this morning. Clearly he's needed an afternoon nap. Bless. His newspaper is folded up next to him, untouched. I think we're the only people in the village who read the *Guardian*.

I do worry about him now in a way that I never did before. I'll leave him for a few minutes longer and make him that cup of tea.

In the kitchen, I put the kettle on, find the tea caddy – which still hasn't yet been given a permanent home – and fuss with some mugs. It was nice to spend some time with Guy Burton. A bit of excitement to liven up an otherwise fairly disastrous day. He seems like a decent chap. Plus he'll be able to give us some good advice on how best to look after our new charges. I hope that in time he'll become a good friend. I think we'll need a few round here, as the neighbours haven't exactly been beating a path to our door yet. But then I'm used to London and we didn't speak to either of our next-door neighbours in all the years we were there. I expected the country to be different but, so far, we've been given quite a wide berth.

The kettle takes its time to boil and I stand and wonder what we might have for dinner. I could whip up some omelettes with the eggs I bought at the market and there's some salad in the fridge. That will do.

Putting the tea things on a tray, I carry them out to the garden. Will is still lolling on the bench, but Hamish wakes with a start and wags his tail. Then recognition shines in his crazed eyes as he realises who I am.

He jumps up and careers towards me. 'No, Hamish!'

Cannoning into my legs, the dog knocks the tea tray clean out of my hands, smashing the cups, the teapot brimming with scalding water and the sugar bowl on the path with a crash that shatters the still of the countryside. 'You stupid bloody animal! Look what you've done.' I take a swipe at him, but he's too quick for me and bounds off again round the garden, barking joyfully.

'Have you seen what this animal's done now?' I shout at Will. 'I'm lucky that I haven't got third-degree burns.'

Then I realise that despite the kerfuffle, my husband is still fast asleep. 'Will?' I go over to shake him, and his Panama slides from his head.

'Oh, Will,' I say. 'My darling, darling Will.' My fingers touch his heart.

Standing there, I stare at my husband. I can't cry, I can't scream, I can't breathe, I can't move. The world has stopped turning.

Then I fall to my knees and rest my head in his lap. All of my worst fears have been realised. It seems that my husband isn't asleep after all.

Chapter Twenty-One

Lying in our bed, I stare at the cracks in the ceiling and there are many of them. Tom, at long last, is fast asleep. But in the next room I can hear Jessica crying softly. I've nursed her all evening and I know that I should get up and go to her again, but I can't move because I, myself, am paralysed with grief.

I can't believe that William has gone. He's left me here in this rambling house – the house that was his choice, his dream – all alone. Helmshill Grange has never felt bigger or more empty. When I realised what had happened, I called 999 and the paramedics came immediately. They confirmed that Will was, indeed, dead.

Then one of the men spoke to our new GP on my behalf. Dr Redman came and made his first house call to us. He was brisk and sympathetic. It seems that my husband has suffered a fatal heart-attack. I could have told the good doctor that much. Despite the pills and potions that were supposed to let William live to a ripe old age, he wasn't getting better. All we had was a brief stay of execution. We both thought that he'd had a reprieve. We were both wrong.

Dr Redman also told me that William wouldn't have felt any pain. I am, it seems, feeling enough pain for the two of us. Then he called the funeral director, and Drake & Sons came and whisked my love away with a practised efficiency and professional courtesy that I wished I had never experienced, but which I've seen far too much of.

Down in the kitchen I can hear Hamish howling and the regular thump of his body as he hurls himself against the kitchen door in anguish. I haven't fed him tonight or the chickens or the sheep or the goats or myself. While my life spiralled downwards around me, my dear son, Tom, made some toast for himself and Jessica. Then we all cried quietly at the table together while they choked it down.

William has gone and I can see no future ahead. What will happen to us now? We were living my husband's dream and it has suddenly and most unexpectedly turned into a complete nightmare. I know no one here and have no idea what to do. Earlier, I managed to call my sister and she's heading up here first thing in the morning. Serena will sort me out. She'll know exactly what needs to be done.

I hear the splintering of a doorframe and then moments later, heavy, doggy footsteps pounding up the stairs. The bedroom door catapults open and Hamish bounds in. He stands by the bedside, whining.

'Missing your master, boy?' I ask tightly. 'You're supposed to be a man's best friend. Where were you when he was dying? Fast asleep at his feet. What sort of a best friend is that?'

Hamish lays his head on the bed and wriggles forward. His crazed eyes look all doleful and he whines pitifully.

'Haven't you ever seen *Lassie*? You're supposed to know these things instinctively and run for help so that you can save the day in the nick of time.'

The dog nuzzles my hand, covering it in slobber.

'Get away from me,' I say, curling into a ball and turning my back on him. 'However you're feeling, I'm feeling worse.'

And the reason is, I'm thinking, Where was I when my husband was dying? I was having tea and flirting with another man.

Chapter Twenty-Two

It seems that Serena couldn't sleep either. So she drove up here at some ungodly hour and now her sleek black Porsche is parked incongruously next to the rusting old Land Rover in the drive. She's fussing round me in the kitchen as only big sisters can. I'm being forcefed a boiled egg even though my stomach is keen to repel it.

'You have to have something inside you,' Serena says sensibly. 'You can't deal with all this on an empty stomach.'

'I can't deal with this at all.' The tears, which are never far from my eyes, start to fall again.

Outside, the rain is pouring down, pounding on the windows and splashing back on itself from the ground. The sky is dark and brooding and it looks as if there's still plenty more rain where that came from. Winter has suddenly come with a vengeance. I should be doing something with the animals, but I can't make myself think what that might be. I don't know if the chickens are in or out of their coop and, what's more, I don't really care.

My sister comes and puts her arm round my shoulder. 'You have to be strong for the children. I'll help you with it all.'

Tom and Jessica haven't yet stirred this morning and I haven't thought to wake them. It's probably best if they sleep as long as they can. I'll get Serena to call the school shortly to tell Mrs Barnsley what's happened.

'Will you come back to London?' Serena asks me.

'This was Will's dream for us,' I say.

'It wasn't your dream,' she reminds me. 'Now you have to do what's best for you and the children.' She sits in the chair next to me and pours herself another cup of coffee. 'You should come home. You need family around you. There's just the two of us now, sis. We need to stick together. Move near to me so that I'm there to help you with Tom and

Jessica.' Serena lives in a swanky flat in the Docklands. She works from seven in the morning to ten at night. My sister takes in the run-down kitchen. 'You can't possibly stay here. It's far too much work for one person.'

'You're right,' I agree, thinking again of the chickens, sheep and the two new goats that are awaiting my ministrations. Everything seems to be taking twice as long. The responsibilities here are too daunting. I could barely dress myself this morning, so how can I suddenly become responsible for a couple of dozen living things? Things that I know nothing about. Serena's right. We can't stay here. 'As soon as the funeral is over I'll put the house on the market. We should look for somewhere in Notting Hill again so that the children can go back to their old school.'

Serena pats my hand. 'I think that would be the sensible thing to do.'

'Perhaps I can get my old job back. Or something similar.' The thought pushes a bright spot into the gloom. 'I'm sure the BTC will appreciate the situation.'

Hamish comes over to me, tail wagging, lead in mouth. 'Not now,' I tell him and he drops the lead on the floor with a miserable look. I feel guilty that I haven't fed him yet and go to the scullery cupboard where we keep his doggy food and mix him up a bowl. He wolfs it down gratefully, chasing the bowl round the floor and decorating the walls with chewed biscuits, splatters of meaty chunks and slobber.

'You have disgusting table manners, dog.'

He woofs at me and spits food across the room. One of my first jobs when I'm up to it will be to take this damn animal back to the rescue place where he came from. I can't handle him and, at the moment, I can hardly bear to look at him because he was here when Will died and I wasn't. It was the dog's fault that I was in Scarsby in the first place. If he hadn't sniffed Maya's bottom maybe she wouldn't have left us. If he hadn't chewed up all our underwear then I wouldn't have had to go into the town at all. I could have dropped Maya at the station and come straight back. If I'd done that, maybe I could have saved my husband's life instead of it gently ebbing away while he was here on his own.

'You'll be okay,' Serena tells me as I head back into the kitchen.

'Yes,' I say dully. People cope. Life goes on. Others depend on me. If it weren't for the children, I'm sure I'd just want to lie down on the floor and die myself. Guilt kicks in. I can't desert Will's charges now. 'I'd better go and feed the chickens and stuff.'

'Need any help?' My sister looks horrified at the thought. In fact, her expression looks exactly like mine.

'No,' I assure her. 'I can manage.' And, pulling on my newly acquired waterproof jacket and Wellingtons, I head out into the downpour.

Chapter Twenty-Three

I'm trying to wrestle antibiotics into Christopher's beady chicken's eyes and I'm wondering why I'm bothering. They'll all be going soon. Will's dream has died along with him and

I don't care if I never set eyes on another chicken again. Though now that the antibiotics are starting to work the hens have more of a chance of setting eyes on me before they go. It looks like I'm never going to have the joy of collecting my own eggs now. It's probably another one of those country experiences that's vastly overrated.

The rain is pounding down on the henhouse and I cry gently as I work. Despite it being morning, the sky is as dark as night. Through the heart-shaped window and the gloom, I see the headlights of a vehicle as it pulls into the drive. I give it scant attention. Whatever it is, Serena is more than capable of dealing with it. I carry along the row of chickens. As they can't see, they all sit on their perches facing the wall which, this morning, makes me feel interminably sad.

Behind me, the door to the henhouse opens. 'Amy,' a voice says.

Looking up, I see Guy Burton standing in the doorway. He's soaked to the skin, hair flattened to his head. 'I just heard.'

'Isn't it supposed to be good news that travels fast?' My voice catches in my throat.

'I'm so sorry.'

I stand, chicken in hand, and don't know what to say. Neither does the vet. It looks like he might want to give me a hug, but I don't think that I could bear it.

'Let me finish that for you.'

'I can manage,' I say. 'I'm just about done.'

'The sheep should be brought inside while it's raining like this,' Guy tells me.

'Oh.'

'Shall I take them into one of the barns? Have you got any hay?'

Shaking my head, I say, 'I don't know.' Will was supposed to look after the sheep. Even though they're old ladies, I'm too frightened to go near them.

'I'll organise some,' Guy says. 'I'll put the goats in with them. They don't like the rain either.'

'Thank you.'

'Amy,' he says, 'if there's anything you need, anything I can do – tell me. Don't be alone in this. Will wouldn't have wanted you to be isolated.'

How does this man, this stranger, think he knows what Will wanted when I, his wife, was struggling to come to terms with it myself? I push away the thought before it makes me weep again.

'I can't stay here,' I tell him. 'Now that Will's not here. The house will be going up for sale. As soon as I can, I'll be taking the children back to London.'

Now it's Guy's turn to look surprised. 'Isn't it a bit too soon to make a decision? I thought you were starting to like it here.'

I think back to the afternoon we spent in the tea room together when I was laughing into those dark brown eyes while all the time Will was slipping quietly out of my life. 'No,' I say. 'I hate it.'

'That's a shame,' Guy says.

'Well. That's life.'

'This place has a lot to offer.'

'You sound like . . .' I was about to say 'my husband' and I stop myself.

'You might see it differently in a few months' time.'

'I hope to be long gone by then.'

'People round here will be sorry to see you go.'

I doubt it. I've hardly spoken to anyone since I've been here. With cleaning the house and unpacking boxes, I've barely ventured out. I'm certain that I won't be missed. Besides, I need my old friends around me now. The friends who I had to struggle to find time to see when I was working. I must let Maya know what's happened too. She'll be devastated. Perhaps she'll come back to us.

'I'd better put the sheep in for you,' Guy says, seeing that I'm distracted, deep in thought. 'I'll come back later with some hay, but I won't disturb you. I'll go straight to the barn.'

'Thank you. You're very kind.'

'Are you sure you don't want me to do the hens too?'

Shaking my head, I say, 'It will be better if I'm busy.'

Then, as he clearly can't think of anything else to say, or has any crumb of comfort to offer, Guy heads back out into the rain and I watch him go.

But will it be better if I'm busy? I currently can't think of anything that will fill this hole inside me. If it wasn't for the children, I'd lie down in this luxury henhouse and let the chickens peck me to death.

Chapter Twenty-Four

The funeral car is here. And it's waiting, engine burbling softly, exhaust fumes puffing into the air. We've managed to capture Hamish, who was bolting round the garden, frothing at the mouth. Now he's safely locked in the scullery, but he's howling the place down. Clearly, he knows that something is happening and, equally clearly, he doesn't like it.

This morning Hamish has had a chewing frenzy – a tea towel, a dishwashing sponge, Jessica's favourite slippers and a pile of clean, folded towels from the scullery have all had the Hamish treatment. I haven't had the time to clear up after him. I haven't walked him for days either as I just couldn't face going out and about in the village and now the dog's a roiling mass of pent-up energy.

'Are you sure he'll be all right in there?' my sister asks nervously.

'We don't have any choice,' I say. 'We've got to go.' I have a quick hunt round the kitchen. 'I can't find my mobile phone.'

'You're not going to need your phone at the church.'

'I'm sure I had it this morning. Now I can't see it anywhere.'

'The vet called again earlier,' Serena tells me. 'He asked if it was okay if he came to the service. I told him it was.'

I nod, gratefully. Despite my continuing guilt when I think of him, it would be good to see him there, to see at least one friendly face. Guy Barton has been quietly slipping in and out of the yard tending to our animals, stealthily making sure that I'm remembering to take the hens in at night. More than once he's saved them from the clutches of the wily foxes who are only looking for the slightest excuse to help themselves to a free lunch.

People I don't even know from the village have been calling me all week to express their condolences – people who didn't even know Will. Which is in sharp contrast to our oldest and supposedly closest friends.

Serena called round all our colleagues from the British Television Company for me, those that we treasured, friends from years ago who have been through all our trials and tribulations with us, and no one – not one single one of them – has been able to make it to William's funeral. Without exception, they cited a whole host of plausible reasons why they were unable to attend the funeral of someone who had once seemed so dear to them, like childcare considerations, work commitments (how often have I used that one myself?), travel difficulties. And I just got the impression that if we'd still been living in Notting Hill and had suffered this tragedy, then I'm sure that they would have been the first to come around. But in Yorkshire we're now out of sight and out of mind. Not even Maya is coming. She says that her new employer won't give her the day off. Old friendships clearly count for nothing when there's a long stretch of motorway in between. My sister tried to convince me to bury Will in London, but I know that this is where he'd want to be. We've been here for such a short time, but I know that he'd want his soul to settle here.

Our friends and colleagues have all sent floral tributes to assuage their consciences. I feel like throwing them on the fire. How could they do this to Will? Did my husband mean so little to them? What a meagre party we'll make for Will's send-off. How can someone who has been so popular in life be so neglected at his death? The people that we cared for have turned out to be nothing more than fair-weather friends. It's at times like this when you find out who your true pals really are.

Hamish howls some more. I give up the search for my phone. 'Let's go. Are the children ready?'

Serena nods. 'They're being very brave.' More than I am. I feel like lying down on the floor and never getting up again. My sister shouts to the children and they come into the kitchen.

I bend down and hug them. Jessica is crying silently. 'I love you both very much,' I tell them. 'Daddy would be so proud of you.'

Then I take their hands – for once Tom doesn't object – and we go out to the funeral car.

Chapter Twenty-Five

I've wanted to come to this lovely little church since we arrived in the village; I just didn't imagine it being in these circumstances. The day is incongruously bright and warm. In the churchyard the trees are hanging onto the last of their autumn coats, their few remaining leaves tinged with gold and raspberry, the rest of them forming a colourful carpet in the churchyard. Will would have loved a day like this. He'd have taken the children by the hand and kicked through the leaves with them, shouting happily. I blank out the image.

We follow the coffin into the church and I find it hard to believe that my husband is lying in there. I keep having to say it over and over to myself – *he's gone and he's not coming back*. I squeeze the children's hands and they look up at me with tearful eyes.

The church has been decked with white lilies and the scent is beautiful. But that's not what takes my breath away. Inside, the pews are filled with people from the village, people that I've barely glanced at over the last few months. Yet they've all turned out to say goodbye to Will. I'm touched that they've taken the time to find space in their busy lives to be here when our friends could not.

We walk down the aisle, our sad little procession, and the sun streams through the stained-glass windows, casting kaleidoscopes of rainbow colour across the floor. This is very beautiful in its own poignant way.

The vicar comes to the front of the altar and the undertaker's bearers place the coffin on its stand. I don't know the vicar, but he called on me yesterday and discussed what I'd like him to say, what readings, what hymns. How could I tell him that I couldn't care less? Now he starts to speak and a respectful hush falls on the congregation. 'We're gathered here in the sight of God,' he says solemnly, 'to celebrate the life of William Ashurst . . .'

I feel my legs start to shake. How will I be able to get through this?

Then, all of a sudden, behind us there's a terrible howling noise. I turn in terror. The shout is out of my throat before I have time to consider where I am or what the occasion is. 'Hamish! No!'

Through the church doors, the dog charges. I dread to think how he's got out of the house, but he has. He barrels down the aisle, knocking us all out of the way and showering the congregation with spittle.

'No!' I shout as I make a futile lunge for him. 'No!'

I see Guy Barton dive forwards, but he's too slow for Hamish. In a masterly body swerve, the dog evades the vet, but loses his footing on the flooring worn smooth by the feet of many worshippers. He slides down the aisle, paws scrabbling against the stone as he goes careening towards the coffin.

The congregation gasp in horror. Hamish starts back-pedalling. But it's too late. He rushes headlong into Will's coffin, where it rocks violently on its hinges but mercifully stays put. The congregation, as one, let out their breath.

Hamish stands on his hind legs and lays his head on the casket, whining pitifully.

I somehow regain the use of my legs and march towards him. 'Hamish, come here,' I shout, all decorum of the grieving widow flown out of the window.

Hamish looks at me, fear in his eyes, and slumps to the ground. Whereupon I hear a familiar sound.

'It can't be,' I say, mouth agog. But it is.

That's my mobile phone ringing. I'd know my ringtone

anywhere. It was mine and Will's favourite anthem. And it's coming from Hamish's stomach. So that's where my phone got to. He opens his mouth to bark and the sound of the phone comes out even louder.

The strains of our much-loved Queen hit slices through the silence and the church is filled with 'Another One Bites the Dust'.

Chapter Twenty-Six

I don't know how we get through the rest of the service, but we do. Guy Barton wrestled Hamish to the back of the church where he tied him to a pew with the belt from his trousers. Apart from the occasional plaintive howl to interrupt the vicar's eulogy, Hamish behaved himself long enough for the funeral to continue, thankfully, without further incident.

Now Hamish is locked in Guy's Range Rover in disgrace and the rest of us are in the small village hall. I assumed that there would only be Serena, the children and me at Will's funeral and had planned to go home and continue the day in quiet contemplation. The village, it seems, has other ideas.

The hall is decked, like the church, with white lilies and everyone has brought food to make up a marvellous buffet of local produce. From the butcher in Scarsby there's a platter of pork pies and a glorious array of cheeses from a shop I've yet to discover. It feels as if it's a welcome party as well as a goodbye, and I dearly wish that my husband was here as he really would have enjoyed it.

A woman called Cheryl who works as a receptionist at Guy's veterinary practice introduces me to everyone. They all seem extraordinarily nice and I realise that I've been churlish to have pretty much ignored them all so far. But then I was too steeped in my own self-pity to make a good neighbour. The children are being fussed over by a lady and gentleman who I think run the village pub. Serena gave them a little plate of food each and I'm relieved to see that they're both eating it while they chat animatedly to the couple. The resilience of children never ceases to amaze me. They have coped so well with today, that I'm extremely proud of them. It seems that it was Guy's idea to hold this get-together after Serena told him that none of our friends were making the journey to Yorkshire, and I think how kind he is to do that for a couple he barely knows. I can see him across the room charming two elderly ladies and it makes me smile in spite of my pain.

When everyone's eaten and many strong cups of Yorkshire tea have been consumed, I stand up to say a few words. 'Thank you so much for this,' I tell them. 'It has meant a lot to me and my family. My husband would have been very grateful for your kindness. He adored life in this village even though we've only been here a short time, and was looking forward to a long . . .' At this point my voice gives up. What William thought was that Helmshill would give us all a long and happy life. Someone else, it seems, had other plans. 'I want to thank Cheryl and Guy for organising this for me as

I'm not sure that I could have managed it myself.' I lift my teacup. 'To William Ashurst,' I say. 'A wonderful man, a loving husband and a caring father. He'll be greatly missed.'

'To William,' my new friends echo.

Ordeal over, I melt into the background and go to seek out Guy Burton. When I find him, I prise him away from his two elderly admirers. We walk to the door of the hall and slip out into the feeble warmth of some winter sunshine. There's a bench by the green and I sit on it and give out a weary sigh. Guy sits next to me. Hamish in the Range Rover starts to bark maniacally. He must be crossing his legs by now. Either that or he'll have piddled in Guy's car.

'I just wanted to say thank you personally,' I tell Guy. 'I really do appreciate this. William would have too.'

'It was the least I could do.'

'Seems as if a lot of our friends were very fair-weather.'

'It might take people a long time to accept you round here, but when they do you're a friend for life.'

I smile wanly. 'I didn't realise how important that was until now.'

'How long is Serena staying?'

'A few more days. She has a very high-powered job. I'll try to find a house close to her when we move back to London.'

A shadow crosses Guy's face. 'I thought you might have reconsidered.'

I shake my head. 'No. The house is going on the market as soon as possible.'

'Oh,' he says.

'Serena's the only family I've got. I need to be near her.'

'Of course.' Guy sighs.

We hear the strains of my mobile phone ringing again from inside Hamish's stomach. I start to laugh shakily. 'Wonder who that is?'

'I'd better take that dog of yours back to the surgery.'

'Surgery?'

'I need to get that phone out of him. I'm not sure that we can trust it to nature. It could be harmful to him.'

'I hadn't thought of that. Will it be expensive?' I hate to think of these things now, but finances are very tight. We haven't yet begun to sort out Will's affairs. And I'd hoped to be able to find some freelance work, but who would I get to look after the kids now if I had to go off to Manchester or somewhere for a couple of weeks at a time? What I need to do is start looking for work back in London.

'Don't worry about that now. You've enough on your plate.'

'You've done so much for us already,' I say, tears welling. I force myself to be brisk and businesslike. 'Just tell me how much it is and I'll settle up with you.'

'I hope that Hamish's antics didn't entirely ruin the day. It was a lovely service. I'm sure that you'll have good memories too.'

'William would have found it very amusing,' I tell him. In fact, my husband would have loved it. 'In time, I probably will too.'

'I hope so.' Guy stands. 'I'll keep the big guy in for a day or two, make sure he's all right. I'll call you to let you know how he's doing.'

'Thanks.' Guy heads off to his car. Hamish goes to bound

out as he opens the door but, this time, is successfully headed off at the pass.

'Be careful with him,' I warn. 'He's a menace.'

'He just needs a firm hand,' Guy says.

He just needs a ton of tranquillisers. I shake my head. Damn dog. He's too much like hard work for me. As soon as he's better, he's going straight back to where he came from.

Chapter Twenty-Seven

By the time Guy got back to the surgery, Cheryl was also pulling up outside.

'That dog looks mad,' she said, as she opened the surgery door.

'He's just a bit boisterous.' Guy struggled to coax Hamish from the car where he'd happily taken up residence in the front seat. He tugged at his lead. 'Come on, boy.' The phone went off again in Hamish's stomach. Amusing as it was, Guy knew he had to get that phone out of there now before it caused a serious blockage that could be life-threatening for the dog.

He'd vowed not to get too emotionally attached to another dog since he'd had to put down his own Border Collie, Robbie, last year. Guy didn't know what it was about Hamish – he was as troublesome as Rob had been bright – but somehow this great lump of a dog had blundered its way into his affections. Perhaps it was because he belonged to Amy who, unfortunately, never seemed to be too far from his thoughts.

Guy went round to the driver's side of the car and, pushing Hamish with all his weight, finally managed to dislodge him from the Range Rover. Immediately, he bolted for the surgery door. Guy chased after him. Inside, Hamish barrelled into the carousel of helpful leaflets that was just inside the reception, scattering pamphlets on cat neutering, dog worming and the joys of rabbit keeping all over the floor.

'Stop that, you monster!' Cheryl cried. She loved that display and could happily spend hours replenishing the information, finding artistic ways to fan the brochures.

Hamish skated round the floor. At that moment, Mrs Evans arrived with her cat, Tabby, who'd come to have a bad tooth removed. Hamish launched himself at the cage, knocking it out of Mrs Evans's hand and causing the door to fly open. Tabby sprang out, claws splayed, spitting. Hamish barked and jumped backwards in fright, sending himself crashing into the aquarium with its excellent display of tropical fish. Hit by a twelve-stone dead weight, the glass shattered on impact, sending a spray of water and tropical fish across the room.

Tabby's bad tooth might have been putting him off his food, but that didn't stop him from catching an Angel fish on the fly and swallowing it down whole. Mrs Evans looked as if she was about to pass out. Hamish barked in delight.

'Get that dog out of here at once,' Cheryl shouted.

'Hamish! Hamish!' Guy made a lurch for him, feet

slithering on the soaked floor. He locked his arms round Hamish and dragged him forcibly towards consulting room one. 'I'll be with you as soon as I possibly can, Mrs Evans,' he said over his shoulder, fixing his professional smile in place. 'Cheryl, can you send the nurse in, please?'

Shutting the door behind Hamish, Guy leaned on it to get his breath. He'd treated enormous cows, raging bulls, kicking horses, but none of them had the strength or ebullience of this dog.

'Hamish,' Guy said, panting as much as his new canine charge. 'You and I need to come to an understanding. If you don't start behaving, lad, you're going to be back in that rescue home before you can say "walkies".'

Hamish barked joyfully at that. Presumably, the only word that had registered was 'walkies'.

'Up on the table then.'

The dog needed no further encouragement and bounded onto the operating table in one leap, wagging his tail frantically.

'You're not going to like this much,' Guy said, as he turned his back on the dog to fill a syringe with anaesthetic. 'In fact, you're not going to like this at all.' He took the precaution of giving Hamish a hefty dose. It was going to take a lot to knock this dog out and he certainly didn't want Hamish waking up while he was trying to extract a mobile phone from his stomach.

Chapter Twenty-Eight

'I can't bear to leave you,' my sister says with a tear in her eye.

'I'll be fine. Don't blub or you'll start me off too.'

Serena laughs. 'Come down as soon as you can.'

'I'm going to try to get in to see my old boss in the next couple of weeks.' As soon as he realises what he's missing, I'm sure he'll hire me again. Then I can start to rebuild our old life in London, take the children back to what's familiar for them, to what they know best, to what *I* know best. How I have longed for this. I just didn't imagine what tragedy would have to occur for me to achieve it. Now, it goes without saying, I'd rather have Will back and stay in this dilapidated old house for ever. But as that's not going to happen, we have to move on. I have to steel myself for a new life without him.

Tom and Jessica hug her. 'Be good for your mummy,' she instructs. 'She needs you to be all grown up.'

My children both nod solemnly and it makes my heart break. I draw them into me and we escort Serena to her car.

We all kiss her goodbye and then wave her off in the drive as the Porsche roars away, breaking up the silence of the morning. As she disappears from view, the van from the estate agents comes and the man makes short work of erecting a For Sale sign while I stand and watch. I hope that the house sells quickly so that I can get away from here as soon as possible.

Back in the kitchen Hamish is lying in his bed. Well, parts of him are. He's so big that most of him spills over the side of it. He's been very subdued since Guy brought him back from his surgery and, if he was like this all the time, I might just be able to cope with him. The dog's wearing a big white collar to stop him pulling his stitches out, but he's clearly unhappy with the situation as he's pawing at it incessantly. The cat, Milly Molly Mandy, is sitting at his head taking the opportunity to systematically bat him on the nose with her claws while she knows he's unable to retaliate. Payback for all the times he's tried to roger her, I'd guess.

While I clean up the now regular pile of shredded mice cast off by the cat, Jessica lies down on the kitchen floor and snuggles up next to Hamish, winding her arms round his big, soft neck. His tail thumps out a rhythm on the floor. 'We love you, Hamish,' she coos. 'We missed you so much.'

Hmm. Not all of us did. I had three blissful slobber-free days. Looking at my daughter, I realise that it's going to be a darn sight harder to take Hamish back to the rescue centre than I'd imagined.

'We'll look after you now that Daddy's not here,' Tom chips in to the doggy love-fest.

Marvellous. Looks like Will has passed on the Doctor Doolittle gene to his children. I feel like shaking my fist at the sky.

The chickens, sheep and goats are all waiting for their breakfast, so I welly up and head out to their respective pens. I scoop the wriggling mice out of the hens' feeder without so much as a whimper. 'Run the other way,' I warn them with a nod towards the house, 'or you'll be kitty litter.'

They head off in the direction of my kitchen and I tut to myself. 'Can't say I didn't warn you.'

The chickens are beginning to recover sight which in some ways is marvellous and in others is problematic. Now they can see me coming at them with their antibiotic drops and scatter in all directions as I approach, so the job takes twice as long. I chase them round, arms outstretched and snatch at them as best I can. They're not half-bald like they were either so they're looking much better. They all have a new fluffy feather coat and really look quite smart. As soon as they're fully healthy then I can get rid of them.

The light is soft on the hills today. It makes them feel close as if they're protecting the house. Some days you feel as if you can taste the air it's so fresh, as if it has an extra ozone molecule. It will be different once we're back in London and breathing in the pollution once more.

I let the sheep out of the barn and into the field. Doris is limping and I make a mental note to ask Guy if there's anything wrong with her. It's going to be the devil's own job to offload these three old dears. They're probably going to have to go to slaughter. I try not to think about that. I can't imagine there'll be many soft touches like Will passing by this way. Who else would want to rescue them? The thought makes the tears rush to my eyes.

'What were you doing bringing us here?' I turn my face up to the sky to ask him. 'I never wanted this, Will. This was your dream life. I'm meant to be in a three-hundred-pound suit and behind a desk, not in wellies and knee-deep in chicken shit.' I look down at said wellies which are indeed covered in crap. 'I feel as if I'm letting you down. But I can't do this. I hope you understand why I'm going back. I won't be able to manage here by myself. I've only just got enough energy to look after myself and the kids. Everything else on top of that is just too much. I have to go back to what I'm comfortable with.'

Then, realising I am alone and no one else is going to do it, I go to check on the tiny goats. They bleat enthusiastically at me. 'Hello, boys.' I'm not actually sure if they are boys. They nuzzle my hand, anxiously. Bless, they really are quite sweet. Will would have been head over heels in love with them. I realise that we haven't even given them names yet. Best not to, if they're likely to be on their way as well.

Cute or not, they're a lot of work. Tomorrow I'm going to call my old boss, Gavin, and find out if I can go in to see him next week. I'll phone the children's previous school too and get them re-registered for the next term. Then I'll look for a place for us to live back in the city smoke. Now that I've got a plan I feel so much more positive about the future. But the tears start to fall again as it hits home once more that it will be a future without Will.

Chapter Twenty-Nine

In the night Hamish has pulled off his collar and has chewed out all of his stitches. He doesn't look any the worse for wear and the wound from his op seems to have healed well enough. I've taken the children to school because I think it's better for them to get back to normal as soon as possible. Strangely, they didn't protest at all. They would have done, had they realised that I had a covert mission to complete this morning.

'Come on, boy,' I say, dragging Hamish into the Land Rover, luring him with a row of the doggy biscuits he enjoys so much. He munches and drools his way into the passenger seat. 'What a mug,' I mutter under my breath.

Tying Hamish's lead to the door handle, I then get in beside him. 'I want no messing from you,' I say. 'Understand?'

He drools on the seat.

Then, with a shake of my head, I crunch the car into gear and rattle off. I can't wait to get rid of this heap either and get back to good old public transport. How I long for the crush of the Tube, the erratic sway of the bendy buses. Just the thought puts a smile on my lips.

In the seat next to me, Hamish wags his tail as we wind our way through the country lanes. Occasionally, he whines along in tune with Radio 2 – the only station I can get on the ancient radio. The route takes us high across the moors, the first time I've been out this way. It's breathtakingly beautiful, a patchwork quilt of colours beneath a vast, untroubled sky.

An hour later and we've clattered and crunched our way over to Malhead. If Scarsby is a one-horse town, then Malhead hasn't even got a horse. There's a rag-tag assortment of cottages grouped around a pitiful main street and not much else. I slow down, grating the gears into third and coast along the road. It can't be far from here. 'Have you any sense of direction?'

Hamish turns doleful eyes on me. I feel a gulp travel down my throat. I wonder if he knows? The thought makes me laugh. Of course he doesn't. He's just a big, stupid old dog.

Then, sure enough, I see a sign. *Malhead Animal Rescue Centre*. That's the one I need. Turning the Land Rover into the unmade road, we bump down the track. Hamish starts a low growl. 'Stop that now,' I say. 'It's like coming home.'

I have a moment of doubt. What am I going to tell the children? They'll hate me if I tell them the truth. I could simply lie, and say that Hamish has run away. They'd be sure to believe that. It wouldn't be the first time he'd tried it.

Pulling up outside the kennels, I think that they don't look too bad. Not really. They're quite pleasant – in a concentration camp kind of way. There are lots of dogs barking and they sound . . . well, they sound sort of upset, unhappy. Hamish growls some more.

I sit and listen to the banging of my heart. My mind is made up. No going back now. Traipsing round to the passenger seat, I untie Hamish and go to scoosh him out of the car. He remains solid as a rock, immovable.

112

'Hamish,' I cajole. 'There are some nice, juicy treats waiting for you.' I lay a trail of doggy treats on the floor, but he won't be conned a second time. I push, shove, rant, rave, coo and curse. Nothing is moving him.

'Right,' I say. 'You can jolly well stay there.' I slam the door on him and march off to find a rescue person.

One in the form of a bottle-blond lady in pink Wellingtons greets me at the door to the main shed of kennels. 'What can I do for you?' She squints into the sunshine.

'My husband came here a few months ago,' I explain. 'He got this dog from you. And well . . .' I try to keep my voice strong. 'He recently died. Unexpectedly.'

'Oh, that's so terrible,' she says, a crack in her own voice. 'You're so young. A tragedy. A total tragedy . . .'

'Yes. Yes, it was. *Is*.'

'Anything we can do to help. Anything . . .' I feel like I'm drowning in her sympathy.

'I'm moving the family back to London,' I continue. 'And we can't take the dog with us. He needs space. Space we won't have.'

'I understand perfectly.' She places her hand on my arm. 'Perfectly.'

'I'm sure Hamish will soon be—'

Her face freezes over. 'Did you say Hamish?'

'Yes, I—'

'The big Gordon Setter?'

'Yes. That's the one.'

'No.' She holds up her hand. 'I'll not have that dog back.'

'But you just said—'

'*No.*'

'Anything, you said. Anything.'

Now both hands are up. 'Not that.'

'Why?'

'He's a disruptive influence.'

'He's a little lively,' I concede as panic fills my chest. 'I'm sure he's settled down a lot in the last few months.' Turning, I gesture back at the Land Rover and, do you know what, I'll swear that Hamish is smiling at me.

'No,' she says. 'We had a devil of a job to rehome him. Do you know how many times he's been back? Do you know how many kennel girls I've lost because he tried to . . .' She purses her lips at me as if it's my fault that my dog has too much testosterone. 'Your husband was the only one fool enough . . .' Then she realises what she's said and stops.

'Well, thank you,' I say crisply. 'You've been very helpful.'

'I'm sorry, dearie,' she concludes. 'I'm sorry for your loss. Very sorry. But I'm not taking that bloody dog back.'

With that she turns away from me and marches off in her ridiculous pink wellies and her blond hair with her roots showing.

I stomp in the other direction and get in the car next to Hamish. He turns his back on me. 'You've just got a reprieve,' I say. 'This is no time to turn moody.'

With that, he lets off the most enormous smelly fart, filling the car with noxious fumes. Even his own nose wrinkles in distaste.

'For goodness sake, Hamish,' I snarl, ramming the Land Rover into reverse. 'You just never know when to quit while you're ahead.'

Chapter Thirty

'I need to call the vet,' I say to Tom. We're watching the sheep in the field. 'I'm pretty sure that Doris's limp is getting worse.'

'I like having pets,' my son says wistfully.

'They're not pets,' I point out. 'They're farm animals.'

'What's the difference?' he asks. 'We look after them like pets.'

'We don't give them names like pets.'

'The chickens have all got names. And the sheep.'

'But the goats haven't got names.'

'They're Stephanie and Blob.'

'You can't call a goat Blob.'

Tom shrugs with a world weariness that's born of surviving on this planet for eight long years. He used to be so full of confidence, but he's been much more subdued and unsure since Will died and I'd love to know what's going on inside his little eight-year-old head.

'Tell Jessica about it,' he says. 'I told her it was stupid. But they've still got names.'

I'm not going to get drawn into this names argument – mainly because I appear to be losing.

'Can we have pets when we're back in London?'

'I don't know. We'll have to ask . . .' For one moment I was going to say 'Daddy' and then I realised that I'm the one who's going to be making all the decisions from now on. The decisions about everything from pets to pensions will rest on my shoulders alone. I get to be the good guy and the bad guy from now on.

Tom looks at me, puzzled. 'Who will we have to ask?'

'Auntie Serena.'

Thankfully, my son doesn't think to question why my sister would be making our pet-ownership decisions.

'What about Hamish? He's a pet.' Said dog is currently slinking round the garden giving me a very wide berth.

What about Hamish? How can I tell Tom that the only reason we've got him at the moment is because the rescue home wouldn't rescue *us*.

'We don't want to leave him here. Or Milly Molly Mandy.' The cat I can just about cope with, despite the fact that her aim concerning the litter tray leaves a lot to be desired. But Hamish? If my dear husband hadn't already died, I'd be wanting to murder him for inflicting that mutt on me. How would we manage him in London?

Turning from Tom, I punch Guy Burton's number into my new mobile as an avoidance technique. Is it a bad sign that he's been promoted to speed dial? He answers straight away with a brisk, professional tone.

'Guy,' I say. 'It's Amy.'

It's true that you can hear the smile in someone's voice and I find myself smiling back as he says, 'Hi. What can I do for you?'

'We've got a problem with one of the sheep. Doris is limping. Can you stop by and take a look at her when you've got a minute?'

'I'm on my way home now,' he tells me. 'I'll be with you in ten minutes.'

And, sure enough, ten minutes later his Range Rover swings into the drive. He has his box of veterinary tricks in his hand and an apple pie that his receptionist, Cheryl, has sent for us. Ever since Will died I've received weekly donations of home-baked pies both sweet and savoury, and regular anonymous donations of freshly picked vegetables which have been left on my doorstep – which makes me feel very humble.

Guy hands over the pie just as Hamish, done sulking, hurls himself at the new arrival and tries to commit a sex act on him.

'Get down, Hamish!' I shout. Hamish does anything but.

Finally, Guy manages to disentangle himself.

'Tom,' I say. 'Take that dog inside.'

My son wrestles the writhing hound over to the kitchen while Guy and I walk back towards the sheep which I've now herded into the barn.

'Still finding Hamish a handful?' Guy asks.

I nod and bite back the tears that are never far away. 'I tried to return him to the rescue home today, but they were too canny to take him back.'

'Poor Hamish,' Guy says.

'Poor Hamish, pah!' Poor Amy, more like. I give the vet a sideways glance. 'Don't suppose that you'd like him?'

'I can take him out while I'm on my rounds a couple of days a week if that would help you out.'

'That would be very kind of you,' I say, jumping gratefully

at the chance of a few hours' peace and quiet without anything being chewed or shagged.

'It wouldn't hurt to give him some basic training either.'

'Can you train a whirling dervish?'

'We could give it a go.' We've reached the sheep. Guy opens the gate to the pen and we go into the barn. He catches hold of a complaining Doris and straddles her.

'Now,' Guy says, 'the problem with old ladies of both the sheep and the human variety is that they have a lot of trouble with their feet. They need their nails trimming regularly and they can be prone to infection between their toes.'

Fantastic. Now I'm going to have to pay to give my sheep pedicures. I chew my lip anxiously. The place is like a money pit. Who knew that keeping a few animals could prove so costly? The bills are mounting up and I'm glad that I'm heading off to London next week. While I'm there I'm going to sort out Will's finances with the solicitor. I'll feel so much happier when I know how much money will be coming in from his pension and life policy.

Guy is examining Doris's feet. 'There's a bit of infection here,' he says after a minute or two of scrutiny. 'I'll give it a good cleanup and then she'll need some antibiotics. I'll look at the other girls while I'm here.' He grabs Delila in an armlock and starts to check her feet too. 'At this age I'll need to give their teeth frequent check-ups too to make sure that they can eat properly.'

Oh, why couldn't Will have landed us with young sheep, little lambs that could have been on our dinner-table by now providing food for us, rather than these old dears who are slowly draining us of much-needed cash.

I watch how much care Guy puts into tending the elderly ladies. 'You must love your job very much,' I say.

'Yes. I guess I do.'

'Well, you're very good at it.' For some reason it makes me feel bashful to say it.

'Thank you,' Guy says with a wry smile. 'If only some of the farmers round here were as appreciative of my talents.' He straightens up and the sheep run away to huddle in the far corner of the barn having had enough indignities thrust upon them for one day. He cleans off his hands under the hosepipe. 'How's the house sale going?'

'We've got the first people coming to look tomorrow.'

'So soon?'

There's only one estate agents in Scarsby – which seems bizarre seeing that they're on every corner in London – but Collier's seem to have done a good job. 'The estate agent says it's a very desirable property.'

'Mike Collier is full of bullshit,' Guy informs me with a nod towards our For Sale board. 'This place was on the market for nearly a year before he managed to offload it . . .' His voice trails away.

'To some mad southerners who didn't know any better?'

'Something like that,' he laughs.

'A year?' I huff.

'Sorry,' Guy says. 'That's not what you want to hear.'

'I'd better get inside and make sure the house is looking as spruce as it can do. I want this place gone – and fast.'

'This would make a lovely family home.' Guy gazes at the house. 'It needs a lot of work, but it would be worth it.'

'Buy the house and I'll throw the dog in for free,' I quip.

119

'Would love to,' he admits. 'But I've no one to share it with. I rattle around in my own house as it is.'

'Stay for supper,' I say impulsively. 'It will be something involving pasta. Nothing fancy.'

'That would be great,' he says, 'but I can't call it a day just yet. Joe up at Brandon's Farm has got a cow with potato choke.'

'I won't even ask what that is.'

'It's a cow that's choking on a potato.'

I smile. 'Of course.'

'I don't know when I'll be back.'

With a shrug, I say, 'Another time then.' I walk Guy to his car as the dusk begins to fall. The nights are closing in fast – most of the light is gone by three-thirty – and I get the feeling that winters will be long and hard here. I'm hoping the people coming to view Helmshill Grange tomorrow – Mrs and Mrs Finnegan – will fall in love with the house instantly and I can be out of here before the worst of the weather sets in. Optimistic, I know, but it's only that thought that's keeping me sane. 'Thanks again, Guy.'

'Any time,' he says, as he drops his vet's bag in the back of the Range Rover and feeds himself into the driver's seat.

I wave as he reverses. There'll be a few things that I'll miss about this place and, I feel awful admitting this, but Guy Burton will be one of them.

Chapter Thirty-One

When Guy got back from Brandon's Farm it was gone ten o'clock. It might have been relatively easy to refuse Amy's offer of supper, but to turn down food prepared by Mrs Brandon took a braver man than he was.

Dealing with the choking cow had been a fairly quick job, as it turned out. The animal had gone into the crush easy enough with a little persuasion and brute force, and he'd managed to get the offending potato out without getting bitten, but Joe Brandon was one of the few talkative farmers round here so that always added a good half an hour to a routine call. Ellen Brandon was also one of the best cooks in the area and was keen to show off her skills whenever he was there. It was, it seemed, Ellen's mission in life to fatten him up as much as it was Cheryl's mission to find him a woman.

An hour after he'd finished the visit, he was still in the Brandons' homely farmhouse kitchen in front of a roaring fire filled with home-made sausages and mash followed by apple pie and a generous dollop of whipped cream, listening to the Brandons tease each other with the ease of people who'd been married for over twenty years.

Now he was back at home. The house was chilly as the central heating hadn't come on and there were no lights burning to welcome him. He sighed as he pushed through a pile of junk mail sitting behind the front door. No welcome in the hillside for Guy Burton.

The only light blinking was that on the answerphone. He pressed the button and listened to the usual raft of messages from people who had vomiting cats, fainting dogs, calving cows. Most of them could wait until the morning, but a couple would probably mean him turning out again tonight. The last call, however, made him come out in goosepimples and it was nothing to do with an animal in need.

'Hi Guy,' the voice said into the darkness. 'I know that it's been a long time, but I thought I'd call and see how you are.' There was an awkward pause on the phone and Guy realised that he could hear his own heart pounding. 'Circumstances have changed for me now and I wondered what was happening in your life. If you want to call me, I'd love to hear from you.' She left a number and then said, 'Oh, this is Laura.'

As if he wouldn't know that. He went through to the living room. The picture windows in here looked out over the valley and the rest of the village. It was his favourite view, the thing that had sold him the house. He could see Helmshill Grange from here, the lights on in the upstairs windows. Amy must be getting ready to go to bed. He could do with an early night himself but, as a vet, that was something he'd given up years ago.

He let out an unhappy huff. Laura, eh? What had made her call him now after all these years? A change of circumstances, she said. Did that mean she was no longer married to his best friend, Craig? The best friend she'd left him for when he'd found them in bed together two months before Laura and he were due to be married? Guy was usually the type to forgive and forget, but some wounds went way too deep.

He hadn't been able to face any of his mates after that. They'd tried to drag him out on the town but, to be honest, he'd had no desire for socialising. He'd lost his love of five years and was raw with pain. Why on earth would he want to go out every night of the week looking for another one to replace her? He'd thought that they were happy, were going to grow old together. How could he have read it so wrong? Craig and Laura carried on as if nothing had happened. So, to his amazement, did his friends and he'd gradually felt himself being squeezed out of his own social circle. That was why he'd come here. To get away from it all. Start a new life. A couple of weeks later, he'd packed up and headed for the hills. He'd been here ever since. And he'd never seen Laura or Craig again.

He sat in the darkness, staring out of the window. What should he do? Did he want to pick up the phone and open old wounds? He'd heard through the grapevine that she wasn't happy with her husband – but then Craig had always had a roving eye and wandering hands. It had been him, loyal and unsuspecting Guy, who'd been the faithful one. Would Laura be calling to say that she and Craig had split and that it had all been a terrible mistake? Did he really want to hear that from her now, after all these years?

Helmshill had been a great place to come to and nurse a broken heart. There was no social life to speak of. All that was required of him was to turn up in the local pub a couple of times a month and make regular appearances at the annual summer barbecue and harvest supper. No hardship in that. No danger in it either. Despite Cheryl's increasingly fervent attempts to pair him off, Guy had stayed resolutely and happily single. It was only when Amy Ashurst had appeared in the village that he'd begun to think that he was missing out on some of the finer things in life. But she was another man's wife and he'd tried very hard to put her out of his mind. Now her circumstances had changed too. Tragically. And Guy had wondered whether his genuine concern for her was entirely altruistic?

He saw the lights go out at Helmshill Grange and he hoped that Amy was managing to sleep well at night.

Guy worried at a ragged fingernail. It was late. He should find out how the calving cow was doing. That was more important than any of Laura's troubles. Guy picked up the phone, calling not his ex-fiancée, but the farmer in question. He'd used his work as an avoidance technique for the last five years, and he didn't see any reason to stop now.

Chapter Thirty-Two

'The estate agent told us of your loss,' Mrs Finnegan says. 'We're very sorry.' She touches my arm. Why do people do that to widows? It doesn't make them feel any better, trust me.

'Thank you. That's why I'm going back to London. We had such big plans for this house,' I say. 'It would have made a lovely family home.'

She's a publisher and he's a lawyer up from Hertfordshire and they're looking for a weekend place where they can entertain. Helmshill Grange would be perfect for them. At least, I'll make them think it is. Actually, I can't imagine why anyone would want to take on a place this size as a second home. But isn't that the trend these days?

I've taken the precaution of locking Hamish in one of the small outhouses. One that I'll have to remember not to show the Finnegans. I thought he might have been howling the place down like the Hound of the Baskervilles, but there's not a peep from him. That should worry me, but it doesn't, so intent am I on flogging my house.

Mr and Mrs Finnegan take in the dilapidated kitchen. 'Oh, my.' She puts a hand to her throat. 'It needs an awful lot of work.'

'Hence the asking price,' I say. 'I'd like a quick sale. And most of the work is purely cosmetic.' If Mike Collier can bullshit, then so can I.

'The estate agent told us that it needed new plumbing, new heating, a new roof, a damp-proof course and new windows.'

So my estate agent has suddenly found his conscience. 'Other than that, it's purely cosmetic,' I say brightly.

'We just hadn't expected it to look so . . .' Mr Finnegan runs out of words as he takes in the room. It's the flattering pictures. Catches them out every time. And I should know.

'Come and see the living room.' In all honesty, this is a great room. It was Will's favourite place in the house. Well proportioned, tall ceilings, French windows that open out onto the garden – if only they weren't rotting away and you were actually able to get them open. I get a vision of him sitting, feet up on the sofa, flicking through the *Guardian* and I push it away to concentrate on the job in hand.

I throw open the living-room door with a flourish. Hamish is in the throes of humping the armchair. His tongue is hanging out. There's a line of drool, pooling on the wooden floor, and his big canine bottom is pumping frantically at my Heal's shabby chic.

'Oh, my word.' Mrs Finnegan's hand goes to her throat again.

'Hamish! Get down!' I shout. 'I'm so sorry about this.' I yank the dog by his collar and disengage him from the armchair. He yelps in dismay at his enforced canine *coitus interruptus*. 'He's normally so well behaved.' He proves this by sticking his nose into Mr Finnegan's bottom.

Dragging him out to the scullery, I hiss at him, 'How did you get in there? Have you dug a secret underground tunnel from the barn? Bloody animal.'

Hamish gives me doe eyes.

'Stop that,' I say. 'It doesn't wash with me. Stay in here and behave. Otherwise I'll have to do something horrible to you.' I shut him into the scullery.

The dog whines pitifully. You'd think it was *me* who was torturing *him* rather than the other way round.

Back in the living room, Mrs and Mrs Finnegan are looking worried. 'I'll show you upstairs,' I say airily and they trail after me while I keep up a stream of nonsensical conversation.

In my bedroom, it's clear that Hamish has paid an earlier visit. The delinquent dog has pulled the goosedown duvet off the bed and has shredded it. The room is full of feathers and they fly into the air anew as I fling open the door. The contents of my underwear drawer are scattered on top of them. My flimsy wisps of expensive lace are even more flimsy now.

'Oh, my word,' Mrs Finnegan says again.

'Very sorry,' I say and slam the door closed. I'm going to kill that dog.

In the children's rooms, the scenes are much the same. Chewed toys, duvets, clothes. It seems that Hamish has learned to open doors. Everything will have to be fitted with child locks from now on.

'The bathroom's very nice,' I try. With trepidation, I crack open the door. Sure enough, the bathroom has remained untrammelled by the hound from hell.

'Oh, my word,' Mrs Finnegan says in dismay. I'm going to have to kill her too if she keeps saying that. 'When was the suite last replaced?'

'Original fittings are very popular,' I say, casting a glance at the chipped, claw-footed bath and the ancient loo. Perhaps Hamish couldn't have made this room look any worse.

The Finnegans turn and start to head back down the stairs. Then my heart jumps to my mouth. 'Where's your handbag?' I demand of Mrs Finnegan. 'Where is it?'

She glances at her unencumbered arm and purses her lips in thought. 'I think I left it in the kitchen.'

Without another word, I barge past them on the stairs. An unguarded handbag is manna from heaven for Hamish. My feet scrabble to get purchase as I skid into the kitchen. Sure enough, Hamish is up on the table enjoying the contents of Mrs Finnegan's handbag.

Tom and Jessica come in from the garden where they've been banished while I show our prospective purchasers around. Though why I thought my children would be the ones to embarrass me, goodness only knows. 'How did Hamish get in here?' I yell.

'He was crying in the barn,' Jessica says. 'So we let him out for a little bit. Then he was crying in the scullery too. He doesn't like being shut inside, Mummy. Daddy wouldn't have shut him inside.'

My heart squeezes at that. Then the Finnegans appear at the doorway behind me and I don't need to turn to see their horrified looks. I can feel them blazing into my back.

'What was in here?' I ask. 'What's missing?'

Mrs Finnegan inches forward, keeping a wary eye on the dog.

'He won't hurt you,' I assure her. Though he might want to shag her if I recognise the glint in his eye.

'Everything's gone,' she says, eyes wide with shock. 'Nearly everything. There was some make-up, tissues, a small purse . . .'

'Call the vet!' I yell at Tom. 'Call the vet!'

Hamish is licking his lips. Can I detect lipstick on them? I turn my attention back to Mrs Finnegan and her now empty handbag. 'Anything else?'

Then, again, there's the unmistakable sound of a mobile phone. This time it's the more romantic 'Stop, Look, Listen to Your Heart'. No mention of listening to the contents of a dog's stomach.

'Oh no.' I fall to my knees on the floor. 'Not again.'

Chapter Thirty-Three

Hamish is on the vet's operating table. I brush away my angry tears and push my hair back from my face. 'I want you to put him down,' I say.

The phone in Hamish's stomach rings again. The dog wags his tail in time with the soulful tune.

Guy's face darkens. 'Why?'

'I've had enough of him.'

'He's a great dog, Amy. He's just a bit . . . lively.'

'He has no brain.'

'Granted,' Guy concedes. 'But that's no reason to consider putting him down.'

I won't be swayed. 'You won't believe what he's done.'

'Well, I can hear that he's dined on another mobile phone.'

'It's worse than that. That bastard mutt has just cost me the sale of my house.'

'And that's it?'

'I haven't got one decent pair of knickers left in the house. He's chewed them all to ribbons. Even my Janet Reger ones.' And Will bought me those for our last anniversary. They were my favourites. And I'll never be able to replace them. That thought alone is enough to make me want to weep.

'You can buy underwear for three quid a packet in Tesco's. Move on. Start buying your pants there. I don't see that as a big deal.'

'You're not me!' I wail.

'Amy, you're not thinking straight. I'll say it again. That's no reason to destroy a perfectly healthy dog.'

'He's not good for *my* health.'

'I've told you that I'll have him for a few hours twice a week. More if I can manage it.'

'And what about the rest of the time?' My voice is getting steadily higher and I realise that the queue of people in the reception area that I've barged past can probably hear me, but I don't care. I want this dog *done* – and now. 'How do I cope with him for the rest of the time? I can't afford to keep bringing him to see you.'

'It's probably a bad time to point out that I haven't yet billed you for any of my calls.'

I fold my arms. 'And it's probably a bad time to tell you that I don't expect to be a charity case.'

Guy's jaw takes on a determined set.

'Right,' he says. 'You want this dog put down then you can do it, because I certainly won't.'

He hauls a surprised Hamish off the table and yanks an even more surprised me by the arm. Guy marches us through the reception area, past a slack-jawed Cheryl and the assortment of open-mouthed owners with their assortment of cats, dogs, hamsters and rabbits and out into the car park that's to one side of the practice. Opening his car boot, he pulls out a double-barrelled shotgun from under the floorpan and brandishes it in my direction – which makes me jump. Hamish barks happily.

Guy thrusts the gun into my hands. 'Have you used one of these before?'

'No.' I can barely find my voice.

He gestures at the barrel. 'That's the dangerous end. That's the trigger. Point that bit at the dog. Pull that.'

'What?' Now I think that the vet is the one who's lost his mind. 'I thought you gave them some sort of lethal injection or tablet.'

'That's just for sick dogs,' he snaps at me. 'If they're perfectly healthy then we just blow their brains out. Or, in this case, you do.'

'I can't do that,' I say, horrified.

'But you expect me to?'

If this is what it takes, then so be it. My hands tremble as they lock round the gun. Sweat comes to my brow and I lick my lips nervously. 'This is ridiculous. I can't shoot a dog in your car park.'

Guy is unmoved. 'Is there a better place?'

A lump sticks in my throat. I can do this. I'll show him.

Gingerly, I point the gun at Hamish. He thinks this is great fun and bounces up and down in front of me, joyously.

'I'll ask you one last time not to do this, Amy,' Guy says calmly. 'Think of your children. They've just lost their father. How will you explain this to them?'

My hands start to tremble. Hamish lies on the ground, rolling over to present his stomach and giving me a great view of his bollocks. Maybe that's where his brains are, after all. My arms are shaking so much that I can hardly hold up the shotgun. Hamish wriggles on his back, his tongue lolling stupidly.

What the hell am I thinking of? Have I gone mad? I can't do this – I just can't do it. And Guy knew that. Of course he did. Lowering the gun, I sink to my knees on the gravel. All my fight seeps out of me. My whole body is shuddering uncontrollably. 'I can't manage,' I say, sobbing loudly. 'I feel so alone. I don't know what to do. I can't manage without Will.'

Guy kneels next to me in the dirt and the gravel. He puts his arms round me. 'Ssh, ssh. Don't cry. Everything will work out fine. It's early days yet. You're bound to feel like this.'

I lean into him and let the tears fall. Then I feel Hamish try to push his body in between us, his big stupid head nuzzling against my chin as he tries to comfort his would-be murderer. 'Get off, you silly animal,' I say. Then I start to laugh, but the crying doesn't stop.

Chapter Thirty-Four

'You must be good today,' I say to Tom and Jessica as they finish their cereal – even though they always are. They both nod solemnly and I love them for it. I pick up two headless mice by their tails and deposit them in the bin. 'And you.' Hamish wags his tail. I'm not sure that I'm overly delighted that Hamish is still in our household, but here he very much is.

Guy has promised me that he will look for someone who would consider taking Hamish on permanently when we move back to London. I notice that, despite sticking up for Hamish, he's not in a busting hurry to do it himself. Wonder why that is? Anyway, whatever happens, there's no way that dog is coming back to Notting Hill with us. How can we? It might break my children's hearts, but it will break mine more to take him.

This morning the offending animal has pooed – whole – a pair of my black lace panties. I'm very tempted not to bin them but just put them through the washing machine. It would feel like some kind of triumph. But I haven't lowered my standards to that level yet.

'Guy is going to look after you all day,' I tell them for the third time in the hope that they'll remember.

They both nod vacantly and I realise that I've exceeded my nagging quota for today.

Of course, I'd booked my busy day in London before I recalled that the school was shut for a teacher training day. I'm trying to be efficient, organised, straight-thinking, but am failing at every turn. Managing without Will is just so much harder than I'd ever thought possible. The pain of his absence seems to get sharper every day. It often felt as if I was shouldering the entire burden of domestic responsibility on my own when we were married, but clearly I wasn't.

I did think about dragging the kids down to Town with me, but that would have been impossible. Serena's away on a conference in Belgium for a few days, so she isn't around to help either. Before I cancelled it all again, Guy, like a knight in shining armour, stepped into the breech. I'm not sure that he knows exactly what he's letting himself in for. He's offered to do the animal duties this evening and I was up at the crack of dawn this morning to do my part.

'Mummy's going to be late home.' I've got a diary full of appointments. First I'm going to see my old boss, Gavin Morrison, to see what opportunities are available for me back at the British Television Company. Hopefully, Jocelyn is making a terrible fist of my job and they'll be only too grateful to give it back to me again. Failing that scenario, there are a couple of other great jobs at the BTC that I've had my eye on for years. This may be the time to start completely afresh.

I've emailed three of my old friends and I'm hooking up with them for lunch at the hot celebrity restaurant 24/7 and I can't wait. It's been months since I've eaten decent food at ridiculous prices. In the afternoon, I have a meeting with the Headteacher of Tom and Jessica's old school so that I can re-register them in time for the new term in January. Not sure what I'll do if the house sale hasn't completed by then, but I'll cross that bridge when I come to it.

Finally, I'm catching up with the solicitor to get my finances in order and sort out Will's affairs. Then I'll know how much money will be available to us and I can make firm plans. A wave of nausea rises from my stomach when I think of doing all this without my husband by my side.

I hear the crunch of Guy's tyres in the gravel of the drive as he swings in. Bang on time. They're all going to drop me at the station first, before Tom and Jessica go off for the day with Guy.

He knocks on the kitchen door and then pops his head round. 'Everyone ready? We need to be moving to catch that train.'

Hamish charges headlong into his saviour. I say nothing as the dog tries to wrangle Guy into the missionary position. 'Down, boy!' Guy tries unsuccessfully. 'Down!'

'Coats on,' I say to the kids who are much more obedient, and then I fling the dishes in the sink for later attention – which means that the cat will probably lick them clean before I get home.

'Okay?' Guy asks breathlessly as he holds the door open for me to climb in his car.

'Yes,' I answer. 'Fine. Thanks for doing this.'

'You're welcome.'

There's a little awkwardness now between Guy and me since I turned into Rambo and wanted to go on a Hamish shooting spree. He handles me with kid gloves in case I should go to pieces again. And I try to avoid thinking how nice it felt to be held by him.

Chapter Thirty-Five

They waved Amy off at the station and then he'd loaded Tom, Jessica and Hamish all back in the car.

The first part of Guy's plan was to wear Hamish out. And maybe the kids too. It was the first time he'd performed babysitting duties and he wasn't sure how easy it was going to be. This morning they could all let off steam. This afternoon he needed them well-behaved. Already, he was sure that was going to be much easier to achieve with Tom and Jessica rather than Hamish.

He'd taken the precaution of buying in supplies so that they wouldn't get hungry – not too much crap, sugar-free fruit juices and healthy snacks such as flapjacks and dried fruit. Hamish sat in the front seat, while Tom and Jessica occupied the back seat as they wound their way out of Scarsby, through the pretty villages, climbing the increasingly steep hills and up onto the moors.

It was a bright, sunny day – which was just as well as the moors could be the bleakest place on earth when it was pouring down with rain and Guy was sure that the kids wouldn't be so easily entertained then. They reached the top and Jessica and Tom jumped out of the car to open the gate that protected the farmers' fields. He inched forwards in the car and the cows that wandered freely across the road, reluctantly moved their bulk back towards the grazing land. When the children were back in the car they headed to the top of Staincliffe Tarn and parked in the scrubby little car park. Today, theirs was the only vehicle there. In the summer, when the hordes of tourists descended, you couldn't move in this place. Now they had the freedom of the moors to themselves and it was at this time of year that Guy loved it the best.

Out of the cosy fug of the car, the strong breeze had a bite to it and he was glad to see that Amy had sensibly given the children warm coats to wear. Hamish jumped out of the car and shook himself, showering them all with slobber.

'Tell me that you're going to be good today,' Guy warned. 'I have a point to prove.'

Hamish woofed and Guy took it as tacit agreement. After all, this dog owed him one. 'Ready?'

The children nodded their heads and they all set off towards the tarn. As there were no sheep around for him to worry, Guy unclipped Hamish from his leash and let him run free. He only hoped that the dog would come back, but he'd taken the precaution of pocketing a few dog biscuits just in case.

White clouds whipped across the sky, buffeted by the breeze. The surface of the tarn shivered in response too. Hamish raced back and ran round and round in circles, tongue flying as he went. Jessica scampered off with him, hands held wide trying to catch the wind, long hair streaming behind her. He wondered if Amy and Will had brought the children up here together. He didn't think so. Maybe they'd just been too busy settling in at Helmshill Grange to explore their surroundings more fully. He was sure that the family had hardly moved out of the village since their father died. He felt so sorry for the kids and he hoped that today he'd been able to take a little pressure off Amy while she did what she had to do.

'Ever skimmed stones?' he said to Tom as they approached the lake.

The little boy shook his head. 'Daddy said he was going to teach me,' he babbled happily. 'But . . .' then his voice suddenly cracked, 'he never did.'

Guy bent down and slipped his arm around Tom. 'Well,' he said, 'I'm probably nowhere near as good as your dad, but maybe I could teach you instead.'

Tom nodded, brushing away a tear surreptitiously. Guy picked up some flat stones. 'These are just perfect. Feel how smooth they are.'

The boy nodded again as he rubbed the stones, his smile slowly returning.

'Take them like this.' Guy showed him how to angle the stones in his hand. 'Stay low.' They both crouched down. 'Then let fly!'

The stone sailed from Tom's hand and bounced once, twice, three times across the tarn.

The boy turned to him with a big grin on his face which Guy was relieved to see. 'Top stone-skimmer!' Guy said and they high-fived each other.

They entertained themselves happily for the next half-hour, Jessica even deigning to have a couple of goes, even though it was a boy's thing. Then they walked round the tarn, Hamish blazing the trail.

'That was fun,' Tom said.

'Bet your dad saw you doing that.'

'Think so?'

'Yeah. I'm sure.'

Tom grinned again. Jessica came alongside him and quietly slipped her tiny hand in his. Suddenly, Guy could see the attractions of family life. He'd been so convinced that he'd wanted to stay a bachelor after losing Laura. It hadn't taken much for these children to find the chink in his armour. Guy smiled to himself. Life on your own wasn't all it was cracked up to be. He was sure that Amy was finding that.

He looked down at Tom and Jessica. It had been a surprise how much fun they'd had together. Amy might not consider another relationship for years and he couldn't blame her for that – so he would be mad to get his hopes up there. But, out of the blue, he was beginning to think that a life that included a couple of kids and a mad-ass dog might not be so bad after all.

'Hungry?' he asked. The kids both nodded as they headed back to the car. So far, it had been a perfect morning. Except that it was clearly too good to last. As he opened the box of goodies that he'd stashed in the boot, Guy could see that someone else had been there before him.

'Hamish!' The dog was slinking away across the car park, belly low to the ground.

All that was left of the snack bars was some half-chewed foil wrappers.

'Oh, well,' Guy sighed. 'Looks like we'll have to go back

to Poppy's for some hot chocolate and chocolate chip muffins.'

By the way the children cheered, that would go down far better than the healthy option. At least he'd tried.

'Hamish,' Guy shouted. 'Get back here now!' And, amazingly, the dog bounded over and jumped straight into the passenger seat.

He was a natural at this, Guy thought proudly. Two angelic children and a near-angelic dog. Why hadn't he tried it before?

Chapter Thirty-Six

I'm sitting in the reception of the British Television Company by eleven o'clock after an uneventful train journey. I couldn't believe how busy the Tube seemed to be this morning. Perhaps I've just got out of practice over the last few months, but I really struggled to cope with all those people squashed in a small space and I couldn't help but think of the journey I'd taken with Will when he'd first had his wobble. I kept getting horrible flashbacks and I was glad to get off.

It seems strange that I have to be escorted to my old office now that my security pass is long gone. Frankly, I can't wait to get back into the fray here. Say goodbye to chickens and hello to celebrities once more. Bye-bye wellies, hello Jimmy Choos. One wall is covered with a bank of enormous LCD televisions screening a wide variety of the station's output. Last night's episode of *Sports Quiz* is among them and I hum along to the familiar theme tune, a pang of longing twisting my insides. I can feel the adrenaline pumping in my veins just being here. Just let me get back behind my desk doing what I do best. This would really help me so much. I'm sure that Will would want me to do this too. He'd know that this was right for me.

Gavin Morrison, my old boss, keeps me waiting for half an hour – which I'm not particularly happy about. I know about the pressures of work and all that, but I've got a schedule to stick to as well. I need to be back on the six o'clock train out of King's Cross station to have any hope of getting home tonight.

Eventually, Gavin's perky assistant appears and escorts me through the security checks and into the building. In his office, Gavin greets me warmly with a hug and an air kiss. I sit down in the chair opposite him.

He rubs his hands together. 'Tea, coffee?'

'A coffee would be great.' Gavin nods at his assistant and, efficiently, she disappears to do her duty.

'It feels good to be back here.'

'Good, good,' he says, leaning back in his executive chair. I fiddle nervously with my hands and try not to.

'We were all sorry – deeply sorry – to hear about William.' He shakes his head. 'Deeply sorry.'

Not sorry enough to get your arse to Yorkshire to support me at the funeral, I think, but instead, I say, 'Thanks. Thanks so much.'

'I expect life will be different from now on,' he says.

'Yes.' I blow out a shaky breath. 'Very different. And that's what I wanted to talk to you about.'

Gavin makes a steeple of his hands and raises his eyebrows.

'I'll be coming back to London now. Selling up. The house is already on the market and we should have no trouble finding a buyer. I could be back by the beginning of the New Year if everything works out well.' I think that's extremely optimistic, but Gavin doesn't need to know that.

'What happened to the country dream? The idyllic life?' Is there a scathing note in his voice?

'I need to be near my family,' I say, ignoring it. 'The house is wonderful, but too big for me to manage alone.'

Gavin purses his lips, but says nothing.

'I was hoping that I could come back. I know that Jocelyn's doing my old job now . . .'

'And doing it brilliantly,' Gavin chips in.

Wonderful. 'But if there's anything else? I recall that you had some new arts programmes in the pipeline . . .'

'Things have changed since you left,' my old boss says.

'It's only been a few short months. I'm still as sharp as ever. I've missed the cut and thrust. I want to get back to it as soon as possible.'

'There have been swinging cutbacks, Amy. You must know that. Don't you read the newspapers?'

Frankly, I haven't been near one in months. 'Yes, yes. Of course.'

'Even *Sports Quiz* isn't safe.'

'But it's been running for years! The viewing figures are consistently high.'

'We've got a new channel controller and he's a ruthless bastard. He's sweeping his new broom into every little nook and cranny. There's a block on all recruitment. Everyone's feeling the pinch. We've got to shed three thousand jobs.' Gavin spreads his hands. 'Three thousand!'

'Yes, gosh,' I say, my heart pounding erratically. He's not going to offer me a job. There's nothing here for me. I hadn't expected that at all. It feels like the bottom is dropping out of my world all over again. I've given this company years of loyal service. I've sacrificed all kinds of things for my career. When Will was in hospital after his wobble, I didn't miss a day. I wonder now if that's something to be proud of. 'That's terrible.'

Gavin stands and I realise that he wants to usher me to the door. I haven't even had my coffee yet. A four-hour journey to get here and he isn't even being civil enough to wait until I've had a drink! I stand up because I don't know what else to do, how to stall him, how to make him see that he must change his mind.

'I'd love to employ you again, help you come back to London. But it's not going to happen, Amy.' He shakes his head, acting the best regret I've ever seen. With a performance like that he should be in front of the cameras, not behind them. 'Even in the short time you've been away, things have moved on.'

'Yes, yes,' I manage to say. 'I can see.'

'Shame you didn't wait for a while.' Gavin gives a humourless laugh. 'You might have got yourself a decent-sized redundancy package.'

Minutes later and I'm back on the pavement outside Television House. I'm stunned. Foolishly, I thought that they'd take me back with open arms. I thought I was a valued employee. And all the time, I was just another number on a page. At the grand old age of thirty-eight, I'm not only a widow, but I'm now on the scrapheap of life. You don't know how worthless that makes me feel.

Chapter Thirty-Seven

After chocolate-based refreshments at Poppy's, Guy piled Tom, Jessica and Hamish back into the car again. Now the children had overcome their initial shyness and were chatting away with him as if they'd known him for years.

He steered the Range Rover out of Scarsby and into the countryside once more. They were going to visit Marty and Gill Bainbridge who had been clients of his since he'd started at the practice. Marty was one of the new slew of television gardeners, a larger-than-life character who had moved to this area five years ago and had been an incomer at the same time as Guy, so there had been a natural bond between them. Marty and Gillian had bought up old Radley's Farm, a twenty-five-acre spread that was kept like a show farm, mainly because every now and again television cameras turned up and filmed pieces of Marty doing farmery-type things on his land for his prime-time programme on ITV.

The Bainbridges had two children of their own – Oliver who was nine years old and Ellie who was seven. The plan was that Tom and Jessica could look round the farm and help while Guy did some routine checks on Marty's animals.

Then Gill was going to give them one of her legendary lunches and, later in the afternoon, when the Bainbridge children were back from their school, which was open today, all four kids could run wild for a couple of hours. Perfect.

The house at the Bainbridges' farm was more manor house than farmhouse – a beautifully proportioned, double-fronted Georgian home, more graceful and elegant than the usual heavy stone buildings of the area. Clearly, Radley's had always been a thriving farm and the Bainbridges had carried on that tradition. Even the yard was clinically clean which made a welcome change from some of the remote hill farms he ventured onto where it was difficult to tell where the pigsty finished and the farmhouse started.

The lawn in front of the house was pristine, mowed into regimented stripes, the borders lush with fading annuals and stoic evergreens – planted as only a TV gardener would. A majestic oak, still clinging to its golden leaves, swept its branches over the vista in one corner. Magnificent stone planters, blooming lavishly, guarded either side of the front door.

Marty and Gill came out to greet them as Guy pulled up behind their new Mercedes 4x4 parked in front of the house. In the back of the car, Jessica's eyes had widened in awe. 'Do you think our house might look like this one day?'

'I should think so,' Guy said. With an awful lot of paint and hard work and even more cash. But there was no doubt that Helmshill Grange had the potential to be equally grand a home.

'I'd like that,' Jessica said breathlessly as she clambered out of the car.

Marty clapped Guy robustly on the back. 'Good to see you, old friend.'

'Good to see you too.' Guy took in the Mercedes, eyeing it enviously. 'Like the new motor.'

'Thought I'd treat myself,' Marty said proudly. 'Took delivery last week. Lively little thing. All the comforts of home.'

'You're getting soft in your old age,' Guy teased.

'We'll maybe take it out for a spin later. Do a bit of boys' tyre-kicking.'

'Sounds great.'

'You boys and your toys. Don't I get a look in?' Gill chided as she hugged Guy. 'We don't see enough of you.'

'I know,' he said apologetically. 'Life is busy.'

'Not too busy to take on someone else's children though?'

He smiled at the inference. 'I'm helping out a friend.'

'We've heard all about the lovely Widow Ashurst,' she whispered. And, in response to his puzzled glance, said, 'I spoke to Cheryl yesterday and she filled me in on all the details.'

'Cheryl, I'm afraid, tends to make up a lot of the detail.' He ushered the children forward. 'This is Tom,' he said. 'And this is Jessica.'

'Well, I'm very pleased to meet you both,' Gill said. 'I hope that you'll have some fun while you're here and then my children will be home later and you can all play together.'

Tom and Jessica smiled shyly.

Gill linked her arm through Guy's and, leading them all back towards the house, said, 'You'll have some tea?'

'We've just had hot chocolate and muffins at Poppy's,' he confessed.

'I do hope that you've left room for lunch.'

'Oh, I'm sure we have.'

'Let's get straight out onto the farm then,' Marty said. 'I'd like you to take a look at the new pedigree Suffolks I just bought.'

'I'll just get the dog,' Guy said. 'He's a bit of a handful, but I think he'll be okay.'

He let Hamish out of the car and the big dog immediately bounded round in circles trying to burn off the energy that had accumulated during a twenty-minute journey in the car.

'See what you mean,' Marty boomed. 'Fine-looking dog though.'

'He's our dog,' Jessica piped up.

'Well, you're very lucky,' Marty told her.

'We've got a cat too,' she ventured now that she was finding her voice. 'She's called Milly Molly Mandy.'

'Come and see our animals,' Marty said. 'You'll like them.' He slung an arm round Tom's shoulder and took Jessica by the hand.

Guy smiled to himself. There was no room for shyness where the Bainbridges were concerned. The day was turning out to be a great success. Maybe he could do this more often, if Amy would let him.

'Come on, boy,' he said to Hamish. 'All you've got to do is behave for the day and everything will be perfect.'

Much later, it was a sentence he came to regret.

Chapter Thirty-Eight

I'm in one of the rash of Starbucks on Oxford Street and I'm nursing my second cappuccino. The place is dirty, strewn with used cups and plates and screwed-up napkins. The staff are run off their feet. I get a pang for the cleanliness of Poppy's tea room and a place so quiet you can hear the clock tick.

I've been here for over an hour and I can't bring myself to move. All I have to do is drain my cup, stand up and walk for just a few minutes down to Charlotte Street and the hot new restaurant 24/7 where I've arranged to meet my friends for a convivial lunch. But I can't do it. My hands are trembling and my heart is beating erratically. And it isn't down to the coffee hit. Two trails of sweat are working their way from my underarms down my sides.

I've known Angela, Lizzy and Justine for years now, but we've hardly been in contact at all since we moved away to Yorkshire. Another case of out of sight, out of mind. I was so looking forward to seeing them – but now? I don't think that I can cope with their sympathetic words and pitying smiles. Especially as they couldn't come to Will's funeral to support me when I needed them. Are these people truly friends of mine?

Perhaps I would have felt better if I'd come out of the British Television Company with the promise of a new job, with the thought that I could step back into my old world, that my life would continue as I used to know it, albeit without Will. But no. It's clear that's not going to be the case. What will I do now? Put out the word on the media grapevine that I'm looking for something – me and the three thousand other people who are about to be unceremoniously dumped by the BTC. I'd counted on the fact that my old colleagues would understand my situation and know the pressures that I'm under. If my old company can treat me so harshly, how can I expect to be able to find a new employer who'll treat me kindly until I find my feet again?

My friends all have great jobs and supportive husbands. How can I sit and listen to their gossip when I feel so outside of their world? What do I have to tell them about? Can I really regale them with tales of horrid Hamish and a bunch of doddery old sheep with bad feet? We're different people and, to be honest, it hadn't hit home until now.

Punching a text into my phone, I tell Lizzy that I can't make it and to give my apologies to the others. It makes me feel terrible as I was the one who was so keen to set up the lunch. Now, I find I just don't have the stomach for it.

Lizzy texts me back. 'Just as well!' she starts. Angela, it seems, has had to cancel as she was too busy at work to escape. Justine had forgotten about our lunch and has arranged to take one of her clients out instead. Lizzy, who at least has bothered to reply, is running late herself and hasn't yet left the office. So much for my thoughts of white wine and sympathy. If I had gone along, I'd have been sitting on my own like a lonely, widowed lemon.

'Another time,' I text back, remembering all the occasions

I too had to blow people out because my work had taken priority. Perhaps our friendship will get back on track when I'm down here again and I've got a job of my own.

So, instead of something wonderful that would probably be pan-fried and drizzled with a fabulous *jus*, I order another coffee and a plastic-wrapped sandwich which a pleasant girl heats up for me. As I eat the synthetic-tasting cheese, I wonder how the children are faring with Guy. I sincerely hope that they're having a better day than I am. I'd like to text Guy to see how they are, but I don't want him to think that I'm checking up on him.

My next stop is to see the Headteacher at Tom and Jess's old school to secure places for them for next term. I hope to goodness that the house is sold by then. The Weston Academy is a very prestigious school and the children were doing so well there before we left. The fees, however, are astronomical and I'd banked on a decent salary to pay for it all. From the price of the uniforms alone, you'd think they were made by Armani.

I clear my own table, even if no one else does, dumping my debris into the already overflowing wastebin. Then I get back on the Tube heading out to Notting Hill.

It seems strange to walk along the roads of my old neighbourhood, and I get a pang of longing. I avoid going past my old home as I just don't think that I could bear to look at it now that someone else is living happily there. What would have happened if we hadn't moved? Would Will still be alive today if we'd stayed put in the smoke? Was it the stress of all the upheaval that actually proved too much for him? Was that the straw that broke the camel's back?

150

Certainly the stress of trying to move back the other way isn't doing me any good.

I reach the school gates and feel shaky as I go inside and ask for the Headteacher. Mr Spalding is brisk and business-like. He runs the school as a tight ship, which is what Will and I liked so much about it. There's no messing with Mr Spalding.

I'm shown into his office and, echoing my pose of this morning, take up a seat opposite him.

'We were terribly sorry at Weston's to hear of your loss,' he tells me.

'Thank you.'

'How are the children coping?'

'They're fine,' I say. 'Tom's a little quieter than normal, which is to be expected. Jessica is coping amazingly well.'

'I'm glad to hear it.'

'They're both looking forward to coming back to London and seeing their friends here. They need to be with things, with people that are familiar. That's why I'm hoping to bring them both back to Weston's.'

Mr Spalding sucks in his breath. He shakes his head. 'I'm terribly sorry, Mrs Ashurst. We would love to be able to accommodate Tom and Jessica at Weston's. They were both excellent students, a delight. We were sorry to lose them. But I'm afraid that we are totally oversubscribed already. I don't need to tell you how popular the school is.' Smug smile. 'We have a very long waiting list.'

'I thought that in the circumstances . . .'

'I would dearly love to be able to help.'

'But you can't?' Or won't.

'I'm afraid not. We have a long waiting list. Imagine the uproar if anyone found out that Tom and Jessica had jumped the queue.'

Yes. God forbid that two grieving children should be given any preferential treatment. But, in my shock, I say nothing.

Mr Spalding stands and shakes my hand. And I shouldn't be quite so stunned this time that I'm being summarily dismissed, but I am.

So, for the second time today, I find myself out on the pavement, dazed and confused. By now I should have had a great job and my kids should have been safely enrolled to go back to their fabulous school. This day is not going how I planned it at all.

Chapter Thirty-Nine

Behind the Bainbridges' house was a huge and very pretty garden, set out with a variety of secluded areas, all carefully planned by Marty and copiously photographed in his range of bestselling books. His perfectly manicured terrace has graced the covers of dozens of glossy magazines. He opens it on two weekends a year for charity and crowds of admiring fans always come to gawp.

'Garden's looking good, Marty,' Guy said, thinking that it put his own neglected patch to shame.

'Photo-shoot next week for *Gardeners' World*. Been working my backside off to get it shipshape. Not easy at this time of year. The ground's as soft as putty.' Marty surveyed his estate with pride. 'Damn pleased with the results though.'

'So you should be. I'll have to get you to come round and give me some tips on mine.'

'Any time, dear boy. Any time.'

Beyond the garden was the farmyard with its assorted barns and outbuildings that somehow managed to maintain a chocolate-box air. The lucky Bainbridge children had their own small petting zoo set out in one of the barns.

Pens containing pygmy goats, rabbits, guinea pigs, two lambs and a handful of squeaking black-spotted piglets were immaculately maintained. Guy never had to worry about the livestock at the Bainbridges' being mistreated.

Tom and Jessica, in raptures, sat on strategically placed hay bales while the rabbits hopped over their legs and the guinea pigs scrambled around them.

'Oh, this is lovely,' Jessica trilled. 'Do you think Mummy would let us have bunnies and piggies at home?'

'We'll have to ask.' How could Guy break it to them that their mother was planning to take them back to London just as soon as she possibly could? That was way beyond his role of babysitting duties.

'I love it here,' the little girl sighed as a rabbit tried to nibble her coat. 'I thought I liked London best, but I don't.'

Maybe this day was going a bit too well, Guy thought. He didn't want to convert the kids into countryphiles if they were soon to be leaving again.

'I need to go with Mr Bainbridge to look at his new sheep,' Guy said. 'Do you want to come along too?'

The children nodded and they all mucked in together to help put the rabbits and guinea pigs back in their respective homes.

'I'll leave Hamish behind,' Guy said to Marty. 'If that's okay with you. He might make the sheep a bit skittish. If I tie him up here, he'll be fine.'

Securing the dog safely to the fence, they all set off across the field to the sheep paddock. They could hear Hamish barking forlornly as they strode away from him.

Marty had bought himself two dozen quality Suffolk sheep, one of the premier breeds of the British Isles that were also known locally as 'black faces' because, unsurprisingly, of their characteristic glossy black faces and ears.

'Think they're good enough to show?' Marty wanted to know.

'They're certainly a fine pack,' Guy agreed.

The two men spent time leaning on the fence, admiring the sheep and the spectacular view of the moors rising up behind the farm.

'We should be making our way back for lunch,' Marty suggested, rubbing his hands together. 'I'm sure the table will be groaning under the weight of food by now if I know my Gillian. Anyone hungry?'

'Yay!' Tom and Jessica cried.

As they headed back towards the house, Guy suddenly realised that he couldn't hear Hamish any more. When had the dog stopped barking? Wouldn't he have started up again when he heard them all approaching?

His heart started to pound as they rounded the corner and saw the fence where Hamish had been so securely tied.

The lead was still firmly attached to the post, but of Hamish there was no sign.

'Oh, no,' Guy breathed as he broke into a run.

'What's wrong?' Marty shouted after him.

'Hamish!' Guy called back.

Tom and Jessica also exchanged worried glances and raced after Guy.

In the garden – Marty's prized garden – Hamish was having a great time. Marty was right. The ground was very soft. Hamish was busy digging himself a crater with his front paws. About the twentieth he'd already completed.

'Hamish!' Guy bolted across the decimated lawn. Behind him he heard Marty gasp. 'Hamish! Stop that now!'

Hamish had no intention of stopping. This was a great game. He snuffled his snout into the mammoth hole he'd just dug.

Guy, Tom and Jessica ground to a halt behind him.

'Eeuuw!' Jessica said. 'What's that?'

Hamish turned, triumphant, prize between his great slobbering jaws.

'It's a mole,' Guy said, feeling terribly faint.

'I've never seen one of those before,' she said, impressed.

'Me neither,' Tom agreed.

Marty came alongside of them, panting. The mole peered blindly at them all.

'Well,' Marty said, when he finally caught his breath. 'I've never had a problem with moles before.'

And Guy didn't like to point out that he didn't actually have a problem with moles, he had a problem with a dog who liked digging for them.

Chapter Forty

I'm in the same situation as I have been in twice already today. Big desk, big chair for the enemy. Little chair, no tea for me.

'Are you absolutely sure?' I ask.

Mr Robert Hilton of Henry, Hilton & Gambon, our family's longstanding firm of solicitors, takes off his glasses and rubs his eyes. 'If Will had still been employed by the British Television Company, then of course, you'd have been in for a large payout. Their life cover policy was very generous.'

'But because he'd left a couple of months or so earlier, I get absolutely nothing.'

Robert checks his paperwork again. 'I'm afraid that's correct.'

'Oh, God.' I grip the arms of the chair. I'd been hoping that there was still a life policy in place to bring us in some much-needed money. With neither Will nor I working since we moved to Helmshill, our savings are now non-existent. But it seems the BTC policy was truncated at the same time as his employment and, for some stupid reason, I assumed that he'd still be covered by *something*. I was wrong. Very wrong. I know full well that Will never got round to setting up a new policy. There wasn't much extra money for life insurance after we'd paid for everything else. With the two of us being able to work together to bring in a bit of money, we might just have managed. Now, with just me left as the breadwinner, a part-time job or some erratic freelance work isn't going to be anywhere near enough.

'Your husband's timing was, I'm sorry to say, most unfortunate.'

'You're telling me.'

'I'm assuming that, in time, William would have made better provision for you all . . .' His voice tails off.

Time was the one thing that my husband ran out of. And, in doing so, he's left me and the children virtually destitute. I pull myself together. That's not strictly true. We are asset rich and cash poor. As a family, we have a fortune tied up in that house, but not a bean in the bank. The place is now a millstone round my neck and it only strengthens my resolve to offload it as soon as humanly possible.

'You do get a widow's pension,' the solicitor continues. 'But I'm afraid it's not going to be enough to bring up two children on.'

He pushes a piece of paper across the desk at me and I pick it up and study the figures. 'No,' I say. 'You're right. It's not nearly enough.'

The only silver lining I can see in this is that it doesn't actually matter that Tom and Jessica can't get back into the Weston Academy, because I could never have afforded it anyway.

What am I to do? The amount of money we're going to get every month isn't even going to cover Hamish's escalating vet bills at this rate. I feel like crying, but I won't do so in front of my solicitor. I won't make my husband the bad guy in this. William would be mortified to think that he'd left us in this situation. Besides, whoever really thinks that today might be their last? He'd probably never given a thought to how we'd manage at Helmshill Grange without him. As far as Will was concerned, we were going to have a long and happy life there together. Hell's bells, I am going to cry now.

Pulling a tissue out of my handbag, I sniff into it.

My solicitor looks distraught. 'I dearly wish that I had some good news for you, Amy.'

My only hope is that I sell Helmshill Grange quickly.

'If there's anything I can do to help,' Robert says, checking his watch.

My time is up and, no doubt, I can't afford Robert's bills any more. Something he'll be well aware of.

I stand and have a last sniff. 'We'll manage,' I say. I don't know how, but that's my promise to my children. Somehow, I'll find a way and we'll manage.

Chapter Forty-One

'I feel terrible,' Guy said for the umpteenth time. 'It's entirely my fault.' And Hamish's, of course. 'Do whatever you need to fix it by next week and send me the bill.' He didn't know much about gardening, but he assumed that it would require a serious amount of new turf to cover up Hamish's mole-hunting excesses.

'Nonsense, nonsense, dear boy,' Marty said magnanimously. Guy wasn't sure he'd be quite so gracious if the boot was on the other foot.

'Please,' Guy implored. 'Whatever the cost. I'll pay the damage.'

The fact that Marty was taking the destruction of his pride and joy in his stride only served to make Guy feel worse. He didn't want this incident to put a dent in a friendship that meant so much to him and was more than happy to throw some cash at it to put it right if that's what it took.

'Accidents happen,' Marty assured him. He even tried a laugh.

'They do when Hamish is around,' Tom said solemnly.

'We can always put back the photo-shoot.' Marty's voice gave a tell-tale waver on that sentence.

Guy wanted to die. Why hadn't he realised that Hamish was more than capable of chewing through a lead? He should have put the dog on a chain – a heavy one.

'More shepherd's pie?' Gillian, however, was quite pale. The rampant remodelling of her garden had clearly hit her harder.

Both children nodded eagerly at the offer – unaware of quite the amount of havoc their dog had created this time – and were duly given extra portions of the delicious meal. Hamish had been banned to the Range Rover in disgrace. During lulls in the conversation you could hear him howling in protest.

The excellent shepherd's pie was followed by a good old English bread-and-butter pudding. But Guy had no appetite. Would it be best, he wondered, if they didn't wait around to meet the Bainbridge children and simply made their excuses and left after lunch?

The children poured thick double cream over their pudding

and tucked in. Guy smiled and ploughed in valiantly. He wished that Hamish would shut up as his constant barking only served as a reminder that he was still around and being troublesome.

What could he do to help Amy to tame this beast? He'd been a vet for years now, yet he'd never come across any animal quite so capable of creating havoc as Hamish was. Guy trawled his memory, wondering if there was some kind of doggy equivalent to Ritalin – the stuff they gave to hyperactive kids to calm them down.

Then Hamish stopped barking and Guy instinctively knew that should worry him more. And it did. There was a moment of perfect silence and then the noise of car tyres on gravel crunched through the air.

'Oh no,' he cried and, abandoning his bread-and-butter pudding, he dived out of his seat and flew to the window. He was just in time to see the Range Rover picking up speed down the slight incline of the Bainbridges' drive. 'Oh no!'

Goodness only knows how he managed it, but Hamish's bumping around in the car must have somehow disengaged the handbrake. Or maybe Guy hadn't put it on as securely as he should have. Whatever had happened, it was too late now. Out on the drive, the Range Rover was gathering pace, very quickly covering the short distance to the Bainbridges' new Mercedes. 'Stop!' Guy shouted. But it was fruitless.

Now, sitting upright in the driver's seat, paws on the steering wheel, Hamish wore a startled expression and was backing away from the windscreen. But once again, Guy was too late. Way, way too late.

The Range Rover, in slow motion, smacked straight into

the back of the Mercedes causing a loud bang, followed rapidly by a delicate tinkling of glass. The Mercedes then, with equally sedate progress, shunted straight into the front wall of the Bainbridges' elegant home.

By this time, Marty, Gill and the children had joined Guy at the window to witness the destruction of the front and rear end of the Bainbridges very new and very treasured car.

'I'm sorry,' Guy said, not daring to look at his friend. 'You won't believe how truly very sorry I am.'

He heard Marty gulp next to him. Then in a voice filled with emotion, he said, 'I *will* be sending you the bill for that one, dear boy.'

Chapter Forty-Two

It takes me five hours to reach the station at Scarsby, giving me plenty of time to think about our predicament on the train. I'm tired, weary and, again, close to tears by the time I disembark. I wish Will was here. I wish I could talk this through with him. But then if he was here we wouldn't be in this mess.

Standing there are Tom, Jessica and Guy even though it's ten o'clock at night and they've got school tomorrow. But I'm deliriously happy that they've all come to meet me, which makes me feel even more weepy. I'd expected to get a taxi back to the house and this is an unexpected and welcome treat. The children run to me and I fling my arms round them and promptly burst into tears. How on earth am I going to look after my babies properly if I can't get a grip on myself?

Guy stands by, waiting, looking sheepish.

'Thank you,' I say to him. 'It was lovely of you to come and collect me. Very kind.'

'Thought you might struggle to get a taxi at this time of night,' he says. 'Did you have a good day?'

I shake my head. 'No,' I say quietly so that the kids don't hear. 'I'll tell you about it later.'

We head towards Guy's car as I ask, 'What about you? Have you all had a good day?'

'Wonderful,' Guy says brightly. 'We've had a great day, haven't we, kids?'

'Yes,' they chorus dutifully.

'Have you both been good?'

My children nod earnestly.

'I made a new friend,' Jessica tells me excitedly. 'She's called Ellie and she's seven. She's got a pony called Snowflake and she let me have a ride.'

'Really?' I raise a questioning eyebrow at Guy and he nods.

'I'd like a pony,' Jessica announces. 'They're cool.'

Well, I think, you've got a mad dog and a serial-killer cat instead. 'No trouble with Hamish?'

'No,' Guy says, but he doesn't meet my eye. 'Not a bit.'

'He ripped up Mr and Mrs Bainbridge's best lawn,' Jessica tells me joyfully. I could have told Guy that he couldn't rely on that one to keep a secret. Her brother doesn't nickname her Blabbermouth for nothing.

'Did he now?' My eyebrow raises at Guy again.

'He just did a little mole hunting,' Guy says tightly. 'Just following his natural instincts.'

'This wasn't by any chance Marty Bainbridge, the television gardener's lawn, was it?'

'He was very understanding,' Guy says. 'No harm done.'

'I don't owe them money?'

'No, no. Not at all.'

We get to the Range Rover and, even in my tired and emotional state, I notice that the front is more crumpled than it was this morning. I stand and study it. Both headlights are smashed and there's a sizeable dent in the bumper. 'Have you had a bump?'

'Just a little one,' Guy replies. 'Nothing to worry about. We weren't in the car at the time.'

'Hamish did that too,' Jessica says with a theatrical sigh. 'He knocked the handbrake off in Guy's car and it crashed into Mr and Mrs Bainbridge's car.'

This time my eyes meet Guy's and I'm sure he can see the twinkle in mine. I can certainly see the caginess in his. 'Sounds like you made quite an impression on your play date.'

'Women,' Tom tuts. 'You weren't supposed to tell, Jessie Blabbermouth.'

'Oh.' Jessica's hand flies to her mouth as her brain kicks into gear. She stares apologetically at Guy. 'Sorry.'

He has the grace to laugh.

'I'm glad that it's not just me who can't control Hamish.'

'It is going to be my mission in life to train that dog.'

'Were the Bainbridges very cross?'

'Not about the garden, surprisingly,' Guy tells me. 'But the Mercedes crashing into the house tested their patience a little.'

'I'll bet.'

'They've invited us back to play again,' Jessica pipes up.

'As long as we don't take Hamish,' Tom adds.

Poor Hamish, I think. He only has to go and visit someone once and no one wants him back again. What am I going to do with him?

'Your day sounds as if it went as smoothly as mine,' I say to Guy with a smile. 'I hope it hasn't been too much of a pain. Don't worry, I won't ask you to babysit again. We'll be out of your hair before you know it.'

We slip into the car. Hamish is sitting in the back seat, tied firmly to the seat-belt fitting. He's drooling and the car stinks of dog. He woofs happily when he sees me. What a bloody nuisance he is.

'Amy,' Guy says softly as we sit next to each other, 'despite everything, I've really enjoyed myself today. The children are fantastic. We've all had a great time together. I'd love to do it again. And soon. Before you leave.'

With that he slides the car into gear and pulls out of the car park. Quite honestly, I'm glad that he doesn't wait for an answer as I really wouldn't know what to say.

Chapter Forty-Three

I tuck Jessica up in her bed after checking it for mouse remains and hand her the headless Bratz doll that Hamish customised. 'Sleep tight.'

'Mummy,' she says thoughtfully, as she strokes the decapitated torso. 'Guy makes a very nice daddy.'

'Does he?' Another statement I don't know how to answer. Which is just as well as my throat has closed up.

'I know that he's not a daddy, but he could be. He taught us how to skim stones and ride a pony and everything.'

'He's a very nice *uncle*,' I tell her, struggling to hold back the tears. 'That's what Guy is. A lovely uncle.'

'When he's here, I don't miss Daddy so much,' she says. My daughter slips her thumb into her mouth and, for once, I don't tell her not to. She snuggles down in her bed, contented and tired from her exciting day. I'll have a devil of a job getting her up for school in the morning, but for now I'm just glad that she's had some temporary respite from her pain.

I look in on Tom again, but he's already fast asleep, duvet thrown off, sprawled on his back, exactly like Will preferred to sleep.

Downstairs, Guy is waiting for me. 'I took the liberty of opening this,' he says, holding up a bottle of red. It's one of William's favourites and that makes me feel incredibly sad, but I say nothing.

'It's fine. Good idea.'

'Gill Bainbridge sent a portion of her wonderful shepherd's pie for you in case you hadn't eaten.'

'She can't have been too cross with you then,' I say with a wry smile.

'I think she was trying very hard not to be,' he admits. 'They're very nice people. You'll have to come and meet them. I put the shepherd's pie in the Aga earlier, so it should be ready now.'

'You'll make someone a lovely wife,' I quip and we both flush. Guy busies himself with my oven gloves. 'Where's Hamish?' I ask, to change the subject.

'Locked in the scullery.'

Then I tune into the scrabbling at the door. The handle has one of William's ties wound round it for extra security. I wonder how long it will be before Hamish can open that door by himself and then I'll have no peace at all.

I take the glass of wine that Guy has poured me and sip it. This feels very strange as this is what Will and I used to do late at night when the kids were asleep. We'd pick at a supper at the kitchen table with a good glass of red to help ease the troubles of the day and talk about nothing in particular. I can't believe that I'll never do that with him again and that so soon I'm doing it with a man I hardly know. Tears fill my eyes.

'Okay?'

Puffing out a sigh, I say, 'Not really. I've had a shitty day.'

Guy puts the steaming shepherd's pie down in front of

166

me, along with a fork and I start to tackle it. It's hot and the potato burns the roof of my mouth, but I continue eating anyway for something to do.

'I can't get a job back at my old company when I naively thought they'd hurl themselves to the floor with relief to find that I was on the market again.' I stab with the fork. 'Who was I kidding? My old boss – a guy who I really respected – treated me like a bad smell. He couldn't wait to waft me away from under his nose.'

'That's very cruel of them in the circumstances.'

I try to shrug it off. 'That's business these days. I should have known. It was stupid of me to think otherwise.' The shepherd's pie is as good as its reputation. The creamy mashed potato and rich lamb is offering up a shred of comfort, and Gillian Bainbridge is clearly a much better cook than me. Washed down with a good glass of red, it very nearly makes me feel human again – so long as I don't think too deeply about our predicament. Sniffing back a tear, I continue to tell Guy my tale of woe. 'The kids' old school won't take them back either. Which is just as well because, as it turns out, I have no money to pay for their fees.' I give up with the shepherd's pie and put my head in my hands. 'Because William had left the BTC just before he died, there's no life cover in place. Nada. Not a sausage. I've nothing but a small pension coming in.'

'Oh, Amy,' Guy says. 'I'm sorry to hear that.'

I force a smile. 'I shouldn't be telling you all this. I've offloaded more than enough on you today.'

Guy's hand covers mine. The heat of it shocks me. It burns me more fiercely than the shepherd's pie burned the roof of my mouth. 'I want to be a friend to you, Amy. A good friend.'

Pulling my hand away, I say crisply, 'You are. You know you are.' This doesn't feel right. It's as if I'm betraying William. 'But I hope you know that a friend is all you'll ever be.'

'Amy . . .'

'I'm still in love with my husband, Guy. I might be on my own now,' my voice trembles, 'but I'm not looking for anything else. I hope you don't think . . .'

'I don't think anything,' he insists. 'I just enjoy being with you and with the children. I know what it's like to be alone. If I can help . . .' Then, abruptly, Guy stands up. 'I'm sorry. All of this came out wrong. I think I'd better go.'

I take a swig of my wine and my hand's shaking. 'I think you better had.'

He goes to the door. 'Call me,' he says. 'I won't bother you any more unless you do.'

'Thank you for today,' I say. 'I really do appreciate it. And thank you from the children.'

But I think the damage has been done. Guy slams the door behind him.

I hear his car pull away and then I can't stop the tears. Does he think that I'm looking for someone else already? Is that what he wants? To get his feet under my table? Well, he might be a charmer and Jessica might think that he makes a wonderful daddy, but it's way, way too soon for me to be getting so cosy with anyone. I might have problems, lots of them, but I can cope. I can cope alone. And I will.

Chapter Forty-Four

It was a very bad idea to get drunk and phone your ex. He knew that. He knew it with every fibre of his being. Guy picked up the phone. It was an even worse idea if you were still *compos mentis* enough to realise that was what you were doing.

Despite his own misgivings, he dialled Laura's number. It was late and she'd probably be in bed. For a fleeting moment, he wondered whether she would be alone.

When he'd come back from Helmshill Grange, having made a complete fist of telling Amy that he would be there for her whatever happened in her life, he'd decided to get very, very pissed. It wasn't something that he did these days. When Laura had first left him, he'd briefly turned to drink as a way of getting a decent night's sleep, but it hadn't worked. Now he was invariably on call and, with a bottle of red wine inside you, doing a caesarean on a calving cow or delivering a lamb with a reluctance to enter the world simply wasn't an option. So the late-night drinking had long since been curtailed.

Tonight, he didn't care. The strong drink route to oblivion was a viable option. It was his assistant, Stephen, who was on call. Stephen who would deal with the varied crises of the livestock of their little part of the Yorkshire moors. Stephen who would crawl back into bed with cold hands and feet to snuggle up to his lovely young wife. That was the worst thing about being single and on call in the middle of the night. When you eventually made it home blurry eyed and freezing, there was no one there waiting for you.

He'd tried for years to pretend that it didn't really matter. Now, he had to acknowledge that it did.

It had been a very strange day in many ways. He'd done a lot of things that he hadn't ever expected to be doing – paying out for a new lawn and extensive repairs on a Mercedes being among them. But who'd have thought that he would have got on quite so well with Amy's children. Okay, her dastardly dog might have done more than enough damage to counter their excellent behaviour, but he'd really enjoyed being with them. Even more worrying, it had made him consider whether the bachelor lifestyle really suited him after all. Wasn't this a rut he'd just slipped into? Wasn't it easier to submerge himself in the world of cats, dogs and farm animals than to form meaningful relationships with human beings? Did one relationship disaster mean that he shouldn't ever try again? In trying to protect himself from hurt, had he simply denied himself the chance of happiness?

Yet look at what had happened when he'd made his first clumsy attempts to try to integrate himself into Amy's family. Complete cock-up! She'd made it perfectly clear that she didn't want him having anything more to do with her. And that was fine.

Except it wasn't really. The reason he'd thrown a passable bottle of red down his neck without tasting it was that it *did* matter to him whether he saw Amy again or not. It *did* matter that he wouldn't now be able to take the kids horse riding or hiking or to Poppy's to fill them up with calorie-laden treats and hear them laugh and squabble and tell him stories.

He should make an effort to meet someone else, think about settling down, perhaps have a few children of his own. Was it so wrong to do that by retracing old ground? Perhaps he and Laura could simply pick up where they'd left off. He'd loved her once. Loved her enough to want to make her his wife – and that hadn't happened with anyone else since. Well, that is until he'd met Amy Ashurst.

Amy still loved her husband and that was how it should be. Soon she was going to be moving back to London and out of his life. He would get over her. He was sure he would. It wasn't any use if only one of them could see that they potentially could have a great future together.

Guy sighed to himself. How long did the grieving process take? Hadn't it taken him years to get over Laura? The sound of her voice on his answerphone had still sent shards of ice to his stomach. And she hadn't died, she'd just buggered off with his best mate. When would Amy be ready to consider another relationship? Next year? The year after? Sometime maybe never. Could he ever even begin to compete with William Ashurst or his ghost?

Guy wasn't getting any younger and now that he'd had this epiphany, he wanted to take some positive steps to changing his life around. If Amy wasn't available, then he'd try his luck with someone who'd made it clear that she was.

Laura answered the phone before he had the chance to further consider the wisdom of his actions.

'Hello,' she said, sounding sleepy.

His heart flipped, spinning back five years, as he heard the familiar tones. 'I hope this isn't a bad time to call,' he said awkwardly.

'Guy?' She gave a delighted little laugh and his heart somersaulted again. 'I never thought that you'd return my call.'

And he realised that this probably wasn't the right moment to say that he never thought he would either.

Chapter Forty-Five

'Is it still the weekend?' Jessica wants to know.

'No, darling.' At least, I don't think it is.

'Are we on holiday?'

'No.'

'Then why aren't we at school?' my daughter wants to know. 'We're learning about a boy who gets his head cut off and is made into an elephant.'

'Ganesh,' my son supplies. 'We did that yonks ago.'

Jessica looks miffed that Tom is better informed than her when it comes to Hindu gods. My son comes over to the table gingerly carrying a bowl of cereal which he puts down in front of me.

'I brought you some Cocoa-pops, Mummy.'

'Thank you,' I say, and push the bowl away to join the cup of tea that Tom has previously made me.

'Hamish is hungry too,' Tom says anxiously with a glance at the dog who's flat out on the floor and currently looks like he's trying to chew off one of his own feet. 'Should I give him some breakfast?'

'I'll do it later.'

'You said that yesterday, Mummy, and I don't think that you did.' Even in this state I can see that Tom and Jessica exchange a worried glance. But there's nothing for them to worry about. Really there isn't. I'll sort it all out.

'Mummy will do it,' I insist. 'Mummy does everything.'

It's nearly noon and we're all still here in our dressing-gowns. Is that such a bad thing though? Does anyone really care? Has anyone missed us?

Actually, I think Mrs Barnsley phoned yesterday to find out why the children weren't at school, but I can't remember what I told her. Or maybe she just left a message on the answerphone. I don't know.

Jessica's hair looks like a bird's nest and I should tell her to comb it or do it for her. My own hair probably looks the same. Who cares? I'm not sure that any of us has washed either. When did I last go in the shower? Perhaps if I did, it would make me feel better.

'Mummy.' Tom interrupts my train of thought. 'No one's feeding the chickens and the sheep. Or Stephanie and Blob.'

'I'll do that later too.'

'If you tell me what to do,' my son says, 'I can do it for you.'

'There's no need, really. I'll see to it.'

Hamish starts to bark and I hear a car crunch into the

drive and it rouses me. Who would be calling here? A moment later and there's a knock at the kitchen door.

'Who can this be?'

'I'll go, Mummy,' Tom says.

'No, no.' I lift a hand and haul myself to my feet. 'Leave it to me.'

At the door there's a smartly dressed couple.

'Yes?'

'We're Mr and Mrs Johnson. We're here to look at the house,' they tell me.

My eyes widen in surprise. 'Now?'

They turn to each other for confirmation, before saying, 'The estate agent told us he'd called you yesterday to make an appointment.'

'Did he?' Funny, I have no recollection of that.

The Johnsons take in my grubby pyjamas. 'Is this a good time?'

'Perfect,' I say and let them in.

'We can come back.'

'No, no,' I assure them. 'Let's do it. I want to get this damn place sold.'

They look slightly taken aback at that. But it's the truth. The sooner I get out of here, the better.

'There are sheep in the drive,' Mr Johnson tells me.

'Really?'

'Three of them,' he says.

'That's Daphne, Doris and Delila,' Tom tells them. 'They should be in the field.'

'I'll sort it out later,' I say dismissively. 'Come in, come in.'

174

Mr and Mrs Johnson check with each other again and then step inside.

'This is the kitchen.' I wave my arm around. 'But then you can tell that. What a dump, eh?'

The Johnsons recoil slightly. 'It certainly needs a little refurbishment,' Mr Johnson ventures politely.

'Needs a bloody torch to it,' I say with a bitter laugh.

'I'm supposed to be at school,' Jessica tells Mrs Johnson. 'But I'm not.'

I look at my children and suddenly realise how scruffy they must look. As soon as the Johnsons have gone, I must do something about it.

'Come and see the living room,' I say, and usher them through the door. Every time I come in here I think I see Will lying on the sofa. Sometimes I think I could actually reach out and touch him. My arm stretches out in front of me. Then I notice what I'm doing and I blink away the image. The living room – a poor choice of name as to me it feels dead, dead, dead – is empty now. As empty as it always is. 'This has a lovely view over the garden. Marvellous. Bloody marvellous.' I just feel so exhausted, I wish they'd hurry up, buy the bloody house and bugger off.

'Are you quite all right, Mrs Ashurst?' Mrs Johnson asks.

'What?'

'You look very . . .' she searches for the right word '. . . tired.'

'Tired?' I start to laugh. Is that what I am? I laugh some more. 'Tired?' Then I sink to my knees on the living-room floor. 'Yes,' I say. Now I'm not sure if I'm laughing or crying. 'I'm so very tired.' I lie on the floor. 'I'm so sorry. I just can't do this. I really can't.' Then I curl up into a ball and I cry and cry and cry.

'Mummy.' I hear Tom's anxious voice by my ear. 'Mummy, get up.'

Mrs Johnson crouches next to him. 'I don't think that your mummy is very well, sweetheart. Is there anyone that you can ring to help?'

'Yes,' I hear Tom say. 'I'll call the vet.'

Chapter Forty-Six

'Mrs Tilsley said she'd seen you with a dark-haired woman in the front seat of your car.' Cheryl folded her arms as she delivered that nugget of information, the day's appointment book forgotten. His receptionist had redone her fake tan and, this morning, she was an alarming shade of Paris Hilton orange.

'Did she.'

'She said you were up by the Bainbridges' place.'

'Really.'

Cheryl wore a smug expression. 'I know it wasn't the lovely Mrs Ashurst because she was in London that day.'

'When you next see Mrs Tilsley,' Guy said with a smile, 'you might want to tell her to pay a visit to Ogilvy's Opticians.'

Cheryl looked at him quizzically.

'That wasn't a dark-haired woman,' he finally told her

176

with a sigh as he leaned on the desk. 'It was Amy Ashurst's dog, Hamish.'

Cheryl tutted. 'Damn,' she said. 'I thought I'd caught you out there.'

'No such luck.'

His good friend puffed unhappily.

'If Mrs Tilsley said that my date looked like a bit of a dog, it was because my date was *actually* a dog.'

'You have very little fun in your life, Guy,' Cheryl complained.

'Tell me about it.'

'Why don't I fix you up with one of my friends?'

'No, thanks.'

'It's not good for a man to live alone.' He wasn't about to confess to Cheryl that he'd recently come to that conclusion himself. It would be round Scarsby before lunchtime and he'd never be able to lift his head in Poppy's Tea Room again.

'I'm not the dating kind,' he insisted.

'That's because you don't make any effort. You could be quite presentable if only you'd shape yourself.'

Guy laughed at that. 'Is there much in the book today?' he asked, in an attempt to change the tack of the conversation and drag it firmly back to the realms of work. He'd already finished his morning calls and there'd been no emergencies as yet. But the day was still young.

'Standard stuff,' Cheryl said. 'Bitch to be spayed. Collie with an arthritic hip. Yada, yada.'

'What time's the first appointment?'

'Not until two o'clock.'

'I'll go and get a sandwich now, then I've got some stuff to sort out in the practice. I need to look at our patients too.' In the cages in the surgery there were a number of in-patients, all of whom needed his attention.

'Think about what I said about seeing one of my friends,' Cheryl said to his retreating back. 'I'm sure there'd be one or two willing ladies.'

He didn't like to tell her that he might have found a willing woman of his own. That would save for another day. For now – briefly, he knew – it would remain his little secret.

He was about to go out of the door when his mobile rang.

'Uncle Guy?' Tom's voice said. The boy sounded worried.

Guy felt his blood run cold. 'What's wrong, Tom?'

'Can you come and see Mummy please.' He sounded like he was crying. 'She's not very well.'

Chapter Forty-Seven

Guy hands me a plate of hot buttered toast and a mug of steaming tea and we sit in my draughty, depressing kitchen together.

'I don't know what happened,' I say, hanging my head. 'I lost it completely.'

'It's hardly surprising,' Guys says sympathetically.

'I can't even blame it on Hamish this time that I've lost another potential buyer for my house.' Having given Guy the customary greeting of nose in the nether regions, the dog now thumps his tail happily on the floor at the mere mention of his name. 'This one I cocked up all by myself.'

'You're being very hard on yourself, Amy.'

'Not hard enough,' I correct. 'How could I have let myself go like that? What about the kids? How can I have neglected them so badly?'

'It was for a few days,' he says. 'A minor aberration.'

As soon as Guy arrived, he took the situation in hand. The children were sent upstairs to shower and get themselves ready for school. I watched as Guy straightened Tom's collar and tenderly combed Jessica's hair and I wept.

The minute they'd left, Guy ordered me into a hot bath and told me to stay there while he made me something to eat. Now I'm dressed, hair freshly washed, and am feeling distinctly more human. I've even put on some mascara.

'The animals haven't been fed or watered either.' William must be turning in his grave to see what I've become in such a short time. I haven't nurtured his dream at all. I've just trampled all over it.

'Don't worry about the animals. It's all sorted now,' he assures me. 'They've come to no lasting harm. Though Daphne, Doris and Delila might not speak to you for a few days.'

I give a teary laugh at that. 'You're too kind to us,' I say. 'And I was horrible to you the other night after you'd done so much for me.'

'I can completely understand why,' Guy says. 'That's not what you need right now. But, if it's any consolation, it was very well intentioned.'

'I know that,' I say with a sad smile. I'm so glad that I

179

haven't messed up this friendship. Guy is the only person I have to lean on here. 'I do know that.'

'All this, it's a delayed reaction,' he tells me. 'You've been trying to cope with everything alone. That's not easy.'

'And look at the sort of job I've made of it.' I feel so ashamed of myself. I'm letting Will down. 'I'm going to call my sister and see if she'll come up here for the weekend. Serena will give me a good talking to.'

'We'll get you back on track,' Guy promises.

'What if I can never sell this place? How will I manage?'

'Maybe you could just lick a few things into shape to help you along.'

'I should do that. But I haven't a clue where to start. It just all seems so overwhelming.' The tears well up again.

'Look,' Guy says, 'this is where I *can* help. There are all kinds of grants available from the EU to help set up small-holdings. I'm sure I could get you some funding to tide you over.'

'You think you can do that?' I sip on my tea, thoughtfully. 'That really would be useful. Wouldn't the fact that the house is on the market make me ineligible for any grants?'

'You let me worry about that. I'll make the application, fill in the forms for you.'

'Thank you, Guy. I do appreciate this.'

'No one here wants to see you struggle,' Guy says. 'You just have to be a bit more open to accepting help.'

'You're so right. I should get out and integrate more. I've been receiving a regular stream of food parcels, I should go round and thank everyone. They've been so kind. We've all been living like hermits and it's not fair on the children.'

'They're really good kids, Amy. They understand. Believe me.'

I only wonder how I can make it up to them for my stupid behaviour over the last few days.

'If you're serious about getting out more, then you should come along to the village hop next weekend. Can't remember what this one's in aid of, but it's normally a pleasant evening, nothing too taxing. It will give you a chance to meet some more of the neighbours.'

'I'll think about it.'

'You should do. People would love to see you there.' Then I see him glance surreptitiously at the clock.

'Guy, I shouldn't keep you any longer. You must have work to do.'

'I have to get back for the afternoon surgery,' he admits. 'There'll no doubt be a queue of herniated hamsters and sickly snakes waiting for me.'

'It's a very good job that you do.'

'To prove that I really am a good person, I'll even take this boy with me for a few days to give you a break.' He flicks a thumb at Hamish.

'You'd do that?'

'Yes.' Guy claps his hands. 'Come on, lad,' he says to the dog, who is immediately on his feet and bouncing happily. If only I had half the energy that mutt has. 'You're going on a little holiday with your Uncle Guy.'

'I hope he doesn't get you into quite as much trouble as he did last time,' I tease.

'You must be feeling better. You're making fun of me.'

'I am. Much better.' I see Guy to the door and, as he

leaves, I reach up and give him a peck on the cheek. 'Thank you.'

'It's what friends are for, Amy.' He returns my kiss. 'Don't forget that.'

And as I wave him goodbye, I realise how much I miss a strong, caring man in my life. William is going to be a hard act to follow.

Chapter Forty-Eight

Guy pulled up outside the row of small farm cottages. He turned to Hamish. 'I have a dilemma now,' he said sternly. 'Are you going to cause more trouble if I take you with me or if I leave you in the car?'

Hamish woofed amiably.

Perhaps he ought to think about getting another dog on a permanent basis, Guy thought. It was good to have the company and made him look less mad when he was talking to himself.

After a moment's indecision. Guy tied Hamish's lead tightly to the headrest. 'Stay here. Don't move a muscle. I'll be five minutes.'

Guy jumped out of the car and knocked on the door of the tidy little home. Moments later a tall, gangling man opened the door, stooping as he did.

'Alan,' Guy said, 'I wondered if you could do me a favour?'

The man stood aside and let Guy pass.

Inside the small lounge it was like a time capsule. Crocheted lace protectors covered the arms of the chintz sofa and graced the top of the highly polished and very dated coffee-table. Alan Steadman was a widower and a retired farmhand. He lived in the same cottage he had lived in with his wife, and had maintained it meticulously ever since she'd died three years ago. Guy saw Alan every now and again at the surgery when his elderly Jack Russell, Bill, had needed some attention. Now Bill had passed on too and Alan cut a forlorn figure. Whatever time of the day, whatever season of the year, Alan could be found wearing a tweed jacket, hand-knitted waistcoat courtesy of Mrs Steadman – God rest her soul – a tie and a flat cap. He'd worked at Brindle's Farm for years and was a valued and reliable farmhand. Now he was retired and didn't quite know what to do with himself. The odd bit of gardening kept him from becoming a total recluse. Alan was a man of few words.

'What can I do for ye, Vit?' he said.

'There's a new incomer, Mrs Ashurst, living up in Helmshill Grange. She's recently lost her husband.'

Alan nodded. Nothing was news in this place.

'Can you spare a couple of hours every day to give her a hand? There are a few animals that need feeding and cleaning. Some odd jobs to get the house looking a bit better. The gate's hanging off. The garden needs tending.'

Alan nodded again.

'I'll pay you, not Mrs Ashurst. At the end of the week. Cash in hand,' Guy assured him. It was always the preferred currency round here. 'But that has to be between us.'

Alan nodded a third time.

'Can you start next week?'

'Aye, Vit.'

'Thanks, Alan. I knew that I could rely on you.'

Guy ducked as he went out of the tiny doorway. How Alan didn't have a permanent bump on the head, he didn't know.

Hamish, still sitting demurely in the car, had managed not to trash anything in his absence.

Guy smiled to himself. Hopefully, that would help Amy out. He could trust Alan to work hard at the Grange. Looking at his watch, he winced. He'd been MIA way too long. Cheryl would have his guts for garters as the waiting room would be full of restless, piddling clients – and that was just the owners. Now he really ought to head straight back to the surgery to see what was waiting for him, and later on he'd fill in those imaginary EU forms that he'd told Amy all about.

Chapter Forty-Nine

Serena is curled up in a throw on my sofa. 'It's freezing in here,' she says, rubbing her arms vigorously. This place is so different from my sister's sleek Docklands apartment. That certainly doesn't have wall-to-wall damp or a constant array of mouse innards in hidden corners.

'I know. Sorry. I need to get some logs or something organised before winter really sets in.' Another job for me to tackle. Topping up her wine I hope that, eventually, if she drinks enough she won't notice the cold.

She slugs down the wine gratefully, hugging the glass to her as if it might thaw out her fingers. 'Feels like it has already.'

'We could go back into the kitchen. The Aga keeps that warm.' Tom, Jessica and I normally huddle together round the stove in the evenings. It's not ideal though. What's the point in having an enormous house when you can't use half of it for fear of developing hypothermia?

'Don't think I could sit upright on those chairs for more than ten minutes, sis. I'm knackered. I'll need to hit my bed soon. Can your woes wait until morning?'

That makes me smile. I'd hoped that my sister would come here offering sympathy and solutions on tap. Still, she's not long arrived after a hideous six-hour drive up here from London to answer my emergency call, so I can forgive her for feeling too drained to sort out my mess of a life for me.

'I'm just glad that you're here,' I tell her truthfully.

'Sounds like the vet came to the rescue before I did.' Serena gives me a sideways glance.

'He's been brilliant,' I say with a heartfelt sigh. 'I really don't know how we would have coped without him.' For some reason, I feel self-conscious even talking about Guy Burton like this. 'He's great with the kids.'

'Hmm,' Serena says, giving me a quizzical look. 'Nothing more you'd like to tell me about this chap?'

I go and sit next to her on the sofa, snuggling into my sister and nicking a bit of the blanket. We cuddle up together, something that we used to do so often as teenagers. Then we were discussing our tortured lovelives long into the night when we should have been fast asleep, sorting out those adolescent problems that seemed so earth-shattering at the time and now seem so simple with the passing of time.

'I'm recently widowed,' I say. 'I've barely begun to grieve and yet I'm finding myself with feelings for another man.' I lean back on the sofa. 'Is that wrong?' Serena strokes my hair and I rest my head on her shoulder. 'How can I possibly feel like that? It seems like a complete betrayal of my husband. I still love William and I miss him so desperately, yet . . .' I don't know how to finish that sentence.

'And does he, this vet, feel the same way about you?'

'I think so,' I admit. 'We haven't had a direct conversation about it. Or even an indirect conversation, if I'm honest with you. The minute Guy made even the hint of an approach, it freaked me out completely.' But – and I'm too embarrassed to admit this out loud – it also made me wonder . . .

'Perhaps it *is* just too soon to be thinking about this sort of thing,' Serena advises.

'It's *definitely* too soon,' I concur. 'But that doesn't stop my brain from speculating.'

We take sips from our wine and gaze into the gloom. The electric light in here is flickering alarmingly, so I've lit a few candles instead. I'm glad of the darkness which is helping to hide my flushed cheeks.

'The thing is,' I say to my sister, 'I have been thoroughly and well loved. I know how great that feels. William, for the best part of our marriage, was a wonderful husband . . .'

'Apart from the bit where he dragged you up here kicking and screaming.'

186

'Apart from that bit,' I agree. I don't point out to Serena that I didn't actually kick and scream, that I accepted Will's dream with a fatalistic resignation. Perhaps if I'd protested more vociferously, I wouldn't be here at all. William would have hated to think that he'd made me miserable. All he wanted to do was what he thought was best for us. 'But having had a lovely husband, I think I can spot a good 'un. And I reckon that Guy Barton fits into that category.'

'Damn,' Serena says. 'Why didn't I see him first? I've not even managed to snare *one* decent husband.'

We both laugh at that. It's fair to say that the course of Serena's lovelife hasn't gone entirely smoothly. She seems only to be attracted to married men now, preferably lawyers, having worked her way through a plentiful supply of gay actors, starving artists and permanently stoned rock musicians – despite having a healthy stream of non-married, heterosexual and solvent males attracted to her.

'He seems very different to Will. I thought you liked your men well educated and erudite – not covered in dog hair.'

'I'm not thinking of him as a replacement. Not at all.'

'Then what's your problem?'

'He's become a very good friend, very quickly. Too quickly. What will people think of me?'

'It's whether *you* feel comfortable or not with it,' she tells me. 'That's all that matters.'

'I wouldn't like them to talk about me behind my back.'

'I would have thought it was that kind of place. Whatever you do, you'll be the subject of gossip. No wonder you can't wait to get away.'

'So, what shall I do?'

'Take it really slowly would be my advice.'

'There's a hop at the little village hall tomorrow night,' I say. 'Guy asked me to go along. Why don't we all go – the kids too – and you can check him out, see if this is just because my emotions are all over the place, that I'm not thinking straight. Is this just me being pathetically vulnerable?'

Panic flits across my sister's face. 'I haven't brought any party clothes.' All thoughts of my inner turmoil having been forgotten in the face of a clothing crisis.

That makes me chuckle. 'I don't think you'll need your Dior here, darling,' I tease. 'Even in your Rock and Republic jeans you'll be overdressed.'

'If you're sure.' Serena doesn't look convinced.

'I ought to go. Say hello to some of the folks in the village. I don't want to appear standoffish. They were all good enough to come to William's funeral and we've been kept in home-made pies and puddings by a variety of the village ladies ever since. My neighbours have been very considerate in small, discreet ways. Would that have happened in Notting Hill?'

'Sounds as if you might be changing your mind about moving away from here,' she notes.

'No, no,' I assure her. 'That For Sale sign is staying firmly in place. It has to. I'm just resigned to the fact that it may take longer than I hoped to sell up.' Though we do have a viewing booked for tomorrow which I'm quite hopeful about.

'And in the meantime, you thought a little fling with the vet might help to ease the pain, you minx?' My sister nudges me in the ribs.

'I've no idea what's going on in my head,' I say flatly. But a fling with Guy Burton wasn't what I'd imagined at all. Far from it. How can Serena even think that? Yet why can't I tell my sister what I really feel? Perhaps because I'm not entirely sure myself. In truth, I can't see anything beyond selling this house. Even if I was available, I don't see Guy Burton as quick-fling material. He's too loyal, too steady for that.

What am I even thinking? William has died and I want to honour his memory. He's the only man I ever loved and that's how it has to stay.

Chapter Fifty

'Get that dog away from me,' Cheryl said as Hamish inserted his nose firmly into her ample bottom and had a friendly sniff.

'Hamish!' Guy chastised. 'Don't do that. It's not the way to win a lady's heart.'

'I hope your courtship technique is better than that,' Cheryl said to him.

It wasn't as direct, Guy thought ruefully, but it might just be every bit as clumsy.

'You should shut him in the Range Rover,' the receptionist advised. 'He caused chaos last time he was here.'

The aquarium had been replaced, but Guy was sure that the rescued tropical fish weren't quite the same. One of them swam sideways now and they all seemed a lot more skittish than they'd previously been. While he wondered whether there was a prozac equivalent for fish, he decided not to tell Cheryl that Hamish was just as dangerous when left unattended in a car.

'I'll take my patients in room one and Hamish can go in the other examining room.'

Cheryl shook her head, clearly unconvinced that this was a good plan.

There wasn't a long list for the surgery this afternoon, for which Guy was relieved, as this was the one night that he wanted to get away on time to attend the shindig at the village hall. He didn't socialise enough in the village – something that was pointed out to him with monotonous regularity. He was also harbouring the hope that Amy Ashurst might turn up. Guy thought that she might have called him this week to let him know that she was planning to come along, but she hadn't. That made it more of an effort to attend by himself, but he was determined to show his face. He hoped that the good animals of Scarsby and the surrounding area didn't have other plans for his social life.

In room one, a friendly black Labrador bitch was waiting for some stitches to be put into a cut paw.

'Hello, Mrs Harris. Hello, Megan.' The black Lab wagged her tail enthusiastically. Mrs Harris contented herself with a beaming smile. 'Poor old girl,' he said to the dog, roughing her ears.

'I thought you meant me, Mr Barton.' The elderly Mrs Harris giggled girlishly.

'Never,' he said with a wink, flirting back.

His client tittered again.

'So tell me, how did Megan do this?' Guy asked her owner.

'On our walk this morning,' the woman answered. 'It was a piece of broken glass. Looks like the teenagers have been drinking in the park again. They don't think of this when they discard their bottles in the bushes.'

'Come on then, Megan,' Guy said, lifting her injured paw. 'Let me have a look at your foot.'

The dog thumped her tail on the table. She was another pooch who'd been a client for some time and was a lovely-natured dog, soft and docile. He cleaned the cut and there was barely a whimper from her. 'Good girl.'

Three stitches and the cut was sealed.

Cheryl popped her head round the door. 'Mrs Harris, I've got your husband on the phone. He's been trying to call you on your mobile, but hasn't been getting a response.'

'Oh, my battery's dead,' she said. 'I forgot to put my phone on charge yesterday. Silly me.'

'You can take the call at the desk.'

Mrs Harris looked at Guy for confirmation. 'That's fine,' he said. Some dogs needed their owners around, but Megan was so placid that she'd be fine without her.

'I'll be just a moment.' Mrs Harris hurried out of the room.

Guy went to the drawer to get some bandages to dress the wound. There were none. 'Hold on there for one second, Megan,' he said. 'Don't move a muscle.'

He went through to the stock room next door and checked in there too. None in there either. Cheryl would need to put an order in on Monday if they were running low. Slipping out into the corridor, he could see that Mrs Harris was still on the phone at reception and so he popped into room two to see if the drawers in there were better stocked.

Guy was taken aback to see that there was no sign of Hamish. He'd tied the dog to his steel operating table with his chain lead. There was no way he could have got free without knocking the table over or causing one hell of a row. Even Houdini couldn't have done that. Yet, somehow, Hamish had managed it.

'Hamish!' he whispered loudly. 'Where the hell are you?' He opened the door to the reception area until he could just see through a slit and peeped out. All looked calm out there. Cheryl would have been bringing the place down by now if Hamish had gone anywhere near her. Guy scratched his head absently. 'Hamish!'

Going through the corridor and back into room one, Guy was even more taken aback to find Hamish there. 'Oh no.'

Hamish turned and grinned at him. A drooly doggy grin. How the hell had he given him the slip like that? Did the dog have the power of transmogrification?

'Get down,' Guy hissed, but Hamish paid him no heed.

And who could blame him. The great lump of Gordon Setter was up on the table doing what dogs like to do best with the hapless Megan as his unwitting partner.

'Out of there now,' Guy said, grabbing at Hamish's joyously pumping rear end. 'At once.'

'Thank you, Cheryl,' he heard Mrs Harris's voice say. 'All he wanted was for me to collect a tea loaf from Allinson's on the way home. Silly old fool.'

Guy heard Cheryl mutter some disparaging remark about men. Time was running out. He dragged Hamish from Megan's back end, causing the dog to yelp in dismay as his impromptu nookie was forcibly curtailed.

'Get in there!' He shoved Hamish into the stock room which he realised could be an extraordinarily bad idea. But he had no choice. 'Eat anything,' he warned, 'anything at all and you are one dead dog.' Literally, if Hamish swallowed half of the stuff that they had in there.

He was trying to settle Megan down again when Mrs Harris breezed through the door.

'Oh,' she said, 'you've waited for me.'

Guy wondered if Mrs Harris had noticed that he was panting as heavily as her dog. If she had, she didn't mention it. 'I just needed to pop and get some bandages and I didn't want to leave Megan alone.'

'She'd have been fine, Mr Barton,' Mrs Harris said with a titter. 'She's such a good little girl, aren't you, Meggy-Meg.'

'I'll be just one minute,' he said as he bolted for the door.

'I need to talk to you about getting her spayed, Mr Burton,' she called after him. Mrs Harris kissed her pampered pet on the nose. 'We don't want you doing the dirty with one of those nasty doggies, do we, Poppet?'

To use another animal analogy, Guy didn't quite have the heart to tell Mrs Harris that it would be a case of shutting the stable door after the horse had bolted.

Chapter Fifty-One

I feed Daphne, Doris and Delila and the two cute goats, Stephanie and Blob, while the kids look after the chickens. The self-sufficient Milly Molly Mandy has fixed herself shrew brains for dinner.

My sister, not surprisingly, made herself scarce when animal duties were being allocated and I realise how quickly I've become accustomed to these chores even though I'm not entirely keeping on top of things. There's a growing list of stuff to do and I make a mental note of it as I head back towards the house.

'Christopher's laid an egg,' Tom tells me, wonder in his voice. My son holds out the little golden oval for inspection. It's our hens' first. And it's a perfect specimen. The egg is still warm and we handle it as if it has been produced by Fabergé rather than a once-scraggy rescue chicken.

All those weeks of squirting them with antibiotics has finally paid off and they've grown into plump, fully feathered and now, it seems, fully functioning hens. Their sight is mercifully restored and they no longer bump into trees or fences or sit staring blindly at the walls in their Ritz-style henhouse. This could be the start of a fruitful production line of fresh eggs every morning. We could sell our surplus at the gate and perhaps add a few much-needed pounds to our meagre household income.

I must be emotionally over-wrought since I feel a lump come to my throat as I cradle the egg and carry it tenderly back to the kitchen. 'We'll hold a raffle,' I say, 'to see who has this for breakfast tomorrow.'

'I don't want to eat anything that comes out of a hen's bottom,' Jessica states, nose wrinkling in distaste. 'I only like the eggs they have in Sainsbury's.'

'Where do you think they come from?'

'Not out of a hen's bottom!'

Oh dear. Our children have become very divorced from their food chain and, when we're not in such a hurry, I'm going to have to sit Jessica down and tell her the facts of life about how her food gets to her plate.

'Come on, come on. We're going to be late for the dance.' I herd my tribe together. 'Let's see what Helmshill village hall has to offer.'

The village hall is already full and bustling with activity when we arrive. Today it's decked out in its Sunday best – even though it's Saturday. It's hard not to think about the last time I was here. Then it was a subdued affair after Will's funeral and the atmosphere tonight is very different. I wish my husband was here to hold my hand. There's a party mood in the air and the disco is playing the Scissor Sisters' latest hit so that the village children can strut their stuff. Tom and Jessica eagerly go to join them.

Each of the little tables has been covered with a paper cloth and sports a bunch of rainbow-coloured helium balloons. My sister took my advice on the dress-down option, but still looks chic in her skinny jeans and black cashmere sweater. I've dragged out some black Ghost trousers that, miraculously, aren't covered with snail-trails of Hamish slobber – possibly the only pair in my wardrobe that aren't – and a silver-grey jersey wrap cardigan that only has a small hole chewed in it. Even the Jimmy Choos are back in service – having been abandoned since I realised that they're unsuitable footwear for feeding animals. Serena has persuaded me to put on my full war-paint and, for the first time in months, I'm feeling good again.

'This reminds me of a school disco,' Serena whispers to me as she hands me one of the glasses of red wine she's bought from the bar. 'I feel as if I should be sneaking in a bottle of vodka in the depths of my handbag.'

I laugh. She's right. There's a quaint, homely feel to the dance and everyone has been so welcoming. People I barely know have come up to ask how I am. Serena, who has never spoken to her next-door neighbour in two years and never intends to, views this as very suspicious.

'How can you bear it?' she wants to know.

'I think it's nice,' I tell her. 'People look out for each other here.' I know that I'll definitely miss this about my country place.

I'm watching my children groove on the dance floor. Tom has, unfortunately for him, inherited his father's appalling sense of rhythm and embarrassing-white-man style of dancing while Jessica would make any pole dancer proud. I'm smiling inanely at them when the door opens once more and Guy Barton is standing inside. A flush goes to my cheeks which has nothing to do with the red wine. He looks smarter than I've seen him before. His normally windswept hair is freshly washed and tousled. It may even be gelled. He's wearing a Ted Baker shirt and black jeans.

'Wow,' Serena says. 'I hope that's not the vet.'

'It is.'

'Damn,' she says. 'I was going to bags that one as mine.'

'You met him at the funeral.'

'He didn't look like that. Or if he did I didn't notice.'

I touch Serena's hand. 'We both had other things on our mind that day.'

'I must have loved my brother-in-law more than I realised,' she teases, 'if I was so consumed with grief to miss eying up the local beefcake.'

My sister is so outrageous. Still, she makes me giggle. 'You're terrible.'

She sips her wine as she studies him. 'I can see why he's sent your hormones into freefall. Mine are doing more than a gentle flutter.'

'He's done nothing of the sort.' She looks at me as if I'm lying.

Guy is all smiles and works his way into the room, shaking hands, clapping backs, stopping to have a word with everyone. He's clearly a popular man. At the bar, someone buys him a drink and then I realise that I'm holding my breath as Guy winds his way towards us.

Serena nudges me in the ribs as Guy comes and stands before us. 'Lovely to see you here,' he says. 'I hoped that you'd come.'

'I couldn't keep my sister away,' I tell him with a laugh.

He holds out his hand and Serena takes it. 'Guy Barton.'

'I've heard a lot about you,' she says in time-honoured fashion.

'All of it good, I hope,' he says back – also in the standard way.

That's enough flirting, I think. Serena's supposed to be sizing him up to see whether he's suitable friendship material for me. Guy turns away from her and surveys the dance floor. 'The kids look like they're having a ball.'

'They're very excited,' I tell him. 'Christopher's laid her first egg.'

'That's wonderful,' Guy says. 'A toast to Christopher.'

We all raise our glasses, clink them together and, in unison, proclaim, 'To Christopher!'

'How's Hamish faring?' I ask.

'He's great.' Guy fails to meet my eyes.

Clearly up to more mischief, then. 'Hmm?'

Guy sighs, knowing he's been rumbled. 'Your dog is currently trying to chew his way out of my utility room.'

'He'll do it,' I assure him.

'That's what I'm worried about.'

'Do you think that you could keep him tomorrow too? I have a viewing on the house at eleven. It would help my chances of a sale considerably if Hamish wasn't around.'

I see his face fall. 'Still determined to leave us?'

Nodding, I say, 'I have no choice.'

'I'm not sure that I should be doing anything to aid and abet your departure,' he says, 'but you know that I will.'

'Thanks,' I say. 'I appreciate it. Come and have dinner with us tomorrow evening, before Serena heads back to the city.'

But, before Guy can answer, the village-hall door swings open and a whoosh of cold air blasts into the room. We turn to see who's making an entrance. Standing there is an extraordinarily beautiful woman. She has a mass of black curls tumbling over her shoulders, pale skin and piercing blue eyes. The woman hasn't gone for the dress-down option. She's wearing a clinging black dress that's the height of fashion – a look that won't hit Helmshill for another five years – and black stiletto boots.

'Oh hell,' Guy says under his breath, and his mouth has fallen open as he stares at her. 'It's Laura.'

He turns to us, his attention still focused on the woman at the door. 'You'll have to excuse me, ladies.'

And before we get the chance to excuse him or not, he's off across the room and taking the woman in his arms. For some stupid reason, my heart plummets to my Jimmy Choos.

'That doesn't look good,' Serena remarks.

'No,' I agree. And I wonder exactly who the hell Laura might be.

Chapter Fifty-Two

Guy was shocked to see Laura standing right in front of him in Helmshill. 'How did you find me?' he asked.

'You're very well known in these parts,' Laura said airily. 'I stopped to ask at the local pub and they told me they

199

thought you'd be over here. I hope you don't mind me coming up unannounced like this.'

'No, no.' Although he wasn't sure if that was entirely true. Laura's appearance had certainly changed his plans for the evening. This made him sound like a teenager, but he'd rather hoped that he'd spend the rest of the dance with Amy, possibly getting the chance to hold her in his arms when the DJ played the slowies. That would have certainly started tongues wagging. Looked like that scheme was out of the window now. But probably just as well as Amy was still so keen to get away from this place. She couldn't feel the same way as he did, if she was so determined to move on. He'd had a broken heart once – courtesy of the woman now standing in front of him – and it wasn't an experience he was in a tearing hurry to repeat.

'I wanted to surprise you,' Laura said.

His ex-girlfriend had said during their initial phone call that she'd have to come up to see Helmshill for herself one day. He just hadn't expected that day to come so soon – or at all, if he was perfectly honest. Wasn't that just the sort of thing that people said? She'd called him last night and had casually asked what his plans for the weekend were. He'd said he'd be at home, but hadn't mentioned the highlight of the village dance or his plans to smooch with a certain Mrs Ashurst if she'd allow it. All Laura had said was that she hadn't much planned. Should that have given him any indication that his ex would high-tail it up here in pursuit of their former relationship? He never knew quite what women meant.

'You certainly did that,' he said.

She laughed. Then her arm slipped into his as she took in the village hall. 'So this is your idea of nightlife?'

'No,' he said. 'My idea of nightlife is a bowl of pasta and some rubbish telly. This is my annual outing.' He wondered if she could tell that he wasn't joking.

'You always hankered after the quiet life.'

'And you always hated it.'

'I've changed,' Laura said softly.

'You look even more beautiful,' Guy told her honestly. The years had been very kind to Laura. Her natural beauty was now more glossy, groomed and her glamour was certainly turning heads in Helmshill and – he suspected – everywhere else that she went. What was she really doing here, traipsing to the outer reaches of the back of beyond to look him up after all this time?

'Is your presence required here?' she enquired.

He shrugged, but he couldn't make lightness come to his shoulders. 'Not especially.'

'Can we go somewhere a little more private where we can talk? We've a lot to catch up on.'

'That we have,' Guy said. 'I'll take you back to my place.' It was with a certain trepidation that the words left his mouth.

With one glance over his shoulder, he saw Amy standing with her sister staring his way. She didn't look as happy as she had done earlier and he wondered if she was okay. Guy thought about waving to her and then changed his mind. He slipped his arm round Laura and steered her to the door and away from the village hall.

Chapter Fifty-Three

When they got back to Guy's house, Hamish was in the living room and had ripped open the feather cushions from his sofa. The dog was woofing joyously around the room trying to catch the feathers in his mouth. The remains of the cat flap that had previously been fixed firmly in the utility-room door was draped around Hamish's scruff like a necklace. Guy groaned. 'How the hell did you get out of there?' Headbutting would be his best guess. Though how Hamish had managed to fit his great bulk through that tiny hole was anyone's guess.

Hamish barked happily, wagging his tail with delight. Showing off even more now that he had an audience, the dog pounced on a pillow and engaged it in a life or death struggle, snarling as he did so. 'That's enough of that, Hamish!'

The dog shook the pillow again. Guy grabbed him by the cat-flap collar and wrenched the pillow from his mouth. Hamish looked crestfallen for a second. Then he turned his attention to Laura instead, and his wet nose went straight to her groin.

'Stop that,' Guy said, trying to pull him back. It was like trying to hold onto a Hummer.

Laura pushed the dog away as delicately as she could. 'I didn't know you had a dog.' She sounded as if she wished he hadn't.

'He's not mine,' Guy said, dragging Hamish towards the kitchen by his collar. 'I'm looking after him for a friend for a few days.'

'He seems very spirited.' For that, read 'really badly behaved', Guy thought.

The lounge looked as if an avalanche had recently passed through it. 'I'll put him in the kitchen,' Guy decided, hoping that Hamish would agree.

Laura had brought an overnight bag with her, so she'd clearly been intending to stay the night. 'My spare room hasn't been used in years,' Guy confessed, hanging on to Hamish. 'It needs a good airing.' Not to mention a good clear-out of all the junk that had found its way in there. It harboured a rowing machine that hadn't been used in anger for at least two years. 'I was going to take the sofa and give you my bed.'

They both eyed the shredded cushions. 'You can't possibly do that,' Laura said. She placed her hand on his chest and he felt his heartbeat accelerate beneath her fingers. The woman who had broken his heart reached up to stroke his face, and her lips found his. This definitely wasn't how he had foreseen this evening progressing, yet despite this, Guy felt his body respond. His ex-girlfriend's lips were warm and sweet on his and he pushed away any thoughts of how they might compare with Amy's.

'What about Craig?' he said when they parted. 'Where does he fit into this picture?'

'We're over,' she told him with a bold jut of her chin. 'History.'

Now wasn't the time to go into the whys and wherefores.

There was plenty of time to have that conversation. Besides, he had enough knowledge of his ex-best friend to imagine what might have happened.

'I'm a single woman again.'

That certainly made things more simple.

Laura glanced at the wreckage in the living room, the sofa covered in feathers, then fixed her eyes on his. 'We could share your bed.'

Would it be madness to sleep with Laura tonight? Didn't they have a lot of talking to do first before they progressed to the next stage? But then it was that sensible streak of his that invariably led to him being left alone. Amy Ashurst was recently widowed. It was obvious that she wasn't in a position to be thinking of another relationship so soon. How long was he prepared to wait around for a glimmer of hope, particularly when that hope would be dashed just as soon as she moved back to London? She hated the country. And he hated London. That was why he wondered if the situation with Laura really had changed – they'd been poles apart in what they wanted. Should that stop him, though, from enjoying her company over the weekend?

His ex-girlfriend made it clear that she wanted him and his lips still tingled from her kiss. It was a long time since he'd made love and in recent weeks it was something he'd sorely missed again. Laura was beautiful, intelligent and funny. It pained him to remember that she was also wildly sexy in bed. He didn't have a long list of conquests to compare her to, but he'd had some of the best sex of his life with this woman. At that moment, with Hamish heaving to escape, Laura pressed her body against Guy's and found his mouth again. Would it be madness to pass up on this opportunity, Guy wondered, clinging on for dear life. Or would it be madness to risk rekindling a flame that had long since died?

Chapter Fifty-Four

My sister and I sit in the kitchen nursing mugs of hot chocolate and hogging the Aga for some warmth. I still haven't come to terms with using the damn thing for cooking, but I've kind of grown to like the atmosphere it creates.

The kids, overexcited and exhausted from dancing all night, have been packed off to bed. Milly Molly Mandy is curled up on my lap, purring gently. Considering I hate cats and she hates humans, this is a major breakthrough. I give her a tentative stroke and she lets me without trying to shred my arm or draw blood from my thighs. Milly Molly Mandy settles further into my lap and, surprisingly, her warm soft body gives me comfort. There are a million surveys that will tell you that owning animals can reduce your stress levels whereas, until now, I've found that owning animals seriously contributes to mine.

'What did you think of him?'

'The vet?' Serena asks sleepily, her head resting on the chairback.

I nod.

'To quote Elvis, he's a hunk-a, hunk-a burning love.'

'Isn't he just.'

'So who's your love rival with the killer figure and expensive taste in clothes?'

'I don't know,' I shrug. 'It could be his sister or some long-lost relative. Isn't that always what happens in this kind of story. There's some terrible mix-up and she's not really a single, hot chick who's available and very willing. And, anyway, no matter who she is, she's not my love rival. There's nothing going on between Guy and me. We're just friends, that's all.' Though I confess that I did think there was a special kind of connection between us. Yet I find now that I know so little about him. He didn't even mention this woman to me. But why should he?

'You said that you'd made it very clear that you weren't interested. You can't blame him for picking up with someone else more malleable. That woman looked very into him.'

'Didn't she?'

'She didn't look like she had two kids in tow either.'

'No,' I agree. She didn't look like she was weighed down by any of the tons of baggage that I'm currently carrying. 'Guy's single and handsome. I don't know why he's on his own. Who can blame him for wanting to see an attractive woman?'

'She wasn't attractive. She was stunning.'

'Is this supposed to be making me feel better?'

'The sooner you sell this place and come home the better,' is Serena's verdict.

Home? Where exactly is that now?

'You're stuck in limbo here,' my sister points out.

206

'Well, I'm hoping that the couple coming in the morning will be keen to buy. The estate agent says they are.'

'Estate agents are not to be trusted.'

'No.' Nor, it seems, are vets. 'But let's hope he's right this time. I want this place to look as spick and span as it can.' Let's also hope that they don't notice that the cupboard doors are hanging off and that there are damp patches on the ceiling. 'Guy is keeping Hamish for the day tomorrow so that he doesn't trash the place or try to commit a sex act on my potential purchasers.'

'Why don't you just get rid of that dog?' Serena says. 'He's a smelly, slobbering pain in the neck.' A fair assessment of Hamish's charms, I think. 'He'll have to go when you head back to London.'

'I know. Believe me, I've tried. That mutt is more indestructible than The Incredibles. Besides, for some reason, the kids adore him.' I have to say that Hamish's varied adventures seem to be doing a good job of distracting them from their grief. Perhaps I have something to thank the dog for.

'Tom and Jessica look like they've settled in really well here.'

'Don't remind me. I'll feel terrible about uprooting them again.'

'You'll come back to Helmshill though.'

'William's here,' I say. 'We'll come back to visit regularly. As often as we can. We're not going to forget this place in a hurry.' Or, indeed, the people we've met here.

Chapter Fifty-Five

'I'll put the dog in the kitchen, then I'll clear up in here,' Guy said.

Laura pressed against him. Her body was soft and yielding. 'Can't we do that in the morning?'

Hamish was frantic, bucking against being restrained. Guy didn't think that he could hang onto him for very much longer.

'Let's go straight to bed.' Her fingers toyed with a button on his shirt, slowly opening it. Her hands drifted lower. Guy felt himself gulp.

'Give me five minutes to sort Hamish out,' he said, 'and then I'll be right with you.'

The dog dragged him through to the kitchen. 'I wish I'd had you as a puppy,' Guy complained. 'You'd be a damn sight better behaved than this.'

Hamish woofed happily.

'We've got company,' Guy continued. Then he lowered his voice. 'I'm about to get lucky for the first time in years. Can't you give me a break?'

The dog was completely hyperactive. He needed a good long walk to run off some energy – maybe it wouldn't do *him* any harm either. But Guy didn't somehow think that Laura would be happy with that suggestion. The thought depressed him. Back in his life for five minutes and already she was silently dictating how his life should be run.

Hamish had, indeed, chewed his way out of the utility room as Amy had predicted. The wood around the place where the cat flap had previously been bore the telltale signs of Hamish-sized teethmarks.

'You are one handful of dog,' Guy said. 'I hate to do this to you, fella, but tonight I need some peace and some privacy.'

He went to his vet's visits bag and opened it up on the table, rummaging through the contents. 'Hah!' Guy found what he was looking for. Doggy tranquillisers. 'This should put you to sleep for the rest of the night.'

Hamish looked at him reproachfully.

'If I could trust you,' Guy said, 'I wouldn't need to do this. But, frankly, you leave me no choice.'

The dog slunk to the floor.

'Don't be like that, Hamish. It's for one night.'

Hamish whined, pitifully.

'Look, what if I hide it in some cake for you?'

His tail gave a grudging thump.

Guy went to the cupboard. It wasn't a particularly well-stocked kitchen. He tried to eat his main meal at lunchtime at Poppy's Tea Room if he possibly could. There was nothing sadder than cooking for one. Inside his one cake tin, there was – fortuitously – a fruitcake. An untouched gift from the wife of an appreciative farmer. Guy couldn't quite remember what he'd done to deserve it. 'What about a bit of fruitcake?'

Hamish drooled in response. Guy peeled the greaseproof

wrapping from the cake. Surely it wouldn't be out of date. Not that a bit of stale fruitcake was likely to trouble this dog's constitution.

Crushing the tablet, Guy broke a piece off the cake and tucked it inside. 'There now,' he said, putting the doctored cake on the table. 'You won't feel a thing.'

Whereupon Hamish made a bolt for the back door. 'Oh no!' Guy shouted. 'Don't do that. You come back here.'

'Finished yet?' Laura's voice came from behind him.

'Not quite,' Guy said over his shoulder. She'd wandered into the kitchen and was standing there looking all sexy and sultry.

'Yum.' Laura's eyes alighted on the drugged fruitcake on the corner of the table. 'I *adore* home-made fruitcake.' She picked up the crumb of cake.

'No!' Guy shouted again, hand outstretched.

Too late. Laura had swallowed the cake.

She looked alarmed. 'No?'

'It's not home-made,' he said in a sickly voice. 'Shop-bought. Wouldn't like you to think otherwise.' There was no point telling her now that it contained enough dope to knock out a small horse. This was exactly the sort of thing that would cause a major argument with his ex. Laura would definitely not see the funny side of this.

'I'm so tired.' His unexpected house-guest stretched. That's a coincidence, Guy thought. The tranquilliser couldn't be working already. Laura gave an enormous yawn.

'Must be the fresh country air,' he tried.

'Mmm,' she said sleepily. And with that, his ex-fiancée slithered slowly to the kitchen floor.

He dropped to his knees next to her. Thankfully, she was still breathing. 'Laura,' he said, shaking her gently. 'Laura, wake up.'

But Laura was already in the Land of Nod, snoring contentedly.

Guy sat back on the floor with a sigh. Hamish came and leaned against him and licked his ear. That was the only action he was likely to see tonight.

'Thank a lot, mate.'

All he could do now was wait. It was his reckoning that his ex-girlfriend should sleep soundly until about noon tomorrow.

Chapter Fifty-Six

I turf our very own serial killer out into the garden, then I give the house a thorough sweep for rodent entrails, headless corpses and cat sick. With Hamish out of the way, I can at least relax a little on the unseemly rogering score.

This morning, I've been up and cleaning since dawn and I have to say that even to my beleaguered eyes, this place isn't looking half bad. I check my watch. Mr and Mrs Gerner-Bernard are due any minute now and my anxiety levels are rising.

On cue, I hear the tyres of their car crunching over my gravel drive. I take off my apron and smooth down my hair.

'You still look a state,' my sister says.

'Thank you.' I didn't sleep a wink last night – I'm not sure why. My mind was busy, worrying about everything and nothing, and it kept me tossing and turning until dawn – when I decided to get up and clean the house instead of lying there fretting.

'Let me show them round.'

'No, no. I'll do it.' By this time the Gerner-Bernards are knocking at the back door. 'I just hope that they've got pots of money and bad eyesight.'

I let my viewers in, all beaming smiles and insincere hospitality. They're a professional couple, up from London, looking for a weekend place to entertain – much like everyone who has so far come to black their noses in my house. They look like the sort of people that I used to mix with in Notting Hill and I don't know why I'm not warming to them more.

'This is lovely,' Mrs Gerner-Bernard gushes. 'It does need rather a lot of work though.'

'Don't we all.' I laugh gaily.

If they think I'm acting strangely or desperately, they don't say so.

Without further ado, I sweep them through the house, taking in the living room, the dining room and the perfectly proportioned study. Today the sun is shining. Light is streaming through the newly cleaned windows. The fading carpet is shown to its best. The gloomy wallpaper sparkles perkily.

'We could do a lot with this,' Mr Gerner-Bernard says, nodding thoughtfully as he considers the pros and cons of my property.

'I'll show you upstairs.' And I do.

All goes well. They coo appreciatively over the bedrooms which are all spic and span if not tastefully decorated. They even make the right noises about the antiquated bathrooms. Tom and Jessica's bedrooms are tidier than I've ever seen them, toys neatly lined up on shelves that have probably never been used since we arrived.

'What's the view like from here?' Mrs Gerner-Bernard wants to know.

'Beautiful,' I say automatically. We all head to the windows and stare out over the Yorkshire moors. The sun breaks through the clouds, dappling the hills with patches of brilliance. I don't think they've ever looked more green and lovely. For some reason, it almost takes my breath away.

'Oh, it is beautiful,' Mrs Gerner-Bernard cries. 'Our friends would love this. Fancy escaping smelly old London every weekend to these wonderful mountains.'

I want to tell her that they're not mountains, but I don't know what constitutes a mountain or what makes a hill. They could be mountains, for all I know. I just know them as moors and suddenly feel very possessive about them. Why is that?

Up on the moors, I can just make out the tiny figures of Tom and Jessica. To get them out of the way, I sent them out with their kite. I can see them now running happily across the hills, red kite flailing behind them. I can't hear their laughter, but I can imagine it. The sound rings in my head. Will they be able to have this freedom back in London? A cold chill clutches at my stomach. In Notting Hill they used to spend half of their lives in front of the television or their computers, or being hot-housed in various classes; now they're out here hail, rain or shine and it hadn't really occurred to me before.

'This is marvellous,' the Gerner-Bernards agree. 'What an idyllic spot. It has such potential. Can we see outside?'

Trailing down the stairs in front of them, all kinds of ridiculous emotions are swirling through my mind. This is *my* house, I think. I don't want to sell it to you. To try to regain a grip on my reality, I blank out their excited chatter.

I show them the Ritz-style henhouse and proudly point out that the chickens were rescued and that I, virtually single-handedly, nursed them back to health. At this point, their eyes glaze over. And I just manage to stop myself from telling them how thrilled I was when Christopher and his compatriots had laid three more eggs this morning – one for each of us – and how my hens are more clever than any others that have ever existed.

Daphne, Doris and Delila chew lazily at the grass. The old ladies are looking very spruce today. 'They're too old to breed,' I tell the Gerner-Bernards. 'They're just pets really.'

'We wouldn't want any of the animals,' Mrs Gerner-Bernard tells me crisply. 'We just want a country house. I don't like animals.'

'I used to feel like that,' I say – and then realise what I'm saying. I *used* to feel like that, but I don't any more. I press on with my sales pitch. 'But when you've had them, it's amazing how attached you become to them. My husband saved these from slaughter.'

I can tell from Mrs Gerner-Bernard's eyes that there would be no reprieve this time for the old dears. They'll be for the chop. Literally. The gulp that travels down my throat is involuntary. 'The goats are very cute.'

'We don't need to see anything else.' The Gerner-Bernards look to each other for confirmation. 'We'd like to put an offer in.'

'You want to buy it?'

'If the price is right. We're cash buyers, so there's no trouble with organising a mortgage.'

'Good,' I say flatly. 'That's marvellous.'

'We'd like to move quickly,' Mr Gerner-Bernard says. He's some sort of hot-shot in advertising and wears the kind of glasses that all those media types do and I've started to dislike him. Intensely. 'We'll want to get the builders in over the winter to knock the place around so that it's ready for next summer.'

'Right.' *Knock the place around*? I don't like the sound of that.

'How soon could you move out?'

'Well,' I say, taken aback at the speed that things are progressing, 'straight away. Though I hoped that we might have Christmas here.' Where did that come from? Why did I say that?

'That shouldn't be a problem,' he says, stroking his little media-type goatee. 'The paperwork's going to take several weeks, even if we push it along. Then Christmas will slow

215

things down, no doubt. I'd like you to be out of here early in the New Year. Say, the end of January.'

'Yes.' My throat is suddenly dry. 'I don't see why not.'

Mr Gerner-Bernard shakes my hand, too firmly. She does the same. 'I'm sure that the estate agent will be in touch with you this afternoon.'

They jump into their big flashy car and roar away. I stand and stare after them.

They're cash buyers and they want to put an offer in. I run my hand through my hair. It looks like I've managed to offload this place, at long last. So, the question is, why isn't my heart singing? Why aren't my feet doing a happy dance?

Chapter Fifty-Seven

'I don't love you any more,' Guy said. 'At this moment, I don't even like you.'

He lay on his back with his arms behind his head. Next to him in the bed, Laura still snored soundly.

Hamish put his head on Guy's chest. 'You'd better get off here soon before she wakes up, because then we'll both be in the doghouse. You realise that you completely spoiled my evening?'

The dog slunk off the bed and skulked out towards the kitchen to see what further havoc he could wreak in there. Hamish was certainly a character, but it was no wonder that Amy was exhausted by him. He was the most full-on dog

Guy had ever come across. Still, it made him smile to watch Hamish the penitent slink down the stairs, tail between his legs.

Guy propped himself up on his elbow and looked at his unexpected overnight companion. He hoped that the Helmshill bush telegraph didn't get hold of this. For some reason he didn't want Amy to know that Laura had spent the night here – even though nothing had happened. If he hadn't inadvertently drugged his visitor, Guy wondered what the situation would be like now. Would things be strained between them, or would the hurt and the years between them have fallen away?

Perhaps it would be better if he was up and about by the time Laura woke. It would be even more embarrassing if they were still in bed together. Particularly as Laura was still fully clothed. Guy had never liked that morning-after-the-night-before moment.

Last night he'd carried her up the stairs and had lowered her into the bed, tugging the boots from her feet, then covering her gently with the duvet. He toyed with returning to the sofa, but figured that she wouldn't actually know whether he was in the bed beside her or not.

She seemed like a stranger to him now, this woman who had shared so much of his life. How many nights had they lain naked in each other's arms – and now he couldn't even begin to think about slipping off her dress so that she'd be more comfortable. But then Laura had been so sparko that she probably could have slept on a washing line and still have had a good night's sleep.

Guy slipped quietly out of the bed. He showered and

pulled on his jeans and a sweatshirt. It wouldn't be a bad idea to clean up all of Hamish's feather mess before Laura surfaced either.

Downstairs in the living room Hamish was lying contentedly among the feathers, trying to swat them with his huge paws.

'Today,' Guy said, 'you and I are going for one *long* walk to try to get rid of some of your energy.'

Hamish woofed happily, clearly liking the sound of the day's activities. Guy fixed the dog some breakfast and then took the Hoover through to the lounge to tackle the Hamish Effect. Guy had just sucked up the last of the feathers when Laura appeared at the foot of the stairs wrapped in his dressing-gown.

'Hi,' she said sheepishly. 'You've made a great job of clearing up.'

'Thanks. Hope the Hoover didn't wake you.'

Laura shook her head, then looked as if she regretted such a vigorous movement.

'Sleep well?' Guy asked as innocently as he could manage.

'I don't know what happened,' his ex-girlfriend said. 'Suddenly, I was just *sooo* tired.' She yawned again, to emphasise the point. Laura still didn't look like she was firing on all cylinders. 'I remember seeing all those feathers and then . . . nothing else. I feel like I've got a major hangover and yet I didn't even have a drink. Did I?'

'No,' Guy confirmed. They hadn't got anywhere near that far on the socialising scale. 'The country air can sometimes

218

have a knockout effect.' He should tell her the truth – he knew that – but somehow he just couldn't quite face it.

'Did we . . . ?' Laura let the sentence trail away.

'No,' he said with a laugh. 'We didn't do that either.'

'God,' she said. 'I feel such a fool.'

'Don't,' Guy assured her. 'It's not a problem. You must have needed the rest.'

'I have been working really hard.'

'Have a shower while I fix you something to eat.' Then he remembered he had no food in other than the stale fruit-cake – which he didn't dare offer in case it triggered Laura's memory – and some equally dried-up bread. 'Actually, Plan B might be better. I need to take the pooch for a long walk. Fancy having some breakfast at a greasy spoon and taking Hamish out?'

'That sounds great.'

'I'm assuming that you're not planning to rush straight off.' There was no way he wanted his ex driving her car for a good few hours yet.

'I'd like nothing better than to hang around for the day,' Laura said. 'Are you happy for me to be here?'

'Yes,' Guy said. 'Of course.'

She smiled at him and blew him a kiss before turning to skip back up the stairs. He watched her go, his own smile failing to reach his lips. But was he really happy to have Laura come crashing back into his life?

Chapter Fifty-Eight

I hang up the phone and turn to my sister. 'It's sold,' I say.

'No way.' Serena gapes at me. 'Someone's crazy enough to take on this place?'

I nod, unable to find my voice. My legs don't feel all that steady.

'Did you get a good price?'

'Not bad.' We'll be going back to live in a shoebox in London, but that's what I want, isn't it? 'Twenty grand below asking price. But beggars can't be choosers.'

'How quickly can they move?'

'They want me out by the end of January.'

'That'll take some doing.'

'At least it means we can have Christmas here.'

Serena looks puzzled. 'Why would you want to do that? You could rent somewhere straight away. I thought you'd have been out of here like a shot.'

So did I.

'You can get all your stuff packed up, anyway,' my sister advises. 'We need to organise you a place in Town. As soon as that's sorted, you can come back. It doesn't matter if this place stays empty for a few weeks. I can help you out with the money side of things until you've got the dosh from the house. There's nothing holding you here.'

'No,' I say, somewhat morosely. 'I guess not.'

Going to the window, I stare out over the moors. What would Will think about my imminent departure? We'll all be leaving behind the house, the life that he'd come to love so quickly. 'Are you happy for me?' I ask out loud.

'Of course I am,' my sister replies, not realising that I wasn't really talking to her.

The clouds are low, sulking. I can't hear anything but the faint rustle of the trees in the breeze. How different London is going to be. I'll have to get used to the traffic noise, the fumes and the crowded places again. Out in the garden I see the children playing. There's an old horse chestnut tree down at the bottom of the garden by the orchard and someone's fixed a rope swing on there. Tom's currently dangling upside down on it, swaying backwards and forwards while Jessica runs round him in circles, arms outstretched, hair streaming behind her. They've enjoyed their time here, I'm sure, despite the tragedy. They're wrapped up against the cold and seeing them looking all pudgy and cute in their Puffa jackets makes me want to go and hug them. I know they've felt the loss of their dad keenly, but they've been so stoic about it all that it makes me so proud to be their mum.

'I should tell the children,' I say to Serena.

'You do that and I'll put the kettle on,' she says. 'We'll have a celebratory cup of tea.'

Pulling on my welly boots and my coat, I go outside. The day's fresh and dry and the chickens are out and scratching about even though they're not that keen on the cold. They need a light put in the henhouse so that it extends their day and they don't get the chicken version of SAD

– or something like that. I'll have to ask Guy for his advice and get my finger out to do it. Don't want my girls going off the boil, so to speak, now that they've finally got the hang of laying. And then I think that I won't need to worry about any of this any more as I'll be out of here quicker than you can say 'townie' and the chickens will be left to face their fate.

Daphne, Doris and Delila baaa contentedly when they see me approach. Is it me or is Delila looking a little bit fatter? Perhaps she's getting more of the hay than the others. She can be a bit of a bully when it comes to dinnertime. I can't bear the thought that the Gerner-Bernards don't want my old girls, but then it isn't so very long ago that I didn't want them either. If only they could meet them and find out their funny little ways then I'm sure the Gerner-Bernards would grow to love them too. Which stops me short. I didn't know that *I'd* grown to love them. I thought I viewed them as a pain in the neck – much like Stephanie and Blob the goats, the scatty chickens, the homicidal cat and that bloody dog.

Speaking of which, it's something of a miracle that Guy hasn't brought Hamish back by now. Either he doesn't mind having his house trashed or Hamish has already been buried under the patio. I check my watch. It's about time I called Guy to tell him that the coast's clear and that the hound from hell can come home. I also need to tell the lovely vet that we'll soon be outta this place. It's not a conversation I'm looking forward to – any more than I'm looking forward to telling the children that we're upping sticks once more.

I stop to rub the sheep's ears and when Jessica sees me she runs over to me, flinging her arms round my waist.

'I love it here,' she says breathlessly. 'Tom and me have run all over the moors with the kite. We went everywhere!'

'Tom and I,' I correct automatically.

'Tom and I,' she mimics with a pout.

We stand together quietly watching the elderly sheep as they chew the grass. The winter sun is a low, milky disc in the sky, but I can still feel its warmth on my face. Slipping my arm around my daughter's slender shoulders, I say, 'How would you feel if we went back to London?'

Jessica drills the toe of her boot into the cold ground. 'I wanted to at first,' she admits. 'I thought it was funny here. But now I like it better. Can we get some rabbits? Christopher would like that.'

'That might not be possible,' I tell her. 'Mummy has to get a job now that Daddy's gone and we can't really afford to stay here.'

'Oh.' Jessica doesn't look too impressed by that.

Tom runs over to join us. He's pink-cheeked with exertion and I can quite honestly say that he's never looked so healthy. My son leans heavily against me, already way too cool for a full-on cuddle.

'I was just asking Jessica how she'd feel if we went back to London.' Tom squirms at my side. 'What do you think?'

'Dunno,' Tom mumbles.

'If we went back to London you could see all of your old friends again,' I say brightly.

'We like our new friends,' Tom tells me.

223

'Well, your new friends could come to see us anytime they like.'

'But they wouldn't,' Tom points out. 'Like none of our old friends came here. The only person we've seen from London is Aunty Serena.'

Don't you just hate it when children come over all logical?

'Daddy's here too,' my son says softly. 'We couldn't leave Daddy behind.'

Tears spring to my eyes. 'We'll never leave Daddy behind,' I tell him. 'Wherever we go Daddy will be with us because you'll always remember the things he used to do for you, what he was like.'

'Why can't we remember him here rather than in London?'

'Oh, darling. I wish we could do that. But I've tried to get some work here and I can't find anything. This house and all of the animals cost a lot of money to look after and we just don't have it.' I hate having to put all this grown-up stuff on their shoulders, stuff that they shouldn't be having to deal with at their tender ages. 'You loved our old house too.'

'Are we going back there?'

'No. Someone else lives there now. But we'll find somewhere nice.'

'Can we stay here for the summer and then go?'

'The thing is,' I say, 'Mummy's already sold the house. Some very nice people want to buy it so that we can go home.'

Jessica bursts into tears. 'I thought this was our home.'

Not sure I've got an answer to that.

'If we go to London,' she sobs, 'can we take the chickens and the sheep and the goats too?'

'And Milly Molly Mandy,' Tom reminds her.

'And Milly Molly Mandy,' she exhorts.

'And Hamish,' my son adds. 'We couldn't leave Hamish behind. Who else would love him?'

Who else, indeed? One of the main reasons I want to go is to see the back of that bloody dog. That and the fact that we have no money, of course.

'I'm not sure that we'll have a garden,' I admit. 'We might have to move to a little flat.'

They both look aghast at that. Tom's eyes stray in tell-tale manner to the vast expanse of the rolling moors.

Crouching down, I gather them both to me. I don't care if Tom doesn't like being cuddled, cuddled he will be. 'You'll love it back in London,' I reassure them. 'You can go to your ballet dancing classes again,' I say to Jessica. 'Remember how much you missed them?'

Her lips tremble a bit at that. Then she trumps me. 'But Guy said I could learn to ride a pony here.'

Thanks for that, Guy.

'You wait and see.' I squeeze them again. 'It will be wonderful.'

Tom and Jessica look at each other dolefully.

'It will be for the best,' I tell them. 'I promise you.' And I cross my fingers, hoping that I haven't made one promise too far.

Chapter Fifty-Nine

Guy and Laura sat on a bench outside the Wayfarers Café, a well-worn eating establishment nestled at the foot of Staincliffe Cove. It was a fine day so the national park was dotted with back-packed walkers striding out. The enormous limestone cliff of Staincliffe Cove was a perfect spot to come when you wanted to leave all your troubles behind. A waterfall tumbled from the top of the cove, its water rushing down noisily to turn the wide brook at its foot into a raging torrent. The couple shaded their eyes against the low winter sun and watched as two climbers, tiny colourful dots in the distance, carefully scaled the sheer slab of rock on ropes.

Laura sighed contentedly. 'I can see the attraction of living somewhere like this.'

'Enough to give up all the bright lights of London?'

She slipped her hand self-consciously into his. 'If there was a good enough reason for me to do it.'

'This is what I always wanted,' Guy said. The magnificence of the scenery never failed to take his breath away. He loved this part of the country with a fierce passion. Guy might not have been a Yorkshireman born and bred, but he reckoned he should have been. He'd never been one for nightclubs, over-priced trendy bars or restaurants. Any day of the week, he'd swap a walk round an art gallery for this.

Laura, on the other hand, had always been a city girl. His

ex worked in marketing. She liked the art-house cinemas, the museums, the buzz, the hustle and bustle. Even if she hadn't done the dirty on him, Guy could see now that their relationship would never have lasted. One of them would always have been compromising by giving up their chosen lifestyle. He wondered whether – now that she was older, wiser and more battle-scarred – she could adapt to life in the quiet of the countryside. Perhaps this too, made it easier for him to understand why Amy was so desperate to get back to London. Some people were born with the rush of the city in their blood, while others longed for the wide open spaces.

The café, one of Guy's favourite places, was the chosen resting spot for many a hungry hiker fresh off the limestone pavements of the Cove or the Pennine Way. Today was no exception and there was an abundance of brightly coloured Goretex and muddy walking boots present.

Luckily, Laura had brought a warm sheepskin jacket with her and they were both wrapped up against the cold. She looked decidedly more chic than the usual walker in her black skinny jeans, cream cashmere sweater and designer label hiking boots. But then Guy remembered that his ex had always had the type of looks that turned heads.

Hamish lay contentedly by their feet trying to eat his own paws, but Guy knew from experience that the Setter's quiet periods were few and far between. As a precaution he'd slipped the dog's lead under one of the feet of the heavy metal table. Laura was giving the old boy a wide berth and it was plain to see that she was not a doggy lover. Still, it was nice to be out here on this glorious day with a pretty woman at his side and a faithful, if deranged, hound at his heel.

They'd both enjoyed an enormously calorific cooked breakfast of bacon, eggs and Cumberland sausages all washed down with a steaming pint-sized mug of tea. Guy was relieved to see that Laura's appetite hadn't been adversely affected by the accidental drugging incident. Even Hamish had enjoyed some tit-bits of sausage.

'If we don't walk soon,' Guy said, 'we won't want to move.'

The winter sun warmed their faces. Beside the café, the brook that fed Staincliffe Tarn burbled speedily by. A dozen or so Mallard ducks plodded hopefully round the feet of the hikers, begging for scraps. It was an idyllic spot and he wondered whether Laura's attachment to London was starting to wane.

'It's lovely here,' his ex-girlfriend said, as if she'd read his mind. Laura leaned back in her chair, crossing her feet in front of her, sweeping her long, black hair from her face. 'I could happily sit in this very spot all day.' She smiled at him and his insides flipped over just as they used to when they'd first met. That, he thought, was a bad thing. 'I'm sorry about last night. I thought . . . I hoped that things would be different between us.'

Guy shrugged, unsure what to say.

'I've thought about you a lot over the years,' she told him. 'Even when I was with . . .' She left the name of Guy's one-time best friend unsaid.

'Were you happy with Craig?' Did he really want to know that? Did he even want to be having this conversation?

'Mostly,' she nodded. 'Although sometimes I wondered whether I'd made the biggest mistake of my life.'

'Why did it all go wrong?'

'He left me for someone else,' she confessed. Laura looked at him beneath her eyelashes. 'Hurts, doesn't it?'

'Like hell,' he agreed.

'I value different things now,' she said. 'I've never met anyone else with the same qualities that you had.'

Why did he think that made him sound like a carpet rather than husband material?

'Me too,' he answered. That was true enough. Until she decided to shag his best mate, he and Laura had been very good together.

Laura's hand squeezed his. Her skin was soft and warm despite the chill in the air. 'Do you think we could make another go of it? Together?'

But before he could answer, Guy felt the table tremble. 'No!' he shouted. As always, it was too late. 'No, Hamish!'

The dog had decided that he wanted to play with the ducks. Right now. Hamish charged across the Yorkstone patio, dragging the heavy picnic table in his wake and scattering hikers still in the throes of their breakfast.

'Come back!' Guy lurched after the table, but Hamish was faster than him and already out of reach.

All squawking and flapping of wings, the ducks fled in alarm driving Hamish to a frenzy of excitement. The panicked Mallards scuttled back to the safety of the brook, not realising that a mere stretch of rushing water would never stop Hamish in his quest. Heavy wooden doors were no barrier to him, nor were heavy metal chains, nor – it seemed – was a picnic table round the neck. Barking wildly, he launched himself into the air, picnic table and all, and landed – splash – in the middle of the stream. The table sank like a stone, dragging Hamish under the water with it.

They sprinted to the side of the brook, Guy ready to dive in. 'Hamish!'

A second later, woofing with glee, Hamish surfaced minus the patio table. He doggy-paddled happily after his new, if rather reluctant playmates.

A gaggle of Goretexed people had gathered to watch. Some tried to retrieve the gritty remains of their breakfasts from the patio.

'Hamish! Come here,' Guy shouted and, surprisingly, the dog paddled to the bank. Guy grabbed him by the collar and hauled him out, whereupon Hamish decided to shake himself vigorously, showering them both with water. The dog seemed none the worse for his ordeal. 'Another lucky escape,' he said to Hamish. 'It's cats who have nine lives, you know. Not dogs.'

Hamish woofed at him.

This was going to be costly, he could tell. Providing a dozen or more new breakfasts was going to make the first dent. 'I'd better go inside and settle the bill,' Guy said, shaking his head.

'Yes,' Laura said. And he noticed that her beautiful face was looking rather stony.

Then Hamish, to show that he was fully recovered from his traumatic ordeal and was newly energised by being back on dry land, decided to treat Laura to a friendly bottom sniff.

It was just a shame that Hamish didn't know his own strength and it was just a shame that Laura was still standing quite so near to the edge of the stream.

She screamed as she hit the water, flailing about. This was an idyllic spot, a place where you could leave all your troubles behind – unless, of course, you took Hamish with you.

Chapter Sixty

I've been neglecting William and I feel terrible. Normally, I go to the cemetery two or three times a week, but my head's been in such a spin that I don't know where the time has gone. On Tuesday I'll get some flowers from Scarsby market and put them on his grave, but for today, I content myself by taking a walk to St Mary's churchyard in Helmshill to see him.

The kids are being entertained by Serena, who's currently trouncing them at *Operation* – my sister is so competitive that she can't quite grasp the concept that it isn't necessary to paste a six year old and an eight year old into the weeds. Character building, is what she'd call it.

Tom and Jessica are still subdued after my bombshell announcement, and I feel just awful about it. In fact, I feel so dreadful that I spent the morning phoning around again trying to find a job in the local area, but to no avail. No one, it seems, has any use for an ex-BTC quiz show producer, however good they might have once been. Serena is trying to jolly the children along and she's making a great job of it. Tonight, she's going home again, making the hideous journey back to London. And I'm dreading it. I'm really going to miss her. Maybe that's why I'm feeling so melancholy.

Opening the wooden lychgate, I let the quiet surround me. A grey squirrel scampers by me clutching a nut that looks like it's been liberated from a birdfeeder. I make my way to William's grave. The headstone hasn't been erected yet as I'm still waiting for the stonemason to finish it. It's my fault it's taken so long as I just couldn't decide what to put on it. How can you sum up an entire person's life in a couple of meagre lines? How will people know how much Will meant to me, to the children, from a few basic dates and details? *Beloved Husband, Loving Father*. That doesn't even begin to encompass what Will was to us. In generations to come, when I'm long gone too, will people come to weddings, christenings or funerals here at St Mary's and glance at his grave as they pass? *William Matthew Ashurst, Aged 42*. Perhaps I should have added, *Taken From Us Too Soon*. They won't know that he was a wonderful cricketer or that he made a mean spaghetti bolognese. Will they care that his favourite tipple was a good red wine or that he liked his chocolate cold, straight from the fridge? Would they smile if they knew how he used to decorate the house with black and orange balloons every Halloween and drape every surface with fake cobwebs and skeletons, playing Michael Jackson's *Thriller* at full volume to make the children shriek with excitement and fear? Would it warm their hearts to know that after more than a decade of marriage he still cuddled up on the sofa every night with his wife for a few snatched moments in their busy lives and that he never minded her putting her cold feet on him in bed? How can I reduce a full and fabulous life to a few lines chipped out on a headstone? I think my husband deserves more than that, but it can't be fitted on a small slab of stone and so *Beloved Husband, Loving Father* it is.

All that marks the grave is the patch of recently turned soil. It has sunk now so that it's nearly level with the rest of the ground. Someone has sown the top with grass seed and by next spring it will have nearly blended in with the rest of the lush, well-maintained lawn in the churchyard. How much does that say about the transience of life?

I sit on the grass next to William even though the ground is cold and damp, knees under my chin. It's still not that chilly for the time of the year, but I pull my coat around me nevertheless. Toying with the grass at my feet, I say softly, 'I miss you.'

The church here is on a small, comforting scale and it's not hard to imagine the christenings, weddings and funerals that have taken place here over the centuries that it's been standing at the centre of this community. Now it's not that well attended, but there are a few stalwarts who keep the place going. The weathered stone is well settled into its surroundings, a constant in a changing world.

'I've been so rudderless without you,' I tell my husband. 'I don't know what to do. Making all the decisions by myself seems so difficult. We're in a terrible mess financially. I've sold the house – your dream home. I don't know how I can do that to you, but I'm trying to do what's best for me and the kids even though I've no idea what that might be.' I pluck up some of the grass and let it fall through my fingers. 'Is this making any sense to you?'

I watch the squirrel charge back and forth. He's obviously found a rich stream of food from somewhere and I'll swear that he's smiling. Nothing else moves in the churchyard. One thing I must do when we get back to London is sit still and watch the world go by. But then, I think, London isn't the kind of sitting-still place.

'And I've had feelings for someone else,' I carry on. 'But you probably know that. In case you don't, it's Guy Burton. The vet. You really liked Guy and I do too. He's been a fantastic friend to me. But I think I let my emotions run away with me because I'm feeling so vulnerable. I've let him get very close to me, to the children. Perhaps that's wrong. I feel like I'm betraying you. Betraying you because I'm moving on, thinking about planning a life without you. How can I do that so soon when you were the sun, moon and stars for me?'

I want to hear Will's voice telling me that everything will be okay, that I'm doing the right thing. But nothing comes. Nothing fills the empty space.

Rain, which wasn't forecast, starts to fall. I hear it pattering on the branches of the trees before I feel it on my skin. At first it's a gentle shower and then, steadily, it grows heavier. My eyes fill with tears. And I lie down on the cold ground next to my beloved William, getting wetter and wetter, and letting the water flow down my face.

Chapter Sixty-One

'This didn't go well, did it?' Guy said.

He'd brought Laura back to his house after her accident, whereupon she'd disappeared into the shower and hadn't reappeared for a very long time. Now she was standing in the living room in clean clothes, overnight bag at her feet. The thoroughly wet designer boots were in a plastic bag.

'It was an interesting reunion.' She had the good grace to try a laugh. Something which had steadfastly eluded her as he'd dragged her out of the icy stream at Staincliffe Cove with the help of another burly hiker and in front of a sizeable crowd.

'I don't suppose that you'll be in a hurry to repeat the experience?'

'We're different people,' she said.

Guy shrugged. 'We were before we parted.'

'It was wrong of me to come here hoping to rekindle what we had. We can't do that – I know that now.' She came and put her arms around his waist. 'Can you forgive me for trying?'

He nodded even though he wasn't entirely sure of Laura's motivation for her trip back in time.

'We could be friends though,' she continued as she toyed with the fabric of his sweatshirt. 'Friends who've been through a lot together and have come out of the other side of it.'

'I'd like that,' Guy admitted.

'You can come to London once in a while to remind yourself how horrible it is. I can come and visit you once a year and you can subject me to torture by Hamish.'

At his name the dog wagged his tail. Guy had thought about locking him in the kitchen in disgrace, but it was pointless. Hamish was an untameable beast and it was wise to work round that – particularly if you wanted your doorframes or furniture to remain intact. 'The dog's going back to his owner this very afternoon.'

'That's Amy?'

'Yes.'

'You talk about her a lot.'

Did he?

'Is there something special between you?'

'No, no,' Guy said with a laugh, but his heart beat faster nonetheless. Just the thought of seeing Amy later today lifted his spirits. 'She's recently widowed. I'm just trying to take some of the pressure off her.'

'You always were very soft-hearted.'

He didn't like to tell Laura that his heart had become a lot more brittle, thanks to her. But that was all water under the bridge now.

'I should be going.' Laura closed her eyes and kissed him softly on the lips. It was a great sensation, but there was no passion behind it – for either of them.

She was a beautiful woman, no doubt. Many a man would be flattered to have her attention, but what he'd once felt for her had now gone. It had been replaced by a friendship – of sorts. He wondered whether he ever would go to London, whether Laura would ever risk the dangers of the countryside again. Perhaps not. And perhaps that was for the best.

Chapter Sixty-Two

When I get back from the cemetery, Serena is peeling potatoes. She looks up from her task. 'You look a bit teary. Okay?'

I nod. 'Just having a good old weep. Feeling sorry for myself.'

My sister puts down the spuds, wipes her hands and comes to give me a hug. 'You're doing fine.'

I'm not so sure about that.

'Get some booze down your neck.' I see that she's already cracked open a bottle to help pass the time while she does her kitchen duties. 'That will make you feel much better.'

She sploshes some wine into a glass for me and I know better than to disobey my sister, so I take a good swig. The wine's smooth, fruity and very welcome. It does actually make me feel better. 'Where are the children?'

'I pasted them at *Operation*. Oh, yes!' She punches the air in celebration of her victory, which makes me smile. 'Now they're watching a DVD. Can't remember what.'

'I'll come and do the carrots.' I open the drawer and search for another apron.

Serena goes back to the sink. 'You had two phone calls while you were out.'

I raise an eyebrow in interest. 'Yeah?'

'One from Guy saying he's going to bring Hamish back, so I asked him to stay for dinner.' She gives me a what-do-you-think-about-that look.

'And is he coming?'

'In about half an hour.'

'That's great. The children will be pleased.'

'Thought it might put a smile on your face too,' she adds.

I refuse to rise to the bait. 'Who was the other call from?'

'Gavin someone.' My heart skips a beat. There's a Post-It stuck on the fridge and she cranes her neck to read it.

'Morrison,' I supply.

'That's him.'

'What did he want?'

'Don't know. Says you're to call him.'

'Now?'

'It's as good a time as any, I guess.'

Peeling away the Post-It, I study it. This number used to be on speed dial in my mobile phone when I worked for him. I ceremoniously deleted it when he ceremoniously gave me a piss-off pill. Sitting at the kitchen table, I stare at the number. Wonder what he wants now?

Before my courage deserts me, I punch in the number. After one ring, Gavin answers.

'Hello, Gavin,' I say, trying to keep my voice steady. 'You called.'

'That arts programme we talked about,' he barks down the phone. 'We just got a green light. Looks like it's going to happen after all. You were on the top of my list. Fancy it?'

'A job?' I say.

238

He laughs at that. 'Yes, a bloody job. Told you I'd come good for you.'

Did he ever tell me that? I seem to remember that he told me in no uncertain terms to get stuffed.

'The pay's a bit worse, but the terms and conditions are the same. It'd be a one-year contract. Up for it? Or are you happy up to your knees in cow pats?'

I feel like telling him to get lost. He treated me so badly, but how can I look a gift horse in the mouth? It was me who raised the prospect of this arts programme with him. How can I turn it down now? Why would I want to? This is the confirmation I need that I am doing the right thing. I always knew that I'd have to go back to London to get into the groove again. Gavin Morrison has just thrown me a lifeline.

'Yes, yes. Of course I'm up for it.' I can't keep the glee out of my voice. 'I've sold my house. When do you want me to start?'

'I'm looking at February-ish.'

'That would suit me perfectly.'

'Good, good,' Gavin says. 'I'll get HR to send the paperwork through. Welcome back on board, Amy.'

'Thanks. Thanks so much.'

Putting down the phone, I turn to Serena. 'I've got a job,' I say. 'Back at the BTC.'

'Fabulous!' She abandons the potatoes again and comes to twirl round the kitchen with me.

'I've got a job!' My heart is pounding high in my chest. I'm back in the ranks of the employable and you just don't know how good that feels.

Chapter Sixty-Three

'I've sold the house,' I tell Guy.

He nods slowly. 'It's what you wanted.'

'Yes.'

Guy brought Hamish back about five minutes ago and already the dog is making out with one of the kitchen chairs.

'Hamish,' I shout. 'Stop trying to have carnal knowledge of the furniture.' The dog completely ignores me. I sigh to no one in particular.

The children, unlike me, are delighted to see the mutt back. Jessica has made Hamish a necklace of pink glass beads which he's wearing with pride, and he has a row of pink hairclips on his ears which he's less impressed with but he's tolerating. Tom has already slipped him three chocolate biscuits that he thinks I don't know about. They say chocolate is poisonous to dogs – chance would be a fine thing! Then I look at how happy they are with Hamish and my insides churn. They're going to hate leaving him behind.

I give Guy and my sister a glass of wine. A small one for Serena as she's driving back to Town late tonight.

'I've got the offer of a job too.' The relief I feel inside at that nearly balances out my guilt. But not quite.

'I'm pleased for you,' Guy says, but he doesn't look it.

'Thank God this place is off your hands. And you'll have

some cash coming in,' Serena says, raising her glass in the air. 'To getting back to civilisation.'

I see Guy's face darken and he doesn't join my sister's thoughtless toast. Some people love this area and wouldn't be anywhere else. She chinks her glass against mine. 'To civilisation,' I echo weakly.

'I don't want sillyvisation,' Jessica pipes up.

'*Civilisation*,' I correct.

'I don't want it,' she repeats, unabashed. 'I want to stay here.'

'Me too,' Tom adds, when no one has even asked him.

What am I to do? How am I to convince my children that they want to go to London, having spent the first few months we were in Helmshill convincing them that what they really wanted was not to be in London, but to be here? It's making my brain ache and it will take more than a glass of passable red to ease it. 'Mummy's got a job there. Aren't you happy about that? Now you'll be able to do all the things you want to do. And we can see more of Aunty Serena.'

'She won't let us win at *Operation*,' my daughter notes, then gives an exaggerated sigh which I take as the end of the conversation.

In the Aga the roast dinner is cooking and it's wafting delicious smells across the kitchen which I view as a good thing. Before I clear off I want to cook at least one decent dinner in this ruddy thing. Everything else I've tried has come out raw or burned or two days too late. We've got a leg of lamb and I hope that Daphne, Doris and Delila can't detect the scent of one of their kinfolk slowly roasting.

'The people who've bought the house seem like a nice couple,' I tell Guy brightly.

'Weekenders?'

'Yes,' I say, feeling guilty about the fact that Helmshill Grange will stand empty for the majority of the time. The estate agent said that all the locals are being priced out of the market and a lot of the houses are being sold to people for holiday homes. That makes me feel bad too. 'But I think they'll be here regularly. They loved it.'

Guy doesn't look convinced. 'They won't keep the animals then?'

'No,' I admit. I think they're planning to spend their weekends with their feet up and a bottle or two of decent Shiraz, not cleaning out henhouses and shovelling sheep shit.

'I'll try to rehome them for you,' Guy says.

'Thank you. Thank you so much.'

'It won't be easy,' he grumbles before returning to his wine. 'By the way, I've organised for someone to come up tomorrow and help you. His name's Alan Steadman. He's lived in Scarsby all his life, in one of the farm cottages. He used to work for Brindle's before he retired.'

'I really appreciate this, Guy.' I open the Aga and check that my roast will be ready before midnight. Hmm. Looking good. 'And it's all funded by this EU grant?'

'Yes,' he says.

'I'm stunned. Not that I'm complaining,' I complain, 'but it's about time I had something out of this bloody government.'

'Alan's a good man. He'll see you right. Give him a list of all the jobs that you want done.'

'It seems such a shame now that we're going.'

'My sentiments exactly,' he says.

I put my hand on Guy's shoulder. His sweatshirt feels soft and warm against my palm and very good. Quickly, I withdraw my fingers. 'You do too much for us.'

'It's my pleasure,' he says. 'The house sale will probably take a while to complete, anyway. Alan will be happy looking after the animals until you go.'

'The Gerner-Bernards might keep the animals on if Alan's here.' Well, I can still hope.

I desperately want to ask Guy about the mystery woman with the movie-star looks who shared his weekend, but I can't. I don't even feel on safe enough ground to tease him about it and he's giving nothing away. He hasn't even mentioned running out on us all at the village hall dance.

Hamish, possibly bored by the lack of romantic response from his chair, comes to lie down at Guy's feet. He huffs, puffs, snuffles and eventually settles. Jessica sidles over, leans casually on Guy's chair and then, in a series of subtle moves, manages to wriggle herself to sit on his knee.

'It's nice to have you and Hamish here,' she says to Guy. Then to me, 'Isn't it, Mummy?'

'Yes.'

He smiles self-consciously at me over my daughter's head. An outsider observer would see this as a perfect domestic scene. No one would ever guess the turmoil and heartache that lie just under the surface.

Chapter Sixty-Four

'Do you know much about pot-bellied pigs?' Cheryl asked.

'Yes. I've dated quite a few in my time,' Guy quipped.

'Very funny. Well, there's one on its way in with an upset stomach,' his receptionist told him. 'It'll be about ten minutes. I said you'd have a look at him before you go off on your rounds.' Cheryl folded her arms across her ample chest and raised her eyebrows. 'Meanwhile, you've got more than enough time to tell me about the black-haired woman who Mrs Tilsley said you had in your car at the weekend.'

Guy opened his mouth to protest. Should a man really be subjected to this, first thing on a Monday morning?

'And don't be telling me that it was Mrs Ashurst's dog again because Mrs Tilsley said that bloody hound was in the *back* seat.' Cheryl gave him a knowing look.

'This time I can't fault Mrs Tilsley's eyesight,' he acknowledged. 'It was my ex-girlfriend who came up from London for a surprise visit.'

Cheryl grinned. 'Ex-girlfriend, eh?' She rubbed her hands together in glee. 'I'll make you into a husband for someone yet. I knew you had it in you.'

'Don't get too carried away, Cheryl. It's not likely to be happening again any time soon. This was definitely a one-off.' It couldn't even be classed as a one-night stand, given the outcome.

His matchmaker looked aghast. 'You can't have scared her off in one weekend. Not even you could have done that.'

'I managed to accidentally drug her so she slept for about fourteen hours straight and then Hamish also accidentally knocked her into the stream at Staincliffe Cove. It wasn't as romantic a reunion as it might have been.'

'You really are a hopeless case,' Cheryl chided. 'Even for a bloke. What am I going to do with you? You're going to end up a sad old bachelor. The sort of man who wears socks with sandals.'

'Thank you for that charming insight into my future. Now I have so much to look forward to.'

'I hear the Widow Ashurst has sold her house.'

'What is this? Some sort of Jane Austen story? "The Widow Ashurst"?'

'Well? Has she?'

'Yes,' Guy conceded with a slumping of his shoulders. 'She has.'

Cheryl tutted. 'That's another one out of the running then.'

Guy sat down on a chair in the waiting room, beneath the new tropical fish tank, and said wistfully, 'I don't want this all round Poppy's Tea Room or on the Mrs Tilsley Telegraph, but I really liked her.'

'I know,' Cheryl said. 'I'm not stupid.'

'What do I do?' he asked, realising even as he did so that it was probably not wise to entrust his lovelife to his well-intentioned but exceptionally nosy receptionist. 'She'll be gone in a matter of weeks.'

'Then you'll have to find a way of stopping her.'

'It would take a minor miracle.'

'Despite your lack of success with the female of the species to date, I believe that you're a very enterprising man.'

'I think your faith in me might be misplaced.'

'Have you told her how you feel?'

'In a stupid, clumsy, roundabout way.'

'Not a good start.'

'No.'

'Then you must become the real-life romantic hero. Sweep her off her feet. Take her roses. Lavish her with compliments. Read her poetry.'

'Poetry? Is that what your husband does for you?'

'Don't be daft. A woman can dream though. That's what we like. All the slushy stuff.'

'I think Amy would run as fast as she could in the other direction if I turned up with roses, spouting poetry.' He also suspected that William Ashurst was the type of man who'd be comfortable reading poetry and he couldn't possibly compete with that. 'I'd rather do things my own way.'

'Stupid, clumsy and roundabout.' Cheryl raised her eyebrows again. 'And I quote . . .'

Then, thankfully, the practice door opened and in shuffled a very miserable-looking pot-bellied pig and his equally pot-bellied master. Why was it that pets always resembled their owners?

'This is Pork Chop,' the man said. 'He's a bit under the weather.'

The pig looked up and sighed heavily. Guy knew exactly how he felt.

Chapter Sixty-Five

A tall, thin man stands at my back door. He's wearing a smart tweed jacket and a tie. His flat cap is clutched in his hands and he's uncomfortable meeting my eye. Hamish is going wild behind me, eager to give our visitor a welcoming chew.

'Vit sent me,' he says curtly.

'Ah. You must be Mr Steadman.'

'Aye.'

'You won't believe how pleased I am that you've come to help.' A feeling of relief floods through me and the poor chap hasn't even done anything yet. I shove Hamish away with my leg as I hang onto his collar. 'I'm not managing terribly well.'

'Aye. Vit said.'

My new helper is a handsome man even now despite his craggy, careworn skin, and would have been quite the looker in his day, I'm sure. He's as neat as a new pin and his whole body exudes calm and containment. You can't ever imagine him being moved to get up and sing in a karaoke bar, or even frequent one. It seems as if a smile doesn't come easily to his lips, but I like Mr Steadman already. 'How do you want to play this? Shall I show you round the place? Write you a list?'

'Tell me what you want, Miss, and I'll get on.'

'I don't even know where to start. You probably know more about this stuff than I'll ever do.' How can I begin to explain that I'm exhausted by the sheer process of getting animals out of barns, feeding them, putting them in again, feeding them, getting them out, feeding them, mucking them out, putting them back in the barn so that they can poo all over where you've just cleaned?

'Leave it wi' me,' he says.

'I can hardly believe that I'm getting a grant for all this.'

Alan Steadman studies his feet. 'I'll take t'dog if it suits.'

'He's mad,' I tell Mr Steadman as I try to dislodge Hamish's nose from my anus. 'Quite mad. You'll never get anything done with Hamish around.'

'Come, boy.' Alan Steadman gives a high-pitched whistle through his teeth. Hamish, looking very confused, wriggles away from me and drops to the floor at Alan's heel.

I'm speechless.

Before I can make my brain say anything else, Mr Steadman strides away, Hamish meekly in step beside him, the picture of obedience. I must be hallucinating.

'Keep him away from the sheep,' I shout after him helpfully. 'He likes to try and roger them. And the goats too.' And anything else that breathes. Or even things that don't.

Mr Steadman raises a hand in response, but doesn't turn round. I watch them go across the yard, my uncontrollable, lunatic hound looking like he's a contestant on *One Man and His Dog*.

Guy was right – my new saviour is a man of few words, but I am eternally grateful that he's here.

Milly Molly Mandy is up on the breakfast-table, licking the remains of the milk out of my bowl of cereal. She complains with an abusive miaow when I swipe her off the table. Are the kids going to want to take the cat with us too? Of course they are. This is shaping up to be a complete nightmare. Tom and Jessica were still quiet this morning when they ate their breakfast, but I hope that they're slowly coming round to the idea of moving back to London.

I should start to think about packing some of the things away, putting our home back into boxes for the second time. The very thought fills me with dread. I'm looking forward to going back to London, getting back to work, in the thick of it again – but it terrifies me in equal measures too. I suspect I've slowed down a lot in the time I've been here. It's going to take some doing, to get back up to speed again. And, while I'm standing here vacillating and working myself up to tackle the chores ahead, I hear the crunch of tyres on the gravel so head to the door instead, glad of the distraction. I'm even more pleased – more than I should be – to see that it's Guy's car parked in the drive.

'Hi,' I say, as I go outside to greet him. It was lovely to have him here last night. He's great company. After dinner, Jessica managed to persuade him to read her a story. *Stories 4 Cool Kids* might not be his cup of tea, but he executed his reading with an impressive degree of enthusiasm. I think my daughter's now his biggest fan. Guy also helped Tom with his homework too. I don't think that my son actually needed any help, but was just feeling a bit left out. He seems to miss Will more keenly than Jess does, or perhaps he just can't hide it as well.

Guy jumps out of the Range Rover. 'Don't be mad,' he says. 'This is purely a temporary measure.'

'What?'

He goes round to the back of his vehicle and opens the door. 'Did Alan turn up this morning?' he asks over his shoulder.

'Yes. He's here now. He's somehow put a spell on Hamish and has turned him into a proper dog rather than a whirling dervish.'

'Then you won't have to do a thing,' Guy promises.

'About what?'

He lifts a small, disgruntled-looking and very wriggly pig from the boot. The vet and the pig look at me earnestly. 'About Pork Chop.'

'Oh no,' I say.

'It will be for a couple of weeks. A month max,' Guy says too quickly. 'He'll be really easy to rehome. How could anyone fail to fall in love with this adorable little thing?'

'I'm not falling in love,' I say. Then I flush. To make me feel even worse, Guy flushes too.

'He's a Vietnamese Pot-Bellied Pig,' Guy informs me. He's black with a cute little snout, chubby legs and, of course, a cuddly pot-belly. And while *I* might be resistant to the creature's obvious charms, I know two small and very impressionable young children who won't be.

'He was brought in this morning. The owner had bought him for his kids as a piglet, thinking that it wasn't going to grow any bigger. Poor old Pork Chop has spent all of his life in the tiny back yard of a terraced house, and now they're bored with looking after him.' Guy lowers the pig to the ground. 'I wish people would think more carefully before they buy these animals.'

I'm absolutely adamant that I don't want any animals, yet I seem to keep acquiring them by default.

'Alan can throw him in with the sheep,' Guy says. 'He'll be fine. No trouble.'

He looks like a whole heap of trouble to me. The pig grunts and shuffles forward to snuffle at my feet. He even gives me a little piggy smile. Oh God. The kids will adore him. My heart sinks. As if I'm not having enough trouble getting them away from here, just wait until they meet Pork Chop.

Chapter Sixty-Six

Alan Steadman has been with me for little more than a week now and already my animals, barns and home are unrecognisable. The yard is swept daily and looks like the sort of yard they have in television period dramas on a Sunday night. The goats, sheep and hens all look happier, healthier and more shiny since Alan arrived. The chickens have indoor daylight which keeps them laying vigorously instead of snoozing the day away. Pork Chop has settled in well and doesn't seem to mind all that much when Hamish, who adores the little pig, tries to mount him on a tediously regular basis.

My windows have been washed inside and out. My garden gate now has two hinges, the fence has had all its missing struts restored, the hedge has been cut, as has the grass. Surprisingly, there wasn't a previously undiscovered tribe of pygmies living in there as I suspected there might well be. In short, Alan Steadman has done all the things that my husband intended to get round to one day but never had the chance to. If Alan wasn't about thirty years older than me, craggy and had an unhealthy attachment to all things tweed, I might just consider falling in love with him. No home should be without a Mr Steadman.

The children have fallen in love with him too. Despite his curt manner, Alan has infinite patience with them and has spent hours instructing them in the ways of animal welfare. It makes me smile to see my slight daughter staggering across the yard with a big bucket of pig nuts for Pork Chop, tongue out, concentration creasing her face. Tom strides round the yard in his wellies in Alan's wake, sticking to his heel like glue and looking every inch the country boy. It's good to see.

Only Milly Molly Mandy is immune to Alan's charms. She is an unreformed character and brought in a headless blackbird this morning and dropped it on the kitchen floor with a smug feline grin to prove her point. Months ago I'd have run screaming from the room; now I just get the

dustpan and brush out and give whatever unfortunate creature that Mils has decapitated a solemn burial in the
swing-bin.

In some ways I feel terrible that Alan has done so much
to the house when it's all going to be for the benefit of the
Gerner-Bernards, but if the EU are paying for it all – which
they seem to be happy to do – then sod it. The Gerner-
Bernards might as well benefit.

I stand back and admire Helmshill Grange in the winter
sunshine as we get into the Land Rover. Everything is looking
just so spruce. Which gives me a pang of something pathetic
– irritating, as today I'm dragging the kids down to London
to look at rental flats. Hamish is fussed within an inch of
his life by Tom and Jessica.

'We'll miss you, Doggy Woggy Doodles,' my daughter coos
into Hamish's neck. I'll swear there's a tear in her eye. 'Be
good for Uncle Alan until we come back.'

Hamish sits there wagging his tail, looking like the model
pet. I am, as yet, unconvinced by this hound's personality
transplant. I view Hamish suspiciously and he wags his tail
harder. Grief. If the kids are going to miss him this much on
a day trip, what will it be like when we eventually leave him
behind?

I've got a list of flats – or apartments as they're now
called – to look at this afternoon. I haven't told either Tom
and Jessica's Headteacher or Guy of our mission today. Mrs
Barnsley doesn't know because she was very keen to tell
me last week how fabulously the children have settled into
the little school, how they're perfect students and a delight

to teach. It makes me feel like a complete heel that I'm even contemplating taking them away from her tightly run educational establishment and throwing their lot in with an inner-London primary school and not a swish public school given our reduced financial circumstances. Once I'm earning good money again, perhaps I'll be able to afford to upgrade them.

I haven't told Guy we're going to London for a whole host of different reasons that I daren't even begin to address.

But I wanted to take the children with me today so that they can gradually become accustomed to our imminent change of lifestyle and I really hope that they're going to enjoy our outing.

'We'll stay the night with Aunty Serena,' I tell the children as we pull away from Helmshill Grange, which is insisting on sparkling in the sunlight.

'Yay!' Jessica shrieks. 'This is so exciting!'

Tom, who is older and clearly wiser to my cunning plan, says nothing as I shoot off down the lane, later than I'd intended to catch the train without stressing. I want the day to run like clockwork. I want us to find a new home in London that we all love. I want my children to be bowled over by the city again and to realise that I'm doing all this for them.

The kids wave madly at the barking Hamish until he's out of sight. And I think that, very soon, we'll be doing this for real, for the very last time.

Chapter Sixty-Seven

Guy pulled up at Helmshill Grange. Alan was in the yard attending to the goats. The vet jumped out of his Range Rover and bounded over to him.

'Vit,' Alan said by way of greeting, and touched his cap.

'Hi, Alan. How's it going?'

'Alreet.'

'Looks like you've worked wonders.' Frankly, it hardly looked like the same place. Everywhere sparkled like a new pin. You could have eaten your dinner off the cobbles in the yard. And Guy wondered whether he might also get Alan to come round and do some work on his own place, which was looking more than a bit neglected these days. His house was too big for one person, but he earned a decent whack from the practice and had no idea what else to do with his money. Living in Helmshill he didn't need a designer wardrobe, flash watch or a sports car. It felt good to have the cash to be able to help Amy out while she needed it.

The upright, elderly man stood back and admired his own handiwork. 'Aye.'

It was rare these days to find someone who took so much pride in their job. 'Is Mrs Ashurst pleased?'

Alan shrugged. 'Reckon so.'

'She still thinks that it's the EU that's paying for all this?'

He nodded. 'Aye.'

'Good, good.' Not that she'd be impressed if she found out that it was him rather than the EU that was actually paying for Alan. Then Guy noticed that Amy's car wasn't in the drive. 'Isn't she around?'

'Gone to London,' Alan informed him. 'Wit bairns.'

'To London?' Funny that she hadn't mentioned it to him. Guy thought he'd sensed that there'd been a renewed closeness between them recently. Perhaps he was wrong.

'Lookin' at flats,' Alan said. 'Shall I do all this if she's off?' He waved his arm around to indicate the work he'd done in the yard and on the Grange.

'Yes,' Guy said with a sigh. 'Hopefully, it will persuade her she might like to stay.'

Alan grunted.

'Want me to take Hamish with me on my rounds? I'm on my way to Cadugan's place to geld one of their horses. They won't mind if I take him up there.' In these days of Foot and Mouth and Blue Tongue and goodness knows what else, fewer and fewer farms liked you taking a dog on your rounds with you. What was once the norm was slowly dying out. But since Robbie had gone, the truth was that Guy missed canine company during his day.

'He's a good dog.' Hamish rolled over on his back, legs akimbo, presenting his stomach for tickling. Alan rubbed it roughly with his foot. 'A bit daft like.'

'He's certainly taken to you.'

Alan shrugged off the compliment.

'Come on, Hamish. Alan's busy. You're coming with me today.' Guy slapped his hand against his thigh to encourage the dog. 'When's Mrs Ashurst back?'

'Tomorrow night.'

'Then I'll take Hamish home with me,' Guy said. 'Save you the trouble.'

To be honest Alan looked a bit disappointed about that, but Guy was sure he'd feel differently when that lethal hammer tail was thrashing round between all the neat little nick-nacks in Alan's cottage.

'Come on, dog,' Guy said. The hound stayed resolutely put at Alan's feet. Guy hauled him up by his collar, but Hamish wasn't to be budged.

'Come, boy,' Alan said and, clicking his fingers, led an adoring Hamish to the back of Guy's car. The man failed to meet Guy's eyes. Hamish jumped in, sat down and curled his tail around him.

Not only had Alan whipped Helmshill Grange into shape, but he'd done the same thing with Hamish. Guy eyed the dog warily. Long may it last.

Before he slipped into the driver's seat, Alan flicked a thumb towards the field behind them where Daphne, Doris and Delila chewed contentedly at the grass. 'One of them old ewe's with lamb.'

'No way,' Guy said.

Alan shrugged. 'Want a look?'

The vet nodded and strode back towards the field. Alan caught hold of Delila – always the more racy of the three – and Guy bent to feel her abdomen. Sure enough, it was swollen. 'She's quite a way on,' Guy said. 'Must have had a romantic interlude just before she arrived here.'

Mr Steadman nodded in agreement. 'I'd say so.'

'Well, well,' Guy said. 'Miracles do happen.' He only hoped

that he could work another one and persuade Amy not to
go back to London.

Chapter Sixty-Eight

The children are aghast. I kick the pile of post away from
the door and take the letting agent's key from the lock. He's
currently sitting downstairs in his car taking a call on his
mobile phone, so we've been sent up here alone. Just as well,
probably.

'This isn't so bad, is it?' I say.

'We can't live here, Mummy.' Jessica's face does look
horrified. Even more horrified than when we first viewed
Helmshill Grange. 'Where would Hamish go?'

Where indeed?

We ease warily into the flat and all take in the pink paisley
wallpaper in the living room – I'm sure my parents had this
in their hall in the 1970s – and the orange swirly carpet.
Not good. Clearly, Linda Barker hasn't been here with her
colour swatch recently. It might not look so bad if the paper
wasn't peeling off the walls and the carpet didn't have the
dirt from a thousand feet trodden into it. Down the hall in
the bathroom, the plastic avocado suite is so bad that it
makes me long for the ancient, chipped, clawfoot bath at
Helmshill.

'Yuck,' Jessica pronounces.

Yuck just about sums it up.

To be fair, the rooms are a good size. But that's where the compliments stop. The rent is astronomical and the area is nowhere near as nice as where we used to live. I can't believe that I'll have to pay so much to get so little. My heart sinks. How does anyone afford to rent in London unless they live ten to a room?

The flat is in an enormous block and, to be honest, the public areas don't look like they're that well maintained either. The lift isn't working and half of the lightbulbs are out on the dingy stairs. It might only be a temporary measure, but we'd be committed to a six-month lease and would I really want the kids to be here over the winter months with the dark nights? The answer is a resounding no. I'd be terrified every time they stepped out of the door. What about when I start my job – how will I manage my childcare arrangements so that I know they're well looked after when I'm not here? I give my fingernail an anxious gnaw.

Only Milly Molly Mandy would like it here as in the grubby kitchen there is plenty of evidence of rodent activity. The cat would be in seventh heaven.

'Don't worry,' I say. 'We've got plenty more to look at. I'm sure we'll find the right one.'

Tom says nothing, but he's gone very pale.

We trail back downstairs before the letting agent has finished his call. 'Like it?' he says as we approach.

'Not a lot,' I tell him. 'Let's hope the next one's better.'

'It's very difficult when you're on a budget,' he says.

What he means is a *meagre* budget and I know that I'll have to cut my cloth accordingly, but neither will I live in squalor. Helmshill Grange might have a lived-in charm, but it doesn't need to be on the condemned list. Did I really just say that?

We've now seen five equally hideous flats. It's late afternoon, pitch dark, cold, and Jessica is just starting to get whiney because she's hungry. I'm feeling pretty whiney myself. Then, when I think I can bear no more of this torture, we pull up outside Lancaster Court. It's an uninspiring block of ex-council flats, but it's in a nice area not far from our old house and the place has obviously had a bit of a face-lift recently as there are new double-glazed window units in each flat and the door of the communal entrance is freshly-painted.

Despite these small uplifting details we still climb out of the agent's car wearily. I don't know why he didn't bring us here first as this seems to be the most suitable. Probably because as well as being the most suitable, it's also the most expensive on his short list. We troop behind him into the hall that, too, has had a new coat of suitably inoffensive paint. The agent opens the door of a ground-floor apartment and we follow him inside.

'Wow,' I say. To be honest, this may be too strong an exclamation, but this late in the day and having viewed too many skanky flats, number 3 Lancaster Court has definite possibilities. Like the outside of the building, the inside has recently been freshened up. It still isn't anything to write home about, but it's a long way from being hideous. It's not damp, it's not mouse-infested, it's not in an area where I'd think my children – and me, for that matter – would be mugged for their mobile phones. Will would hate to think of me and the kids squashed in here, but I can't think of that right now. I have to cut my cloth accordingly.

Is it within our budget? Of course not. But it's not too way out of it either.

'This will just be temporary, until Mummy's working properly again. But do you think that we could live here?' I ask the kids.

'Yes,' Jessica agrees readily. I think she's so desperate to stop viewing flats and get to the sanctuary of Serena's splendid apartment that she's forgotten that she doesn't want to move from Yorkshire at all. 'Hamish would like it here.'

'He'd love it,' I assure her. 'There's a little park just across the road where we could walk him.'

'Ah,' the agent says. 'One slight snag with that. The landlord doesn't allow pets – other than goldfish.'

I can see that Hamish would be considerably more trouble than a goldfish. Damn. I want this place. It's the only flat we've seen that's even remotely suitable for our pocket. What am I to do?

'Go and choose which bedroom you think you'd like,' I say to the children, and Jessica – always the wily one – skips off to bags the best one. Tom shuffles his feet along the shiny laminate floor in her wake. My son is worryingly quiet.

When the children are safely out of earshot, I lower my voice and say conspiratorially, 'I'm not actually planning on bringing our dog here. But my children don't know this yet. I'd be grateful if you didn't mention it.'

'Ah,' he says, tapping the side of his nose. 'Mum's the word.'

Mum's the bitch, I think, feeling dreadful at my deceit. Despite that, I ask, 'Where do I sign?'

Chapter Sixty-Nine

Guy pulled into Cadugan's yard and was met by their efficient nineteen-year-old stable girl, Jade. She flushed as he got out of the car to greet her as she always did, which Guy thought might mean that she had a crush on him. Cheryl would know if it was that or if she was just a shy teenager. If she wasn't less than half his age, he could have been interested. She was certainly a fine-looking girl. Hamish clearly thought so too, and the minute he was out of the Range Rover, he charged at her, drowning the poor thing in slobber and canine affection. So much for Alan's calming influence. The effect seemed to disappear the minute the saintly Mr Steadman was out of view.

The wind whipped over the moors, scudding the clouds across the blue sky. Jade brushed the hair from her eyes and tried to retie it with a scrunchy. In doing so, she dropped the scrap of pink material on the floor whereupon Hamish paid her the ultimate compliment of eating it.

'I'm sorry,' Guy said. 'Let me give you the money to get another one.'

'No, no.' Jade tried a laugh. 'It doesn't matter.'

'I'm afraid he's a bit boisterous.' In other words, completely out of control. 'I'm on a tight schedule today. Want to take me up to see the horse and I'll get on with the job.'

They walked together through the yard to the far end and then into the tidy stables where Cadugan's fine range of horses were housed. Guy knew them all by name now and he patted the ones who had their noses stuck over the stable doors, murmuring low greetings as he went.

They stopped at the last stall. 'This is Ladies' Knight,' Jade said. She stroked the horses. 'You're a good lad, aren't you?'

In the stall, a fine young stallion stood, pawing the ground nervously. He was a year old and rich chestnut in colour.

'He's a fine creature,' Guy agreed. He patted the horse, letting it get to know him. 'Let's do it,' he said. Then Guy washed his hands under the nearby cold tap and dried them off, before sedating the horse with a hefty belt of anaesthetic straight into his jugular vein. It was wicked stuff which immobilised the standing horse enough for it to be operated on. A few drops of the drug would be enough to knock a man out permanently – and that was why Guy always had to carry an antidote to the powerful sedative in his visits bag, in case there was ever an accident and he somehow managed to inject himself.

Then it was time to wash and disinfect the gelding's scrotum, never his favourite job. Not surprisingly, a skittish horse could still kick out now and do Guy's own goolies a severe mischief.

Jade held the other end of Ladies' Knight and cooed soothingly at him to calm him down. Guy gave the horse a local anaesthetic and then made a bold incision through the skin to each testicle. It was times like this when he wondered why he hadn't become an accountant or a lawyer. What sane person would want to spend their days up to their elbows in horses' knackers? There had to be better ways to earn a living.

He then removed the testicles with an instrument that was, quite rightly to his mind, called an emasculator. For some reason, Guy always gave a sympathetic wince as he clamped down. It seemed a shame that Ladies' Knight's stud days were over before they'd even started. The testicles were thrown in a bucket for disposal. He gave the horse a pat on the rump for being well behaved. 'Brave lad,' he said.

Even after all these years, it made Guy shudder to geld a horse. There was no way that he'd ever be able to consider a vasectomy.

'It's down to you now, Jade,' Guy said as he finished up. 'The wound needs to be kept clean for the next ten days. Get Mr Cadugan to give me a call if there are any problems.'

'Right, Vet.'

'Come on, Hamish.' He whistled to the dog who was messing around by the bucket of testicles. 'Come away.'

He opened the back door of the Range Rover and Hamish hopped in.

'Dog looks a bit wobbly on his back legs,' Jade noted.

Guy shook his head. 'This animal is always up to some sort of trouble.' He got into the car. 'See you next time, Jade.'

She waved him away and Guy set off winding through the narrow lanes back towards Scarsby and his afternoon surgery. He turned the radio up and whistled tunelessly along as he drove. It was a fine day. No rain. Blue skies. Air cold and crisp. 'What a day, boy, eh?'

He might have expected that to elicit a bark from Hamish,

but there was no response. Guy flicked a look in his rearview mirror. All he could see was Hamish's four legs sticking up rigidly in the air. From all his years of veterinary experience, he could tell immediately that was not a good thing.

Guy pulled up sharply at the side of the road and sprinted to the boot of the car, grabbing his visits bag. He yanked open the back door. Hamish was still immobilised, legs akimbo, eyes glazed, tongue lolling. It looked as if he'd had some kind of seizure. Guy's phone rang. Bad, bad timing. He was tempted to let it go to voicemail, but you never knew what might be urgent in this game. 'Guy Burton,' he snapped as he answered.

'It's Jade,' the girl on the other end of the line said. 'Ladies' Knight's testicles have gone from the bucket.'

So that was what was wrong with Hamish. He must have scoffed the horse's testicles, and the anaesthetic in them had been enough to knock him out. Good Lord, Hamish could have eaten enough for it to prove fatal. 'Thanks, Jade. You're a lifesaver.'

Without further hesitation, Guy loaded a syringe with the antidote and injected Hamish. Minutes later, Hamish gave a slurred bark and gazed drunkenly at him.

Guy sighed with relief. 'That was a close call, Doggers. Don't ever do that to me again.' The dog turned and nuzzled his muzzle into the vet's hand. 'You are a walking disaster, Hamish. Did anyone ever tell you that?'

Hamish woofed happily, still sounding inebriated.

Guy had never wanted a brandy so badly. How could he have forgiven himself if anything had happened to Hamish? That would have been a great way to woo a woman, to kill her dog. Even Cheryl wouldn't believe that one as a court-ship move.

Chapter Seventy

Serena has moved into her spare bedroom for the night to accommodate us *en famille*. There's a single inflatable mattress on the floor which she's currently blowing up with the help of her Nicky Clarke hairdryer. The room is cramped, with her state-of-the art and incredibly expensive vibro-gym taking up most of the space.

My sister has kindly vacated her double bed so that Tom, Jessica and myself can all squeeze into it. Already it's clear that we couldn't stay here for more than a night or two. It's too much of an inconvenience for her. This is an apartment definitely designed for solo living. We'll have to go straight from Helmshill Grange to our new flat whether we want to or not.

'Are you sure you're doing the right thing?' Serena whispers to me while I busy myself putting a clean pillowcase on her pillow.

I check that the children are still riveted to her 42-inch plasma television and Wii. They are. 'It's not exactly salu-brious,' I tell her, lowering my own voice too, 'but it's not that bad either. It will get us back to London.'

'And that's still what you want?'

I look up. 'Why wouldn't it be?'

She shrugs. 'I don't know. I just thought the country life might be suiting you. You don't look too bad on it.'

I'm not exactly sporting rosy red cheeks as plump as apples, but perhaps I'm not looking quite as gaunt as I did after Will died. Whether the country air suits me or not, needs must. 'I have to work, Serena. This is the only offer of a job I've had. I've drawn a big fat nada round Helmshill. Jobs are few and far between even in Scarsby, unless I want to become a waitress in Poppy's Tea Room.'

'There are worse career moves.'

Folding my arms over the pillow, I say, 'This isn't like you. I thought you wanted me back here in the land of the living. I thought you'd be eager to push me up the corporate ladder again.'

'It's not all about work, is it?' she replies with an uncharacteristic lack of ambition. 'Look at this place. It's a shoebox – a nice shoebox – but the majority of my income goes in keeping its tiny roof above my head. That's madness. Isn't quality of life more important?'

'Now you're sounding like Will.'

Serena flops down onto the bed. 'Perhaps he had a point. I'm in the office at six in the morning, rarely home before eight – except when my sis is visiting – and what do I get for it? Sod all.'

'Apart from an enormous salary.'

'There are only so many pairs of shoes that I can buy, Amy.'

Going over to the vast expanse of picture window, I stare out. There's nothing but concrete, steel and glass. It's an attractive manmade landscape, but it can't compete with the

Yorkshire Moors. Even I can see that. I can't spot a blade of grass or a plant anywhere. Despite the double-glazing, I can hear the hum of the traffic a dozen floors below us, punctuated by the occasional irate and blaring horn. How different it all seems to the peace and quiet of Helmshill. This, that was so familiar to me, now seems so alien. I shake my head, clearing it of the thought.

'I can't back out now,' I tell her as I turn away from the window, 'even if I wanted to. The house has been sold. I can't let the Gerner-Bernards down. I hate people who do that. Plus I've just signed a six-month lease on the flat, starting from the end of January.' I've even given the letting agent a hefty deposit to secure it as he assured me that the 'desirable' Lancaster Court apartment wouldn't stay on the market for long. Of course, I bought right into his spiel. Nothing on earth could have persuaded me to spend another depressing day looking at over-priced dumps. I deftly skipped over the clause that stated in bold letters NO PETS ALLOWED. 'We'll have Christmas at Helmshill Grange and then we're out of there in the New Year. I'm sure this is the best thing to do for the children.'

My sister looks unconvinced and that unnerves me. 'And what about Guy?'

I shrug. 'What about him?'

'One thing I've learned from my extensive loveless years on this earth is that good men are hard to find.'

'I thought the phrase was "hard men are good to find"?'

'That too,' Serena grins. She secures the valve on her blow-up bed and winds the flex round her hairdryer. 'I'm being serious here. You like him. He likes you. Maybe more.'

I hold up a hand. 'It's way, way too soon.'

'It's too soon *now*,' she agrees. 'What I don't want is you turning around in five years' time and thinking it's too late.'

'I'm dreading telling him,' I admit. 'I don't know why that is.'

'You're my sister,' she says, 'and I love you. But sometimes you can be very thick.'

'Guy will understand why I'm doing this. I'm sure he will. We both have to do what's right for now and not think about what might or might not happen in the future.'

And I only hope that I'm right.

Chapter Seventy-One

The next afternoon, the children say nothing as we drive from the station back to Helmshill Grange, which I view as a bad thing. The excitement of seeing their favourite aunt has long since worn off during the tedious train journey. The sun is setting on the day and the landscape looks mellow and sleepy. We're the only car on the road as we slowly wind our way home. The only noise is the whoosh of the tyres on the tarmac.

I spent the morning negotiating to have the children taken on by the local school nearest to our new flat. It's a long way from the Weston Academy for Children with Rich Parents. Tom and Jessica's new primary school is a vast, sprawling block of 1960s concrete, with a million children of a hundred different nationalities – not quite on the scale of the homely, cottage style of St Mary's. Despite that, I had to beg for a place. It makes me go cold at the thought of sending them in there alone every day. But the Headteacher at Queensway seemed straightforward and sensible enough, if not quite as forceful and in control as Mrs Barnsley. They say that you shouldn't judge a book by its cover and although Queensway is a hideously battered old tome, the results there are good and my children are accustomed to working hard at school. Plus I have to look at this as a short-term measure. It won't be for ever. Once the coffers are full again we can move from the flat to a more salubrious house and the children can go to a more salubrious school.

Guy's car is in our drive as we pull in and my ridiculously impressionable and romantic heart skips a beat. I do wish that it wouldn't do that, but despite what my head thinks, my heart seems to feel differently.

As the kids barrel out of the car, I can see that Alan is finishing sweeping the yard and our friendly vet is gently escorting Delila and her cohorts into the barn for the night. 'Hi,' he says as I approach. 'Can I be the first to congratulate you on your impending baby?'

I look at him, puzzled.

'Delila,' he says. 'Looks like she had a little romantic dalliance just before she came here.'

'She's having a baby?'

Guy nods.

'Are you sure?' Then I realise that he's a vet and he probably is. 'But I thought she was too old and knackered.' Much like myself.

'Miracles can happen,' he tells me with a shrug. 'I can't believe we didn't spot it before. She's due very soon.'

I wonder what will happen to Delila and her baby when the Gerner-Bernards take over this place and I have to get rid of all the animals. I should be delighted for the old girl – Will, I know, would be doing a proud-parent happy dance – but it just seems like one more problem and I sigh out loud without really meaning to.

'You sound weary,' Guy says. 'Long day?'

'We've been down to London.'

'Alan told me.' He leans on the barn door. 'Successful?'

'I've taken out a lease on a flat,' I tell him starkly. 'From the end of January.'

He nods, but says nothing. My mad dog weaves his way across the yard and I feel a pang of guilt.

'Has Hamish been good?'

'Marvellous,' he says.

'No problems?'

He shakes his head a bit too vehemently for my liking. 'None at all.'

'He looks a bit drunk.'

'Does he?' The hound is definitely unsteady on his legs. 'Can't think why.'

My children hurl themselves at the dog and knock him flat to the ground. Makes a change for it to be that way round.

'Alan will sort him out,' I say with a shake of my head. 'Alan will sort everything out. I'm so grateful to you for fixing me up with this grant. When does it run out?'

Guy avoids my eyes. 'It should see you up until you leave.'

'Fabulous. It's been such a relief.'

'Good. Good. I hoped it would be.'

And then, I don't know why, but it suddenly hits me. 'Which agency did you say it came from again?'

'Er . . .' Guy says. 'Can't quite remember. Would have to look at the paperwork. Brain like a sieve.'

Something in his tone sets alarm bells ringing louder in my head. My sister's right. I *am* thick. Folding my arms, I study the vet intently. 'It isn't the government who's paying for Alan's work here, is it?'

'Er . . .' he says again, glancing round to see if there's an escape route. There isn't.

'You're paying for all this.' I wave my arm around the spick and span yard, take in my spick and span house.

'I'm just helping out.'

'Oh, Guy,' I say. 'You can't do this for us. *Why* would you do this for us?'

'I wanted to,' he answers flatly. 'I could see that you were struggling alone. It helps Alan out too. He's been bored out of his head since he's been on his own and retired.'

'How could you lie to me so convincingly?' I ask.

'I knew that you wouldn't accept my help or my money if I offered it straight out.'

'Am I so stubborn?'

He nods at me.

'You're such a good fibber,' I complain. 'I bet you're not even a real bloody vet.'

We both laugh at that and it breaks the tension.

'Why?' I ask again. 'Why did you do it?

This time Guy meets my eyes and his stare makes my

272

mouth go dry and my throat constrict. 'Because I hoped it would make you stay here.'

And there's nothing I can say to that.

Chapter Seventy-Two

I don't know where the time goes, but Christmas is upon us before I've had time to blink. It's Christmas Eve and the children and I are decorating the tree. Alan has been to one of his friends' farms and has brought us the most fabulous specimen of blue spruce which is currently filling one corner of the living room, its scent imbuing the space with the fresh tang of pine. Saint Steadman has also chopped us an enormous pile of logs for the winter and a fire is currently toasting the room, filling it with a warm glow. Milly Molly Mandy is curled up in front of it, spark out. Even serial killers, it seems, take time out at Christmas. Her claws flex and her feet paddle in her sleep. I'd bet you a fiver she's dreaming about flaying some unsuspecting rodent alive. The central heating is also on full blast to try to scare away the damp. I'm trying not to think about the resulting oil bill and am luxuriating in the rare cosiness instead.

Standing back, I admire the tree. I have to say that Helmshill Grange has never looked so fine and it gives me a pain in my heart to think of it this way.

Tom hangs a bag of chocolate coins on the tree, making

one of the huge branches droop under its weight. 'Can I have one now please, Mummy?'

'Save a bag,' I say. 'You and Jessica can share it after your tea.'

I loved the glittering gold bags of chocolate coins as a kid. They were always my favourite decoration – a trait that I've passed on to my own two. Despite the fact that I'm not a huge fan of Christmas, I love the process of decorating the tree, getting the ornaments out of their boxes, dusting them off, discovering treasures that I'd forgotten about in the intervening months. This year I'm making a big effort for Yuletide. Even though money is tight, I've spoiled the children. They've been through an extraordinarily difficult time and I want to reward them for how well they've handled it all. A pile of gaily wrapped presents is waiting to go under the tree just as soon as we've finished our handiwork. There's an X-Box for Tom, a surfeit of tasteless Bratz stuff for Jessica that she'll adore. There are clothes, chocolates and silly stocking-fillers to make them smile.

There's an enormous wrapped present for the both of them from Alan too, and only I know what it is. Bless him, he confided in me that he's handmade them a wooden sledge. It's like a work of art, with their names meticulously carved on either side. They've never had a sledge before and I'm sure they'll love it. Glancing out of the French windows, I can see that the snow is still falling heavily, coating the ground with a soft blanket of white. I can't remember when I last saw snowfall like this. I'm not sure that the children have seen it at all. It's been years since we had anything more than a few flakes in London and it really looks magical outside. I hate to admit this, especially at this late stage, but part of me is sorely going to miss this place.

The Bainbridges have forgiven us our trespasses – or our dog's trespasses, in particular – and Gill has kindly made us a beautiful wreath for our front door. They've brought presents for Tom and Jessica too which is just so kind of them. If only we were staying I'm sure that we could have become firm friends. Everything looks so truly wonderful. There's only one thing – one person – missing from this Christmas to make it perfect.

I check my watch. We're all going to the family service at St Mary's tonight. Alan's joining us, so is Guy, and they're both going to be our guests for Christmas lunch tomorrow. It will be strange to have Christmas without William – it was the time of year he loved the most. He adored the whole thing, from dressing the tree to flaming the Christmas pudding to our traditional family walk on Boxing Day – but we're just going to have to make the best of it. My sister Serena arrived just ahead of the snow – also laden down with presents for the children. She's now upstairs having a hot shower and a glass of good red wine that I've liberated from Will's stash to revive her.

'We'd better be making a move,' I say to the children. 'We don't want to be late.' What I mean is that we don't want a pew at the back near the draughty door. 'Are we nearly finished?'

They both nod and come to stand next to me. I slip my arms around my kids and cuddle them to me. It's at times like this when I still miss my husband the most. Gradually one ticks off the milestones – first Christmas without him, then it will soon be our wedding anniversary, Will's birthday, my birthday, the kids' birthdays, perhaps a holiday on our own and, eventually, somehow, we will have managed to survive for a whole year without him. The thought makes a lump come to my throat and we have to get out of here before I cry.

Ushering the children through to the kitchen, I get them to start the lengthy procedure of putting on boots and coats and hats. 'Serena,' I call out. 'We need to go.'

I check on Hamish who's currently locked in the scullery. There was no way that we would have got the tree decorated with that pest around. He's still alive, but complaining loudly at such inhuman treatment. I give him a cursory fuss and then re-wedge the chair against the handle so that there can be no escape. He whines even more abjectly from behind the door.

The turkey, fresh from Tunliffe's Farm courtesy of Guy, is sitting on the work surface. I cooked it today in the Aga, which I've finally mastered just in time to be returning to a bog standard electric number, so that we can have some warm turkey sandwiches after the Christmas service, another family tradition that was Will's idea. Plus there was no space for the turkey to languish in the fridge until tomorrow as it's an enormous bird and the shelves are already full and groaning with festive food. I lifted it out of the oven half an hour ago and now it's tightly covered with tin foil. Briefly, I consider giving Hamish a bit to placate him, but decide that would only encourage him.

I boot and suit myself, ready for the elements. I'll swear it was never this cold in London either. Serena appears, still managing to look chic in arctic-style gear. She has on Ugg boots, brown jeans and an off-white padded jacket with a hood trimmed with chocolate-coloured fur. I've tried to spruce myself up too and am wearing my black Joseph trousers, a red cashmere sweater and a big black coat that I hardly ever wore in Town, but which has seen much service over the last few weeks.

'We won't be long,' I shout to the dog over my shoulder. 'Try to be good, Hamish.'

Then we all step out into the falling snow and I close the door behind me.

Chapter Seventy-Three

Guy strode into the churchyard. The snow was thick and deep. It looked like one of those scenes that you saw on Christmas cards, the quaint church with the orange glow from the stained-glass windows, the dark skeletal trees tipped with frosted snow, sparkling like diamonds. The snow-covered moors loomed in the background; it would be a raw night to be up there and Guy hoped that no one had an emergency that he had to go out to. The problem with dealing with the animal kingdom was that it didn't observe festive holidays.

What an idyllic picture this was, though. It made him glad to be living in Helmshill and, at this moment, he couldn't imagine being anywhere else. By the path he could see Tom,

Jessica and Amy's sister. Amy was on her knees next to Will's grave, placing a bright red poinsettia in front of the headstone which looked incongruous in the monochrome scene. He saw her wipe a tear from her eye and she stood up to cuddle the children. The joy he'd experienced at seeing her dissipated. She was still very much another man's wife even if that man was no longer here. It would serve him well to remember that.

He slowed his pace, giving them a minute to compose themselves and then, when he saw Amy risk a tearful smile again, he strode up behind them.

'Is this cold enough for you?' he asked.

She turned towards him and the warmth of her smile took his breath away. Try as he might to control his head, his heart had somehow gone seriously awry. 'It's fabulous,' she said. 'Like a winter wonderland.'

He wanted to take her hand, but daren't, so they walked side by side into the busy church. The congregation might be a little reticent on a normal Sunday, but the high days and holidays brought out the good folk of Helmshill in force. Alan had come up from Scarsby and was already inside the church, sitting at a pew alone, and as they all slipped in beside him, the man parted with one of his rare smiles.

This just felt so right, Guy thought as he sat on the hard pew, hands clasped in front of him in an attempt to emulate prayer. After being alone for so long it was as if a ready-made family had been delivered directly to his doorstep and had lifted him from the loneliness he hadn't even realised that he'd embraced. What could he do to keep it like this? That's all he wanted. Amy, the kids, her sister, even Alan. He wanted them all to be his family now, and he couldn't bear the thought that Amy didn't share, maybe didn't even know about, his dream.

The vicar led the service, Christmas carols were sung, the voices of the villagers ringing out bright and clear in the church. Halfway through singing 'Silent Night' he had to stop. The notes simply wouldn't come. It had brought a lump to Guy's throat and a tear to his eyes. He was getting sentimental in his old age. Amy was next to him and he glanced towards her. She had stopped singing too and tears were rolling down her face. He wondered what was going through her mind. Was she thinking about her husband? Was she wondering what might have been? Was she even having second thoughts about leaving all this behind?

Surreptitiously, he took her hand in his. Blow what the villagers would think, if any of them noticed. She needed comfort and he was the one who wanted to be there to give it to her. Amy didn't move it away. Instead, she looked gratefully at him, soft blue eyes flooding, and that look pierced his soul.

The words *I love you* were lingering unspoken on his tongue, longing for release. Well, for now, they would have to stay there.

Chapter Seventy-Four

We walk back along the path from the church, exchanging hugs and Christmas greetings with various villagers, oblivious to the silent, steady fall of snow. There are powdery drifts against the headstones, and the poinsettia I placed with Will earlier is already heavily tipped with white.

There's a warm glow inside me and, for the first time, I'm happy to acknowledge that I'm part of the community here now. Guy held my hand throughout the church service and I don't know whether it was to comfort me or for some other entirely more scary reason, but it felt good, too good.

He stands in front of me now. 'I'll see you tomorrow,' I say and I kiss him tenderly on the cheek. 'Come about noon. Serena's brought a couple of bottles of decent champagne. We can get legless before lunch.'

Guy laughs and I realise that it's a sound I'm growing to love, which frightens me and thrills me in equal measures. 'I'll look forward to that.'

Alan, wrapped up in an overcoat that looks like it dates back to the war, hovers behind us. I kiss him on the cheek too, but am not sure whether he enjoys it or not. He touches his face where my lips have been and, movingly, tears spring to his eyes. Maybe it has been too long since anyone kissed him. 'We'll see you tomorrow too, Alan.'

He nods and strides off into the night and I can hardly bear the thought of him going back to his cottage alone on Christmas Eve. I look at Guy and feel the same way. Perhaps I should have invited them both back to the house now for warm turkey sarnies. But I guess that I should also spend some time with Serena as we haven't had a chance to talk since she arrived.

'Tomorrow, then,' I say brightly.

Guy leans in and kisses me, his hands on my arms, even though we've already done this bit. His aim is slightly off and he brushes my mouth before he connects with my cheek. The warmth of his lips takes me by surprise and, like Alan, I almost lift my fingers to touch the spot. Our eyes lock and, for some reason, I find it hard to tear myself away.

'I'm freezing my butt off here,' Serena says, clapping her hands together and bringing some much-needed reality back to the moment. 'Are we ready to rock?'

'Coming, coming,' I say, flustered as I break free from Guy's embrace. 'See you tomorrow.' I wave over my shoulder as I walk away.

Tom and Jessica are way ahead of us already and I fall into step next to Serena.

'Hmm,' my sister says, regarding me quizically. 'Tender moment there.'

'Yes,' I reply. 'Thanks for your timely intervention.'

'Sorry. Didn't realise until I opened my big mouth.' She gives me a squeeze. 'Plenty of time for a re-run.'

'Not really,' I say. After all, our time here at Helmshill Grange is rapidly coming to an end.

I've left lights on all over the house so that it would look warm and welcoming on our return. I have to say that the Grange looks lovely, very festive. The heating's still pumping out too for all it's worth so, for once, it will be like a sauna inside. This is one Christmas where I want to feel toasty and pampered and content.

The kids start to throw snowballs at each other, shrieking as targets are hit.

I nudge Serena. 'Come on,' I urge. 'Let's show them how this is done.'

Giggling like schoolgirls, we both grab handfuls of snow

and hurl them at the kids, who scream with delight. Then they round on us and give us a good pelting. Somehow Serena turns rogue and ends up on their side and all three of them chase me back to the house, showering me with snow while I shout and run, breathlessly. It's a long time since I have felt so carefree. I look back at the kids, my sister, Helmshill Grange. This is a wonderful moment that I'll always cherish.

I reach the back door first and, still laughing and panting hard, push it open. Then I stop dead in my tracks. It takes a moment for the scene to register in my brain. The laughter stops in my throat and turns to a cry of, *'Oh no!'*

Chapter Seventy-Five

On the floor in the middle of the kitchen is the turkey. The tinfoil is shredded, as is the bird. Torn lumps of the meat litter the floor. Our Christmas lunch looks like it has been shaken to hell and back. I can feel my face darken and my blood boils. Hamish! Wait till I get my hands on that flaming animal. The chair wedged against the scullery door is lying toppled on its side and the door is open. That wretched dog is better than Houdini. How has he managed to get out again?

It's clear that it is not all Hamish's work though. His accomplice is currently lying on the kitchen table languidly licking turkey grease from between her claws and from round her mouth. Milly Molly Mandy pauses in her ablutions and gives me a disdainful look.

'Get off that bloody table before I skin you alive,' I shriek, just as the kids and Serena come in behind me also laughing and panting with exertion. They too pull up short.

Milly Molly Mandy thinks twice about acting cool and shoots off the table, scarpering through the living room at warp speed.

'Oh no,' Serena says behind me in a echo of my own sentiments.

At that moment, I hear Hamish bark happily in the living room. I storm towards the noise, yanking the door open, the warm glow of Christmas spirit quickly evaporated. The sight that greets me is even worse than in the kitchen. My beautiful blue spruce tree that we all lavished such tender loving care on decorating is up-ended in the middle of the floor. Hamish is currently worrying the fairy from the top who's clamped firmly in his jaws, silver crown and filigree wings askew. His low, rumbling growl is laced with joy.

'Dear God.' My hand goes to my mouth.

All of the presents have received the Hamish treatment. Ripped wrapping paper is littered round the room, all over the carpet, on the sofas. Tom's X-Box has been gnawed beyond recognition and Jessica's Bratz paraphernalia has been chewed into a thousand slobber-covered pieces.

The gaudy paper has been torn from Alan's hand-crafted sled and there are Hamish-sized teethmarks all over the wood. And the little glittering bags of chocolate coins, ridiculously, irrationally, my very favourite thing, have all been dragged from the tree and lie half-chewed and spat out on the carpet, their golden wrappers shredded, the chocolate all but gone.

'Oh,' Jessica says in a small voice. 'Naughty Hamish.'

Suddenly, I'm mobilised from my paralysis. 'Right! That's it!' I charge at Hamish and, to his surprise, grab him roughly by the collar. His eyes nearly pop out of his head. 'Get out. Get out of here now.' He starts to whine as I yank him to the door. Even a dog as small-brained as Hamish can't mistake the fact that this time he's in deep, deep shit. This time he has over-stepped the mark. 'I want you out of my sight.'

'Amy . . .' Serena tries to still me, but I'm having none of it. I push past my sister, hauling the reluctant dog behind me.

His feet scrabble on the floor as I drag him through the kitchen and he tries in vain to sit down. I round on him. 'You have ruined my fucking Christmas,' I scream. 'All I've done, all I've worked for and you've ruined it, you stupid animal.'

'Mummy,' Jessica says, and I can tell that she's crying.

I turn and behind me the blanched faces of my children stare back at me. I don't think they've ever heard me swear before, and certainly not like this. But a red rage has descended on me and I can't help myself.

'This dog is going,' I tell them. 'I have tried, but I've had enough of him. I can't deal with him any longer.'

Somehow, I manhandle him out of the kitchen door. There's no way he's getting back into the house this side of New Year. He's done enough damn damage for one day. The snow is thicker now and Hamish howls as I push and shove and tug him towards one of the outhouses – the one with the biggest bolt across the door.

Despite his protests, I somehow manage to get Hamish

into the secure brick building. 'You can damn well stay here until I decide what to do with you.'

Hamish lowers his head, his doleful eyes pleading with me. Well, it's a bit too bloody late now. 'Don't give me that crap,' I shout at him, arms flailing. He backs away from me, cowering. 'You weren't *just* playing. You're a destructive monster. I have six mouths to feed tomorrow. Did you think it was funny to eat my turkey? Did you enjoy it, you canine bastard? What am I going to do now, thanks to you? What are *we* going to eat?'

It feels as if all that I've tried to hold together over the last few months has suddenly been swept away. I'm shaking and I can't stop. Behind me I can hear Tom and Jessica crying softly as they stand shivering in the yard and let the snow fall on them.

'We love him, Mummy,' Jessica sobs. 'He didn't mean it.'

'I can manage without an X-Box,' Tom adds tearfully.

I ignore their pleas. I think I'm justly berating a big, useless, slobbering shite of a dog. They think I'm laying into Helmshill's answer to Scooby Doo. Well, I'm the grown up. I'm the one who's right. Hamish tries one last, valiant wag of his tail.

'It doesn't work,' I spit at him. 'I hope you're pleased with yourself, you stupid mutt. It's curtains for you now, mate. This is over and I've won.' And I bang the door behind him, giving it a kick for good measure, and I make sure that the bolt is firmly secured.

Now I'm going to have a drink, a double brandy, scrape the irretrievable turkey off the floor and think about what

I'm going to give my guests for Christmas lunch and how I'm going to get rid of that accursed dog.

Chapter Seventy-Six

When I wake up on Christmas morning, I'm a damn sight calmer. I cried and cried and cried last night, and now it's as if all my emotion is spent and I have a clearer perspective on what happened. If it wasn't so heartbreaking and so achingly expensive I might even be able to see the funny side of Hurricane Hamish's destructive streak. Maybe in years to come. Okay, so there's no turkey and no presents, but that at the end of the day is a minor hiccough. Worse things happen at sea. No one died.

And that's really what my outburst was about last night. It wasn't entirely down to Hamish's Christmas frenzy, it was more to do with the stress that had been piling up over my job, the move to London, the worry of looking after the children by myself, the fact that life is never going to be the same again. My dog's dastardly behaviour was just the straw that broke the camel's back. I had tried so hard to make it perfect and then . . . I'm not going to go there again. But, I have to admit, after a good rant and a good cry I feel so much better. Now I'm just feeling shamefaced and will have to set about a damage-limitation programme.

The hens, thankfully, don't realise it's a special day so there'll be plenty of eggs. Omelettes for Christmas dinner could work. I'll have several glasses of champagne with the others and we'll all laugh heartily about it. There's no way I'm going to let it spoil today.

Milly Molly Mandy is curled up at the bottom of the bed fast asleep and drooling on my favourite duvet. Clearly the cat wasn't overly rattled by my unusual outburst.

'Morning, Mils,' I say, and inch a foot out of the duvet to give her a rub. 'Up for some more turkey today?'

She opens one eye, regards me icily and then closes it again. Normal service resumed.

This is the first time I've woken up alone on Christmas Day for many years, but you know, I feel all right about it. I stroke Will's side of the bed even though it's empty. He's still here with us every day and always will be. I know that. Instead of grieving for what I've lost, I should count my blessings. I've got my health, I'm relatively happy and I've got two wonderful children who make my life worthwhile. I may not be the world's best parent, but they're growing up to be nice, responsible kids despite my inadequacies. They never give me a moment's trouble.

Glancing at the clock, I see that it's nearly eight even though it's still dark outside. Just goes to show that Tom and Jessica are growing up. Normally by now they'd be up and in our bed, demanding presents, dragging us from our sleep. Or perhaps they've stayed in bed because they know that this Christmas there are no presents.

I feel terrible that I blew up like that. It was unacceptable and I must apologise to them at once. That bloody dog will be the death of me, I'll swear. But it looks like I'm stuck with him as a permanent member of my family. I'm going to make sure that Hamish has plenty of time in the outhouse in which to consider the stupidity of his ways – even though it is Christmas Day and already I can feel my resolve weakening.

Stretching and yawning, I heave myself out of bed preparing for the rigours of the day. While there's still a modicum of peace and quiet, I sneak into the shower and let the hot water play over me, reviving my tired body. Hopefully, there'll still be some hot water left for Serena when she gets up – which I realise is not entirely in the spirit of Christmas, but then my sister has plenty of hot water for the other 364 days of the year, whereas I do not.

After showering and dressing I go down into the kitchen and start to make preparations for breakfast. Just something light as I don't want anyone to spoil their lunch. And then I remember that lunch isn't going quite according to plan. Only Hamish and Milly Molly Mandy are going to enjoy the remains of the turkey. Still, the croissants and pain au chocolat I bought should fill a hole until then. I just hope that the hens have been prolific in their egg production to make up for the shortcomings on the fowl front as I don't want to be popping a couple of them in the Aga.

The kettle whistles to let me know that it has boiled and I take Serena a cup of chamomile tea. She's only just woken and is still luxuriating in her bed. 'Don't think that you can stay there for long,' I warn. 'The minute the kids get up your life will no longer be your own.'

'I'm looking forward to it,' she says. 'Thank goodness I hadn't had time to put my presents for them under the tree. At least a few things escaped Tornado Hamish. They'll still have something to open.'

It took us ages to clear up the mess in the living room last night, but we righted the blue spruce which didn't seem too much the worse for wear after its ordeal. With a bit of solicitous titivation we even managed to get it fairly near to looking like its former glory – apart from the seriously chewed fairy. When the kids had gone to bed we sneaked Serena's presents downstairs and placed them under the tree.

'You're an angel.' I give my sister a warm hug. 'Happy Christmas. Let's have a lovely day together.'

'Mmm,' she says. 'It will be wonderful. I'm not a big fan of turkey anyway.'

'Don't,' I say with a laugh. 'I've tried so hard to make everything perfect.'

'Have a few drinks. Chill out. Don't worry. All your guests should be grateful that they're here whatever you serve up. I'm sure we'd have all been spending it on our own being maudlin otherwise.'

'Think I should get the kids up yet? It's not like them to lie in this long, although we did have quite a late night.' And Jessica was still sobbing when she went to bed, I think guiltily. 'I'll give them a knock.'

First I head to Jessica's room. The morning is dark and gloomy, outside the snow is still falling and by now it's getting quite deep. I nibble anxiously at my lip. Guy will be fine to get here as he can walk to our house, but I hope Alan doesn't have any trouble getting through to Helmshill in his car. Surely the roads must be starting to become impassable by now. Maybe the people who live up here are more used to these conditions. From my point of view, I'm happy that we're all going to be safely tucked up for the day with no need to venture out into the elements.

'Come on, Sleepy Head,' I call out as I enter Jessica's bedroom. She's completely buried in the duvet, burrowed down like a little dormouse. I sit down on the side of the bed and shake the mound. 'Don't you want to see if Santa's been?'

Then my blood runs cold and I whip back the duvet. Instead of Jessica, there is a pile of carefully arranged teddy bears and dolls beneath the cover. 'Serena!' I cry out and then fly across the hall and into Tom's room, heart pounding erratically.

I can already tell as I go through the door that the hump in the bed is not my child. Sure enough, that too is a pile of soft toys. 'Oh, God,' I say under my breath. 'Where the hell are they?'

I look out of Tom's window into the yard and instantly see that the door of the outhouse that imprisoned Hamish is flung wide open and is swinging on its hinges. It seems that my children have launched a secret operation to liberate the damn dog.

'What's the matter?' Serena comes up behind me, pulling her dressing-gown around her and trying to smooth down her hair. She too stares out of the window, yawning. 'Where's the fire?'

I turn to her, my eyes welling with tears and blurt out, 'The kids are missing.'

Chapter Seventy-Seven

I phoned Guy, who phoned Alan, and now they're both here. 'It looks like they've taken the dog and gone,' I say, managing to control my tears.

'They can't have got far,' Guy says in a reassuring tone. 'The weather was terrible last night.' And then I see the two men exchange a worried look and that sets me off weeping again. My babies could be out in that.

Serena and I donned our boots and heavy coats the minute we found that Tom and Jessica had gone AWOL and made a thorough search of all the outhouses and barns just in case they were still in the vicinity of the house or tucked up safely behind a bale of straw somewhere. How often are kids that go missing found asleep behind the sofa or under their beds – right? It was worth a look, but they're nowhere to be seen.

Tom has left his mobile phone on the kitchen table. The one time I need it in an emergency and it's lying here impotently. How sorry am I now that I didn't give into Jessica's demands for a phone, citing her unreasonable youth as an excuse? It would have been more than her street cred was worth for her to have left it behind.

There's been a lot of fresh snow so we can't see any footprints leading away from the Grange to give us a hint as to where they might have gone. 'This is all my fault,' I explain tearfully to Guy. 'When we got back from the church last night, Hamish had trashed the house.'

'It seems to be his speciality,' he says enigmatically.

'This time he did a particularly good job,' I sigh. 'He'd devoured the turkey. Wrecked the Christmas tree. Half-ate most of the presents. I completely lost the plot, locked him in the outhouse and, effectively, told the kids that he had to go.'

He purses his lips. 'Seems as if they had other ideas.'

'Where did they think they were going to go with him? Do they really think I'm so heartless?' My eyes meet Guy's and I think back to the day when I begged him to put Hamish down. God, how could I do that? What a cow.

'We're wasting valuable time,' Guy says. 'Where do they go and play on the moors when they go out? Chances are they've headed there.'

'They stay pretty close to the house usually.'

'Maybe they've become disorientated in the snow. It's easy to do.' Guy runs his fingers through his hair. 'Do you want us to do an initial sweep before we call the police, or do you want to ring them straight away?'

'Police?' This makes it seem so much more serious. 'You don't think anyone's taken them?'

'No, no,' Guy says. 'But I'm worried about how long they've been out there and whether they're properly dressed.'

'Their coats and boots have gone.' At least they should have gloves and hats with them too as I always insist that they keep them in the pockets.

'Have you any idea what time they might have left?'

I shake my head. 'Serena and I went to bed just after

midnight. I checked on them then and they looked to be sound asleep. I'd had a few drinks.' More than a few. How bad do I feel about that now? 'I stayed awake for about another hour.' Don't need to tell Guy that I was crying into my pillow. 'Then I was out for the count.' Not exactly the sleep of the just, more the sleep of the pissed.

'They could have been out most of the night.'

I chew anxiously at my fingernails. 'That's not good, is it?'

Guy's face is grim. 'The sooner we find them, the better.'

'Oh, God,' I say. 'I'll never forgive myself if anything has happened to them.'

'Don't worry,' he tells me. 'We'll bring them back safely.'

I can only hope and pray that he's right.

Chapter Seventy-Eight

The sky is lightening now as I set off across the moors with Guy, Alan and Serena. We are all grim faced and unappreciative of the beautiful pink and peach wash that the sunrise is bringing to the grey sky.

I've wrapped up tightly against the cold but, to be honest, I'm sweating now inside my coat and I can feel it trickling beneath my arms and down my back. My mouth is dry with anxiety. My heart is racing. This is the first time since Will collapsed on the Tube that I've felt true full-on fear. What if we don't find the children? What if something terrible has happened to them? What if they never come home? How would I forgive myself?

'We'll split up,' Guys says. I can't tell you how grateful I am that he's taking charge. It feels like my emotions are scattered to the four corners of the earth and I'm incapable of rational thought. All I can think is that my children are out there, lost in this snow, and that it's all my fault. 'That way we can cover more ground. Serena, you go with Alan.'

Mr Steadman nods solemnly and says nothing. My sister goes to stand next to him.

'If we haven't found them within the hour, I'll call the police.'

A sob rises in my throat at that.

'But I'm sure we will. It won't come to that,' Guy adds hastily. 'Let's get a move on. The sun's coming up now, that will make it easier.'

Alan and Serena set off in one direction. Guy takes my hand and we stride off in the other, only the sound of the snow crunching under our feet breaking the silence.

'I think they usually take their kites up this way,' I say, realising that I've never spent time out on the moors with my children even though they love it so much, and that makes me feel like a terrible and neglectful mother all over again.

The snow is deep and is coming halfway up my boots. If it didn't seem so treacherous it would be truly gorgeous out here today. We stride out over the steadily rising hills and I'm struggling to keep up with Guy's pace, but adrenaline is firing me on.

We call out their names. 'Tom! Jessica!' The sound echoes back, emptily, at us.

After half an hour we've found nothing, not even a foot-print. I sink down to my knees. 'This is hopeless,' I say. 'They could be anywhere. What if they're miles from here by now?'

'I don't think they would be,' Guy states. 'It would have been hard going last night. I still can't think that they'll be far away.'

Heaving myself up, I start to cry again. Guy folds his arms round me. Tears course down my cheeks. He brushes them away with his thumb. 'Crying won't find them,' he says. 'We've got to keep going. Feeling up to carrying on?'

I nod and start off up the hill once more. Then I hear a noise. 'What was that?'

'I didn't hear anything,' Guy says.

'Ssh.' I strain to hear it again. Sure enough, there it is. From out of the void comes the faint and muffled sound of a dog barking. 'It's Hamish.'

We stand stock still and Guy listens intently. There it is again. I'd know that bark anywhere. 'By God it is,' he agrees.

The sound puts wings on our feet and we hurry in the direction of the barking. I punch Serena's number out on my phone. 'I think we might have found them,' I pant as we race across the moors. 'Come this way. We can hear Hamish barking.'

My legs are aching with the effort of hill climbing in the thick snow which is forming into drifts in the light breeze. The sound of the barking gets louder as we push on. Then, as we round a corner, I catch a glimpse of Jessica's pink coat next to a huge limestone boulder.

'They're here,' I say joyously, and run towards the flash of cerise.

Sure enough, my children are huddled together beside the rock. They're both lying lifelessly, covered by a frosting of snow. They look like something out of a fairytale. And not a good one. Hamish's barking continues unabated, but I can't see him anywhere. I drop down on my knees next to the children, rapidly followed by Guy.

'Jessica. Jessica! Tom! Wake up. Mummy's here.' I catch hold of my daughter's hand and rub it vigorously. At least she had the sense to put her gloves on, something I'm grateful for, but they, like the rest of her clothes, are wet through. She struggles to open her eyes but, thankfully, there is movement there. Guy does the same for Tom and my boy too soon stirs.

Don't panic. Don't panic, I tell myself as I rub my daughter's arms and legs. *Don't lose the plot, they need you calm, they need you in control* – but I can't help the tears from falling.

Jessica starts to cry too. 'We were frightened, Mummy. It's so cold out here and it was very dark.' She's shivering and I hug her to me.

'You're safe now,' I murmur into her hair.

Tom seems in worse shape. He looks sleepy, out of it, and hasn't spoken yet.

'Tom. Tom!' I try to bring some colour to his frozen cheeks. 'Mummy's here.'

Slowly, my son revives too though he's shaking uncontrollably. 'Hamish,' he says, worry creasing his young brow. 'He was trying to take us home because we were scared.

He knew the way and everything, but he fell down a hole and we didn't know what to do.'

We both tune into the dog's barking again and Guy runs over to where the sound is coming from. 'He's here. I've found him,' he shouts back at me. 'He's fallen down a ravine in the limestone.'

'Can't he get out?'

'He's hurt,' Guy says, and my daughter bursts into tears. He sprints back to us. 'Let's get the kids home and warm them up, they're half frozen to death.' He stops short, appalled at his choice of words, but I know that they nearly are. I'm not exactly *au fait* with the symptoms of hypothermia, but I know that they're beyond mere cold and this is potentially very serious indeed.

At that moment Serena and Alan appear running across the snow to us. They're another welcome sight.

'Thank God,' Serena breathes and she hugs me more tightly than she ever has before.

'Help me to carry the children,' Guy says to Alan, who obeys without a word though I see a lone tear making its way across his craggy cheek. 'You take Jessica.' Which Mr Steadman does, lifting her as if she weighs nothing at all.

'Here's my phone.' He tosses it to Serena. 'Phone the doctor. Tell him to meet us at the Grange. Urgently.'

Serena also does as she's told without hesitation.

Guy hefts Tom into his arms. My boy lies there listless and unprotesting.

'What about Hamish?' Jessica mumbles. 'Don't leave my doggy behind.'

'We'll come straight back for him,' Guy promises her. 'Just as soon as we get you home.'

'Mummy,' she cries, 'don't leave Hamish.'

'He'll be fine. He'll wait here for Uncle Guy,' I assure her. When she doesn't stop crying, I say, 'I'll check on him for you.'

The dog's bark is becoming more hoarse and I wonder if he's been barking all night. I run over to the edge of the uneven limestone path which is covered in snow, hiding lethal dips, hollows and plunges. Peering down to where Guy said that he'd seen the dog, I can see that Hamish is seriously hurt. He's lying on the snow at the bottom of a deep cutting and I'm shocked that the snow around him is lividly stained with his blood. His back leg is at an unnatural angle and even an amateur could diagnose that it's broken. Hamish looks up at me and barks pitifully. He even manages a wag of his tail, which turns on my waterworks again.

'We'll be back, boy,' I tell him. 'We'll come for you just as soon as we can. Hang on, Hamish.' Then I whisper, 'Please don't die.'

Chapter Seventy-Nine

Dr Redman's 4x4 is pulling into the drive at the same time as we hit the garden coming back from the moors, children still borne in Alan and Guy's arms. I haven't seen Dr Redman since Will died and the association makes my blood run cold.

It seems this time we have averted a tragedy in the nick of time.

'Thank you for coming, Doctor.'

'No problem,' he says, even though he's been dragged away from his family's Christmas celebrations.

We all bundle into the house. 'Serena, crank up the heating.' My sister disappears into the scullery where the boiler is and, a second later, I hear the pipes clunk into life. 'Let's take the children straight upstairs into my bedroom.'

Alan and Guy do my bidding and take Tom and Jessica up to lay them both on my bed. Milly Molly Mandy, who doesn't appear to have moved since this morning, lets out a disgruntled miaow at the intrusion on her privacy. Dr Redman has followed us and as he comes through the door, he instructs, 'Get them straight out of those wet things and into something dry. Quick as you can.'

'Their pyjamas are in their rooms,' I say to Guy, and he disappears to go and find them. Moments later he comes back, by which time the doctor and I have stripped the children out of their sodden winter clothes and are rubbing them down with warm towels.

'Do you know how long you've been outside?' the doctor says to Tom.

My son shakes his head. 'We got up before everyone else to sneak out.'

'What time was that?'

He turns tearful eyes to me. 'You're not in trouble,' I say. 'Just tell the doctor.'

'It was three o'clock.'

'Good,' Dr Redman says. 'Not too long. But long enough.'

I slip the soft pyjamas onto their ice-cold bodies while the GP now bends over them and checks their pulse, their eyes, their temperature. He takes out his stethoscope and listens to their hearts and it's a good job that he doesn't put it to my heart as it's pounding so hard that it might just blow his ears off. When he's finished, he turns to me once more. 'Give them hot drinks, something sweet. And plenty of carbohydrate. Keep them tucked up in bed, nice and warm for the rest of the day.' He speaks in crisp, efficient tones. 'They'll probably want to sleep for a few hours,'

'Will they be all right?' I'm wringing my hands together.

'Mild hypothermia,' he says. 'I'm sure that they'll be right as rain by tomorrow. Children have amazing recuperative powers. Another hour or two and it could have been a different story.' He regards me grimly and I find it hard not to cry again.

'Thank you,' I say gratefully. 'Thank you for coming out on Christmas Day.'

'Don't suppose that you planned on spending it like this?'

'No.' I shake my head.

'Warn the children about the dangers of going out on the moors unprepared.'

'I'm sure they'll have learned their lesson.'

'You put your feet up too,' he instructs. 'You look exhausted. Let someone else do the cooking.'

I daren't tell him that whipping up a few omelettes is about as strenuous as our Christmas lunch is going to be. I tuck Jessica and Tom into bed. Milly Molly Mandy stretches, stands, strolls across the bed and curls herself up next to Jessica. My daughter reaches out a hand to stroke her and then slips the thumb of her other hand into her mouth. She's going to have buck teeth when she grows up if she keeps doing that and it will all be my fault for putting her through so much stress as a child. Serena comes in with a tray bearing mugs of hot chocolate for them, which I'm sure on this occasion is exactly what the doctor ordered. There's plenty of hot buttered toast piled on a plate too.

'I'll be on my way,' the doctor says and I follow him downstairs, Guy and Alan close behind me.

'Merry Christmas to you all.' Dr Redman waves a hand. It's clear that he's eager to get back to his home now. 'Don't hesitate to call me if there are any problems. Any at all. I'll find my own way out.'

When he's gone, Guy says, 'We'd better go back for Hamish right away. He looked in bad shape.' The vet worries at his lip. 'It would be a lot easier if there was any form of road access up there.'

'Take Alan's sledge,' I suggest. 'You won't be able to carry him.'

'Good idea.' Guy nods. 'It'll be slow but I can't see why it wouldn't be effective.'

'Who'd have thought that your present would have come in handy quite so soon,' I say to Alan, resting my hand on his arm.

'Aye,' he says and his voice is thick with emotion. Alan pulls off the remains of the Christmas paper from his sledge. He doesn't remark on Hamish's toothmark customisation.

'Thank you, Alan. I have no idea what we'd do without you.'

The strong, silent man studies his feet.

'I might be a while,' Guy tells me. 'I'll take the dog straight to the surgery. His leg looked bad. He looked like he'd lost a lot of blood.'

Panic seizes me again. 'He will pull through?'

'Any other dog and I wouldn't give it much of a chance,' he answers with a shake of his head, 'but this is Hamish we're talking about.'

'Call me,' I insist. 'Let me know how he is. The children will be worried.' So am I. Worried sick. 'Bring Hamish back safely.'

'We will.' Guy squeezes my hand. 'Don't you worry.'

'Be careful.' I reach up and stroke Guy's face. 'Thank you. Thank you so much.'

'I'd better be going,' he says. 'I'll be back just as soon as I can.'

The two men take the sledge and go back out into the snow to rescue the injured dog and I can only wait and hope.

Chapter Eighty

Now that they had a trail of footprints to follow it was easy enough for Guy and Alan Steadman to retrace their route back to Hamish. They trudged silently through the crisp snow, Guy thinking how much he'd enjoy a walk like this if only the circumstances were different.

Hamish had looked in pretty poor shape to him. The amount of blood around him was bad news and it was lucky that the dog had survived the night. He only hoped they were going to be able to get down to Hamish and complete the task of hauling him back up the slope on the sledge. He'd taken his vet's visits bag and some rope from the back of the car to lash the dog to the sled if they needed it. Guy hoisted the weight of the rope onto his shoulder.

Thankfully, Alan Steadman was alongside him, dragging the heavy wooden sledge in his wake. His companion was more than man enough for the job. Disguised beneath that long, lanky frame was a body of pure muscle and, for a man of his age, he had incredible strength – emotional as well as physical, it would seem. He had been a rock in helping to find the children and bring them home.

Guy felt wrung out after taking the kids back to the Grange. Thank God they'd found them in time. He'd tried not to convey to Amy just how worried he was about the state they might find them in. Youngsters could succumb to hypothermia so quickly in conditions like this. He couldn't help but feel that, this time, they'd had a very lucky escape. Hopefully, this scrape would teach them not to be so foolhardy again.

He'd been glad that he'd been there to come to Amy's aid. She was distraught, as any mother would be, and he wanted to protect her from that. The kids were home safely and had, by some miracle, come to no lasting harm. Now all he had to do was bring the dog home too.

As they pushed on into the rolling hills of the Yorkshire moors, he could hear the faint barking of Hamish once again. The dog's voice sounded hoarse now, weak, and he'd probably strained his throat from barking for so long. Either that or he was fading fast.

They reached the edge of the drop where they'd left Hamish and looked over. The dog was still lying prone on the snow. Was it Guy's imagination or had the pool of blood that surrounded him grown significantly larger? The dog had broken his back leg, that was obvious enough; he only hoped that the fracture hadn't nicked an artery too. If it had, they were in serious trouble. It was clear that they had to get Hamish out of there and back to the surgery just as soon as they could, or the dog could bleed to death.

'Ready?' Guy said to Alan.

'Aye, Vit,' the man replied with a nod.

'We're coming, boy,' Guy shouted down to the dog and got a feeble wag of a tail in return.

Together the men clambered down the steep side of the culvert, edging their way over the limestone boulders, lowering the sled as they did, inching their way further and further into the bottom and towards Hamish.

Ten minutes of strenuous descent later, hot, sweating and out of breath, they finally reached the dog.

'Hello, boy,' Guy said, roughing up the hound's floppy ears. 'What have you been up to then?'

Hamish gamely tried to raise himself, but couldn't and he let out a whimper as he fell back against the snow, though his tail pounded happily at the sight of Alan. Hamish's breathing was shallow and he was covered in deep cuts which he must have sustained on his fall. It looked like the dog was suffering from hypothermia too.

Guy examined the break. It was bad. The fracture was in the middle of Hamish's thigh bone and the jagged edges of the break were sticking through his skin. Years ago, if a dog had come to him in this condition there would have been no choice but to put him down. Now, thankfully, things were different and Hamish at least had a fighting chance. But if Guy didn't get this fixed soon then the dog could still end up losing a leg. Guy opened his visits bag and rummaged inside. 'I'll give him some pain relief and an antibiotic injection,' he told Alan. 'Because the fracture's open there's a risk of infection. That could kill him as quick as anything.' Guy filled a hypodermic and then eased it into the muscle on Hamish's rump. The dog whimpered and the vet rubbed the area soothingly. 'Don't hold it against me, boy. This will make you feel better soon, I promise.'

In his bag there was a wad of cottonwool and some bandages. He took them now and gently bound the fracture to try to support the leg. It wasn't perfect, but it might at least give Hamish some comfort. It was going to be a bumpy ride back.

Guy stood up and surveyed the rocks around them on all sides. 'We're never going to carry him out of here, Alan,' he said as he assessed the desperate situation. 'We're going to have to lash him to the sledge and haul him out. You up for it?'

'Aye,' Alan said grimly.

'Let's lift Hamish together.' They positioned the sledge as close as they could to him, then slid their arms under the dog and in unison hefted him onto the sled. The dog weighed a ton and Guy was glad that Alan had crafted such a useful present for Tom and Jessica. Guy had no idea how they would have managed without it. Any longer and Hamish's life could be in serious jeopardy. It was touch and go as it was.

They tied the dog tightly to the sledge and, for once, Hamish lay still and let them do what they had to without complaint except for a whimper or two when his broken leg was knocked in the process. 'Good lad,' Alan said soothingly as they secured him, stroking Hamish gently. 'There's my good lad.'

The two men climbed back up the ridge, hauling the heavy sledge complete with Hamish behind them. They had no option but to take it slowly, inch by inch, but eventually they reached the top. The worst part was over. Guy and Alan stood panting at the top and Hamish gave a weak woof, clearly also glad that the painful, jolting progress up the rockface had stopped. There was still a long way to go, but it would be easier from here on in as the route was mainly downhill back to the car. Now the race was on to get Hamish back to the surgery in time to save him.

Chapter Eighty-One

I'm sitting in the bed between my children, Tom snuggled under my arm on one side, Jessica on the other. 'You must never do that again,' I tell them as I stroke Jessica's hair. 'Mummy was so worried about you.'

'We thought you were going to hurt Hamish,' Tom says tearfully. 'We didn't want you to do it.'

'I'm so sorry.' I squeeze my son. 'I was so cross with him

that I lost my temper. I'll never do that again. I love Hamish.' Did I really just say that? Yes, I did. And I mean it. Our life might be a damn sight quieter without Hamish in it, but suddenly that doesn't seem to be an appealing prospect. He's brought some fun and joy into the children's lives when they've really needed it. 'I don't want anything bad to happen to him.' How true that is now. I'm desperately worried that Guy and Alan won't be able to get the dog out of that treacherous ravine in time. My blood turns to ice when I think that the children could have fallen down there too. If we were staying here I'd have to make sure that they were better schooled in the ways of outdoor pursuits and safety. As it is, we're heading back to London where they're more likely to get hit by a bus or mugged. That doesn't sound like a great prospect either.

'They're here!' my sister shouts from downstairs. 'They're bringing Hamish back.'

I shoot out of the bed, hotly pursued by Tom and Jessica. 'You have to stay here,' I tell them, marvelling at how quickly they're recovering after some well-aimed hot chocolate and plenty of toast. 'You must rest.'

'We have to see Hamish,' Tom says firmly. 'He saved us.'

'Okay,' I relent. 'But you must wrap up warm and go straight back to bed afterwards.'

Flying downstairs, we gear up in the kitchen, the children putting on layer upon layer over their pyjamas while Serena keeps an eye on their progress. We're kitted up and are outside just in time to see Guy and Alan hauling the dead weight of Hamish into the yard. Stupid dog that he is, he still tries to bark and wag his tail.

'Oh, Hamish,' Jessica cries and runs to him.

Guy and Alan stop where they are and the men wipe the sweat from their brows. 'Hard work,' Guy pants.

My children crouch in the snow next to the dog, fussing and petting him.

'How's he doing?' I ask Guy quietly.

'Not great,' he admits. 'But he's a fighter. We should get him straight back to the surgery. Alan's going to come with me.'

I reach out and touch Guy's arm. 'Come back as soon as you can.'

'I will,' he says.

'I'll cook you both up the best festive omelette you've ever had.' And I know that I owe this kind, strong man so much more, but I can't say that now or I'll cry again.

He laughs. 'I'll hold you to it.'

'Children,' I call out to Tom and Jessica. 'Let Guy take Hamish now. He has to go and mend his broken leg.'

'Please be careful with him,' Tom pleads as he gives the dog a last, loving stroke.

'I will,' Guy assures him.

'We couldn't live without him,' Jessica adds.

And that's true enough. If Hamish survives – and I just pray that he does – it looks like he's coming to London with us after all.

Chapter Eighty-Two

When they arrived at the surgery, Guy unlocked the door and flicked on all the lights. Unusually, they had only one patient in residence over Christmas so the place was virtually deserted. He could hear Fluffy, a hedgehog who'd also been brought in with a broken leg, rummaging about in his cage. The little animal had been here for over a month now. He was all healed and it was time for him to leave. But Fluffy had become so accustomed to human contact – Cheryl's in particular – and his luxury diet of cat food, that Guy just couldn't see him surviving in the wild now. He should be hibernating, not living in a centrally heated, one-room comfortable apartment with several doting attendants. Who in their right mind would want to go grubbing about for slugs in the cold after this? They couldn't possibly think of turning him out yet. It was a problem that they'd have to address in the New Year. For now, Guy had more pressing matters to deal with.

For some reason Guy also switched on the lights of the Christmas tree which Cheryl had spent hours lovingly decorating. They twinkled at him – red, green and gold – but failed to make the practice look any more festive. On the desk there were boxes and boxes of chocolates, all brought in by grateful customers. Cheryl had tipped some into a glass dish and, without thinking, Guy automatically unwrapped one and ate it without tasting it either. 'Chocolate?' he said to Alan.

The man shook his head.

'It's the closest you'll get to dinner for a while.' Guy threw him a Quality Street anyway, then flicked on the CD player that was behind the desk. Soon, Cheryl's selection of Christmas carols drifted out through the speakers. He'd need something to soothe him while he carried out this particular operation. Ridiculously, he felt as if he was going to be operating on his own child. Even worse, it took him back to the day he'd had to put his own dear dog to sleep. Hopefully this operation would have a better outcome.

The mellow sounds of 'God Rest Ye Merry Gentlemen' filled the reception. Again, it would be some time before he and Alan got any rest. Although he could currently see the attraction in getting very, very merry when they'd finished.

Guy sighed to himself. They'd better get moving. Hamish had coped well so far, but he didn't want to risk delaying any longer. It seemed unnecessary to call in a practice nurse when Alan was here with him and was sure to make a reliable assistant. 'Up for a spot of veterinary nursing?'

'Aye.' Alan nodded.

'Let's get our patient in then.' They went back to the car and between them carried Hamish into the surgery and hoisted him up onto the table in Guy's consulting room.

The vet scratched his head. If it was any other patient, he'd have given the dog intravenous fluids to counter the

310

shock and would have left him to stabilise overnight before operating. But this was Hamish and so much more seemed to be resting on his recovery that he didn't feel able to wait that long.

He scrubbed up and had Alan do the same, both donning green surgical gowns while Hamish waited patiently. Guy fixed Hamish up to a drip while he took an X-ray of the fracture. Thankfully, when he looked at the break in the cold light of a clinical setting it didn't seem nearly as bad as he'd expected. The dog would need a metal fixator put in place to help it heal, but it was definitely do-able. The fixators might look like medieval instruments of torture, but they worked like magic and it was amazing how well dogs tolerated them, even though hideous bits of metal were left sticking out through their skin while they did their job. Dogs who weren't Hamish, of course. Although currently, the dog in question was being the model patient.

'Good lad,' Guy said, and gave Hamish a loving stroke.

The femoral artery was intact, thank God, which was what he'd been most worried about, and it looked like the majority of the blood loss had been caused by the multiple cuts that Hamish had sustained as he'd tumbled down the rockface. Most of them were superficial, and a few stitches would put the worst of them right.

'I'm going to give him an anaesthetic now so that I can fix this leg, Alan,' Guy said.

The dog looked trustingly into his eyes. 'We need you to give this your best shot, Hamish,' Guy said. 'And we'll do the same.'

He gave the dog an injection into his front leg and within

seconds Hamish was fast asleep. 'I need you to hold Hamish tight while I put in this breathing tube. Here, like this.' He showed Alan what to do and was surprised to see tears rolling down the man's face. 'He'll be fine,' Guy said. 'He'll be just fine.'

Alan wiped the tears away with the sleeve of his scrubs. 'Aye, Vit.'

There was sweat on his own brow. Alan stroked the dog's head lovingly.

'Ready?'

'Aye,' the man said. 'Get on wi' it, Vit.'

'Right.' Guy took an unsteady breath. Never in his life had he wanted a dog to pull through as much as this one. He picked up his scalpel. 'Here goes.'

Chapter Eighty-Three

Alan and Guy sat in the recovery room watching Hamish sleeping off the effects of his anaesthetic in one of the big cages while they systematically worked their way through a box of Heroes.

'We'll spoil our dinner,' Guy said.

'Aye,' Alan agreed and ate another chocolate.

Their surgical scrubs had been dispensed with and all Guy was waiting for now was to see Hamish wake up. This dog was indestructible, he was sure. He'd come through the operation brilliantly. The vet smiled to himself. He liked it when operations had a happy ending. Guy felt a strong bond to this crazed handful of animal and he got up and ruffled Hamish's floppy ears affectionately. The dog stirred in his drug-induced sleep and twitched his front paws.

Already, he'd phoned Amy to let her know that Hamish was fine. He could picture her now sitting anxiously in front of the Aga at Helmshill Grange with the children by her side waiting for him to come back. It was a nice, comforting image.

'Did you like being married?' he said to Alan as he still fussed with Hamish's ears.

'Aye,' the man replied.

'You'd recommend it?'

'Reckon so.'

Guy turned to look at his very efficient and capable nurse, but Alan was intently studying the contents of the box of Heroes.

'Do you miss Mrs Steadman?'

'Aye,' Alan said. 'Every single day.'

'I'm sorry I didn't really know her.'

'She was grand.' Alan looked up and met Guy's eye. 'Give it a go, Vit. Reckon you'd be good at it.'

For Alan, that was the equivalent of delivering the Jonathan Dimbleby lecture.

'I'd like to,' Guy admitted. 'I'd like to very much.' He let out a heartfelt sigh. 'But what if Mrs Steadman had been in love with someone else, someone who wasn't actually around but was there in pretty much every way? Would you have waited for her, or would you have given up hope and found someone else?'

Alan's gaunt cheeks coloured up and he studied his shoes. 'Don't know, Vit.'

Clearly that was an emotional conversation too far for the man. Then Alan pointed at Hamish, glad of the distraction. 'Dog's up.'

Sure enough, Hamish was rousing from his sleep and looked quite bright, considering his ordeal. He gave them an enthusiastic woof and his tail thumped against the bars of his cage.

'There's a good lad,' Guy said, as he went to pet the dog. 'None the worse for your ordeal, eh?'

Alan came over to fuss Hamish too. Guy could see that the man was crying and he felt tears on his own face.

'What a couple of silly old farts we are,' Guy sniffed.

'Aye, Vit.'

He put his arm round the elderly man and clapped him on the back. Relief washed over Guy and, more than anything, he wanted to be with Amy. He wanted to be with her right now. Technically, he should stay here for a few more hours and monitor Hamish, just to be on the safe side. But, damn it, it was Christmas. How could he spend the night here? How could Hamish?

'Fancy risking putting our backs out again?'

Alan waited to find out how.

'I think we'll take this fellow home,' Guy said. 'No one should be in hospital at Christmas. Not even a dog.'

Alan smiled. A rare event.

'One other thing.' He held up a hand to Alan and then rushed out to where Fluffy was still shuffling about in his cage. The little hedgehog stood up on his newly mended back legs and scrabbled at the glass when Guy appeared and let out a grunt in greeting. He could swear that Fluffy was getting more like a dog with every passing day. Guy was sure that Amy wouldn't mind feeding one more mouth at Christmas. 'Want to come on an outing, Fluff?'

He picked up the cage and took it back through to where Hamish and Alan were waiting. 'Let's go and get our Christmas dinner,' he said.

Chapter Eighty-Four

'We just have to wait now and see,' Guy says. 'But he looks like he's going to be fine.'

Alan and Guy have hefted Hamish into the kitchen in a big wire cage. He's lying inside it looking quite perky despite the horrible metal contraption that's attached to his broken leg, and his tail is beating time against the bars of his temporary prison. He looks just like Hamish should – ready to be out of there and ripping up the house as soon as he can.

'Thank goodness.' I feel like sagging to the floor with relief. The children go crazy, huddling round Hamish and cheering, my earlier attempts to keep them tucked up and resting in bed having failed. To be honest, I'm just grateful that they seem to be none the worse for their ordeal.

It's late afternoon now and we've all been sitting in the kitchen, huddled by the Aga waiting for news. And, at long last, we've been joined by Alan, Guy and the star of the moment, Hamish. I hope I'm not speaking too soon, but now our Christmas celebrations can finally start. Which is usually the cue for the roof to cave in or a meteor to hit the yard. I pause for a moment, tensed, but I'm relieved to find that nothing happens. You don't know how good that feels.

'Alan made a lovely nurse,' Guy teases.

Saint Steadman flushes and studies his boots.

Even though Alan isn't one to wear his heart on his sleeve, he looks drained by the events of the day and his craggy face is paler than it normally is. Despite that, he still insisted that he was the one who went outside into the cold to sort the animals out for me, securing the chickens for the night and tending to the sheep including the expectant mother, the goats and Pork Chop.

I allow myself a little tear and Guy gives me a hug. 'Thank you.'

'Glad I could help,' he says. Guy looks exhausted too and I think it's about time that I got those omelettes on the go before we all nod off.

'I have a confession.' Guy glances sheepishly at Alan. 'There's another little visitor here if you'll have him.'

Alarm bells ring, but I know that I can deny him nothing. He has saved my children and has saved my dog. Even if he's brought a bloody great boa constrictor to visit then I'll smile and welcome it.

He goes out to his car again and comes back with a cage with a hedgehog in it. 'This is Fluffy,' he tells us. Of course, the children go into raptures.

The hedgehog's extraordinarily cute, but I still eye it warily. 'Aren't they riddled with fleas?'

'This one is flea-free and very nearly house-trained.' Guy turns on the charm. 'He'd make someone a lovely pet.'

'Oh, Mummy,' Jessica trills. 'Can we keep him?'

'You wouldn't have to do anything,' Tom adds, seeing that this is a contributing factor to the residence of all of our charges.

'For the time being,' I say evasively. Guy might be the saviour of all mankind, but I will kill him for this. How can we take on a hedgehog now?

So my daughter lets Fluffy out of his cage and he trundles like a mini-tank across the kitchen floor. Milly Molly Mandy narrows her eyes and spits at him.

'Alan, sit down near the fire,' I instruct. 'I can't thank you enough for all that you've done for us.'

I kiss him on the cheek and hug him warmly and, this time, he succumbs to my embrace. 'Can I get you a drink? I reckon you've earned one,' I say.

'Aye, lass,' he says, and I pour him out a glass of Selbies' Strong Ale, a local beer and his favourite tipple according to Guy. He takes off his cap and stretches out in the armchair, luxuriating in the warmth. Milly Molly Mandy eyes his lap covetously and, sure enough, pounces before padding round to find the most comfortable spot and curling up with a contented purr.

I splash out some champagne for the rest of us, even giving Tom and Jessica an inch of fizz in the bottom of two flutes. 'To Hamish,' I say. 'May he get better soon.'

'To Hamish,' we all toast and raise our glasses. The object of our good wishes howls his approval.

I throw back my champagne, thinking that I've earned it too. 'I'll get the dinner on,' I say. 'I bet everyone is starving.' There are assenting murmurs all round.

The chickens have been busy and, thankfully, there are enough eggs for big, duvet-sized omelettes for all of us. I've also got a big block of local cheese, so we can have some of that grated in them too.

In an effort to take my mind off the trauma of the day, I spent part of the afternoon setting the Christmas-table in the dining room in lavish style with my fine bone china and crystal glasses that I unpacked for the first time, even though I know I'm going to have to pack them all again straight away for our move. There's a strategically placed fan heater in there too, to try to chase away the last of the chill. Already there's a big roasting pan of potatoes browning nicely in the Aga and a pile of vegetables steaming on the top of the stove. I go over to the working end of the kitchen, get my mixing bowl and start breaking the freshly laid eggs into it in batches of three. A moment later, Guy comes up behind me. 'Can I help?' he asks.

'You've done more than enough,' I tell him thankfully. 'It's your turn to relax now and let me look after you.'

'And what about you, Amy?' He rests his hand lightly

on my shoulder and I can feel the warmth of it searing through my sweater. 'Who will look after *you*?'

'I'm fine,' I assure him. But my voice is more wobbly than I would have liked. I turn to face him and we're inches apart. I can feel the warmth of his breath on my face.

'I wouldn't have been able to bear it if anything had happened to the children or to you.'

'Thanks to you, we're all fine.'

I'm thinking that if we were alone, if we weren't in a room full of people, that he might just take me in his arms and kiss me.

Instead he looks at me sadly and says, 'I'm going to miss you when you go away, Amy Ashurst. I'm going to miss you more than you'll know.'

And I have a horrible feeling that I'll feel exactly the same.

Chapter Eighty-Five

'Why did the turkey cross the road?' Tom reads out his cracker joke. 'Because it was the chicken's day off.'

After too much booze we all find this hilarious and laugh uproariously.

'I don't get that,' Jessica complains.

'It doesn't matter, sweetheart.' I kiss her hair. 'It's not really that funny.'

'Then why are you all laughing so much?'

'Because we're all glad that you're safe and well.'

'I don't get grown-ups either.' She slumps forward at the table, head in her hands, perplexed by the mysteries of the world. To be honest, even if I understood them myself, I've had way too many glasses of champagne to be able to explain them to her.

Outside, the snow is falling again, but inside we're all warm and snug and happy. Only thoughts of my dear husband are marring the enjoyment of the day. How different this Christmas has been to the one before where Will was, as far as we were aware, fit and healthy; there was no heart problem looming large, no mention of a better life in the country. I push my mind away from dwelling on this, but raise my glass and silently make a toast to Will, telling my husband how much I miss him and that I've never stopped loving him.

Across the table, Guy catches my eye and he gives me a melancholy smile, raising his glass too as if he's reading my mind. This has certainly been a Christmas Day to remember.

The omelettes were a resounding success and, frankly, I'm not even sure that I'll bother with a turkey in years to come. Though, judging by the way Milly Molly Mandy has stuffed her face all day, the turkey is pretty good too. I wonder whether Fluffy might like some and then I realise I'm behaving like a big, old animal softie once again and wonder what happened to the hard-bitten, pet-hating, cynical me. Where on earth did she go?

I turn to my children who seem to think I've forgotten it's past their bedtime. 'It's about time that you two went off to bed.'

'It's early yet, Mummy,' Jessica whines. 'And it's Christmas Day.' Then she stifles a yawn.

'And you spent half the night out on the moors rather than in your beds. You should be tucked up again by now.'

'But I want to stay with Guy and Uncle Alan.' She curls into my side in supplicant pose.

'We're going now too,' Guy says diplomatically. He's persuaded Alan to spend the night at his home, so that the man could enjoy a few glasses of Selbies Strong Ale and not have to drive home. Alan is looking pleasantly contented. 'We'll probably see you tomorrow.'

'But what about when we move to London?' Jessica says. 'Then we'll never see you again.'

'We'll come to London,' Guy assures her. 'Won't we, Alan?'

Alan doesn't look too sure about this turn of events.

'All of our friends said that when we moved here,' my astute child points out. 'But they never did.'

'Enough chatter,' I tell her, not liking the way this conversation is progressing. 'Bedtime. Kiss Guy and Uncle Alan.'

My child slips away from my side and does as she's told, throwing her arms round both of the men for good measure. 'You are the closest thing I've had to a grandad,' Jessica tells Alan solemnly and his eyes fill with tears. Neither Will's parents nor mine were alive by the time Jessica was born and you just assume that they don't miss what they've never had. Seems I was wrong again.

'Night, lass,' Alan manages.

'Thank you for bringing Hamish home,' she says, before a yawn overtakes her again. I turn her round and aim her in the direction of the stairs.

'I'll be up in a minute to tuck you in,' I tell my daughter.

Tom also hugs the men and follows his sister without a quibble. He must be completely exhausted. I bet they'll both be asleep before I even get up there. I feel a yawn coming on myself.

'Can we help you to clear up?' Guy asks. 'We can't leave you with all this mess.'

I shake my head. 'Wouldn't hear of it. Serena and I can take our time. The dishwasher is, thankfully, one of the few things here that works properly.'

'Then we'll take our leave now,' he says, 'and you can put both of the kids to bed.'

Both Alan and Guy rise and we all hug and kiss before they leave. Alan, voluntarily, takes Serena in his arms, though he flushes when he does so. Amazing what several glasses of Selbies Strong Ale can do in lowering a man's defences.

I see them both to the door. The snow is thick again and now that my children are safely inside I no longer see the menace in the scenery. The flakes drift lazily down, blanketing the ground, covering the tracks of Alan's sledge. Perhaps we can take the kids out on it tomorrow if they're up to it – then, I think, they're not the ones who are likely to be suffering.

'Thanks, lass,' Alan says gruffly and he sets off down the drive, cap pulled down on his head. 'Thanks for a grand day.'

I think that's the only time I've heard him utter two consecutive sentences and I'm genuinely touched. That's the equivalent of Alan stripping naked and doing a happy dance on my lawn.

Guy lingers, then shouts after his companion, 'I'll catch you up.'

Alan waves a hand in acknowledgement.

'I've had a grand day too,' he says to me. Snowflakes are landing on his hair making it curl madly and, irrationally, I want to reach out and brush them away.

'It was you that made it turn out all right,' I tell him gratefully. 'I can't thank you enough. After losing Will, how would I have coped with losing the children too?' My eyes fill with tears.

'Don't think about it,' Guy advises. 'They're home now, that's all that matters.'

'I hope Hamish will be okay.'

'He seems just fine,' he reassures me. 'I'll leave him in your capable hands tonight. Have a look at him every couple of hours if you can. If there looks to be any problem, anything at all, then give me a call and I'll be right back. I'll be over anyway to check on him first thing in the morning,' he promises.

I don't tell Guy that I plan to get my duvet and curl up on the floor and sleep next to Hamish. Well, you can't be too careful, can you?

'Despite everything,' I say quietly, 'I have enjoyed today. I've enjoyed having you around and Alan.'

'And I've enjoyed being here. You have a lovely family, Amy. It's nice to feel like a part of it.'

'Thank you.'

Guy looks deep into my eyes. 'Oh Amy,' he breathes. 'I could so easily fall in love with you.' Then, before I can say anything, he turns and runs down my drive, chasing after Alan and leaving me to stare after him, mouth agape.

323

Chapter Eighty-Six

Barely a month after Christmas and I'm packed up and ready to go. I've taken the bull by the horns as I haven't yet exchanged contracts on the house with the Gerner-Bernards, but I feel that I can't delay the move any longer. I want a few weeks to get myself sorted before I start back at the BTC. The children have already missed a couple of weeks of the new term at Queensway and I want them to settle into their new school as soon as possible. I'm sure everything will be fine with the sale. The conveyancing has been done and the solicitor says that everything is moving along very well, and the Gerner-Bernards have already had a stream of builders coming through to look at the place to 'knock it into shape'.

The removal van is parked on the drive and two accommodating young men are loading up my life's possessions to cart them all the way back to our new pad in London. That's not strictly true, since some of the furniture and stuff is having to go straight into storage as there isn't anywhere near enough room in the flat we've rented for all this junk we've accumulated over the years. Some of the boxes I haven't even opened since we moved into Helmshill Grange all those months ago. If I put them into storage it means that I can go through the boxes a couple at a time and get rid of anything that's now surplus to requirements – that's the theory, anyhow.

There's still piles of Will's stuff that I haven't been able to face going through. I still have all of his clothes, his sports equipment – even the squash racket that has never been used although he was always going to get round to it – his collection of Queen memorabilia and a stack of dusty biographies that have yet to be thumbed and now probably never will be. I don't suppose that I'll be needing the excellent volume *Keeping Chickens* by Audrey Fanshawe now either. And, though it seems stupid to take it all with me, that's exactly what I'm doing.

It's not a bright, sunny day for our departure from Helmshill. There's a cruel bite to the wind, miserable clouds hang low over the moors and even the sky looks depressed. I was up and out before the kids woke up this morning and I went to visit Will's grave. I put a new wreath of twigs interlaced with acorns on there that I bought in Scarsby because I knew that it would last for a while. It gives me a pang to think that we might not get here for several weeks. Who will look after Will while we are away? The reality of all that I'm leaving behind is starting to hit home.

I stood there for ages, but I just didn't know what to say, so I came home and collected my hens' eggs for the final time, packing them in polystyrene boxes ready to take in the car with us. I only hope that the rattly old Land Rover will make it all the way down the motorway; the first thing I'll have to do when I'm in London is get rid of it and buy something more suited to city driving and less covered in cow poo.

I'm due to start my new job on the arts programme in the middle of February, which will give us a couple of weeks to settle in before I go out into the big, bad world of work again. Gavin Morrison is proving very elusive as he's tied up with this massive sweep of redundancies that's all over the media at the moment. I haven't had my employment contract either, despite hassling the HR department twice a week. But then I remember how useless they were when I worked there before, with three women trying to do the work of ten. Plus I know that they're also snowed under with extra work at the moment – probably too busy firing to think about hiring. I'm so grateful that they're even taking me on when they're getting rid of so many people. If it wasn't for the lure of this job, I really would be having serious second thoughts about this.

In some ways I wish there was another solution, but I know that I can't stay here, so we just have to get on with it. Now I'm standing and watching the lads load the last of the boxes and waves of nausea keep washing over me. I pull my jacket around me but it fails to keep away the chill.

The children are helping with the packing up and Jessica is sobbing quietly while doing it. Do you know how much of a heel that makes me feel? Hamish is tied up to the tree closest to the yard with a sturdy rope. He's barking manically. Apart from the Frankenstein-style fixator on his hind leg which he keeps trying to chew, our demented dog appears to be none the worse for his ordeal. Unfortunately, his brush with death hasn't helped to calm him down any. I thought it might have taught him some sense, but no such luck. How on earth we're going to manage to get him all the way to London without disaster is beyond me. And quite what we're going to do with him when we get there is another matter altogether. With his fracture, he's confined to short walks on the lead and is supposed to be kept calm. Fat chance. Guy has promised to pop by and give me a sedative for him before we set off. I might take one myself. But it's really great that Guy is coming here because at least it gives me a chance to say goodbye to him – something I'm not exactly looking forward to.

The vet and I haven't managed to be alone together since Christmas Day. Nor has he mentioned what he said to me, and I wonder whether he's regretting it now and it was purely down to a heady mixture of the heightened emotion of the day and the drink talking – always a lethal combination if you ask me. We've both been maniacally busy. Me with packing up. Guy with keeping the practice going single-handedly as his partner, Stephen, has the flu. I think, in some ways, we're both avoiding each other.

'Nearly done, missus,' one of the removal men tells me and I pull myself away from my reverie.

'Right. Thanks.' We need to set off soon, I know that. As it is, it will be dark by the time we get to London.

Milly Molly Mandy – who is also now coming to London with us – has been captured and is sitting in a travel cage awaiting her fate, hissing crossly at the indignity of her treatment. The endangered rodent population of Helmshill are, I'm positive, breathing a collective sigh of relief at our cat's imminent departure. I'm not sure that I dare go and look at the other animals that we're leaving behind. The chickens that I nursed back to health are a particular sticking point. I can feel my eyes tearing up whenever I even dare to think about them. Fluffy is also proving to be a tear-jerker. Who would have thought that this prickly little hedgehog could have wormed his way under all of our skins. He's taken to following Jessica round the house like a shadow and sleeping snuggled up in a pair of her old pyjamas under her bed. Unfortunately, Fluffy is having to stay behind too. How can you have a hedgehog as a pet in London? It's just not going to happen. Then I see that my daughter has climbed up onto the fence and is peering over in the pen where the sheep and Pork Chop are currently held, and think that I must join her for one last round of goodbyes to the animals that have somehow become an integral part of our lives even though I never wanted any of them.

Jessica's standing on the second slat of the fence and is leaning over to feed Pork Chop some pig nuts from the bucket that's always kept handy for him. The chubby Vietnamese Pot-Bellied Pig has settled in well and has also already charmed his way into the affection of my children, and I have to admit that I quite like him too. He's a friendly and well-behaved little soul and I hope that Guy is able to find him a good home. The same goes for our other charges. Delila is as fat as a house now and is due to give birth to her lamb at any moment according to Alan and I guess he'd know about these things. Daphne and Doris are out here on their own as Delila is taking a mid-morning nap in the barn.

Saint Steadman is here and is busy around the yard. He's also been carefully avoiding me since Christmas – although with Alan it's harder to tell. I think he's going to find it more difficult to watch us leave than he'd care to admit and doesn't want any emotionally loaded conversations or hysterical scenes. The children are very fond of him and I know that he's grown very attached to them too in his own dour, unde-monstrative way. He's agreed to stay on until the animals have gone and the Gerner-Bernards move into the Grange. I try not to think of it as tears well in my eyes and I don't want them to. Not today.

I sidle up to Jessica and slip my arm round her shoulders. 'All right, honey?'

She shakes her head. 'Why can't Tom and I stay here with Uncle Alan and you can go to London to work and send us money?'

My daughter says it as if it is such a reasonable proposi-tion that I wonder why I haven't considered it myself. 'But Mummy would miss you both so much, darling.'

'I'd miss you too,' she says, unmoved. 'You could come home at weekends. Hamish likes it better here.' On cue, the dog woofs his agreement. Never work with animals or chil-dren, they say. Now I can see why.

Tom is climbing in the branches of the oak tree at a worrying height.

'We need to be going soon,' I shout up to him.

'I'm climbing the tree for the very last time,' he yells back. 'Because I'll never be able to do it again.'

'There are trees in London.' Not many in the part we're living in, I'll admit.

'Yes,' he says. 'But you won't let me climb them there.'

I sigh. He's probably right. They'll never have the freedom in the city that they've enjoyed here.

Then Alan comes across the yard. For Alan, he's hurrying. 'Delila's starting wit' bairn,' he tells us, flicking a thumb towards the big barn.

'Yay!' Jessica shouts. 'A baby!' And she charges off towards the sheep.

Tom scrambles frantically down the tree, scraping the knees out of his jeans as he does and shouting, 'Wait for me!' He, too, bolts up to the barn.

'Comin', Mrs A?'

'Yes,' I say. 'I'm coming.' And, despite a thrill of excitement, I think this is all I need. This, of all things, is all that I need.

Chapter Eighty-Seven

Guy arrived just as Alan was delivering a lamb for Delila. Tom and Jessica were watching, rapt. Amy, he noted, was looking decidedly green around the gills. Guy couldn't help but smile to himself. Try as she might, she'd never make a natural farmer. And that, of course, was why she was heading away from the hills and back to the city smoke. His heart was heavy with the knowledge of her impending departure. By the look of the removal lorry, they were just about ready to go. Time, it seemed, had run out for them.

Since Christmas he'd tried not to think about it. He'd been aided considerably in that process by having the majority of animals in Scarsby and the surrounding areas fall ill all at once. Then his assistant, Stephen, had compounded the problem by getting the flu himself, leaving Guy to cope single-handedly at one of the busiest times of the year. As a result, he'd been in the practice shortly after six every morning and was rarely getting home before ten at night. Then there were the call-outs that punctuated the night. It didn't leave a lot of time for courting, as he pointed out regularly to Cheryl, who was continually berating him for not making time to see more of Amy. Guy felt that he had a perfectly good excuse. Cheryl said he was using it as an avoidance technique. And, much as he hated to admit that his receptionist and self-styled lifecoach might be right, perhaps Cheryl had a point. What was he to say to Amy now, after he'd blurted out his feelings to her like a gauche schoolboy? Let's face it, even gauche schoolboys probably did better than that these days. Amy hadn't said anything in return, but then he'd scurried away, mortified by his unrehearsed and spontaneous outpouring of emotion – unaccustomed as he was to sharing his feelings with anyone these days. The other side of the coin was that by the time he had pinged his microwave dinner for the night he was virtually incoherent with tiredness and more than once had spent the night fully clothed on top of his bed, unable to stay awake long enough to go through the tedious procedure of getting undressed. Whenever they had snatched a moment together, they had never been alone or the timing had been wrong to have anything more than a cursory conversation. The opportunity to pour out his heart to her, or to find out how she felt about him had never happened – and perhaps it was just as well.

The two removal men, tasks completed, came and gazed over the fence too.

'Come on, girl,' Alan gently coaxed Delila. Guy had to

say that it wasn't looking good. The ewe was straining but nothing was happening. 'You can do it, lass.'

The sheep turned doleful eyes on him and let out a complaining baa. Guy pursed his lips. 'How long has she been going?'

'Nearly an hour now. Want to take over, Vit?'

'I'll have a look.' He scrubbed up under the tap in the yard, before sliding his hand inside the ewe. All he could feel was a little tail and bottom. It was clear that the lamb was presenting breech. 'She needs a bit of help here.'

Guy felt for the lamb's hind legs and then, holding them tightly, he pulled the youngster out backwards. A grey slithery mound plopped lifelessly to the floor. Alan cleared the mucus from its mouth, then he swung the lamb backwards and forwards, trying to get it to breathe.

'Nothing, Vit,' he said, alarm in his voice.

Guy held the lamb and rubbed vigorously at its chest to stimulate breathing. Still the tiny creature didn't move. 'Water,' Guy said over his shoulder. 'I need water.'

Amy quickly put a bucket down next to him and Guy flicked the cold water all over the lamb which, thankfully, gasped its way into life at the shock. It seemed a brutal way to make your entry into life, but it usually did the trick.

'Oh,' Jessica cried. 'It's lovely!' The little girl and her brother were crying and if Guy wasn't mistaken, Amy was shedding a tear too. Perhaps even the removal guys were a bit watery eyed as well. When you were so used to delivering lambs it was hard to remember the miracle of watching your first birth.

It was a tiny lamb and weak. Its breath laboured in its

little chest. The animal vainly tried to stand on its stick-like and wobbly legs, but couldn't support its own weight. Guy didn't rate its chances much. He looked at Alan and the man nodded his agreement without him having to speak. To get some warmth for the lamb was paramount. 'We need to get it warmed up. Can we put it in the Aga, Amy?'

She looked at him in horror. 'You're going to cook it?'

He laughed. 'Not intentionally.' Then he was serious again. 'It might not last otherwise. We need to get it warmed through. It's totally against health and safety regulations and there's probably an EU directive against it, but nothing does the job better than a night in the stove. Right, Alan?'

The man nodded. 'Aye, Vit.'

'I thought that was a country myth.'

'No.'

Amy shrugged her acceptance. 'Then let's do it.'

'I'll tend to the ewe, Alan,' Guy said. 'You see to the lamb.'

Alan tenderly picked up the scrap of a lamb and carried it towards the house.

Jessica ran behind him. 'We can't leave Delila with a sick baby,' she said to her mother. 'We'll have to go to London another day.'

Amy looked at him for support.

'She's right,' Guy said. 'Can you stay another day or so?' It was wrong, he knew, but he'd clutch at any straw that kept Amy here for even a minute longer.

Chapter Eighty-Eight

I call Serena and arrange for her to be at the new flat to meet the removal lorry and I give her the men's mobile numbers in case of emergency. She can't believe it when I say that our delay is caused by a crisis with a newborn lamb. My sister definitely thinks that I've gone soft in the head. I tell her that we'll see the lamb through the night – hopefully – and that we'll be in London tomorrow *without fail* to be reunited with our furniture.

While I'm doing this, Alan and Guy are making a bed for the little lamb and are slotting him into the front of the Aga. Grief, I just hope they can work this bloody oven better than me otherwise he'll be medium rare in no time. I wonder whether I should shove some rosemary in next to him just in case. Just kidding.

'A lamb,' Jessica intones reverently. 'We have a little baby *lamb* in our kitchen!'

I must admit that it's a first for me and it seems so right and fitting for this place to be nurturing the struggling newborn.

Thankfully, I rescued the box with our kettle, mugs, toaster and the last few bits from the fridge in it from the removal van before the men drove off taking the rest of our worldly possessions with them. It's late for them to be leaving and it will be well into the evening by the time they get to London, even if they have a clear run. I might not have much money left, but I'll make sure that they're well compensated for their inconvenience.

There's nothing else left in the kitchen or the rest of the house for that matter. Not knowing what else to do, I put the kettle on. I'm tired and we've got no food and I'm beginning to wonder whether this was a wise idea.

'I'll run Alan home,' Guy says into my reverie. 'Then I'll pick us up a Chinese take-away in Scarsby and I'll collect some bedding on the way back.'

I wasn't sure what we were going to do about sleeping arrangements. Looks like the kitchen floor is going to be our bed for the night.

'Is that okay?' he asks. 'You and the kids can stay at my place while I sit here with the lamb, if you'd prefer.'

My heart surges at the thought of this big, strong man sitting here to tend to this tiny scrap as it clings precariously to life. 'You think I'm going to get these two away from this little wretch?'

'Probably not.'

'*Definitely* not,' I tell him.

'Sit tight until I come back,' he instructs. 'Call me if the lamb shows any signs of worsening.'

I'm not sure that it could look much worse than it does. The poor thing is shivering like mad despite being wrapped in a fleecy towel that also escaped the clutches of the removal men, and being slowly roasted on a low heat – though the oven door is open, so hopefully he can't come to too much harm.

Guy and Alan head to the door and as they leave, Mr

Steadman turns and doffs his flat cap to me before he disappears. It occurs to me that it could be the last time that I see Alan and I want to run after them. I had plans to say so much to Mr Steadman, to pass on my heartfelt thanks for all that he has done for us, how I now consider him a family friend, how the children will miss him like mad, but there never seemed to be an appropriate moment. I wanted to hug that rough brown tweed coat to me and tell him how much we all care for him. But with a man like Alan, perhaps it was best that these things went unsaid. I'm sure he knows how much he has come to mean to us without me going all slushy on him. I should write to him when I get home. I should write on a regular basis. I can't bear the thought of anything happening to him and us not knowing. Then I think 'home'? Am I already viewing London as home?

I fold up the children's coats so that they can sit on them by the warmth of the Aga, then I crack and go into the scullery to fire up the central heating once more. During all this Hamish has been the model of good behaviour – well, if you consider full-on barking and trying to strangle yourself with a rope good behaviour. Now he's clearly getting bored and hungry. I hope that Guy remembers to bring some dog food back with him when he gets the Chinese take-away as we've nothing else to feed Hamish on; The removal men are now heading down the M1 with his bowl and tins of meaty chunks. Though I'm sure Hamish wouldn't object to dining on spare ribs and pork balls tonight.

'Sit down, Hamish,' I tell him. 'Your pacing about is driving me nuts.'

'Come here, boy,' Tom says, slapping his leg, and the dog goes to settle down next to him, half-smothering my son with his bulk.

Fluffy, having won a brief reprieve from going back to his home in the veterinary surgery, is keeping himself amused by shuffling happily round the kitchen floor. The children can't take their eyes off the lamb and I don't know what to do with myself so I wander through the empty rooms of Helmshill Grange. I wonder what the Gerner-Bernards will do with the house. Will they countrify it? Will they turn it into a minimalist shrine to Dulux matt white emulsion? There's been a lot of builders striding about here with tape measures, tutting.

The days are so short now that already the moon is up and shining through the French windows in the living room.

'If only you'd left us with some dosh,' I say out loud to Will. 'I might have been tempted to stay here. Despite everything, we've had some good times.'

I sit in the middle of the floor in a patch of bright moonlight. 'I don't want you to think that I'm leaving you here,' I tell my husband. 'We'll come back to visit. I think I'm doing the right thing for the kids.' Though that argument somehow sounds so hollow now. 'And I have to work. I have no choice. There's nothing here for me and Gavin's so keen to have me on board at the BTC again. It will seem funny, but I'm sure that we can pick up our old life. It'll be just like having you back.' The tears roll down my face. 'I really have enjoyed my time at Helmshill Grange. Thank you for dragging me out to this beaten-up old place in the country. If only you could have stayed here with me.'

Then I cry and cry and cry. I cry because I don't want to leave here and because I can't stay. I cry because I want to do the right thing by my kids and because everything I do turns out wrong. I cry because I still love my husband and because if I stay here I might just fall in love with someone else too.

Chapter Eighty-Nine

Guy lifts the lamb tenderly out of the Aga. On his trip he has somehow managed to find some formula milk for the poorly infant.

'I've got some colostrum from one of the other farmers,' Guy tells me and I assume that this is a good thing. 'I've brought some glucose to give it too.' He certainly came back to the house laden down with carrier bags.

Now he produces an empty wine bottle and fixes a teat to it. 'Mix up some of the formula and put it in here.'

I do as I'm told and minutes later hand the bottle of formula milk back to him. Snuggling it in tightly to his chest, he tries the lamb on the bottle and the tiny animal sucks hungrily on the teat.

'Come on, you two,' he says to the children. 'You can do this.' They sidle up to him and Guy gives the bottle first to Jessica and then to Tom. Their eyes are alight with delight as the lamb continues to feed undaunted.

'Oh, Mummy,' Jessica breathes, gingerly holding the big

bottle in her small hand. 'When I grow up I want to be a vet too.'

Marvellous. I'd always hoped that she'd be a lawyer or an astronaut. Now I'm looking forward to a lifetime filled with the scent of animal wee and fur all over my best clothes. Though I have to say the lamb does look incredibly cute. I only hope that it survives the night. If the way it's drinking that milk is anything to go by, then it's going to give life its best shot.

'Mummy, come and feed the lamb,' Tom urges, and Guy holds out the wine bottle for me. Not to be the killjoy, I go over and take the bottle, slipping it into the hungry, searching mouth. The lamb tugs eagerly, its scrawny body wriggling in Guy's arms and, for some silly reason, my eyes fill up with tears.

'I'm going to call him Stuart Little,' Jessica says, voice still laced with wonder, 'because he's little like Stuart Little.'

'Stuart Little's a mouse, stupid,' my son points out helpfully.

'Don't call your sister stupid,' I say.

'I don't care.' Jessica is defiant. Hands on hips, chin jutting. 'That's his name now.'

That's all I need. Now we're naming animals that we're going to leave behind.

I hand the lamb and the bottle back to Guy, surreptitiously wipe my tears away with my sleeve and, after giving my hands a good scrub, set about dishing out the Chinese take-away that Guy has collected. He's also brought four plates and cutlery from his home for us to use. Plus he arrived with two sleeping bags, a couple of double duvets and some pillows to make up our beds for the night. Clearly, Guy is planning to spend the rest of the night with us and I feel so grateful for that.

Not forgetting Hamish, he also brought dog food for our hound and a bowl. Having eaten, our troublesome hound is now slumbering soundly in front of the stove. He looks the very picture of contentment, his ears and paws twitching madly as, no doubt, he gets up to all kinds of mischief in his dreams. I look at the dog and for the first time feel a strong wave of affection for him, maybe even love. It's taken all this time, but Hamish is finally entrenched in my heart and he really is one of the family now. Milly Molly Mandy, glad to be liberated from her small travelling cage, is stretched out along his belly also fast asleep. Partners in crime, I think.

The lamb, now fed and looking a little stronger, is popped back into the Aga while we kneel down in front of the stove with plates heaped with delicious Chinese food. 'I wish I hadn't packed away all the wine now,' I say.

'Ah,' Guy says. 'Forgot about that.' He puts down his plate and pads over to another carrier bag by the door. 'A decent red, two glasses and a corkscrew.'

I laugh. 'You really did think of everything.'

'As I've got you here for one more night, I thought we'd take advantage of it.' Then we exchange a glance that's full of regret for what might have been.

He breaks away first and busies himself with opening and pouring the wine, sloshing healthy measures into each glass. Then he hands me one and clinks his own glass against it.

Guy sits down next to me, closer this time. My cheeks are glowing and not only with the heat from the stove. It seems bizarre in a house that's so empty that we can feel so cosy.

'This is very good wine,' I say as I take a swig. 'I'll certainly sleep tonight.' And that makes me flush even more.

'To London,' he says.

'To London,' I echo flatly.

Chapter Ninety

The children's eyes grew heavy the minute they'd finished their food. Too much excitement for one day, I think. They've no pyjamas, so I get them to strip off their jeans and jumpers so that they can sleep in their little T-shirts and pants. I wonder what the progress is of our furniture and belongings and vow to give Serena a call just as soon as the children have dozed off.

Guy and I lay out one of the duvets on the floor for Tom and Jessica, then cover them snugly with the other one.

'I like sleeping in the kitchen,' Jessica says with a yawn. 'Can we do it more often?'

'Yes, of course,' I say, hoping that she'll have forgotten all about it in the morning. I kiss them both and tuck the duvet round their necks. 'Sleep tight.'

The thumb goes into my daughter's mouth. 'Can Guy read us a story?'

'No books,' I remind her.

'He can make something up.'

I glance at Guy with a smile and he shrugs that he's up for giving it a go. He slides along the floor until he's next to the children. 'I could tell you a story about a pretty little girl who grows up to be a vet.'

Don't encourage her, I think.

'What about the boy?' Tom mumbles sleepily.

'What would a young boy want to grow up to be?' Guy asks softly.

'A farmer,' Tom says. 'With lots of sheep. And some black and white cows.'

Bloody hell. What have I done to these children? I've taken two townies and turned them into a pair of straw chewers. Or perhaps the country gene that lay latent in their father for so many years has simply been released earlier in them. How are they going to like it now, back in our cramped London flat? And my head spins as I wonder for the hundredth time whether I'm doing the right thing.

While Guy starts to tell his story to my children, I turn off the main light so that just the warm glow from the stove and a couple of spots under the kitchen cupboards keep the gloom away. Going into the scullery, I make a quick call to Serena who tells me that the furniture has just arrived and, despite the fact that they must be exhausted, the removal men are cheerfully unloading it. All of the boxes are clearly marked, so all my sister has to do is direct them to the right rooms and I can do the rest when I get there tomorrow. I blow a big kiss down the phone and tell her that I owe her before hanging up. Then I puff out a wobbly breath. Tomorrow. Tomorrow I'll be in London.

I clear the plates away, running them under the tap to clean them as best as I can without the aid of Fairy Liquid or a dishcloth. I can hear Guy telling the children of rolling fields and magical animals, and it makes me smile to myself. My heart contracts when I think that one day he'll make a lovely dad.

When I've stacked the plates so that they'll drain, I turn round to see that both of the children are flat out. Guy is still telling his story, even though his audience are long gone to the Land of Nod.

'Job done,' I whisper to him.

He glances at the children and seems surprised to see that they're both soundly asleep.

'You realise that I'll now have to make up the second instalment.'

'I'm sure you're more than up to the job,' he says as he stands and stretches.

'How's the patient?'

Guy checks on the lamb. 'Also sleeping like a baby.'

'Good.' Imagine the tears now if anything happened to Stuart Little. I hope he'll be up and reunited with his mother by the morning, then I can leave without feeling *too* hideously guilty. 'More wine?'

'Hmm. Great.' Guy takes the two sleeping bags and sets them out side by side, folding them so that we can sit near the Aga and keep an eye on our charge. I refill his glass and hand it to him. He takes his place on the sleeping bag and I sit down next to him.

'I used to be the doyen of sophisticated parties,' I tell him. 'Now look at me.'

'You'll be back to that soon enough.'

I will, I guess, and I wonder idly whether it will hold the same appeal for me now. Have I changed so much since I've been here? I certainly don't think I would have given house room to a sickly lamb in my former life.

'I'm glad you stayed,' Guy says. 'Somehow it felt like you were rushing away. It's been nice to spend this time together before you go.'

I study him in the soft light. 'You are such a nice man,' I say. 'Did I ever tell you that, Guy Burton?'

'And you're a very lovely woman.'

'I feel I've really messed this up.'

'I know this sort of conversation scares you, but do you think there might have been something between us if you were staying?'

I nod. 'In the long term. We might have become close over the last few months, but you know that I can't possibly consider a relationship so soon. It wouldn't be fair.'

'No.' He paused, then said: 'I don't want to lose touch with you or the children though. When you all come up for the weekend, you're more than welcome to stay with me. There's plenty of space in my house. You know I'd love that.'

'I'm going to miss you,' I tell him honestly. 'You've been very good to us.'

'I'll miss you too. And the children.' He glances sadly at Tom and Jessica. It would be impossible to replace their father, I know that, but Guy has been there quietly and steadfastly for them throughout our time at Helmshill Grange and that means more to me than you could know. 'I know that you're having second thoughts about all this. Is it really too late for you to pull out?'

'I've already signed the contract on the house,' I tell him. 'The Gerner-Bernards are due to go to their solicitor to do the same as soon as possible. I'm not sure what the delay is. I'd hate to let them down now. They seem to be mad keen to move into the house.' Though I wonder how much of it will be left of its heart once they've stopped knocking it about and have got rid of all the animals. 'Plus I've taken out a six-month lease on the flat. I can't back out of that either without it costing me a packet.' I sigh. 'And, at the end of the day, I can't afford to stay here. There's no work up here for me and I need the money. There's no way round that. I have a great job in Town to go back to. That's the reality of our situation.'

'There's really no other option?'

I shake my head. 'And I'm looking forward to getting back to work, producing programmes.' I've gone over the brief with Gavin Morrison and already I'm putting ideas together in my head. 'It's what I do best. It will stretch me again. Stop my brain cells from dying.' Or dwelling too much on my loss. Then my business brain kicks in. 'Oh, can I ask one last favour?'

My friend nods. 'The Gerner-Bernards are coming up to take a final look around and do some measurements later in the week. I've given the estate agent a key, but he's been completely useless so far. Can I leave a spare with you and tell them that you'll be here to let them in?'

'Of course.'

'Thanks. That's another weight off my mind.'

Unexpectedly, Guy reaches up and his fingers gently brush my cheek. 'You look tired.'

'It's been a long day.' My voice sounds tremulous.

Guy's lips find mine and he kisses me softly. This is the first time I've kissed another man since Will died and, despite my qualms, I return the kiss hesitantly. It feels so strange to have the taste of unfamiliar lips on mine. I'm quivering inside.

'Lie down next to me,' he says when we part.

And, while I stand, he flicks out the sleeping bags. I slip into mine fully clothed and he does the same. Then, against my better judgement, we inch together until my back is snuggled up to him. I haven't played spoons with anyone else other than my husband, but this feels nice and cosy. Guy's body, even through the thick down, is warm against mine and I can feel his heart beating or maybe it's my own. His arm slides round my waist, pulling me close to him. I didn't realise how much I've missed a man's touch. At this moment, I think that I would be quite happy to spend the rest of my life here on the floor in this bare kitchen in Guy's strong arms. But it's not to be and that thought is going to keep me awake all night.

Chapter Ninety-One

Waking at dawn, the view that greets me is a graphic reminder that Hamish is a boy dog. 'For goodness sake, you unseemly mutt, get your bits and pieces out of my face.' I push him away, but not before he's run his lollopy tongue over my face.

As I wipe the slobber off, Hamish plods off only to plop himself down on top of both of the children with a doggy huff. Neither of them stir.

I push myself up and peer through the window. All is still dark outside. My back hurts from sleeping on the hard stone floor and I try to massage it with both hands. My head aches and my bum is numb; one of my legs is completely dead. Guy is still fast asleep on his back, arm lifted above his head. What on earth was I thinking about, cosying up to him like that? Blame it on the wine, the warm fire and a lamb roasting in the oven, a need inside me that can't ever be filled.

Wriggling myself out of the sleeping bag, I know already that I'm going to feel like death warmed up on the drive down to London today. I try to rub some life into my leg. It was a really, really bad idea to delay our departure even for a sickly lamb. We should have gone yesterday, made a clean break while we could. Now look how complicated things are. I'm cross with myself – just as well as I have no one else to be cross with.

'Hi.' I turn to see Guy looking up at me. His hand touches my arm. A wave of guilt washes over me. Did I really spend the night watching this man sleep next to me? 'Sleep well?' he asks.

'No,' I say, more sharply than I'd intended. I hardly slept a wink actually. All night, when I wasn't looking at Guy, I tossed and turned, wondering what I was doing.

'Do you need to get up right away?' He reaches out for me.

'I've got so much to do,' I mumble, moving away. 'We ought to get on the road as soon as possible.'

My guest sits up briskly and rubs his hands through his hair while he stares at me. 'On the road?'

'Yes.'

There's surprise in his voice when he says, 'You're not still planning to go to London?'

'Of course I am. Why?'

Guy looks hurt. 'I thought after last night . . .'

'What?'

His eyes fix on mine. 'After last night, I thought – I hoped – that you'd stay.'

'Stay? Whatever gave you that impression? We had a cuddle,' I say. 'And a kiss.' I push away the image of Guy's mouth on mine. 'Which was wrong of us. Wrong of me. I'm still a married woman, Guy.'

'Amy? Why are you being like this? Did you get out of the wrong side of the sleeping bag?'

'I can't stay here,' I say. 'You know that. Even if I wanted to, what difference would it make?'

'What happened during the night to turn all this on its

head?' He looks puzzled. How is he to know that I spent the night berating myself for even considering that I might be happy with another man. It will be so much easier for both of us if I can keep Guy at arms' length – which is what I should have done all along, of course.

'What would William think of me?' I say. 'I'm the mother of his children, for heaven's sake. He wouldn't want me cavorting with someone else.'

Guy risks a smile at that. 'Whatever we did, Amy, I assure you that it couldn't be classed as "cavorting".'

I don't deserve happiness, I think. Life isn't that kind. It's cruel and it steals love away, it doesn't hand it to you on a plate. It's easier to stay rooted in this miserable morning greyness than consider what might happen if I move on. I'm not ready to do that yet. Perhaps I thought that I was, but I'm not.

'I thought that you'd grown to love Helmshill Grange?'

'Look at it.' I wave my arm round the kitchen which has plenty of shabby, but no chic. 'It needs a fortune spending on it. A fortune I don't have. I'm just doing what has to be done.'

He looks stunned. 'What on earth do you want from life, woman? No one else will tell you this, but I think that you're making one big mistake.'

Hands on hips now. 'Oh, really?'

'The kids are happy here. *You're* happy here.'

'I'll decide where I'm happy, and the kids. You've been great with them, Guy. Really great. But you're not their dad, and you never will be.'

At that he recoils. 'Well, that lets me know where I stand.'

349

'I'm sorry that I've misled you into thinking that it could be any other way, but I think it's best if we have a clean break. My emotions are all over the place and this just seems like one complication too far.'

Guy eases himself out of the sleeping bag and stands up. 'I think that I've outstayed my welcome.'

I daren't stop him. I cannot stop him now.

He glances at the Aga. 'The lamb looks as if he's okay,' he says. 'I'll take him back to Delila before I go.'

'Thank you.'

'I'm sure that Alan will keep you up-to-date on their progress. If you're interested.'

I stand there frozen to the spot, just about holding it all together.

Guy moves towards me, uncertain now. 'Amy . . .' He looks like he's about to launch into another sensible speech about how I should run my life. Then he lets his arms fall by his side, a look of resignation on his face. 'I hope that life back in London is all you want it to be.'

'I'm sure it will be.'

He casts a look at Tom and Jessica still asleep on the floor. 'Give the children my love. Tell them . . .' His voice fails. 'Tell them that I'll miss them.'

And with that he scoops Stuart Little into his arms and heads to the door.

'They'll miss you too,' I say, but Guy has already gone.

Chapter Ninety-Two

'You look like something the cat spat out,' Cheryl told him.

'Thank you, oh kind and wise receptionist.'

'You look like you slept in those clothes too.'

'I did,' Guy said, then he went through to the examination room and quickly closed the door behind him before Cheryl had a chance to find out why.

If he was lucky, he told himself, he might be able to string this out until lunchtime before someone came in and told her that he hadn't been home last night and that he'd spent the night at Helmshill Grange. Actually, lunchtime might be stretching it. A story as juicy as that would be round Poppy's Tea Room by, say, Guy glanced at his watch, eleven o'clock at the latest. Until then it was his secret. Let the good people of Scarsby and district think what they would. No one really knew what had gone on between him and Amy. To be honest, he was a bit unsure himself. Last night he'd been convinced that they had a future together. This morning he was a man thwarted once again in love, watching the only woman he cared for drive away from him, and, frankly, he hadn't a clue what he'd done to change that.

The consulting-room door was flung open. 'Stick insect,' Cheryl said as she ushered in an impossibly thin and concerned-looking family clutching a mesh enclosure, and slammed the door behind them.

Guy rubbed his hands together and checked his appointment schedule. *La famille* Felix now stood before him, according to his notes. 'Now Mrs and Mrs Felix – what can I do for you?'

Mrs Felix pushed one of her two waiflike children forward. Another family that looked like their pet.

'Twiggy's not well,' the little girl said, an unhappy tremble in her young voice.

Guy took the mesh cage from her and set it carefully on his table. He studied the forest of foliage inside the structure but, for the life of him, couldn't see a stick insect in there. But then the stick insect or *carausius morosus* – to give the insect its correct title – was the master of disguise. Guy peered intently at the branches. Any one of them could have been Twiggy. 'Can you just point Twiggy out to me, please?' Guy said.

The girl and her family regarded him with disgust. As one, they pointed at the mesh. 'There!'

'Of course.' Still looked like nothing but a bunch of twigs to Guy. 'And what do you think is wrong with the little fellow?'

Again the scornful looks. 'Twiggy's a girl.'

'Ah, yes. I can tell that now.' Clearly, stick insects were not his specialist subject. Thankfully, he didn't come across them often enough for it to be a problem. In this kind of rural practice it was more pertinent to know your way round the working end of a cow.

'She's listless,' the mother supplied. 'And off her food.'

A bit like the rest of the family perhaps, Guy thought. He removed the lid of Twiggy's home and gently eased out the main branch. Sure enough, after a great deal of scrutiny, there between the leaves he managed to pick out the beautifully camouflaged and elusive insect.

He carefully lifted it out and balanced it on his hand. It was hard to tell, but it looked perfectly healthy to him. How exactly did you determine whether a twig with legs was unwell?

'You haven't changed her diet recently?'

Much shaking of heads.

'These are very sensitive creatures,' he intoned. 'As I'm sure you know.'

Much nodding of heads.

Guy wracked his brain to think back to what he knew about stick insects when all he really wanted to do was think about the night he'd spent with Amy and the joy of holding her in his arms, even though it had been a very chaste encounter. And then try to work out what had gone so very wrong.

The vet scratched his head and blew out a perplexed breath.

'Do you think it needs an MRI scan?' the family quaked as one.

'No, no,' Guy said. 'That would cost an absolute fortune.'

'Nothing is too much for our Twiggy,' the father declared solemnly.

This was probably the type of guy who would rush into the blaze if their house was burning down to save Twiggy. Guy sighed wistfully. If only someone cared about him so much. Now that it seemed he might have stumbled across such a person, she was currently heading away from him down the M1 motorway.

Last night he'd thought that perhaps he and Amy could have tried to have a long-distance relationship, but was that really ever going to be viable? Didn't distance put an unsurmountable strain on even the best of partnerships? How could he begin to woo her (to use an outdated term), with more than two hundred miles between them when he couldn't even manage it in the same village?

Guy looked down at Twiggy perched on his hand. Perhaps he should give all this up and go in hot pursuit of his love. Say goodbye to the moors and set up a high-falutin practice in a well-heeled area of London – preferably close to Amy and the children – where he could spend his days in a cosy consulting room examining the stick insects of the rich and famous, fixing the broken legs of £4 hamsters and charging £400 for the privilege. He could treat chihuahuas wearing cerise pink coats, and Bengal cats with diamond collars, and not spend half his life with his arm up a disgruntled cow's bottom. A dedicated emergency vet service would deal with all of his out-of-hours calls while he went home at five o'clock, rediscovered the joys of cooking, started watching all of the soaps and spent an entire night in his own bed and not in a draughty barn with an arsey farmer who was reluctant to pay his bill. There was a certain appeal in that even though it wasn't what he'd joined the world of veterinary practice to set out to do. Would it be worth considering, so that he could be near to Amy? Guy stared out of the window to catch a glimpse of the rolling moors that surrounded Scarsby. Trouble was, it was just so damn beautiful here. Leaving would be nigh on impossible. Could he simply walk away after it had taken so long to build up his reputation in these parts? Would his assistant want to buy out the business? He was young, still inexperienced in many areas. Would it be too much for him to handle? Could Stephen even get the money to enable him to take over? Would Amy even want him to do that? After what she'd said this morning, it seemed unlikely.

'What shall we do, Doctor?'

The question from Mrs Felix pulled his mind back to his meagre stick insect knowledge. 'I think Twiggy may be dehydrated,' he said, after feigning deep thought. 'The symptoms are classic. Take her home and spray her enclosure regularly. Keep an eye on her and come back in a few days if there's no improvement.' Though quite what he'd do if they did reappear, he wasn't exactly sure.

There was a collective sigh of relief from the Felixes and Guy lowered Twiggy gently back into her home. He ushered them out of the door, wearing his best professional smile, but he knew that it didn't reach his heart. Cheryl gave him a look to turn water to ice as she caught his eye. As soon as she was out of the way he'd check the diary to see when his next weekend off was rostered. He needed to go down to London and examine Hamish to see how he was getting on with his fixator, if nothing else. Who was he kidding? He was simply trying to conjure up an excuse to see Amy again. While his receptionist continued to try to freeze his blood with her stare, he could do nothing but think how he could make things right again.

'It's nothing serious,' the family told Cheryl with obvious joy before they left.

He only hoped that this wasn't one of those cases where the Felix family would turn up next morning with Twiggy flat on her back on the floor, legs in the air. That, like the woman you love leaving town for ever, was always a bad start to the day.

'What's up next?' Guy asked, rubbing his hands together keenly.

'Mrs Harris.' Cheryl nodded across the reception area and sure enough the good lady and her lovely dog, Megan, were sitting there waiting patiently for him.

'Hello, Megan.' Guy bent to stroke the dog. He had a terrible flashback to what had happened last time the poor animal had paid them a visit. A close encounter of the Hamish kind, that's what. Guy shuddered to think of it. Instead, he smiled at the bitch's owner. 'What seems to be the problem this time, Mrs Harris?'

The lady looked round, concerned, and lowered her voice to a whisper even though there was no one else but him and Cheryl in the waiting area. 'I think Megan's "with child", Mr Burton,' she intimated. 'And I've absolutely no idea how that happened.'

But, unfortunately for Guy, he did.

Chapter Ninety-Three

When we arrive in London the light is fading and it's bucketing down. So much for the milder climate of the south. It's taken us hours to crawl here across Town, grid-locked in traffic from the north of London – nearly as long as it took us to whizz down the motorway from Yorkshire.

Whilst trying not to tear out my hair, I drive round and round and round, hoping to find a parking place for the Land Rover. Eventually, we find one miles away from the flat and I'm going to have to be out here at some ungodly hour in the morning to move it before the clampers come along. I'll have to get on to the council about a resident's parking permit first thing tomorrow, before I am given a yellow boot.

Milly Molly Mandy has made the journey an interesting one by puking up all the way here. The car pongs of cat sick. Hamish hasn't stopped barking since Birmingham, unlike the children who stopped speaking to each other shortly after we passed Leicester Forest Services. This was shortly after my younger child stopped crying about leaving Stuart Little the Lamb behind.

As the flats of Lancaster Court have a no pets policy – in capital letters on the lease agreement, I seem to recall – I'm going to have to move heaven and earth to get Mils and Hamish inside unseen. How would I have fared with a damn lamb? Pet smuggling won't be so difficult in the case of a small cat cage, I think. Our feline friend will simply get a towel thrown over her. But how the hell am I going to get a great lump like Hamish indoors without any of the neighbours noticing? The dog wags his tail at me as if reading my thoughts. 'Oh, Hamish,' I say, a note of exasperation creeping into my voice. 'What am I going to do with you?'

I have all this to worry about – and yet has anyone given a thought to what might be going on in *my* mind? No. I have driven away from my husband's dream life, riven with doubts and wracked with guilt.

'Come on,' I say to the kids. 'We're here. Just a short walk to the flat.' Well, short-ish. At one point I thought we were going to end up parking back in Yorkshire. How had I managed to forget all these delights in the months that I've been away?

Out of the car and I get the scabby car blanket from the boot and throw it over Milly Molly Mandy's cage. She miaows in complaint and I know that I'll get a set of claws in the leg later when I'm least expecting it as repayment for her undignified treatment. Tom hauls Hamish out onto the pavement and the dog immediately wees up the parking meter we've stopped next to and then barks out his relief to anyone who cares to listen. He gives a cursory chew at his fixator which is still firmly in place and we set off towards the flat, me and my ragamuffin bunch of companions looking like we've fallen off a flitting. As we get round the block from the apartment, I shrug out of my coat and throw it over Hamish, who promptly shrugs it off.

'No, no, you silly dog,' I tell him. 'You've got to wear it.

We need to disguise you to get you into the flats.' I pull the coat over him again. This time he tolerates it. Fantastic. I stand back and regard him. Great. Now he looks like a dog disguised as a dog in a coat. Sighing, I think, Sod it. We can't go through this every time he needs to go out for a wee – unless we only take him out in the dead of the night. Now there's a thought.

I clamp my hand over his muzzle in an attempt to stop Hamish signalling our arrival with his customary barking as we cover the last part of the street and head up to the front door. The block looks much more utilitarian and drab than I remember and my spirits don't lift. We have no choice now that we've come this far though and, with that thought in mind, we go inside.

Once we're in the flat, I'm relieved to see that Serena has done a great job with the furniture. On first glance it doesn't look too bad, even though there are a load of cardboard boxes piled into the living room and there's not much space left on the kitchen floor either. Give me a couple of days though and this will be looking fine and dandy. Oh goodness, I do hope so.

Tom and Jessica hang behind me. 'Are we really going to live here?' my daughter asks. 'It's not a joke?'

'No, darling,' I said. 'It's only for the time being, but this is where we live now.' She looks as if she's about to burst into tears. 'You said you liked it when we looked round.'

'I didn't *like* it,' she insists. 'But it wasn't as horrible as everywhere else.'

'We'll make it homely in no time,' I assure her.

She gives me her all-adults-are-liars face.

Then the doorbell rings and rescues me. Hamish barks as usual, and as I go to open the door I have a momentary flash of blind panic. Suppose it's the landlord come to check that we're all right? Suppose, even worse, that he wants to come inside to check if we're all right? We're going to have to find a secret hiding-place for Hamish and Milly Molly Mandy, should the occasion arise. And gag Hamish. Why did I not consider until now just how much noise he's capable of making? Something else for me to think about. It's too late for now though, I'm already at the door and, if it is the landlord, he will have already heard Hamish's greeting. I open it a crack and then breathe out a sigh of relief when I realise that it's only my sister standing there.

'What?' she snaps when she sees the look on my face. 'Did you think it was someone come to mug you on your first night back in the smoke?'

'I thought it was the landlord,' I say, 'and, as we've got two illegal immigrants here, I was starting to panic.'

'Oh, cripes,' she says. 'Forgot about that.'

'Well, I hadn't.'

I let her in and she gives me a bunch of flowers and a kiss while trying to dislodge our hound from her leg.

'It's not too bad, is it?' I ask.

Serena wrinkles her nose. 'It's horrible,' she whispers. 'I couldn't believe it when I saw it yesterday. Whatever possessed you?'

'Price,' I tell her. 'There was nothing else in our budget that wasn't on the condemned list. At least this is clean and newly decorated.'

'Fabulous. If beige is your favourite colour.'

'Beggars can't be choosers,' I point out.

'Oh, sis,' she says. 'Have you really done the right thing? You've left that massive house for this?'

'You were the one encouraging me to come back to London.'

'I was, wasn't I?' Serena agrees. 'Wonder why I did that?'

'You tell me.'

As a distraction technique, she nods at the flowers. 'Think you might find a vase in this lot?'

'Not now,' I say, suddenly very weary. 'I'll put them in the sink for the time being.'

The kids have disappeared into their respective bedrooms to stake claim to their toys again. As my sister talks to me I rummage about in the boxes in the kitchen to find the kettle; I'm absolutely gasping for a hot drink. I picked up some milk and bread at one of the service stations even though our pit stops on the way down were as brisk as they could be because you can't leave Hamish in the car alone for more than three minutes without him trying to eat it.

'You will like it here?' Serena says, chewing her lip. 'Not here, *per se*, but back in London, I mean?'

'I do hope so.' The kettle boils. Not a moment too soon.

'How did you leave things with Guy?' she asks.

'Badly,' I tell her. 'I think that he wants more than I can offer.'

'That's a shame,' she offers. 'He looked like a keeper to me.'

I shrug as if I'm unconcerned, but I am concerned, I just can't afford to show it; I can't afford to feel it. 'I'm just looking forward to getting back to work, getting back to the

life we used to have.' I try a laugh, but it sits uneasily. 'Bring
it on!'

Chapter Ninety-Four

It's eight o'clock and still dark when we sneak Hamish out
of the flat for his morning constitutional in the little park
across the street. The dog limps a bit on his newly mended
back leg but, thankfully, he seems undeterred by this minor
handicap.

The small green space is tiny and hemmed in by railings
all round that need a new coat of paint, but Hamish
immediately becomes demented even though he's still
supposed to be having only light exercise, and strains to
be let off the lead. There's litter strewn everywhere and I
hope that there aren't any discarded junkies' needles or
used condoms in it. I realise the only thing we've had to
watch for out on the moors is stepping in a minefield of
poo from a variety of creatures. The dangers are of a
different sort entirely here and it's funny how soon you
forget that. Once, not so very long ago, I would have
wandered round a park like this and would have thought
that it was quite pleasant.

After a couple of days getting used to the flat, Tom and
Jessica are due to start their new school this morning, and
it's fair to say that neither of them are looking forward to
the experience. My children's faces would indicate that they're

about to go to the guillotine rather than a modern, inner-city primary school.

Reluctantly, I acquiesce to my dog's demands and let Hamish off the lead even though that's against vet's orders. My heart squeezes as I think of Guy, but I push the thought away. My hound immediately charges away like a speeding bullet, not realising that before long he's going to careen headlong into the railings that bound the other end of the park. I'm probably going to be wresting his head out of them before long. Can just see it coming.

'It will be okay today,' I reassure my children as they trail morosely in my wake.

Jessica sighs. 'This isn't exactly Yorkshire, is it?'

How am I going to deal with her when she's sixteen rather than six? I shudder to think.

'Give it a chance,' I encourage her. 'You didn't like St Mary's either when you first started there.'

My daughter chooses to ignore this comment, realising for once that her mother just might be right.

'I didn't go to sleep,' Tom says with a weary yawn. 'The cars were noisy and kept me awake.'

Me too. By dawn, lorries were thundering past our window, trying to shake the glass out of its frames. How different from being woken by nothing but the sound of tweeting birds. Still, I'm sure we'll get used to it. This flat is not our permanent home. It's a temporary measure, that's all. Plus we all used to live in London before and managed to sleep perfectly well. I'm sure we did. Now my eyes feel like they're being sandpapered by my eyelids. Don't quite know how I'm going to stay awake for the rest of the day. Excess caffeine is probably the answer. I used to live on artificial stimulants when I was a high-powered executive before; I doubt it will be any different second time around.

At the end of the park, I hear a commotion. And, although it's dark and I can't quite see what's going on, I know instantly who's causing it. 'Come on,' I say to the kids. And, as one, we charge off towards the sound of Hamish's joyous barking. When our dog is sounding at his most happy, it's when I become most worried.

Sure enough, as we reach the end of the path, we come upon Hamish. My unruly mutt is currently trying to roger a prissy-looking little dog that might or might not be a Pomeranian. Whatever it is, it's clearly not enjoying the rather robust sexual attentions of a rufty-tufty, twelve-stone Gordon Setter. Nor, it seems, is the dog's owner. The woman is small, elderly and is wearing an old-fashioned, buttoned-up coat with a fur hat. She's currently battering Hamish around his rather thick skull with a pink rolled-up umbrella. Hamish, gamely, is clearly thinking that this is a pleasant addition to the experience. He woofs in appreciation.

'Is this your dog?' she screams at me.

For a moment, I consider denying Hamish, but I have the damning evidence of a dog leash in my hand. 'I'm sorry,' I pant breathlessly as we all dash up to interrupt Hamish's bit of fun.

'Get him away from my Lou-Lou,' she shouts. 'Just get him away.'

I haul Hamish off the poor, traumatised Pom and clip his lead on again. 'He's only playing,' I say brightly.

'*Playing?* He was trying to force himself upon my poor

little girl! I will get you and that thing barred from this park if he does that again,' she warns, wagging a bony finger at me.

Hope she's not one of my near neighbours. I'd forgotten just how unfriendly people in London can be. We can't have Hamish banned as this is the only bit of greenery near to us. From now on I'll have to keep him on a tight leash. Poor Hamish, I think.

'Sheep and Pot-Bellied Pigs are one thing, Hamish,' I whisper to him as he whines miserably when the object of his unrequited love limps away. 'You've got to remember that dogs round here are soft, southern shandies. You'll have to modify your courtship behaviour or you're going to get us into a lot of trouble.'

Unperturbed, my dog pees on the nearest tree. What on earth's going to happen to Hamish when I go back to work? Lots of people leave their dogs at home all day, but those dogs aren't Hamish. I'm not going to be able to leave him in the flat all day without him trying to eat it, and I certainly can't take him into the office with me. Can you imagine the chaos he'd cause? Something else it seems that I haven't quite thought through.

It pains me to have to admit it, but I can't manage without help. I called our ex-nanny's mobile phone again to see if Maya could come to my rescue in the short term, as I could certainly do with her calm, efficient help now – but a tinny electronic voice told me that the number I was calling was out of service. Perhaps her employers have given her a whizzy new phone or something. Or she changed her number to stop me calling her and begging her to come back. And I realise that I feel hurt that she's never got in touch with us at all since Will died.

Before I do anything else, I must go into the nearest employment agency today and fix myself up with a reliable nanny and bulletproof dogsitter with nerves of steel.

Chapter Ninety-Five

'Get a move on, you two.' I encourage my children to be speedy with their breakfast by tidying up around them. Wanted the jam? Too late, back in the fridge. I haven't been able to eat anything myself, as my stomach is too nervous. Instead of feeling like a seasoned professional embarking on a new stage in her career, I feel as if I'm going to my first day at school – and it helps me to understand how daunting this must be for Tom and Jessica.

This is the first time I'd realised how leisurely our start to the day was at Helmshill Grange, with the school at the end of the road and me not having a tight timetable to stick to. 'We need to leave in five minutes,' I tell the kids. 'Less.'

They both slide down from their stools at the work surface and head towards their coats. Good, good.

'I want you to behave too.' I wag my finger at Hamish, who has already found his favourite spot in the kitchen, lying exactly where we all trip over him. His tail pounds the floor. I never thought I'd hear myself say this, but he seems a bit quiet this morning. My alarm went off at some hideous hour so that I could sneak the dog out of the building and across the road to the park before anyone else was awake. He did his business without fuss, didn't try to roger anything, not even the benches, no towing me behind him like a waterskier while he went to investigate some wonderful smell he'd discovered, no rolling in something completely unsavoury. It was like walking a different dog. 'You okay?' I ask him and he rolls doleful eyes at me. 'I don't want you eating the flat while we're out. Get it?'

I take the listless thump of his tail as tacit agreement.

'All you have to do is hang on until lunchtime and Kati will be here to take you out for a long W.A.L.K.'

My visit to Au Pair Positions was a great success. The very helpful young lady in the agency fixed me up with an Estonian girl – the aforementioned Kati – who's now gainfully employed to look after Jessica, Tom and Hamish. Milly Molly Mandy, as always, can look after herself.

Kati is a slim blonde with slightly scary eye make-up and more holes in her ears than a colander, but otherwise seemed like a perfectly pleasant specimen of human nature and competent to boot. She's over here ostensibly as a language student, despite speaking five different tongues fluently already. Our new au pair is supposed to be as reliable as rain in summer, marvellous with children, a lover of animals – even Hamish, it seems – and could beat Jamie Oliver hands down in a cook-off. I snapped her up immediately.

'Have you got your lunches?' The children nod miserably as they stand there waiting for me. 'School won't be so bad today,' I promise them. 'The first day is always the worst and you've cracked that. It will just get better from now on.'

They both look unconvinced by my optimism and my heart breaks for them. 'We'd better get a move on.'

Barricading Hamish in the kitchen, I then tie the door handle to the one across the hall with a scarf, so that he can't escape. I can only hope that he's still like that when Kati arrives. As soon as I can afford to get a better place, I will find somewhere with a garden – and a six-foot perimeter fence with razor wire on top and maybe a guard tower. Anything else and Hamish will be out of it.

Tom and Jessica are hustled out of the door for another day of torture at their new school. They'll be there way too early, but I want to make sure that they get there safely before I go off to work. It's still dark and this road is too busy for them to walk along alone. The traffic is whipping by and it's so loud that we can't hold a conversation, so I just grip Jessica's hand and tow her along at my pace.

Outside the school, I kiss them both goodbye. Tom lets me as there are currently no other pupils around to witness it. 'Go straight indoors,' I instruct. 'Remember to wait for Kati at home time. She'll be here to collect you and take you back to the flat. Okay?'

They both nod.

'Got the key, Tom?'

My son produces it from his pocket to show it to me. I thought I'd better give him a spare just in case Kati doesn't turn out to be quite as reliable as she seems and manages to lose hers.

'Guard it with your life.'

He nods again.

'I love you,' I say. Grief, I'm tearing up. I hug them both

to me. Tom is less impressed this time. 'I hope you have a better day today. Wish Mummy luck too.'

My children mumble something at me that I think is supposed to spur me on to greatness. 'Now scoot.' I turn Jessica round and give her a playful slap on the bottom to set them on their way. Watching them walk into the school together, I brush the tears away with the sleeve of my coat. They look too tiny to be going into such an enormous building on their own.

Pushing down a wave of nausea brought on by nerves, I try not to think about that now, as if I don't scoot myself then I'm going to be late on my first day. And I don't want Gavin Morrison to think just because I'm now on my own with two kids to bring up that I can't cut it.

Chapter Ninety-Six

From the depths of the packing boxes I've managed to root out some suitable work attire. I've chosen a silver-grey wool wrap cardigan and black trousers. The heels are back in business and I'm in full war paint for the first time in months.

I think I look like a contender, but I can't believe how terrified I am. You'd think that I'd been out of the work environment for years rather than months – albeit quite a lot of months. The British Television Company offices seem suddenly to be filled with sparkly, bright young things who make me feel as old as time itself.

Gavin Morrison stands as I'm shown into his office. He holds out his hand and I shake it.

'It's good to be back,' I say.

'Good to have you back. Though you might find there've been a lot of changes while you've been away.'

'I'm sure I'll get straight into the swing of things.' I take a seat while he paces the room. 'My only concern is that I haven't had a contract of employment yet, even though I've hassled the Human Resources lot.'

'I know,' Gavin says. 'We'll sort that out later. My assistant will take you down there.'

I don't remind him that I know perfectly well where the HR department is.

'I wanted to float a few things by you first.' He stares out of the window into the courtyard in the middle of the building. I used to love sitting out there for ten minutes in my lunch break when I could, to escape the stifling central heating or the freezing air conditioning. 'The brief has changed slightly since I offered you the job.'

This, I don't like the sound of.

'We've decided that the arts programmes need to be more commercial.'

Ah, the dreaded dumbing down that the BTC is so often being accused of.

'We've brought in a new chap, Lawrence Holmes, to spear-head the new initiative.'

I smile to myself. I'd forgotten how much Gavin likes the jargon.

'You'll report directly to him.'

Oh. I thought Gavin would be my boss, as he used to

be. I guess this is one of the first changes I'll have to live with.

'He's just next door, I'll buzz him to come through.' Gavin goes to the phone on his desk. 'Lawrence, Amy Ashurst is here. Can you spare a minute now?'

'What's his background?' I don't think that Lawrence Holmes is a BTC man.

'He's a hot shot. Been out making and selling commercial programmes in the States for the last few years. Lawrence is the brains behind *Celebrity Wedding Day*, *Celebrity Change My Style!* and *Celebrity Three Little Words*.'

Gavin is clearly impressed. I'm not. I think they're three of the most banal programmes on television and, let's face it, there's a lot of banality to choose from.

While I'm still digesting this information, Lawrence Holmes strides into Gavin's office. He's sharp-suited and slick. A handsome bastard. I stand and he grips my hand like a vice, almost wrenching my arm from its socket as he shakes it. Then he sits on the edge of Gavin's desk and fixes his eyes on me. Lawrence is young, edgy and ambitious and I wouldn't want to be on the wrong side of him although he's all smiles now. 'Welcome on board.'

'Thanks. I was just saying to Gavin it's good to be back.'

'It's a different kind of BTC now, Amy,' he says crisply. 'Let's just get that clear from day one. There's no room for sloppiness.'

Hmm. Charmer. I can already tell the direction the arts programmes are going to take. We'll be doing *Celebrity Watch Paint Dry* before you know it.

'All the years I was exec producer of *Sports Quiz*, I was

known for running a tight ship,' I tell him. 'I'm sure we'll work well together.'

'I hope so.' Lawrence glances at his watch. Rolex. 'I'm in meetings all day, but I'll catch up with you at the restaurant tonight.'

Alarm bells ring. 'Restaurant?'

'I emailed you yesterday about it.'

'At home?' I haven't even got the computer out of its box yet, let alone checked my email. Things like that were William's department. I don't have a clue where to start. 'I didn't receive it.'

Lawrence frowns and then tuts. 'We've got a party of clients over for a couple of days from the USA. We're taking them to La Strada tonight.'

Wow. I'd love to go to La Strada. It's about as far removed from Poppy's Tea Room as you can get. Then suddenly without warning, I get a pang of longing for the low-key delights of Scarsby.

'You need to be there,' Lawrence continues as I rally my scattered thoughts. 'I'm hoping some free-flowing champagne will help to cement Anglo-American relationships and lead to some great deals.'

'I'm really sorry,' I say. 'But it's probably too short notice for me now.'

Lawrence Holmes's frown deepens.

'I have two children,' I remind him. 'I'd need to organise a babysitter. We've only just arrived back from Yorkshire. I can see if my au pair can stay on this evening, but it's her first day and I can't promise anything. I don't know anyone else I can call on to help me without a bit more warning.'

I could try Serena too, but I don't have high hopes. My sister normally needs several days' notice to sort out her diary.

My new boss purses his lips, clearly unhappy at this unexpected development. 'This is a regular feature of our work,' he points out. 'I thought you'd be aware of that. Next week we have two of these things, maybe three. Is it going to be a problem?'

I can see my first black mark being mentally scored against me.

'No.' I shake my head while thinking, Yes, it bloody is! I used to do this sort of thing all the time when Will and I worked here, and we sorted out the details between us – even if co-ordinating our diaries was sometimes like a military operation. But this is my first day, for heaven's sake. Can't a girl get a break?

'I'll leave this with you, Amy,' Lawrence says. Then he strides away. 'I hope that you'll be there.'

'Wow,' I say to Gavin when he leaves the room. 'He's a force to be reckoned with.'

'Think you can work with him, Amy?'

Looks like I don't have much choice in the matter and I'd guess from Gavin's behaviour that he's found himself in the same boat. 'He'll be eating out of my hand in no time.'

'I hope so. Lawrence is the future of the BTC.'

Then God help us all, I think.

Chapter Ninety-Seven

'How's Delila?'

'Champion, Vit.' Alan nodded.

'And the lamb?'

Alan nodded again. The newborn was currently enjoying being bottle-fed by Alan and was looking sturdy and strong. He sucked hungrily at the plastic teat. There was nothing much wrong with Stuart Little now. Clearly the night in Amy's Aga did him the power of good. Another happy ending.

'Everything all right with the rest of the animals?'

Alan shrugged. 'Can't find homes for them.'

'No.' Guy blew out a worried breath. He'd tried himself, phoning round everyone he could think of who might be up for an orphaned animal, but no one wanted to take on Pork Chop or even the goats or the sheep. At the eleventh hour, someone would probably step forward and rehome the chickens – fingers crossed – but what would happen to the rest of them? Perhaps he'd have another word with the Gerner-Bernards when they arrived. Seeing the new lamb might soften their cold, townie hearts. Guy glanced at his watch. He'd taken an hour or so off from his rounds to see them today so, hopefully, they should be here before too long. He'd promised Amy that he'd let them into the house while they took some measurements for curtains or carpets or some such, then they were due to go into their solicitors and sign the contracts later in the day.

Five minutes later and a smart Mercedes pulled into the drive. The Gerner-Bernards got out, all smiles. Guy hated them instantly. The husband sported a black 'Teddy Boy' jacket with bright red lining and those rectangular spectacles like art critics wore on *The South Bank Show*. The wife was in a flowing purple velvet number that brushed the floor, and had hair that was an alarming shade of pink. He couldn't see them fitting into the village at all. But then, hadn't he thought that when he'd first clapped eyes on Amy and Will? Still, it was clear a few minutes after talking to Will Ashurst that his primary concern had been to assimilate into village life and embrace the country ways – odd though they might well be on occasions. Somehow, he just wasn't getting the same vibe from the Gerner-Bernards and the poor couple hadn't even opened their mouths yet.

He held out his hand and they shook it. 'Guy Burton,' he said. 'I'm a friend of Mrs Ashurst. I said I'd let you in.'

'Where's the estate agent?' Mrs Gerner-Bernard wanted to know.

Hello, nice to meet you too, he thought. Clearly the woman wasn't keen to talk to the local yokels. Guy gritted his teeth. 'He should be coming, but he's not the most reliable sort,' he admitted. 'Most people round here operate on Scarsby time, which can run an hour or more later than Greenwich Mean Time. That's why Amy wanted me to be here so you wouldn't have a wasted journey.'

'Hmm,' she snorted, and with that Guy opened the kitchen door and let them inside.

Mrs Gerner-Bernard wrinkled her nose as she stood in the centre of the room and surveyed her soon-to-be new home. 'It looks even worse now that it's empty,' she trilled.

'How can people live like this?' Mr Gerner-Bernard wanted to know. 'It's barbaric. Positively Dickensian.'

Guy wanted to kill them already. And these horrors were going to be his new neighbours?

'The builders will soon have it right,' Mrs Gerner-Bernard assured him.

'Are they starting on the underpinning first?' Guy queried.

They both spun round and stared at him as if they'd forgotten he was there at all.

'Underpinning?' they said together.

'Your survey picked up the mine-shaft? Surely?'

To Guy's delight, they looked at each other blankly. 'Mine-shaft?'

'This area's riddled with them,' he informed the trendy couple. 'You might be lucky though. It might not be directly under the house.' Guy kept his expression as neutral as he could manage. 'It could just be under the yard.'

'No one mentioned this,' Mr Gerner-Bernard said, frowning.

'Really?' His face was the picture of innocence. 'It's well known round these parts. Might not give you any trouble for years though.'

They looked relieved at that.

'Then again . . .' Guy rubbed his chin and sucked in his breath.

'I'm surprised Mrs Ashurst didn't tell us,' the man said. 'She seemed like a decent sort.'

'Oh she is,' Guy assured him. 'But then she was *desperate* for a quick sale.'

Their frowns deepened.

'But maybe I'm worrying you unnecessarily,' he said lightly. 'Perhaps the great fissure in the earth isn't serious enough to trouble your property.' He smiled sweetly at them. 'Yet.'

The Gerner-Bernards looked frozen to the spot.

'Don't let me hold you up in taking your measurements,' he said politely. 'I'll just wait in the yard with the animals until you're ready. And please don't worry about them still being here either. They'll all be gone by the time you arrive. As you don't want them we're sending them all to slaughter.'

The Gerner-Bernards recoiled at that. 'Let's . . . let's get a move on,' the wife whispered, and together they shot through to the living room.

Despite Amy's harsh words on the morning she left, Guy was still convinced that she'd fallen in love with Helmshill and the Grange. No matter how much she tried to deny it. He sighed to himself. If only there was a way . . .

A scant ten minutes later and they were back in the kitchen. 'Thank you,' Mrs Gerner-Bernard said stiffly. 'We've seen more than enough.'

'Good,' Guy said. 'I look forward to welcoming you to the village. It takes people a long time to warm to strangers round these parts, but when we do, we'll never be away from your door. You can count on that.'

He gave them a friendly wink and Mr and Mrs Gerner-Bernard held hands together tightly.

Strangely, they rushed away after that. And when they'd gone, their Mercedes purring off into the distance, Guy leaned back on the fence that bounded the yard. He regarded Helmshill Grange, massaging his chin thoughtfully as he did. It was a fine house. Despite Alan's ministrations, it was still looking a bit dilapidated, but there was nothing insurmountable. No mine-shaft running beneath it, for instance. He grinned to himself. That was a very cruel thing to do. All the Grange needed was a serious cash injection of about twenty grand, give or take a few bob, which could transform this place into something quite spectacular. The house had been an integral part of the village for many years. It should be a family home, filled with children and animals, not a bland showcase for some arsey posh people to do their entertaining.

He'd tried his best to put the Gerner-Bernards off the place. Had it worked? He should know soon enough. Amy would kill him if she knew what he'd done, but it was hard to stand back and watch while some more 'incomers' moved in, to use it only as a weekend place. And maybe that was when Guy had decided that he wouldn't.

Chapter Ninety-Eight

I've been calling Kati's mobile phone all day to see if she'd be available to babysit for the children tonight, but I'm getting nothing but voicemail. After leaving a dozen messages, she still hasn't called me back. Now I'm worried. I've tried Serena too, but she's in a conference and unavailable, so I texted her instead.

Even though it's my first day back, I'm going to have to leave the office early in order to meet Tom and Jessica from school. If I can't get hold of Kati, how can I be sure that she's going to be there to collect my children? I glance at the clock. Three-thirty. I try Kati's phone for the millionth time. A big fat nothing. Now I'm going to have to explain my plight to Gavin and then fly to get to the school in time.

Just at this moment Lawrence bowls in. That's all I need. 'Amy . . .'

I hold up my hand. 'Lawrence, I have to leave. Now. I'm really, really sorry. My au pair's let me down and my children will be standing outside the school with no one to collect them.'

The full Holmes frown is bestowed on me again.

Then my mobile phone rings and his frown becomes a great line of furrows as we're technically not allowed personal telephone calls during working hours either. 'This could be from her,' I say, and I pick up anyway.

'Hello, Mrs Ashurst. It's Wayne at Collier's here.' The estate agent.

'I'm busy right now,' I say reluctantly. I hope he's phoning me to say that the sale of Helmshill Grange has finally been completed. That would certainly be a weight off my mind. 'Can I call you back?'

'I won't interrupt your fun, Amy,' Lawrence says with raised eyebrows. Then he strides away, slamming the office door as he leaves.

I sigh and speak to Wayne as I shrug on my coat, grab my bag and make for the door. 'I hope you've got some good news for me,' I say wearily.

'Er . . . 'fraid not,' he says, clearing his throat. 'The Gerner-Bernards should have gone to their solicitors this afternoon to sign the contracts.'

'But they didn't.'

'That's a correct assessment of the situation,' he agrees. 'They said they needed more time.'

'Time for what?'

'I was unable to obtain that information, Mrs Ashurst.' Estate agent speak for 'I'm as clueless as you are.'

'So when *are* they going to sign?'

There's an uncomfortable pause at the other end of the line, then, 'I'm not in a position to answer that.'

I puff down the phone at him. 'I don't need to tell you that I have to get this sorted out as soon as possible.'

'I understand that,' Wayne tells me.

'Get back to me as soon as you can.' I hang up and check

380

the time. It's nearly quarter to four already, so I fly out of the office and practically run up towards the Tube as fast as my heels can carry me.

It's only a few stops but, at this rate, I'm not going to make it in time. Before I go underground, I punch the number of the school into my phone and, when the secretary answers, I explain my predicament. 'Can someone keep an eye on the children until I get there, please?'

'I think that the children have already left,' she says. 'I'll dash outside now and call you right back.'

The train rattles through the tunnels while I stand and gnaw my fingernails to the quick. How can I have been so stupid, to have trusted someone else with my children? They'll be outside in the dark waiting for Kati, terrified when she hasn't turned up.

As soon as I burst out of the Tube station and am overground again, my phone rings. 'They're not here,' the secretary tells me. 'I've looked everywhere, but I can't see them. I'm sorry, Mrs Ashurst. We'll keep looking.'

Now my mouth is dry, my heart's pounding in my chest and, suddenly, I can't stop the tears from streaming down my face.

I kick off my heels and run down the road as fast as I can, arms pumping, calves screaming in pain. If they've decided to walk home by themselves, I might just catch them up. I thought I'd taught them so well. I thought they would have gone back inside to tell one of their teachers that no one had come to collect them. Why have they wandered off into the night alone? I think back to the time they went out onto the moors with Hamish. I hope they haven't taken this opportunity to try to walk back to Yorkshire.

I'm almost back at the flat and I still haven't seen them. They should be on this road if they've walked home. The lights of Lancaster Court are burning bright ahead of me. Then I see that there's a light on in our window too. Did I leave it on this morning? My legs sprint faster and I can feel my blood pressure soaring through the roof.

I fumble with my key, then burst through the door. Hamish heralds my arrival with a frantic bark and frenzied bouncing. I fight my way past him.

Falling into the living room, I'm convinced that it will be as empty as the grave and, at the very least, Tom and Jessica will have been abducted by paedophiles on their way back from school. Instead, I find them sprawled on the sofa, amid the unpacked cardboard boxes, watching *Happy Feet* on the DVD with a glass of milk and a biscuit each. My sobbing is renewed and I rush to them, hugging my children to me.

'What's wrong, Mummy?' Jessica asks, with one eye still on the dancing penguin in the background.

'Your feet are bleeding,' Tom tells me as he tries to prise me off him.

I look down to see that my tights are ribboned and my feet are raw.

Behind me a voice says, 'Hello, Mrs Ashurst. You are home very early.'

I nearly jump out of my skin. 'What are *you* doing here?'

Kati stares at me, confused. 'I thought that was our arrangement. I have collected the children from school.'

'You did?'

'Yes.'

'But I've tried to call you all day and have just got your voicemail.'

More confusion. She shrugs. 'I don't know why.'

I punch her number into my phone. Kati's phone doesn't ring, but the robotic voice answers.

She takes the phone off me and looks at the display. 'You have one of the numbers wrong, Mrs Ashurst. You have been calling another person.'

'I have?'

'Why are you crying?' my daughter wants to know.

'Nothing, nothing.' I cry louder. How can I hold down an executive position when I can't even get a simple phone number right? 'I'm being silly.'

Jessica looks at me as if to say that's nothing new.

'Shall I phone Guy?' Tom wants to know, his face anxious. Perhaps my son thinks that I'm going to pot again. Perhaps I am.

Pulling myself together, I wipe my tears away. 'No. No. I've just missed you today. That's all.'

They both look at me warily.

'Our new school's very smelly,' Jessica says with a pout. 'I don't think that I want to go back there tomorrow.'

How can I tell them that I feel the same way about my new job? How can I tell them that my new young, thrusting boss scares the life out of me? How can I tell them that I want to be at home for them, to care for them myself, not to leave them with an Estonian au pair, no matter how reliable she seems to be?

Hamish comes up and pushes his muzzle into my hands, whining as he does. Even the bloody dog looks miserable and I cry even more at the sight of his hideous metal frame poking through his skin. It's my fault he's in this state. It's my fault that my children are at the mercy of strangers while I go out to work.

I'm a crap dog owner and a crap mother. Tears prick my eyes again. And I realise that I'm struggling to do this. I'm struggling to do this alone.

Chapter Ninety-Nine

Amy had called him last night. Completely out of the blue. They hadn't been in contact since she'd moved back to London and he'd missed her more than he ever could have imagined. His joy at hearing her voice had, however, been short lived. 'She sounded so miserable on the phone,' Guy said.

'So you're just going to drop everything and go to London to see her?' Cheryl asked incredulously.

'Yes,' Guy replied. Frankly, he was worried sick about Amy despite her reassurances that she was fine. She certainly hadn't sounded fine. He was glad that she'd phoned him when she was feeling down, but it was torture to be so far away from her and unable to do anything useful to help.

His receptionist rolled her eyes. 'It must be love.'

'It must be,' he agreed.

'Good for you,' she said with a smile. 'About time.' She leaned on the desk. 'You realise that there'll be a lot of very irate clients this weekend.'

'Yes,' he said. 'But it's about time that I put myself first. Stephen and the guinea pig population of Scarsby can, I'm very sure, manage without me for two days.'

'Is this really you?' she teased. 'Or have you been abducted by aliens and given a brain transplant?'

'This is really me. The *new* me.'

'Then you should be making tracks, otherwise you'll spend the entire weekend sitting in traffic.' Cheryl stood up and hugged him. 'You'd better come back.'

'I'll see you on Monday morning,' Guy assured her. 'Bright and early.'

His spirit and heart felt light as he jumped into the Range Rover and headed out towards the motorway. It had been years since he'd been back to London. Five years, to be exact. He'd fled from Town after his relationship with Laura had broken up and he'd never looked back since. The big city lights no longer held him in thrall and he wondered if he'd feel differently, now that he was going to see Amy and the children. He couldn't believe how much he'd missed them all in the time that they'd been away. How on earth was he going to cope with their absence longterm?

It was true that Amy's phone call had worried him. She'd sounded on the verge of tears and it seemed that going back to her old company wasn't all that it was cracked up to be. The children didn't like their new school and, according to Amy, even Hamish wasn't being Hamish. Only Milly Molly Mandy, it seemed, was unfazed by the upheaval. But that was cats for you every time.

Guy had lain awake all night worrying about her, which prompted his decision to do his knight in shining armour impersonation. Cheryl had been suitably impressed and he only hoped that Amy would feel the same too. She'd certainly sounded relieved when he called her first thing this morning to tell her that he was planning to head straight down to see her.

It was dark now; he'd been sitting in traffic for hours and had long since developed hundred-yard stare. How different this was to pottering round the green lanes of the dales and moors. He'd forgotten that this number of cars actually existed.

Finding Amy's flat was easy enough, but locating a parking space was less so. Frustratingly, he was still circling her place a quarter of an hour after arriving. He felt like abandoning his vehicle in the middle of the road. How did people do this every day? Then he got lucky and squeezed into a space that he didn't actually think was big enough to accommodate the Range Rover. He was feeling ragged by the time he pressed her doorbell, but the sound of Hamish's frenzied barking lifted his flagging energy levels.

The block of flats looked depressingly dreary and it was hard for him to form a picture of Amy and the children having a cosy family life in this bleak place. Then Amy opened the door and her smile nearly broke his heart. She looked drawn, pale – as bad as she had just after Will had died – and he wanted to take her in his arms right there on the doorstep. Instead, he just said, 'Hi.'

Thankfully, Amy was less reticent. 'You made it,' she said as she hugged him. His muscles were tight, tense after the long drive, and her body felt soft and warm and oh-so-good against his. 'I was so worried that you'd have a terrible journey.'

It had been fairly horrendous but he didn't want to bother her with such trivia now. 'It's good to see you,' he said, and it was alarming to hear his voice cracking with emotion.

Before she could say anything else, both of the children barrelled out of the living room and flung themselves at him, Jessica jumping into his arms, shouting, 'Yay!'

'Your biggest fans have missed you too.'

'And I've missed you all.'

'We hate London,' Jessica said candidly. 'We want to go home.'

And he wanted to take them home – back to Helmshill Grange – but he wondered whether Amy would ever buy into that one.

Chapter One Hundred

Hamish is bringing the place down. 'Ssh, dog,' I say, as I open the kitchen door a notch. 'Calm down, for goodness sake. You'll get us evicted.'

I hang onto his collar as he bounces out to greet Guy. 'No pets allowed,' I tell our newly arrived guest. 'I can see why now.'

Every wag of Hamish's powerful tail destroys something – albeit unintentionally. Though I have to say that this is the liveliest I've seen our hound since we arrived. If I'm honest, I could say the same for me and the children too.

I'm so glad that I called Guy this week and that there's no bad feeling between us. I hadn't expected him to rush down here, but I'm so pleased that he did.

Hamish escapes my clutches and bounds to give Guy his friendliest nose-up-the-bottom doggy version of a hug. Guy bends to fuss him and nearly gets knocked over in the process. Hamish is beside himself with excitement and we should take him out for his walk soon otherwise there'll be a puddle on my already skanky carpet.

'Hello, boy,' Guy says, ruffling his ears. And to me, 'He's looking well.'

'He's been as miserable as sin since we got here,' I tell him. As have we all. 'You've certainly perked him up.' Ditto the rest of us. But I don't voice that opinion out loud.

It feels so good to see Guy here, if a little bizarre. His waxed jacket and checked shirt look strangely out of place in a Town setting, and he seems even bigger than I remember, in our tiny flat. He looks more stereotypical 'country vet' than I've ever seen him and, for some reason, that makes me smile.

He runs his hands over Hamish's flanks. 'Leg looks like it's holding up well.'

'He's got a slight limp,' I say, 'but it doesn't seem to be bothering him too much.'

'The fixator might be niggling,' Guy offers. 'That's why he might be a bit down in the dumps.'

'I think it's being holed up in this place,' I say, lowering my voice so the kids can't hear. 'And who can blame him?'

Guy looks around him. He says nothing, but I can tell that he agrees with the sentiments.

'I've arranged for Serena to come and watch the children tonight so we can go out,' I continue. 'I hope that you're feeling up to it after the long drive?'

'Great,' Guy says. He looks down at his jacket. 'I have brought some city clothes with me so I won't embarrass you.'

'I'd never feel embarrassed with you.' Then I flush at my forwardness as our eyes meet. 'I'll put the kettle on and show you your room.'

'You're having my bed,' Jessica says proudly, making it clear that she was ear-wigging on our conversation.

I'm putting my daughter in with me, so that Guy can have her room. I only hope that my child doesn't wriggle as much as she usually does or I won't get a wink of sleep for the next couple of nights. 'You'll have to share the bed with a selection of soft toys, I'm afraid.'

'That's fine,' he laughs, and I can't believe how much I've missed that sound.

'It's not much,' I say, as I show him Jessica's little box room. His face takes on a worried frown.

'Are you happy here?' he asks.

'No,' I admit. 'I'm completely miserable.' Then I say nothing else as those stupid tears threaten to spring into action once again. 'But it will do for now. I don't plan on staying here for ever.' Before I turn on the waterworks, I choke out, 'I'll leave you to settle in,' and beat a hasty retreat to the kitchen.

Swiping Milly Molly Mandy from the work surface, I flick the kettle on, making tea while Guy is busy in the bathroom. He reappears just as I'm putting in the milk. 'I need to walk Hamish before we go out, if that's okay,' I say.

389

'I could do with stretching my legs.'

We look at each other over the tops of our steaming mugs. 'It really is good to see you,' I tell him quietly. 'I didn't expect you to come down so soon.'

'It took Cheryl by surprise too.'

We laugh at that. 'You realise that we'll be the talk of Poppy's Tea Room next week,' I warn him. 'And what they don't know, they'll make up.'

'That's true enough.' Guy sips at his hot tea. 'Alan sends his love.'

'How is he?'

'Fine.' Then he stares directly at me and asks, 'Missing Helmshill?'

I nod and a terrible sadness creeps over me. 'More than I'd like to admit.'

Chapter One Hundred and One

Guy had forgotten that restaurants could be so busy. Even though Amy had booked a table, it wasn't ready for them by the time they arrived and now they sat squashed together on vertiginous stools at a crowded bar while they waited for it to become vacant. His stomach growled with hunger and Guy recalled that it had been a long time since he grabbed a sandwich at one of the motorway service stations.

This was tedious. Every minute, his elbow was jogged or someone trod on his foot. This was also exactly the sort of place that he hated. The sound bounced round the room off the stripped wooden floors, making the noise level so high he was barely able to hear what Amy was saying.

All the women looked sleek and high-maintenance – like Laura. He could just see his ex loving this place. All the men were wearing designer shirts, not tucked in, with skinny jeans. He felt dowdy and old fashioned in his button-down shirt and boot cuts, and previously he'd never even considered himself to be concerned by such things. As he looked round at them he wondered how many of them would be capable of castrating a bad-tempered bull though.

'This place is very trendy,' Amy shouted unnecessarily. The only good thing about it being so packed was that it meant she had to put her mouth right close to his ear to be heard.

'I can see that,' he shouted back. Guy decided that he didn't do trendy any more. These days he was built for comfort, peace and quiet. A pint and a chilli con carne at the Helmshill Arms was about his level. This was far too stressful to be considered relaxing. He'd wondered if Amy would have slipped easily back into her London ways, but she seemed ill at ease too. Perhaps having taken the girl out of the city, the city had been taken out of the girl. Guy could only hope so.

'Someone at work recommended it,' she yelled. 'Maybe we should have gone somewhere quieter.'

He was just about to suggest that they cut their losses and leave when a waitress came and told them that their table was ready. Guy helped Amy down from her stool and took her arm as they followed the waitress through the crush.

Before they'd left for the restaurant, they'd found ten

minutes to take Hamish for a quick walk round a scruffy little park opposite the flat, sneaking the dog out under a dark blanket. It wasn't too bad for Hamish at the moment as his exercise needed to be limited, but he'd need more space to run free than this as soon as his leg was fully healed. This was no place for a big dog. No wonder Hamish was miserable.

'Perhaps we can go up to Hampstead Heath tomorrow,' Guy suggested as they sat down. Already he was sick of the smell of exhaust fumes and was desperate for some fresh air. He felt claustrophobic, hemmed in. How on earth did people live like this permanently? How had he done it once?

'That would be nice. I could do with a long walk.' Amy sighed as she said, 'This week has been a nightmare.'

'Sounds like the job isn't working out, from what you said on the phone.'

Amy shook her head. 'I've got a young boss, who seems keen to change the world. Or rule it,' she told him. 'He seems to want me in the office morning, noon and night. The rest of the team are under thirty and have no commitments. I don't think he understands that I have another life outside of work.' She sighed wistfully. 'After spending so much time with the children at Helmshill I'm finding it hard to leave them with a nanny, even though she's Mary Poppins reincarnated.' She swigged at her drink.

That was another thing. The prices here were eye-watering. Something else you forgot when you lived in the country.

'It would be a lot easier if I had the money from the sale of the house,' Amy continued.

Guy felt himself go hot under the collar.

'For some reason the Gerner-Bernards are delaying signing the contracts and I can't get any sense out of the estate agent.' She shrugged her frustration. 'I don't know what can be wrong. They seemed so keen on it. Now it appears that they've gone off the boil.'

'Perhaps it will sort itself out soon,' Guy said evasively. Amy would kill him if she knew what he'd been up to, and he felt guilty at the thought of his actions.

She looked across at him and smiled. 'You're not loving London, are you?'

'Does it show?'

She giggled at that.

'I'd forgotten how busy it was,' Guy explained, joking, 'Did there used to be so many people here?'

'Don't ever see yourself becoming a townie again?'

He shook his head.

'I hope we can stay in touch, Guy.' Amy's hand rested on his arm and her fingers burned through his shirt to his skin. 'It would be nice if you could come down to see us every now and again.'

'I'd like that.' Before this, he would have thought that he'd have moved heaven and earth to come down to London to see them as often as he possibly could, if there was any chance, no matter how tiny, of him and Amy getting together.

But the truth of the matter was that he didn't really believe it now. Would he want to spend his weekends down here in Amy's horrible, depressing flat? If they both had demanding jobs, exactly how many weekends would they be able to wangle together? He'd thought that he could give up his life in Helmshill and move here permanently, if that was what

Amy wanted him to do, but now he wasn't so sure. It would kill him to live here – that was an odds-on certainty. Did he love her and the children enough to give up all that he cherished? He had thought that he did. He had been so absolutely sure. But now that he was here, the reality of the situation had hit him full force and the question was a lot more difficult to answer.

Chapter One Hundred and Two

This is my second week of work back at the British Television Company and my third cocktail party, the third night in a row. It's Thursday and I'm absolutely knackered. I cannot wait until Friday comes around so that I can slob out in front of the telly with the kids instead of being forced to make small talk in loud bars to people who have had too much to drink. I seem to have lost the art of trivial conversation. Didn't I used to enjoy doing this? I'm sure I did, but for the life of me, I can't now see why.

We're at another 'in' place to go. The hot ticket. To me it just looks like another packed bar even though we have it for our company's exclusive use. Didn't I once find the buzz of the city energising? Now I feel that it's sapping all of my strength. God, I've found this week so hard. None of my colleagues seem to find this so tiring or so mind-numbingly tedious. They all look as fresh as daisies and as if they're having the best fun of their lives.

I've reached the age when a quiet drink in a country pub with a roaring log fire is more my sort of thing than standing crushed in a place where painting everything stark white and providing chairs that are impossible to sit on is considered the height of chic.

Kati, our new au pair, is doing a sterling job and she's fabulous with the kids, but I'm paying out an absolute fortune every week for childcare. It's eating an enormous hole in my salary, and the cost of living back here is truly scary. I haven't had time to sit down and do the sums properly – once again, that was Will's forte – but I feel as if I'm barely breaking even. It might not even be that good.

Serena has promised to look after the kids for me a couple of nights each week to ease the burden, but that means she'll have to make sure that she's out of work early, which is nigh-on impossible for her even if the spirit is willing. I've haven't even had the time to contact my old friends yet, never mind reacquaint myself with the babysitting circle. How would I manage to reciprocate when it was my turn, now that I'm on my own? I can't rely on neighbours here as I might have done in Helmshill. How the hell do you make instant friends in a cold, impersonal city like London? A place where you might not speak to your immediate next-door neighbour for thirty years.

The man next to me guffaws at something that has been said and I try to switch back into the conversation and not dwell on how much my feet hurt or my legs ache or my head throbs. My companion is a high-flying executive for an Italian television company. I'm supposed to be talking to him about a raft of programmes with titles too ridiculous to say out loud – all new ideas from the crazed mind of Lawrence Holmes – and I wonder for the millionth time whether I'm really cut out for this any more. My ideas and Lawrence's are, creatively, poles apart. Would I be happy working on the sort of programmes that would make up our department's output? Programmes such as *Celebrity Art Exhibition*, *Celebrity So You Wannabe a Writer?* and *Celebrity Interior Design Challenge*. Every single one of them populated by people who've been tossed off *Big Brother*.

I had a lovely weekend with Guy – you won't believe how much it lifted my spirits. We took the children and Hamish up to Hampstead Heath and let them run around for a few hours, all of us enjoying the wind in our hair. It felt so good to be out of that cramped flat and in the fresh air.

But now that Guy's gone back to Helmshill, I feel quite down again. It could be weeks before we're able to see him again. I need to visit Will's grave too. I thought being back in London would somehow make me feel closer to my husband, but I simply feel more alone. At this rate, when will I manage to get up there? I'm so exhausted by the time that Friday comes around that I hardly have the energy to move all weekend, let alone flog up to Yorkshire and back.

I could tell that Guy didn't enjoy being in Town again – and who can blame him? He said it was years since he'd been in the city, and that he was surprised how much it had changed. Frankly, I feel like a fish out of water after having been away for less than a year, so I can fully understand how Guy must have felt.

The man next to me howls with laughter again and I force a wide grin even though I've no idea what's been said. Then

I feel his hand on my backside and he turns his leery face towards me. In case I'm tempted to think that he's done this in error, he then grabs a handful of buttock and squeezes.

'Get. Your. Hand. Off. My. Arse,' I say through gritted teeth in a voice that's audible just to him. This may be acceptable behaviour in his country – though I doubt it – but it certainly won't wash with me. The man's English is limited but what he can't understand in actual words he can tell from the tone of my voice and the fire in my eyes. His hand drops away, he shrugs insolently and turns his back on me to talk to another one of my colleagues.

I don't care if it's still early. I've had more than enough, and I'm fuming. There's no way that I need to put up with that kind of behaviour. I slug back my drink – at least the champagne is good – and head for the cloakroom to retrieve my coat.

As the cloakroom attendant hands over my things, my boss appears out of the men's room. Lawrence Holmes looks taken aback as I struggle to shrug on my coat and he marches over to me.

'You can't go now,' he says.

How do I tell him politely that I can't get out of here quick enough?

'I've had it for tonight,' I say. 'My feet hurt. My head hurts.' My heart hurts. 'And I've just been goosed by one of the Italians.' I hold up my hands. 'That's me done.'

His face hardens. 'Amy,' he says, 'I have to tell you that I'm beginning to doubt your commitment to this job.'

'You know what, Lawrence?' I reply, hands on hips. 'Me too.'

Then I flounce out of the door and, as I can't face the bloody Tube either, hope I can hail a cab quickly to take me home.

Chapter One Hundred and Three

'It did not go well.' I tell Serena my sorry story when I get back.

My sister puts on the kettle and utters suitably soothing noises as she makes me some chamomile tea. I slip off my shoes and enjoy the pain of the cold tiles on my bare feet.

'Every company wants their pound of flesh these days,' she reminds me.

'I don't mind giving a pound of flesh, but I do mind having my bottom groped. That's definitely more than a pound!' We both laugh at that. 'It's not as if he was even attractive.'

This was to be my big chance at getting back into the cutting edge of television, steering a raft of popular arts programmes to the small screen. I didn't envisage working for a megalomaniac barely out of his teens, nor of producing programmes that wouldn't tax the brain cells of an amoeba.

'I've got some more bad news for you,' she says. 'I think Hamish has eaten some of your pants.'

I sigh. 'That's the least of my worries.'

'I caught him in your underwear drawer,' she continues. 'He was looking very sheepish and I'll swear I saw some white lace disappear down his throat.'

'Looks like my dog might be getting better.' I nurse the cup of chamomile tea to me. This stuff had better be strong if it's going to be able to relax me. 'Have the kids been good?'

'Angels,' she says. Then she looks sadly at me. 'They deserve better than this.'

'I know.' I let out a wobbly, stressed breath. 'I'm working on it. Really I am.'

'If there's anything I can do to help,' my sister slips her arm round my shoulder and squeezes tight, 'you only have to ask.'

Then the doorbell rings and my stomach plummets, because I just know that at this time of the night it's not going to be something to cheer me up. 'What now?' I say, and then plod out to open the door.

Hamish starts up a crazy bark. 'Hush, hush,' I tell him, finger to my lips. He gives a low growl instead and I shove him into the living room and close the door behind him.

A woman is standing there in the stark communal hallway. She's tiny, Chinese and very polite. 'I live upstairs,' she tells me, helpfully pointing upwards.

I haven't actually met anyone else who lives in the block yet – so typical in London. Could be another five years before I'm on nodding terms with any of them.

'So sorry to trouble you,' she says, 'but I have to tell you this.'

I'm all ears, but I think I know what's coming.

'Your dog is howling all day long,' she continues, looking embarrassed that she's had to raise the issue. 'I am a nurse. And I work night-shift. During the day I must sleep.'

I can hardly deny Hamish now, can I, when he's just done

his favourite party piece. 'I'm really, really sorry,' I say, and I am.

'I do not think that you are allowed to keep dogs here. I do not mind. I love animals. But I do not think that other neighbours will be so kind. He is very noisy.'

Yes, that's Hamish all right. 'I do apologise. I'll try to keep him quiet. We're only here on a short-term let,' I explain. 'We'll be gone before you know it.'

'Thank you,' she says. 'I know that you will deal with the situation.'

I close the door and lean against it. What can I do? Gag Hamish? Turn the television up so loud that all they can hear is *Bargain Hunt*, *60-Minute Makeover* and *Place in the Sun* rather than my dog? But then I'm upset to hear that Hamish is distressed while we're all out. He's got so used to having us all around that it must be lonely for him. He was clearly overjoyed to see Guy last weekend. And he wasn't the only one.

I worry about Milly Molly Mandy too. She hasn't been out at all since we got here, as I'm terrified that she'll be run over on the busy road or that she'll escape and never come back. She looks lethargic and disinterested in her modest surroundings and, with her penchant for disembowelment, was never intended to be a house cat.

Most of all I worry about the kids. They're not settling in well at their new school, although I appreciate that it's early days yet. My children already seem to look paler and less robust, the country colour having fled from their cheeks.

I go back into the kitchen.

'You look like you've seen a ghost,' Serena says.

'My neighbour is complaining about Hamish,' I tell my sister.

'Haven't they got anything better to worry about?'

'It's fair enough, I suppose,' I say wearily. 'We're not supposed to have pets here.'

Serena comes and puts her arms round me. 'It will be all right,' she says. 'I promise you. Everything will be all right.'

But, you know, I'm not sure that I believe her.

Chapter One Hundred and Four

Bad news – like buses, it seems – comes along in threes. At eight-thirty the very next morning, just when I'm selecting Hamish's television viewing for the day in the hope of keeping him quiet, my phone rings and it's the secretary from Queensway, Tom and Jessica's school. The Headteacher, she says, would like to see me urgently but can offer no further information as to the reason for my summons.

Immediately, I call Lawrence's PA and explain to her that I'm going to be late this morning. If my boss is already cross with me, then let him stick that in his pipe and smoke it too.

I chivvy up the children and we set out towards the school. The traffic thunders by us on the road. I try to talk to Jessica, but I can't even hear myself think, let alone hold a sensible conversation about whether or not she's done her homework.

At the school door, I say goodbye to them, remembering

not to kiss Tom, then I tell the receptionist that I'm here to see the Headteacher. There's paint peeling off the walls in the hall and I don't recall seeing that when I was here before. Perhaps I'm seeing London through different eyes now than I did then. If I am, it all looks horrible and dirty and down-right depressing.

In her worn and slightly grubby office, Mrs Richards offers me a cup of tea. Even though I'd love one, I refuse because I can't afford to hang around too long. 'I've asked you to come in, Mrs Ashurst,' she says, 'because I'm worried about Tom and Jessica.'

You're not the only one, I think.

'They don't seem to be settling in well,' Mrs Richards continues. 'Are they unhappy at home?'

'It's been a very traumatic year for them,' I explain. 'We uprooted to the country, then they lost their father and now we've upped sticks again to come back to London to be near my family. I've had to become a working mum again. That's never easy when you're on your own.'

'Hmm,' she says, lips pursed. 'I can see that it's rather a lot for them to cope with.'

'Yes,' I say meekly, all of my guilt buttons having been pushed.

'And for you too.' She smiles softly at me which makes me feel even worse. 'I'm afraid that Tom and Jessica aren't having a much better time here,' Mrs Richards continues. 'They're being bullied.'

'Bullied?'

'I can assure you now, Mrs Ashurst, we're doing all that we can to stamp it out in the school, but this issue does raise its ugly head every now and then.'

Don't remember her mentioning this at the interview when she was keen to extol the virtues of her school.

'You see, as new pupils arriving halfway through a school year, Tom and Jessica are prime targets.'

'They never said anything.'

'They're lovely children, Mrs Ashurst,' she tells me.

I know that, and I want to weep because of it. I hate to think of some streetwise little oik pushing my kids around when they're already feeling vulnerable. I hate the fact that they haven't felt able to tell me about it.

'What can I do?'

'Just be supportive of them. We're trying to keep on top of the situation here,' the Headteacher assures me again, 'but I wanted to let you know that they are having a hard time at the moment. We'll do everything we can to help them.'

'Thank you,' I say. 'I appreciate you calling me.' Why am I being so polite when I really want to scream at her to get her scabby pupils under control and then go and snatch Tom and Jessica from their classes?

'We'll keep in touch,' she says, and stands up to shake my hand. A frown crosses her brow. 'Are you sure that you're all right, Mrs Ashurst?'

'I'm fine. Thank you.' Then as I leave her office, I check my watch. I've got to fly like the wind. I'm an hour late for work already and I know that I'm not going to be able to stay late tonight as neither Kati nor Serena are available for babysitting duties and I have to get back for the children. Wonder what Lawrence Wonderboy Holmes will think of that?

Who cares? I want to spend time with my kids. They need

me more than some poxy television company. Let Lawrence Holmes swivel on it.

Chapter One Hundred and Five

Without heed of the expense, I manage to hail a cab outside the school and jump in it. I lay my head back on the seat, close my eyes and try to absorb what Tom and Jessica's Headteacher said to me and how I can help them get through this.

Twenty minutes later and I'm swinging through the chrome and glass doors at the BTC. As I try to sneak to my desk unnoticed, I see the dreaded Lawrence Holmes coming out of his office and he heads me off at the pass.

'Can you spare five minutes to have a word with me?' he says. His sarcasm isn't lost on me.

'Of course, Lawrence.'

He steers me back to his sumptuous office. An office just like the one I used to have.

'Sit,' he says, talking to me like I talk to Hamish.

I sit. Lawrence strides up and down in front of me wearing his 'concerned' frown. I have never previously come across a man with such a wide range of forehead furrows. Already, I know many of them too well.

'I'm sorry to say, Amy, that we won't be extending your trial period.'

Trial period? I didn't know I was on one.

He folds his arms and stares at me. 'If you'd like to clear your desk you can leave now.'

I also fold my arms. 'This is because I object to one of our clients groping my bottom?'

'I don't think there's any point in us discussing this issue. We're not sure that you're a team player and here at the British Television Company we need team players.'

Team players! You need bloody mindless slaves with no homelife, I think, but say nothing. There's no use in arguing with someone like Lawrence and, to be truthful, my return to the fold has not been quite the homecoming I envisaged.

My heart was never in this job from day one, though I don't think I've done badly enough to be given the boot. If Lawrence had one iota of compassion he'd understand my problems. But he doesn't. The man has a calculator where his soul should be, and all he knows are targets, ratings and sales. This isn't for me. I want to make programmes with integrity. I want to work with people with integrity. In my time, I was a damn good producer and I deserve more than this.

I have no argument for Lawrence though. I'm too exhausted, too crushed to be able to fight my own corner.

Holding up my hands, I back out of the door. 'Thanks,' I say. 'Thanks for nothing.'

Bad news, it seems, comes in more than threes. Before I know it, I'm out on the street and stunned. It's not yet ten o'clock and I've found out that my beautiful children are being bullied and I've been sacked.

In a daze, I get onto the Tube, heading back towards home.

Hanging onto the overhead bar, I let my body move with the sway of the train and my mind go into freefall. I've come back here to try and pick up my old life and, suddenly, it's all crumbling round my ears.

Before I know what I'm doing, I'm out on the street and walking towards my old house in Notting Hill. It pulls me up short. I didn't mean to do that. I just did it on autopilot, before I remembered that I didn't live here any more. Since we've been back I've done all that I can to avoid coming here. I've even taken a circuitous route to give this place a wide berth.

It's dry today, for a change, but windy along the street and I pull my coat around me, aware of the swirling dust stinging my eyes. Now, standing outside the place that was my home for many a happy year, I feel even more like an alien. A hick up from the sticks. I stare at the house, hands jammed into my pockets to keep them warm, as if it's somewhere that I don't know every nook and cranny of, every creak and groan. I know that the utility-room door is warped, that a breeze blows through the study window, catching you in the back of the neck as you sit at the desk, and I know that the thermostat on the radiator in the family bathroom needs replacing.

They haven't done much to the house, the new people. There are two smart black pots either side of the front door bearing wind-scorched bay trees, but other than that it looks pretty much the same. But I know that the rooms – which made the house our home – would now be unrecognisable. There'll be new furniture, new books, new cutlery, new covers on the beds, a different range of foods in the fridge. All the small things that defined us as a family are gone. I wonder, if the house could look back at me, would it think the same thing? Would it think that I looked pretty much the same on the outside? Would it realise that everything inside has changed, that nothing is familiar any more?

Desperately, I want to go back inside to try to reach out to the past. But the door is closed to me, there's no one at home. More than the new plot in the graveyard that I tended, or the emptiness in my double bed that I feel so keenly, this brings it home hard to me that this treasured part of my life is now gone. It's the past. It's over. What I had will never be mine again.

I tried so hard to re-create the old life – for me, for the children – without ever realising that even if everything had turned out perfectly and even if I'd done the impossible and claimed back my house, my beloved job on *Sports Quiz* and had managed to get the children places at Weston's again – *it still wasn't going to bring Will back to me*. My old world meant security to me; somehow I thought if I got that back then I'd manage better without my husband and everything would return to how it had been.

Of course, I was hideously mistaken. Things can never be the same. A smart job in London and a flat with a trendy address is never, ever going to bring William back, it's never going to give my children back their beloved father. All the time I think I've been making plans, moving on, and all I've been doing is trying to move forwards by going back.

My eyes fill with tears and I realise that there's no trace of Will here. He's not in London any more. There are no traces of him in the restaurants we used to go to, the places we used to love. My husband's in Helmshill now. That's where his heart is. That's where Will is. And it hits me like a body blow that I'm not.

Feeling my wedding band on my finger, I take my hand out of my pocket to look at it. The shiny gold symbol always felt like a part of me; now I feel like a fraud for wearing it. Slipping the ring from my finger, I let it fall into the depths of my pocket. I'm not a married woman any more. I'm a widow. A single parent. Alone.

Chapter One Hundred and Six

As I go into the block at Lancaster Court, the letting agent is coming out. We both do a double-take. Then he flushes bright red.

'Hello,' I say, unable to keep the surprise out of my voice.

'I'm here with an eviction order,' he says briskly. And then I notice the bulky brown envelope in his hand. 'From the landlord. Your neighbours have complained to us. The dog has to go by the weekend or you're out.'

'Ah.' My poor dog. I sigh and take the envelope as he holds it out for me. 'Hamish isn't a pet. He's a member of the family.'

The letting agent looks unimpressed by this. So kick me out on a technicality.

'You'll lose your deposit,' the agent explains. 'If you go.'

'Right.' That's an awful lot of money.

'I'm sorry,' he says. He doesn't look it.

'Me too.'

Then he scuttles away, banging the door behind him and leaving me to think, Am I really sorry?

With a leaden heart, I let myself into the flat. In the living room, Hamish and Mils are lying side-by-side on the sofa watching *The Jeremy Kyle Show*. They both look up when I walk in. Hamish slides off the sofa, wagging his tail and rubbing up and down my legs.

'I'm thinking of selling you both to a glue factory or some laboratory that does hideous animal experiments,' I tell my pets, but they fail to look terrified. Perhaps they now know that I'm all bluff and bluster. 'If I don't, we'll all be homeless. Any other ideas?'

Milly Molly Mandy yawns and returns her attention to a lesbian grappling with her ex-husband for reasons I know not why on the small screen.

'I need a nice cup of tea,' I tell Hamish as I divest myself of my coat. 'You won't believe the morning I've had. It's been hell. What else could possibly go wrong?'

Then, before I get as far as the kettle, my mobile rings. Why, it's Wayne the estate agent calling all the way from Yorkshire! Surely good news now!

'Mrs Ashurst,' he says. 'I've some very bad news.'

I just about manage to stop myself from laughing hysterically down the phone.

'The Gerner-Bernards have decided not to go ahead with the purchase of Helmshill Grange.'

My inclination to laugh dissipates instantly and instead I

suck in a sharp intake of breath. 'They can't back out now. Not at this late stage.'

'They're very sorry,' Wayne says, and I wonder whose side he's on.

'Give me their telephone number,' I demand. 'I want to call them.'

'I can't do that, I'm afraid.'

'I want to call them and make them realise exactly what they're doing.'

'I've tried everything to persuade them otherwise, Mrs Ashurst, but they wouldn't change their minds.'

'What can I do?'

'We'll remarket the property,' he says. 'Straight away. Perhaps you'd consider reducing the price?'

'I need time to think about this,' I tell Wayne the Wonderboy. 'I'm struggling to take it in.'

But as I hang up, I know exactly what I have to do. I have to go up to Yorkshire and find out what's going on. I forget about my cup of tea and, instead, go into the bedroom and pull an overnight bag out of the wardrobe. I throw some stuff in for me and then go through to the children's rooms and do the same. My coat gets shrugged back on. 'Come on, you two,' I say to Hamish and Milly Molly Mandy. 'You're coming as well.'

Mils makes a break for it as I bring in her travel cage, but I grab her, kiss her on the nose and, while she's still in a state of shock at my unexpected affection, slide her inside. I put Hamish on the lead and my dog promptly enters into the spirit of adventure by barking like a loon and doing jumping jacks even though he's not supposed to. Banging the flat door behind me, I struggle down the road, going as fast as my legs will carry me with my baggage and my pet posse. The Land Rover is just round the corner and I load it up with our gear. Minutes later, I'm outside the children's school.

'Do not eat one single thing,' I say to Hamish before I fly inside.

The receptionist looks up as I burst into the school. 'I'd like Tom and Jessica Ashurst out of school, please. A family emergency has come up.'

Without further question, she springs into action and five minutes later, while I'm tapping my feet impatiently, my children appear.

They're carrying their coats and have worried looks on their faces.

'Why do we have to come out of class, Mummy?' Tom wants to know.

'Are we going to the dentist?' Jessica looks deeply unimpressed by this idea.

'Mummy has a few problems she needs to sort out. We're going to Yorkshire,' I tell them. 'Back to Helmshill Grange.'

'Hurrah!' they both shout and race out towards the car.

And, despite the fact that my problems are stacking up, my heart feels lighter than it has done in days and I race after them.

Chapter One Hundred and Seven

'I could fix you up with a date,' Cheryl suggested.

'I don't need a date,' Guy insisted. 'We've been down that route before and it was a complete disaster.'

'It might stop you moping around like a love-sick teenager.'

'I'm not moping around.' Although he had to agree that he *was* feeling rather too much like a love-sick teenager for his own good.

'You're just too fussy,' his receptionist puffed.

'I am,' Guy agreed. 'And I also happen to have found someone that I want to be with all by myself.'

Cheryl made another disparaging noise. 'I don't like to point this out,' she said, 'but the lovely Mrs Ashurst is at the other end of the country.'

'I'm working on that,' he told her.

'You'd better not be thinking about leaving us to go south.'

'No,' Guy said honestly. 'That's not in my masterplan.'

'Glad to hear it.'

He sighed to himself. He could only hope that Amy would be pleased to hear what he had in mind. 'Now, let's get down to business. What's in the book for today?'

Cheryl reeled off the list of appointments. 'Two cats to neuter. A budgie with some sort of growth on its beak. A dog with diarrhoea. Oh, and Mrs Harris is coming in. Megan had her pups a few weeks ago.'

That stopped Guy in his tracks. 'Why did no one tell me?'

'Why would you want to know?' Cheryl looked puzzled, as well she might. One or more of their clients' pets had pups practically every day of the week and he never took a personal interest in them. How would Cheryl know that this was different?

'Stephen had a look at them. Did their injections and all that. Now she wants you to check them over just to make sure they're all right. Have you got a problem with that?'

'No, no.' He felt a guilty gulp travel down his throat. How the hell was he going to be able to bill Mrs Harris for this? For what Hamish had done to her poor, unsuspecting bitch, he at least owed her this one on the house.

'You've gone all pale.' For reasons that Cheryl wasn't aware of he felt more than a little responsible for Megan's pups.

'I'm fine. Perfectly fine.'

'I've squeezed her in,' Cheryl continued, unaware of the cause of his discomfort. 'Mrs Harris should be here at any minute.' On cue, a shiny new Vauxhall Corsa pulled up outside. 'Oh, look. She's here now.'

He watched, frozen, as his client eased herself out of her car, toddled round to the boot and opened it. She struggled to lift a cardboard box out.

'Don't just stand there,' Cheryl scolded. 'Go and help her!'

Mobilised, Guy shot out of the door and into the car park. 'Here,' he said to Mrs Harris. 'Let me help.'

'Oh, thank you, Mr Burton,' she said gratefully. 'They might only be a few weeks old, but they weigh a ton.'

Guy took the box from her arms and stared inside. Shocked, he nearly dropped it on the ground. There could be no doubting the parentage of these pups. Peering back at him, all barking squeakily, were six miniature versions of Hamish.

'They're quite a handful,' the elderly lady said with a sigh. 'I can tell you.'

Guy could well imagine.

'They've got me run ragged.'

And, if their father was anything to go by, it was only going to get worse. What a shame they hadn't inherited their looks from their boisterous father and their personality from their placid mother.

The little glossy black and tan bundles were climbing over each other, trying their best to escape from the confines of their box. On a cute scale of one to ten, the pups were up there at eleven. One licked his finger with its soft, tickly tongue and Guy felt his heart melt.

'Still,' she said, 'I've got offers for four of them already. They'll soon be off my hands.'

He lifted the pup up. It licked all over his chin. It was a dog, the biggest of the bunch.

'That one's the most lively, Mr Burton. We've nicknamed him Trouble. I think he'll grow into a fine dog.'

He couldn't believe he was about to say this, but he did anyway. 'Mrs Harris, is this one taken?'

Chapter One Hundred and Eight

It takes me five hours to drive back to Scarsby. The children have behaved like angels all the way. Even Hamish and Milly Molly Mandy have been no trouble at all. It's as if they know.

Now we're in striking distance, on the last leg of the journey. I ease the Land Rover up the twisting lanes, over the steep hills, taking roads which decrease in size with every turn away from the motorway up to Scarsby. The moors are spread out before me, stark in their winter array. For miles and miles, I can see nothing manmade but the threads of the low, meandering drystone walls and the odd, lone farmhouse. A hawk hovers patiently by the side of the road, waiting for its lunch to appear. I turn off the radio and all I can hear is the plaintive whistle of the wind past the car.

'Nearly there.'

'Yay!' Tom and Jessica shout together. Hamish wakes up and barks.

Before I go up to the house, I screech to a halt right outside the estate agents. 'Wait here,' I say to the kids. 'I won't be long. Don't let the dog eat anything.'

Wayne, the youthful estate agent, looks up, shocked, as I burst through the door, making it reverberate on its hinges. This is the most excitement Scarsby has seen in months.

'Mrs Ashurst.' His spotty face blanches as if he's seen an apparition. 'I was going to c . . . c . . . call you,' he stammers before I can say anything. 'Honestly, I was.'

'What on earth is going on?' I snap. 'How can you have lost this sale? Do you know how important it was to me?'

Wayne holds up his hands. 'I've got some good news,' he bleats. 'It looks like we've got another buyer.'

That stops me in my tracks. I flop into the seat in front of his desk. Now it's my turn to be stunned. 'Oh. So soon?' That's good news, isn't it? I should be thrilled. Instead, my heart beats in panic. This sale could still go through.

The estate agent recovers some of his composure. He shuffles papers about on his desk and tries to look like he knows what he's doing.

'The client has just gone up to the house. You've only missed him by a few minutes.'

'I'll go straight up there,' I say, standing as I do. 'I'll show him round.' Do *your* job, I think. It seems that I came back not a moment too soon. 'Give me his name.'

The agent flushes again. This man should never play poker. 'I'm afraid that I'm not at liberty to do that.'

'Why on earth not? He wants to buy my house, I damn well want to know who he is.'

'He's asked that he remain anonymous, for the moment.'

'Is this man seriously interested or is he just a time-waster?'

The agent shrugs. 'He seemed genuine enough.'

I wonder whether it's one of these soap-star types from Granada in Manchester. They're all buying up country properties out here. Though, frankly, I don't give a toss who buys it as long as it goes quickly. No, that's not strictly true. I care very much who lives at Helmshill Grange – even though I shouldn't.

'Call him,' I instruct, and wag my finger at him for good measure. 'Tell him that I'm on my way and not to move without seeing me.'

'I'll do that right away, Mrs Ashurst.'

I can present Helmshill Grange in its best possible light. Let's see if I can't secure a sale within the next hour!

Chapter One Hundred and Nine

'What do you think?' Guy asked.

Alan put down his spade and Guy handed over the puppy, who promptly weed with excitement as he licked at Alan's face.

Neatly avoiding the puddle that was forming on the ground, Alan lifted the tiny, wriggling dog and studied its face intently. 'It's reet like Hamish.'

'Yes,' Guy said. 'This is Son of Hamish. But I wouldn't want that to be common knowledge, otherwise we'll be slapped with a paternity suit.'

Trouble squirmed in Alan's arms. 'Friendly little tyke.'

'He's called Trouble.' The two men exchanged a knowing glance.

'I can't believe I've taken him on,' Guy confessed. 'I must be mad.'

Alan didn't disagree.

'I'm hoping that you'll help me to look after him.'

Alan didn't disagree again, which Guy took as a good sign.

'If it was possible, would you be prepared to stay on at Helmshill Grange permanently?' Guy asked Alan.

A faint whisper of a smile threatened the man's lips. 'Aye, Vit.'

'You've enjoyed your time here?'

Alan nodded, before elaborating with, 'Aye.'

This place had become like a second home to Alan, who worked way longer than the hours that Guy paid him for. Some days he seemed reluctant to go home at all. Alan might not say much, but he clearly had become very attached to Helmshill Grange and the animals he cared for. It was costing Guy a small fortune to keep the place running, but it was worth it. He only hoped that Amy would agree.

Guy looked round the spotless yard. In his pen, Pork Chop snuffled around next to the two goats, Stephanie and Blob. In the paddock Daphne, Doris and Delila happily chewed at the sparse winter grass while the newborn lamb, Stuart Little, gambolled happily in the field, going from strength to strength every day.

Guy leaned on the fence and took in a breath of the cold, clear air. Any man would be happy to make Helmshill Grange his home. This was a beautiful setting, the house in its own land, nestled cosily at the foot of the brooding moors. How could the Gerner-Bernards have pulled out of buying such a place? Guy smiled to himself.

'Shame the townies aren't moving in now, eh?' he said to Alan.

'Reckon you've summat to do wi' that, Vit.' Alan tapped his nose knowingly.

'Mrs Ashurst must never get wind of that, Alan, or I'll be toast.'

'Secret's safe wi' me, Vit.'

'At least all the animals have got a reprieve.'

'Aye.' Already their new addition had fallen asleep in Alan's arms. The elderly man carried him to Guy's car and laid him gently in the front seat.

'I'll have to call Amy later,' Guy said absently. 'See how things are going in London.'

Then they heard the familiar rattle of a Land Rover and seconds later, Amy swung the car into the drive. Guy's heart lifted. What had brought her back to Helmshill without notice? Amy hadn't told him that she was planning to come back for a visit. Maybe she'd decided that she couldn't wait to see him. Guy hoped so. He wanted to run to take her in his arms and kiss her passionately. Well, he could dream.

Then he wondered how she'd take the news he was about to give her and he stayed where he was, shifting nervously from foot to foot. 'Looks like I won't have to wait that long.'

Chapter One Hundred and Ten

As we round the last bend before Helmshill comes into view, I get the urge to burst into tears and a lump comes to my throat. Strange as it may sound, this feels like coming home. I remember the first time we came here and I thought that Will had lost his mind bringing us to a place like this. Now, having spent just a few weeks back in London, I think that I've lost my mind in wanting to leave.

'We're home!' my daughter shouts and I couldn't agree more with her. Hamish pees in the footwell in excitement, but even that can't dampen my mood.

Turning into the drive, my spirit soars further when I see that Guy's Range Rover is parked there. That threatens to open the floodgates completely and I don't think that I've ever parked and been out of the car so quickly before.

I don't care what people think, but I rush into his arms and bury my face in his neck. It feels so good to see him. I knew that I'd missed him desperately this week, but I didn't realise quite how much.

Hamish goes berserk. He careens into Guy, barks maniacally, then when he spots Alan he sprints across the yard, ears flapping, feet scuttling on the cobbles, to take a flying leap at his hero.

'Whoa, boy,' is all that Alan says as he catches Hamish at full tilt and I have no idea how he remains standing.

I untangle myself from Guy's arms and he goes to give Tom and Jessica a hug. My daughter, I note, clings tightly to him.

'I didn't know you were coming back,' Guy says over his shoulder.

'Neither did I.' All I want now is a cup of tea. I feel so exhausted after the drive and everything else that's gone on. 'The estate agent called this morning to say that the house sale had fallen through. I've just stopped by there on the way here and now he tells me that there's another buyer interested.' I glance at my watch. 'He's supposed to be here now, according to Wayne.'

'Hmm,' Guy says.

'How long have you been here?'

'Half an hour or so. I brought a visitor to see Alan. Seems quite timely now.' Guy goes to his car and opens the door. There, curled up on the seat, is the cutest puppy I've ever seen. The children are wide eyed with adoration.

Guy lifts him up and the puppy opens his eyes sleepily.

'Oh, my God.' My hand flies to my mouth. 'It's a mini-Hamish.'

'Yes,' Guys says.

'How did that happen?'

'Usual way,' he tells me, but doesn't elaborate. No doubt I'll find out the full story later.

The puppy yawns and starts to wriggle. 'Meet Trouble,' Guy announces.

'He's yours?'

'For my sins.'

'Have you learned nothing, from all of Hamish's escapades?'

Guy shakes his head. 'Clearly not.'

'I love him,' Jessica says, and Guy hands Trouble over to her. 'He's so sweet.'

He is sweet, I have to agree. But I know exactly what he'll grow up to be like.

'So,' I say, 'this chap who's supposed to be looking at the house hasn't turned up then.'

'Er . . .' Guy says shiftily. I regard him quizzically. 'That chap would be me.'

'*You!*' I can't quite get my head around this. No wonder the estate agent was keeping schtum. 'You want to buy Helmshill? Why?'

'Look at it,' he says, sweeping his arm round the yard. 'I couldn't bear to see it go to someone else. Especially not some arty-farty Londoner wearing arty-farty specs.'

I laugh out loud. 'You can't buy it just because of that!'

'What would have happened to the animals?' He lowers his voice. 'To Alan? This is his life too now.'

And I do know that Alan Steadman has invested a lot of time and energy into looking after this place, more than he ever needed to. Would the new owners have appreciated that?

Guy comes to me and puts his hands on my arms. 'I know this is perhaps not what you want to hear, but I think that we could be good together. In time.' He sighs. 'There, I've said it. I know that you still love your husband, you always will, but I think that you could find room in your heart for me too. We could have a great relationship, Amy – I adore your children – and I want to give that a chance too. If you

422

think we could have one. How much more difficult would it be, with me being here and you being there? Don't you think we deserve a chance at happiness together?'

'Yes,' I finally admit – to Guy and to myself. 'That's what I want too.'

'I want to buy the house for you to live in,' he says. 'Come back from London. It was horrible to see you there, to see the children and Hamish cooped up in that awful flat.'

'The flat's not so awful,' I say defensively. Then I remember that, actually, it is.

'Come back,' he implores. 'Live at Helmshill again.'

'How can I? I lost my job this morning, Guy. I have no income. We're about to be turfed out of "that awful flat" because the neighbours have complained about Hamish's barking, and the kids are being bullied at their new school. Don't you think that I'd come running back here if I could?' I only have to look around me to realise that I've made a terrible mistake in trailing us all back to Town.

'You'll have the money from the sale,' he rushes on. 'Then you can rent it back from me. For heaven's sake, Amy, you can have the place for nothing.'

'I can't do that.'

'That's exactly why I'm suggesting that you rent it. At a nominal fee. You know that I don't want anything from you. I have more money than I know what to do with. The practice is doing well and my expenses are low. What else do I have to spend my cash on? Please,' he begs, 'let me help you.'

I can feel my resolve crumbling. Is there any way that I could come back here and make it work?

'We can sort out the details later. Just say you'll come back.'

'How would I earn a living?' This has been the block all along. I have no skills that I can offer to the community around here. I'm a television producer and that's neither use to man nor beast when you live in the country.

'We'll work something out. I promise you.'

My head's swimming and my brain won't do joined-up thinking. I can't believe that Guy has been planning and plotting all this for us. And I realise that he really does love us. He loves us all. Me, the kids, Hamish, Milly Molly Mandy, Doris, Daphne, Delila, Stuart Little, Stephanie, Blob, Fluffy the hedgehog, all of the chickens and Pork Chop. And Alan too. I don't think I've left anyone out. It's totally overwhelming.

'Phew,' I say, massaging my temples. 'I can't quite get my head round this. I need time to think about it all.'

'Take all the time you need,' Guy says. 'Just say yes.'

If only it were so easy, I think. If only it were so easy.

Chapter One Hundred and Eleven

I leave the children happily feeding the goats, stuffing Pork Chop with his favourite pig nuts and becoming reacquainted with Stuart Little the lamb, all supervised by Guy and Alan. While they're occupied, I take the opportunity to walk out into the garden by myself.

I'm dressed for London, still in my work suit and light coat, so I'm cold and wish that I'd thought to bring my padded jacket, a woolly hat and some thick gloves with me. At least I remembered to pack sensible clothing for the children. I pull my coat around me against the chill and, oblivious of my ridiculously inadequate shoes, set out over the grass.

In the garden, I go and sit on the bench where Will died. Which is something that I haven't previously been able to do. Now there's a comfort in sitting where my husband liked to sit, Hamish snoozing at his feet. I stroke the bench, absently, as if I can somehow touch Will again through it. I feel so much more connected to him here than I did in London. All the time I was there, I was so frazzled that I couldn't talk to him at all.

So much has happened in the last year that I feel dizzy with the thought of it. The last thing I want to do is rush into something else, but the draw of this place, of Guy, is much stronger than I thought.

The old oak tree looms over me, looking less benign but just as sturdy without its dressing of leaves. The grass is lush, green from all the rain. I look out over the landscape, the ancient unspoiled moors, and I think that someone who sat here a hundred years ago, more, maybe the very first owners of Helmshill Grange, would have seen the very same things that I'm seeing now. From the fields, the silence is punctuated by the comical baa of the sheep and the lowing of nearby cows. In a few months this place will be alive again. Little blue damselflies will hover over the boggy patch in the corner of the garden that could be the perfect home for a pond if I ever got organised. The flowers will be coming out in force and so will the bees and the butterflies. Last year I was too stressed, too unhappy to enjoy those small wonders. I hope this year that it will be completely different. If we come back, I want to spend time sitting on this bench, spending time with nature, spending time with Will. I smile to myself. I'm saying the things that my husband used to say. The same things that I used to scoff at. Perhaps William would be proud of me. I hope that he would. It's beautiful here already, but there's so much more I could do. There's so much potential. If only I'd thought to watch *Gardener's World* once or twice. Perhaps I'll start now. Maybe Marty and Gill Bainbridge would help me too.

'What do you think, Will?' I say out loud. 'Did you hear Guy's offer? Should I try to stay here?'

How good it would be, to hear the sound of my husband's voice again. 'I want to do what's best for the children and I know that you wanted them to have a less stressful life than they would in London. I can see that now.'

I curl up my knees and lean my head on the back of the bench. 'Do you know how much I loved you?' Now the tears start to fall. 'Did I ever tell you enough? I never thought, never imagined that I'd find anyone who could make me feel like you did. But I'm in love with Guy. I feel so lucky. He's been so good to us, Will. He adores me. He adores the children. He even adores that damn dog. And I love him – as much as I did you. How can that be?'

Now the sky's darkening as dusk is falling. Soon lights will be going on in the village, little pinpricks of warmth in the gathering gloom. I wonder where we'll stay tonight as there's nothing left in Helmshill Grange and it will be days before the gronky old heating system will thaw the place out enough to make it habitable once again. Maybe Guy will let us camp out at his place. I don't even have to think about it really, already I know the answer to that. He'll be delighted to have us and he'll make us feel safe and warm and loved.

'I'm worried that it's too soon. But look at what happened to us, Will. We thought we had forever together and we were wrong.'

I could make Tom and Jessica and me into a tight little impenetrable unit, able to cope, self-sufficient, letting no one else inside. I could harden my heart against love, close off these feelings I have for Guy. But that wouldn't be good for any of us. I want my children's lives to be filled with the type of love and laughter that only a father-figure can bring.

The light's nearly gone now and the temperature is dropping steadily with the departure of the sun. Soon it will be too cold to sit here speaking to my husband.

'I want to be with him. I hope that's okay with you.' I take a deep, shuddering breath. 'I just have to work out the practicalities. I know that you wouldn't want us to struggle on alone. I'd like to think I'll be carrying on part of your dream and that you'd approve of what I'm doing. I know you always wanted to run a bed and breakfast . . .'

Then I pull up short. *Bed and breakfast*? The last thing on earth that I would have ever considered! It's just not me. But, sometimes, things change, people change. I thought television was my life, but I was wrong. I giggle to myself and a thrill of excitement runs through me. Bed and breakfast, eh? I might just have hit on a solution to my income dilemma. My husband would smile at that.

'Thank you, Will.' I blow a kiss into the air. I know, just *know* that my husband will always be here with us – for me, for the children – and there's a great comfort in that. It's strange, but suddenly I don't feel that he's left us, after all. 'You knew what was right for us all along. I'm just sorry that it took me so long to see it. I love you, Will,' I say to the darkening sky. 'Thank you so much for bringing us here.'

Chapter One Hundred and Twelve

'I'm not going back to London,' Jessica states as I approach. 'And neither is Tom.'

My son, hiding behind his sister's bravado, nods in agreement. They climb down from the fence by the garden where they've clearly been plotting, little knowing that I've been doing some plotting of my own. Tom has Hamish's lookalike puppy nestled in his arms. Trouble, I can see, is chewing a hole in his new school jumper. That puppy has got to be a chip off one old block. God help us all.

'Really?' I say.

'You can do what you like,' she adds, hands on hips. 'But we're staying here. Daddy would have let us.'

I have no idea why she talks like a thirty-five year old, but it makes me smile to myself.

'Well, that's fine then. I'd better send for all of our things.'

They look at me open mouthed. My ready agreement will probably turn my daughter into a power-crazed monster, but I'll deal with that later. I wonder what the removal men will think when I ask them to bring all our stuff back so soon. I wonder what Guy will say too.

'Come on, then.' I beckon them after me. 'Let's go and tell Guy our news.'

We find him with Alan, still in the yard even though the light is failing. Alan is putting the animals to bed for the night. It's nice to think that Mr Steadman will be around for a while to watch over them.

I sidle up next to Guy as he leans over the gate watching Alan at work. 'It's a deal,' I say.

He spins round to look at me, surprise and joy on his face. 'You're staying?'

'Looks like it.'

'You really mean it?'

I nod. 'I'm going to run Helmshill Grange as a bed and breakfast. If I can get approval from my new landlord, of course,' I tease.

'That's a great idea.'

My mind is rushing ahead of me and I'm having trouble marshalling my thoughts into a cohesive stream. 'I'll use some of the money from the purchase to do it up and then we can pay you rent – perhaps on favourable terms at first, then we can increase it as the business grows. How does that sound to you?'

Guy takes me in his arms. Even in the darkness I can see that his eyes are sparkling with tears. 'That sounds just wonderful.'

'You think it will work?'

'We'll make damn sure that it does.'

Excited laughter bursts from my lips. 'We're going to be busy, Alan,' I shout to Mr Steadman. 'I've got lots of plans for this place.'

His face breaks into an uncertain smile.

'You up for it?'

'Aye, Mrs Ashurst,' he says, a catch in his voice. 'Reckon I am.'

'Good. I'm not sure that I could manage it without you.'

He smiles shyly and returns to forking over the hay, clearly overcome by the emotion.

The children come and join in our hug.

'Does that mean I can have a pony if we're staying?' Jessica pipes up.

'Don't push it,' I tell my daughter. But I think that somehow one will turn up here whether I want it to or not.

'Thank you,' I say to Guy. 'Thank you for making this happen for us.'

Then Hamish bounds over and sticks his nose up my bottom. 'Hamish!' Damn dog. I laugh and tears spill over my lashes. And I know that from now on, everything is going to be all right.

Chapter One Hundred and Thirteen

They say that every cloud has a silver lining and this is ours. Out of terrible grief and upheaval, I've come to appreciate a different, kinder, quieter way of life. In following my husband's dream, I had no idea that it would eventually become mine too.

I'm turning off the heating in the scullery for the night when I see a glimpse of black lace peeping out of Hamish's bottom. 'I wondered where they'd got to.'

'Come here, mad dog.' Hamish whimpers, legs quivering, as I extract my pants, inch-by-inch from his backside. Holding as little as I can, I fling the pants straight into the washing machine and put them on to boil. I've long since given up buying new underwear and simply re-wash those that Hamish has eaten. I find that Marks & Spencer's knickers are the ones that are least troubled by Hamish's digestive processes and boil washing, so buy all my pants online from there now.

When I've washed my hands, the dog follows me upstairs. As well as indulging Hamish's fetish for lacy pants, I've also long since given up trying to shut him in the scullery for the night. We were just getting through too many doors. The only way to get any peace is to let him sleep on the bedroom floor. Our hound's fixator has long gone now and you'd never know that his leg had been broken at all. If his back end is a little weaker than it once was, it certainly doesn't stop him from doing anything. More's the pity.

Poking my head round Jessica's door, I can hear my daughter breathing heavily in deep sleep. She loves being back at St Mary's School and Mrs Barnsley is pleased to see both of her star pupils back. The children can walk to school alone now without me having apoplexy, but I still find time to take them most mornings, enjoying the talks we have while we trundle along the quiet, green lanes.

I close the window in her room, shutting out the cool breeze that's sprung up. It's been a long, hot summer here at Helmshill Grange and we've all enjoyed the garden. The borders have been a riot of colourful cornflowers, cranesbill, bees and butterflies. Now we're sliding slowly into autumn once more and the weather is starting to turn.

Fluffy the hedgehog – now in permanent residence here – pokes his head out from under my daughter's bed and then joins me and Hamish as we go to check on Tom.

My son, too, is sleeping soundly in his bed. I draw the duvet over him where he's kicked it off. My soulful, anxious boy is much more relaxed now that we're safely ensconced back at Helmshill. He's made new friends in the village – two lovely boys called Alfie and Zack – and goes out on the moors with them every weekend flying his kite. He too is thriving at school, and to see the children both so content like this makes me realise that, finally, I have made absolutely the right choice. I'm only sorry that it took so long and caused so much pain.

The sale of the house went through quickly and without a hitch. Guy Barton was the model buyer! Plans for the bed and breakfast are coming on well. I've applied to the council for planning permission and we're just waiting for that to come through, then we're raring to go. First of all, I'm going to do up three rooms and see how I go from there. I've had quotes from builders to sort out the ancient plumbing here and install extra en-suite bathrooms. Alan is going to help with the handiwork – of course. Where would we be without Saint Steadman? Alan rarely goes home now until it's time for him to sleep. He has dinner with us every night, usually gets roped in to do the children's homework and then he's back first thing in the morning in time for breakfast. As a grandad substitute he's doing a sterling job.

We were out in the garden together today, discussing the first project on the agenda and I realise just how much I've come to lean on him. Alan's going to transform the boggy bit in the corner to a small pond. It will make a lovely spot for a couple of ducks, maybe some geese too. I'm going to do it as a kind of memorial for Will, because I think that he'd really like that.

Nearly a year has gone by since my husband died and I can hardly believe it. His presence here seems stronger than ever and we all love it, even Guy who never has one moment of resentment for the other man who will always be in my life. He has been a rock for me and for the children. I was so lucky to have been loved by Will, but I've also learned in the last twelve months that the heart can heal and can love again.

I open the bedroom door, Hamish padding behind me, followed by the little tank of Fluffy, who shuffles straight under the bed to curl up for the night. He's probably the only hedgehog who's up and about all day, then sleeps at night.

My darling Guy is already under the duvet. 'I wondered where you'd got to,' my live-in landlord says with a stifled yawn.

'Hamish has been at my pants again.'

He raises his eyebrows. 'Lucky old Hamish.'

'I'll be five minutes,' I tell him. 'I bet you're whacked. I've just got to brush my teeth.' The practice has been busy. Stephen has bought into the business now and they're even thinking of taking on a third partner to lighten the load. Guy wants to be able to spend more time with Tom and Jessica, and you don't know how glad that makes me feel. After much discussion, he's rented out his own house to a new GP who's come to join the surgery in Scarsby, and moved in with us just a few weeks ago. Despite living on his own for so many years, I can't believe how easily he's adapted to the hustle and bustle of family life. Guy assures me that he loves every minute of it. Even when I make him do breakfast duty.

In the bathroom, I shrug out of my clothes and quickly climb into my fleecy pyjamas. Although it's still mild during the day, the night-time temperature doesn't allow for filmy negligées, but Guy doesn't seem to mind. I dash into the bedroom, braving the chilly floorboards and ignoring the shredded mouse remnants which I promise myself to deal with in the morning. Jumping in beside him, I nudge Milly Molly Mandy out of the way, and she miaows her disgust at being so rudely disturbed.

'I spoke to Marty earlier – the pony's going to be arriving

on Monday,' Guy says as I wriggle in next to him, rubbing my icy cold feet on his legs. I must buy some new slippers when I'm next in Scarsby. Fur-lined ones. 'Is that okay?'

'Do I have a choice?'

'No,' Guy admits. 'But I'm sure you'll love her.'

And, you know, I probably will. But not half as much as my daughter will.

Our ever-growing brood has now been expanded to include two rabbits – a glossy black one for Jessica, a snow-white one for Tom – and some more bedraggled hens which means I'm back on antibiotic duty again. We're even looking at a couple of alpacas to put in the top field. Not bad for someone who isn't an animal lover, eh?

At the foot of the bed, Trouble is already snuggled down for the night. Hamish plods round in a circle on the rug until he finds his maximum comfort spot, then he flops down with a heavy sigh.

'There's going to be no room in here for us soon,' I grumble.

'Did you ever think that you'd be sharing a bed with two dogs, a cat, a hedgehog and a vet?'

'No.' I ease myself further under the duvet until Guy's warm body is next to mine. He slips his arm round me. 'Did *you* ever think that you'd be sharing a bed with a woman whose underwear had been through the digestive tract of a dog?'

'No.' Guy lifts himself up on his elbow, until he's leaning over me. He kisses me hotly. 'Did you ever think you'd make love to a man who'd had his arm up a cow's bottom?'

'No,' I breathe sexily. 'I never thought that.'

He undoes the buttons of my fleecy pyjamas, slowly,

one by one. Already my body is in ecstasy. His hands are warm on my breasts. He kisses my throat, my face, my ear. Then I feel his tongue, hot, probing and . . . slobbery.

'Hamish!' we shout together. 'Get down!'

If you enjoyed *The Difference a Day Makes*,
you don't have to wait for more!

Carole Matthews' new novel,

Calling Mrs Christmas

is out now.

Read on for the first two chapters, and join Cassie as she
takes you on a romantic and emotional rollercoaster ride in
the brand-new festive novel from readers' favourite, Carole
Matthews.

Chapter One

Perfume ads on the telly. First it's Charlize Theron, strutting and stripping her way through some mansion until she's wearing nothing but J'Adore and an alluring smile. Next it's Keira Knightley overacting 'fun' for Coco Mademoiselle. Finally, for Chanel No. 5, it's the stylised Red Riding Hood advert that's been doing the rounds for years with the best-looking wolf you've ever seen. It's only when these luscious advertisements grace our screens that you know the giddy, helter-skelter rundown towards Christmas has finally begun in earnest.

All three advertisements have been screened in a row and it's barely mid-morning. I missed most of the ads last year. At least, the daytime ones. I hear myself sigh. It's a bad habit and I've been doing it a lot lately. This year, as I am an unemployed, redundant couch potato, I am running the entire gamut of Christmas commercialism. It's the first week of October and already Stacey and Jason are extolling the virtues of Iceland's pre-prepared party food.

There is much laughter, much over-indulgence in these adverts, much that is red and gold and glittering. Which is all very lovely. I'd usually buy right into it. Except there'll not be much partying at our house this Christmas. Very little, if any, party food from Iceland – or elsewhere – will be bought. Our table will not be replete with festive delights. Our Christmas tree will not be surrounded by half a ton of presents. It will be a big contrast to last year. I stop the next sigh that threatens to escape.

'Budget' is the watch word of the moment. Closely followed by 'cutbacks'. Last Christmas we had a great time. As is expected, the table groaned with food, the booze flowed, we force-fed ourselves an excess of Quality Street. All the usual things. Wonderful. But last year I had a job. This year I don't. And there's the rub.

This Christmas, any tightening of the belt will be entirely down to our dwindling finances and not, for once, caused by the calorie overload of the festivities. I have now been out of work for a grand total of eight months, four days and, checks watch, three hours. It's fair to say that no one seems to be missing the great contribution that Ms Cassie Smith, age thirty-five, of Hemel Hempstead in the fair county of Hertfordshire has made to the cut-throat world of commerce.

I switch off the television and stare at the walls of the flat. This place has become my prison and my refuge all at once. I hate being trapped in here all day with nowhere to go. Yet now when I get the chance to go out, spread my wings, I'm frightened. My heart pounds, my mouth goes dry and my palms sweat at the thought of stepping out of my comfort zone. Do you think that's how budgies feel? Do they desperately want to fly free, but as soon as that cage door is open, they freeze? If it is, then I feel so sorry for them. I used to be sure of my place in life, but my self-confidence has dwindled just as fast as our meagre savings.

My job, I have to admit, wasn't fantastic. I grumbled about it a lot. To anyone who would listen, really. But, my goodness, how I miss it. I would give anything to be complaining about hauling myself out of bed on a frosty morning, scraping the car windscreen, blowing on my fingers to keep warm, muttering about the crap office coffee. Instead, when Jim gets up for work, I simply turn over and go back to sleep. No need to get up. No need to rush. No need to do anything. No need to be here at all.

I worked as a secretary and general dogsbody for a small

engineering company specialising in component design and fabrication. The price I paid for daydreaming in school. But I was good at my job, efficient. People liked me. I was a dedicated and diligent dogsbody. I could turn my hand to anything and frequently did. Sometimes it felt as if I was running the flipping place. Jim and I went to my boss's house for dinner. Three times. He opened champagne. I always went that extra mile, my boss said. He said I was indispensable. In fact he said it the very morning before he called me into his office and told me that, from the end of the week, I would be surplus to requirements. Not enough people, it seemed, needed components designed or fabricated.

I push my misery aside and phone Jim. Just the sound of his voice can pull me out of a downward spiral. His mobile rings and rings. My other half, for his sins, is a prison officer based in the Young Offenders' Unit at Bovingdale Prison. He can't have his phone with him when he's on duty, but I'm hoping that I might catch him on a break when he tries to go out to his locker if he can, snatching a few minutes to listen to his messages and look at his texts. He never used to go out to his locker during his shift when I was at work because I never had time to phone him during the day. We did all our catching up on the evenings when Jim's shifts allowed us to fall exhausted onto the sofa together. Now I spend my entire life on the sofa – primarily alone – and Jim is conscious that he's my lifeline to the world, so he checks his phone as often as he can.

As I think it's about to go to voicemail, Jim picks up. 'Hi, love,' he says, sounding harassed. 'A bit busy right now. Just got a call on the radio. Can I ring you back later?'

'Yeah.'

'Was it anything important?'

'No. I'm just bored.'

'OK. Catch you when I've got a spare mo. Love you.' He hangs up.

'Love you,' I say to the handset.

And that's the trouble when you're not busy. Everyone else is. I switch the television back on. The John Lewis advert. Something sentimental to have you reaching for the tissues as usual. The Argos ad. Then Boots who seem to be trying to guilt mothers into excess present buying. No wonder vulnerable heartstrings are stretched to breaking point. Soon everyone but me will be wrapped up in Christmas. A time when all sensible spending goes out of the window and everyone racks up the debt on their credit cards to pay another day. Well, we can't do that this year.

To be honest, I didn't particularly worry when I was made redundant although, equally, I wasn't exactly overjoyed, as in my view I'd done my best for the company and I believed they were happy with me. But then I thought I'd get a job really easily. I'd waltz straight into another company who'd love me and appreciate me more. Who doesn't need secretaries? What sort of company doesn't have a dogsbody on which to dump all their most depressing and unwanted tasks? Who doesn't want someone to mollycoddle and care for all the staff and their various crises? An office angel. I assumed that the local paper would be filled with opportunities for someone with my skills and experience. It seems that I was wrong.

Chapter Two

I stare at the clock. Nearly ten minutes have passed since I last looked at it. Jim still hasn't called me back. In fairness, he has a very busy job. Unlike me, he works in a growth industry. No shortage of customers in Jim's company. No chance of anyone saying that there isn't enough demand for *his* skill set. The Young Offenders' Unit at Bovingdale is already overflowing and there's a steady stream of thieving, drug-dealing, car-nicking, house-breaking kids that they can't even begin to accommodate.

But no matter how much I hate being unemployed, I couldn't for all the money in the world, for all the tea in China, do a job like that. My Jim is a saint among men.

We've been together for five years now, meeting in a less than salubrious bar in Watford just after my thirtieth birthday and just after I'd decided that true love would never find me. There he was, standing with a pint of Magners in his hand, and for me – for both of us – it was love at first sight.

Sometimes, you just can't put your finger on what causes that strength of attraction, but you know that it's there. It's not that Jim Maddison's an oil painting. I wasn't bowled over because he's a dead ringer for Matthew McConaughey. He doesn't have that kind of movie-star looks. His hair is cropped close, which makes him look a lot scarier than he actually is. From his time in the army, he's got tattoos on his toned biceps. A heart and a rose entwined on one side. A skull with flowers growing through it on the other. Between his shoulder blades there's a colourful phoenix and I love to trace the outline of them on his skin when we're lying in bed. He's stocky, not that tall, has a face that's too pale as he spends his working days locked indoors and we haven't had a holiday in the sun in years. But my Jim has the kindest eyes you'll ever see. They're soft, grey and always have a twinkle in them. He smiles much, much more than he frowns. When it comes down to it, Jim's just an uncommonly nice guy and it radiates from every pore he possesses. Everyone adores him. Me included. Jim is the epitome of the word 'solid' and, since the day I met him, I know what it is to be loved, to be cared for.

By the end of our first week – a week when we saw each other every night – we'd decided to move in together. Just like that. No ifs, no buts. I knew instantly, instinctively, he was The One.

I'd had a few relationships in the past, but no one had ever made me feel the way Jim did. It wasn't that he showered me with flowers or diamonds. Quite the opposite. Present buying isn't Jim's forte. He isn't romantic in a showy way at all, but I watch him sometimes when he's making me some toast or a cup of tea. I see how much care he takes. He's knows that I like my toast well done with loads of butter right up to the edges of the bread. He frowns in concentration as he makes sure that the jam is spread really thinly, exactly the way I do it myself, and that it's cut in triangles, not sliced straight across. He puts his feet on my side of the bed to warm it before I get in. He opens doors for me, walks on the traffic side of the pavement and pulls out my chair in restaurants. To me, that's love. It's not roaring down the street in a Ferrari, it's not skydiving out of a plane with an 'I LOVE CASSIE!' banner trailing behind you. I think it's the constant, quiet things that tell you that it's real love. And I feel that I am very loved.

My dad cleared off when I was young. I barely remember him, but something like that leaves its mark and I've always felt wary about getting too involved with men. I always expected them to let me down and, invariably, they did. It got to the point where I hardly dated at all, didn't really trust men. With Jim it was completely different. This might sound mad, but it was like finding the other half of myself. From day one, I knew that I could trust him with my life, that my heart would never be mashed by him. If that sounds corny, then so be it. He is truly my soulmate.

We can spend hours just sitting reading together or walking

through the woods. There's never any drama with Jim, I don't have to worry about where he is or who he's with. Jim isn't one for nights out on the lash with the lads; he'd rather be at home with me than anywhere else. And that's all I want too. Just to be with Jim. We're content in each other's company. We don't need the high life, we're happy exactly as we are.

If it wasn't for Jim, I don't know how I would have survived the last year. He's been my only brightness, always there with the right words to cheer me up or knowing when a well-timed bar of chocolate would lift my spirits. When I was made redundant, I thought I'd take a couple of weeks off, have a bit of a rest. A 'career break' I laughingly called it. After all, I'd been in work constantly since I was sixteen and there was no rush to find something else. I'd been given a month's salary as a pay-off. Yeah, thanks for that.

Then, when I'd caught up on the ironing, and the flat was so spick and span that it looked as if Anthea Turner had been through it, and I'd watched all the films I'd been meaning to watch but hadn't got around to, I applied for jobs. There weren't as many of them as I'd expected and some, I felt, just weren't right for me. I was surprised when, having sent off a rash of my splendid CVs, I got only one interview. I was even more surprised when I didn't get the job. I thought the interview had gone so well. Seems I was wrong about that too. After that setback, a little bit of panic set in. I catalogued all our DVDs and old CDs alphabetically and then applied for more jobs. This time I was less choosy. Got one interview. Got no job. And so it went on.

I signed on. Was given Jobseekers' Allowance, went to a workshop that showed me how to present my CV properly and then applied frantically for anything with the word 'vacancy' attached to it. Still no luck.

When the spring morphed into summer and I was still terminally unemployed, I began to lose my nerve. The few interviews I did have went badly. A lot of firms that would normally employ secretaries seemed to have embraced an age where managers did their own donkey work or made use of university graduates who had a degree, thirty grand's worth of debt and were desperate. Instead of 'unpaid slaves', they called them 'interns' and insisted the posts were great and necessary work experience for their CVs. But whatever it was, it meant that people like me – who actually wanted paying – went down to the bottom of the pile.

I don't mean to sound sorry for myself. But I am. Very sorry. I don't want to be like this. I look at the television, at the snowy scenes, at the promises of unfettered festive happiness, at the excessive consumerism, and I want to be part of it. I love Christmas. I want to embrace all of its tacky indulgence. It's my time of year. Perhaps sometimes I let myself get a bit carried away – Jim said the flat looked like a flipping winter wonderland last year – but it's supposed to be like that. I don't want to be thinking of getting a meagre Tesco Value chicken rather than a big, fat Kelly Bronze turkey. We can cut back on present, that's no hardship. It's the little things that make Christmas special. But I don't want to miss out on the atmosphere.

This is the only difficult part of my relationship with Jim. We never have enough money. We might not aspire to the high life, but we've never actually had the money to try it. Funds are always tight. Even when I was gainfully employed we didn't have a lot left to splash around, and now my not working is a terrible drain on us. Our desires are fairly modest, but I feel as if I've been on a budget since the day I was born. We don't want for much but, sometimes – just sometimes – it would be nice to treat ourselves without having to count every penny. Surely Christmas is one of those times?

I don't catch what the advert is for, but there's a mother on television, dressing the Christmas tree, two mop-haired children and a dog from Central Casting at her feet. Presents are piled around the tree, which sparkles brilliantly. A beautifully set dining room table replete with ravishing food is in the background. Carols soar to a crescendo and Daddy comes through the door to his perfect family and his perfect Christmas. A sigh rises to my throat. Surely there must be someone who needs extra help at Christmas? Doesn't everyone try to run round doing ten times more than they normally do? There *must* be a role for me out there. My ideal job, my *raison d'être*, is organising stuff. What a shame that I can't get paid for celebrating Christmas!

Then something inside me clicks and the most brilliant idea hits me like a bolt out of the blue. A grin spreads over my face. I could be a part of this. I don't have to sit here on the sidelines and let the joy of Christmas pass me by. I can embrace the commercialism and bring in some much needed extra cash. I can do something about it.

My mind is whirring with the kernel of an unfocussed plan when the phone rings. Jim's at the other end. That means it must be his lunchtime and here's me still in my pyjamas. Well, all that's about to change. No more slobbing around the house feeling sorry for myself, I'm going to launch myself back into the world with a vengeance.

'Hey,' he says. 'Sorry I couldn't speak earlier. I was on my break, but something kicked off. It's total madness here today.'

It's total madness where Jim works *every* day. While we're talking about money, they don't pay him nearly enough for the stress he has and what he has to put up with. That's another one of the reasons why we're still renting this tiny flat and both drive clapped-out cars. I want to do my bit. It's not fair on him. I want to get out there again in the big, bad world of paid work. I don't want our life to be like this, constantly living from hand to mouth. I hate having to accept benefits from the government just to get by. We're young, we're resourceful. We shouldn't be in this situation. I know I can do more. And I might just have a plan as to how.

'Are you OK, Cassie? Still bored?'

'No,' I say.

I can feel myself beaming widely. It's as if a terrible fog has suddenly cleared from my head. A light bulb has gone ping-diddy-ping in my brain and it's burning brightly. I let out a bubbly laugh, a sound that I'd forgotten I could make.

'You'll never believe this,' I tell him. 'But I have just come up with *the* most brilliant idea.'

Chapter Three

By the time Jim comes home in the evening, I'm buzzing. I pounce on him the minute he swings through the door of the flat, twine my arms around him and give him a big kiss.

'Hey,' he says. 'I like a welcome home like this.' Even though he looks weary, he takes me in his arms and returns my kisses. 'What have I done to deserve it?'

'You've just been you,' I say. 'All these months I've been a terrible moody cow and you've stood by me.'

'You've lost your confidence, Cassie,' he says softly. 'That's all. You'll get it back.'

'I have,' I babble. 'I'm just so excited about this idea.'

'Tell me about it again. I couldn't concentrate properly at work,' he admits.

When I talked to Jim on the phone I rushed through my explanation of my plan, babbling like a loon. To be honest, it was all just forming in my brain as I was speaking and I must have sounded like a mad thing. As always, when he's at work, I could tell that Jim had only one ear to the conversation. Now that I've had time to mull it over properly and put some thoughts down on paper, I still think it's a great idea.

Jim drops his bag to the floor and I help him take off his jacket.

'I was watching television this morning.' As I always do. 'It was nothing but Christmas ads.'

'Already?' Jim looks as if he has a heart-sink moment.

'It'll be upon us before we know it,' I remind him. 'That's why I have to act fast.'

'It seems to come round more quickly every year.' He puffs out a tired breath. 'So what's the master plan, Dr Evil?'

'I want to offer a complete Christmas planning service,' I remind him.

Jim untangles himself and we go through to our titchy kitchen where I've got dinner on the go. It's Wednesday and we've got tuna risotto, which, if humanly possible, is even less glamorous than it sounds. Just think, if I could get this business off the ground, we could upgrade to prawns! We could eat meat more than once a week.

'What on earth does that involve?'

'Everything,' I say, excitedly. 'Putting up trees, writing cards, baking mince pies. I could buy presents and gift wrap them. I could put Christmas lights up outside houses. Well, maybe you could do that bit.'

He raises his eyebrows at that.

'A lot of people are into that whole over-the-top decoration now and it's a total pain, putting lights up and taking them down every year. That would be a great service. I could do their food shopping, organise parties. That's just for starters. I'm sure there's a lot of things that I could do that I haven't even thought about yet.'

'Hmm . . .' He rubs at the shadow of stubble on his chin.

'You know what it's like,' I rush on. 'Everyone has eight million things to do before Christmas. If you're not careful, then it just becomes a lot of hassle rather than being the most wonderful time of the year.' I remember to pause for breath. 'If I could take the pressure off people, for a small fee, then it's a win-win situation. Some people will pay anything for the perfect Christmas.'

Jim looks thoughtful. 'You love doing all that stuff anyway.'

'I do.' I used to adore getting ready for Christmas. My favourite job in the world is wrapping presents. And I think I'm good at it. Good enough, with a bit of polishing, to provide a professional service. 'I'd try to offer everything to take the stress out of Christmas. So all the client has to do is pay up and have fun.'

'It sounds like an awful lot to take on, Cassie.' There's a concerned frown on his brow.

'I know. But I have to act fast. People lose all sense when it comes to money at Christmas. If I'd ever had the cash to spare I'd have bought in help myself. I've just never seen anyone offer it. Certainly not round here.'

Jim purses his lips. 'That's true enough.'

'It's a niche market that I think I can explore.'

'Are you sure you wouldn't just be better off looking for another office job?'

'I've tried that, Jim. There's nothing out there.' I stir the risotto and add some more herbs to try to inject some excitement into it. 'I've got my name down for seasonal work at a dozen different shops, but I've heard nothing yet. Even retail outlets are cutting back. Where there are vacancies they're filling them from a list of regulars. No one even wants me as a shelf-stacker.' He knows how hard it's been. 'At least I could try this. If it doesn't work out, I've not lost anything but my time.'

'Starting your own business is always tricky. You know what it's like out there at the moment. The current climate is hard for everyone.'

'This will be for a short period only. It's purely a seasonal thing. Everyone goes raving mad at Christmas. We all like a bit of festive escapism. Buy now, pay later. Batter the credit card. We've done it ourselves. That's what it's all about.'

Not to put too fine a point on it, I'd like a bit of that action too. I can't sit here on my bottom all through the winter, eking out our measly income and feeling miserable. If I can work hard for the next couple of months, cash in on Christmas, then we'll at least have a little bit more money behind us to start the new year. If it goes well, I could maybe think of another business idea or, at worst, go back to the Job Centre with my head held high.

'You could look at commuting into London,' Jim suggests. 'There must be jobs up in town.'

'I'd have to leave at some ungodly hour in the morning, get home late at night. The cost of the rail ticket is extortionate now. With your shifts, we'd never see each other.' Plus, from what I've heard, I think that the city of London is probably suffering from intern overload too. 'I'm also frightened of rejection again,' I admit to Jim. 'At least with this, I sink or swim on my own merits.'

'That's what I'm worried about. You've had a tough time, Cassie. I don't want you to take on too much.'

I chew my fingernail. My first doubt creeps in. 'You don't think I can do it?'

He wraps his arms around me and hugs me tightly. 'Of course you can do it. It's simply a question of whether there's the business out there.'

'I'd like to try.'

'Let me go and have a quick shower, then we can talk some more about it.'

Jim is always conscious that he smells of the Young Offenders' Unit, which is a pungent mix of teenage boys, institutional food and despair. I think he also likes to wash work out of his hair the minute he comes home. I don't care what he smells like, I just feel safe in his arms.

While he hits the bathroom, I fiddle about, pulling the table out from the corner of our living room that doubles as a dining room, and then set it. One thing about my being at home is that we do now eat together at the table rather than slum it with a tray on our laps, watching the telly in a stupor. The only downside is that by the time Jim comes home I'm usually pacing the floor with anxiety. Waiting for someone seems so much worse when you haven't been anywhere yourself.

Catching sight of myself in the full-length mirror in the hall as I bustle about, I realise that the last few months haven't been kind to my appearance either. I've let myself go, no doubt. I've never been slim, but now I'm definitely curvier than I should be. Too many hours spent on the sofa. No visits to the gym. To economise I gave up my membership months ago. To save money

I've also not had my hair cut since January and it now graces my shoulders. Jim says he likes it longer, but I can see that it's out of condition and, at the very least, the ends need trimming. Thankfully, there's no grey showing in my brunette hair – not like my dear sister who's been dyeing hers for years – so I don't feel the need to have it coloured yet. My complexion is usually good – very peaches and cream – but now my skin looks dull, tired. My green eyes have lost their sparkle. I felt pretty once, but not any more. I huff sadly at my own reflection.

Jim's standing behind me. 'You still look beautiful to me.'

'I feel old and fat and forgotten.'

'You're none of those things,' he insists. 'You're my gorgeous girl.' He hugs me and I rest my head against his shoulder. What would I do without him?

'You must be starving.' Jim gets a free meal at lunchtime and he tries to fill up then, but I know the food is not all that it might be. 'Sit yourself down. I'll get dinner.'

I shoot into the kitchen to sort out the risotto. When I had my brainwave, I was actually motivated to go to the supermarket and buy the tiniest piece of Parmesan cheese I could find as a treat to liven it up. I grate some on top and make the dish look as respectable as possible with a sprinkling of parsley.

'Hmm. Looks lovely,' Jim says as I put it down in front of him.

It doesn't, not really. It looks exactly like what it is – a dish knocked up quickly and on the cheap. But he's always so incredibly kind and encouraging.

'It won't always be like this,' I say and tears spring to my eyes.

Jim takes my hand. 'Do you think I'll love you any more if we have steak for dinner every night?'

'Yes.'

'Mmm. Maybe you're right.'

I kick him under the table and he laughs. After he's said, 'Ouch.'

The flat's OK really. The block's a bit tired. Built with all the style the 1970s could muster, it looks like the sort of square, grey lump that you'd imagine more akin to Stalingrad or somewhere Communist and depressing. The windows need replacing as a howling gale comes in around the edges and our communal stair-well could best be described as functional. I'm sure we could make a bit on the side by renting it out as a set for slasher movies. It would be perfect.

We've lived here for two years now. The landlord's a bit of a twat too and, as is the way, we have to make two dozen phone calls before he'll deign to come out and fix anything. Usually, Jim just ends up doing it. We try to make the best of it and have the place as nice as we can. But it's not home, is it? Not when you're renting. It's still always like living somewhere you don't really belong. I didn't think this was where I'd be at this stage in my life. I thought I'd be happily married, have my own home, maybe even a couple of kids. I didn't think that I'd still be scratching an existence in rented accommodation with a baby about as distant a prospect as a trip to the moon. I want to marry Jim. I want to marry him on a tropical beach with colourful flowers in my hair and white sand and waving palm trees. That's my dream. I don't want a massive church bash with three hundred guests and a disco. I just want me and Jim and the sand beneath our feet. But how am I ever going to achieve that if I can't even get a job as a secretary? Which turns me back to the plan in hand.

'So, do you think I should give this business a go?' I desperately need Jim's approval, otherwise it's dead in the water. I don't have the nerve to do this without his backing.

He plays with his fork in the risotto. Today he seems more wound up than normal when he comes home from work, as if he could do with a good glass of red. But, for reasons that you're now well aware of, there won't be one. 'We've nothing put away now, Cassie. It's all gone and the credit cards are maxed out.'

'I'm well aware of that, Jim,' I say more crisply than I mean to. 'Surely that makes it even more critical that I do something? I'd try to keep the outgoings to a bare minimum. A lot of the services I'm going to offer won't need any outlay at all.'

He doesn't look convinced. 'Even if it takes off, it would more than likely stop dead in January.'

'I know. But if it goes *really* well, then maybe I could carry on doing a similar sort of thing for the rest of the year. Event planning or something. There's always Valentine's Day and Easter. Mother's Day too. It's just that Christmas is The Big One.' I touch his hand. 'I feel that I have to try. It would get me out of the house. Get me involved in life again. I'm going mad being at home all the time. I feel worse than useless.'

'I can tell that it's got you all fired up again.' He smiles at me. 'That's good to see.'

'Can I go for it? Will you support me?'

'Of course I will. You know that I'll do all I can. Whatever you do, you'll be brilliant at it.'

'I love you.' I reach across the table and squeeze his hand. 'Thank you for your faith in me.'

'So,' he says, 'have you got a name for your brilliant new venture?'

'Yes, I have,' I say proudly. 'Calling Mrs Christmas!'